THE CROW

REVISED AND UPDATED

THE CROW

The Life, Death, and Rebirth of a Classic Film

BRIDGET BAISS

APPLAUSE
THEATRE & CINEMA BOOKS

Essex, Connecticut

APPLAUSE
THEATRE & CINEMA BOOKS

An imprint of Globe Pequot, the trade division of
The Rowman & Littlefield Publishing Group, Inc.
4501 Forbes Blvd., Ste. 200
Lanham, MD 20706
www.rowman.com

Distributed by NATIONAL BOOK NETWORK

Library of Congress Cataloging-in-Publication Data Available

ISBN: 978-1-4930-7411-2 (pbk. : alk. paper)
ISBN: 978-1-4930-7412-9 (electronic)

 The paper used in this publication meets the minimum requirements of American National Standard for Information Sciences—Permanence of Paper for Printed Library Materials, ANSI/NISO Z39.48-1992.

To my husband, Sean, for his unwavering love and support through the trials of authorship and beyond.

CONTENTS

ACKNOWLEDGMENTS

DEEP GRATITUDE TO MY DEAREST FRIEND Steve Gold, who lent his expert editorial skills and creative imagination to this edition. Thanks for always being almost superhuman.

An eternal thanks to the late Francis Megahy and Peter Fenton for their confidence in me. Without their support, this book would not have been written.

A very special thanks to the legendary special effects makeup artist Lance Anderson for his generous support and allowing his personal, behind-the-scenes photos to be printed in this book.

And, my sincere thanks to all those I interviewed:

Lance Anderson, Ken Arlidge, Clyde Baisey, Roberta Bile, Bryan Carpenter, New Hanover County District Attorney John Carriker, Charles M. Coleman III, Angel David, Rochelle Davis, Greg Gale, Mark Galvin, Mike Gibbons, John Goldwyn, Bobby Griffin, Vick Griffin, Ernie Hudson, Charles "Chunky" Huse, Jeff Imada, Attorney James Janowitz, Ian Jessel, Attorney Robert W. Johnson, Michelle Johnson, JB Jones, Randall LaFollette, Darryl Levine, Bai Ling, Larry Madrid, Paul Maslak, Laurence Mason, Frankie Nardiello—aka Groovie Mann, Claudio Miranda, Jeff Most, James O'Barr, Sandra Orsolyak, Wilmington Police Sergeant Brian Pettus, Arianne Phillips, Graeme Revell, Cornelia "Nini" Rogan, Robert L. Rosen, Sofia Shinas, John Shirley, Chad Stahelski, Rachel Talalay, Robert Zuckerman, and Larry Zanoff. Thanks also to those, whom I have not mentioned, who spoke to me off the record.

INTRODUCTION

THE *CROW* HAS HAD MANY LIVES.

It has enraptured fans for three decades, spawned three feature film sequels and a TV series, and now, a big-budget remake expected to be released in 2024.

My journey with *The Crow* began one unusually stormy evening in May 1994. My best friend, a fellow UCLA Theatre, Film & Television alum, dragged me through the rain-slick streets of Los Angeles into a Westwood Village movie theater to see *The Crow*.

I had only a moderate interest in seeing the film, but Steve (a brilliant screenwriter who has gone on to a career in animation working with some of the world's greatest living science fiction authors and illustrators) convinced me it was worth our time, seeing the edgy film and last performance of someone he considered a bright, gifted, and promising young star, Brandon Lee.

I was impressed and intrigued by the film and the charismatic Crow character, and Steve and I discussed the story and various scenes late into the evening over heaps of shawarma at our favorite college haunt, Falafel King.

My original commission to write this book came about on an unlikely occasion. It was a festive New Year's Eve dinner in 1998, at what was the eclectic, celebrity-filled Les Deux Café in Hollywood, owned by enigmatic artist Michelle Lamy, where she and her husband, fashion designer Rick Owens, also lived and had their studio. While celebrating the evening with the late film director Francis Megahy, McLaren Formula One racing chief Ron Dennis and his wife, Lisa, and film producer and longtime friend Scott Wolf, London publisher and friend Peter Fenton approached me with the subject.

When he told me he had noticed a tremendous international interest in anything to do with the movie, I was quite surprised. Four years after it had hit the screens? But I was intrigued, and we began to talk about the possibility of me writing a book on the making of the film.

My career, up to this point, had consisted of playing some small roles in movies and TV shows, acting in professional theater, and producing television documentaries and print journalism. Then, in 1996, I established myself as an international television reporter specializing in the entertainment industry. I had always thought at some time I would write a book, but at some vague, unspecified, and future date. Then, after I had done some research, some reading, and seen the movie again, a couple more times, I became fascinated by the subject of *The Crow*.

For a start, I had forgotten just how compelling the look of the film was. I had just seen *Dark City*, the most recent film from Alex Proyas, *The Crow*'s director, and I immediately noted many visual similarities. This stood out particularly in *The Crow*'s stunning opening shot, as the camera flew over clearly a miniature city—dark, gloomy, and full of mystery and danger.

I quickly discovered that *Crow* merchandise was hot: Comics, T-shirts, calendars, toys, and photos were all big sellers. And online, there were a number of fan sites with high traffic. Even after the release of the second, much less successful *Crow* film, *The Crow: City of Angels* (1996), anything to do with the original film was still a hot commodity at conventions and book fairs and with retailers around the world.

So, in January of 1999, I agreed to write the book, and I set myself on a course that, for a year, changed the rhythm and structure of my otherwise extroverted life. I had no idea that the journalist's key characteristic, persistence, would become so vital.

The research itself turned out to be a much bigger challenge than I could have imagined. I came up against endless layers of suspicion and hostility, and I was always having to defend my own credibility.

The tragic on-set accident that killed Brandon Lee cast a pall over the lives of many of the cast and crew, many of whom remain affected by it to this day.

When I started the book, I naturally tried to interview every single person I could reach who had been involved with *The Crow*. I soon found that simply tracking down the members of the cast and crew was difficult. Some of them had dropped out of the fickle movie industry, while others apparently had their own reasons for being hard to find. Their elusiveness was not hard to fathom, since the last time many of these people were contacted by any journalist was immediately after Brandon Lee's fatal shooting.

So, I wasn't entirely surprised, but my patience was to be sorely tested. One key member of the production team, who had since gone on to work on some of Hollywood's biggest movies, arranged for and canceled interview dates no less than five times, often with less than thirty minutes' advance notice, or without notice at all.

Nevertheless, many people close to Brandon Lee did speak with me candidly and at length. Many of them felt it was finally time to have their say about what had happened during the shooting of the film, which had been kept something of a mystery. For many, it was a much-needed release. By talking about it, they hoped to finally heal the tragic wound caused by the young actor's death.

I went to the North Carolina town of Wilmington, where the movie was shot, and found a startling degree of paranoia about *The Crow*. I was barred from entering the studio lot by its nervous general manager, who told me that I should "stop snooping around" and that I would be "hearing from" his attorneys. But also in Wilmington, I met some of the nicest, warmest people I have ever encountered.

In Los Angeles, I returned home one night to find a sinister message on my answering machine. An anonymous male caller warned me that if I didn't abandon writing my book, "it could make trouble for me."

Some of the people from whom I requested interviews were instantly and openly hostile, others tried to intimidate me, while others even went out of their way to prevent their colleagues, who had been connected with the film, from speaking with me.

Chief among those who would not talk to me was the director, Alex Proyas, who is renowned for rarely speaking to the media. After many contacts and several conversations with his co-producer, they both declined on the grounds that I could not surrender editorial approval of my book to them. At one point, they even inquired if I would be willing to co-author my book with one of the movie's screenwriters to whom they have remained close.

This disappointment was only made more frustrating when they then asked their friends, *The Crow*'s production designer, art director, cinematographer, and first assistant director, not to speak to me. Some of this group have continued to work together, others have not. But whatever the loyalty these filmmakers have to Alex Proyas, it prevented most of them from ever hearing my requests.

Nevertheless, I did manage to interview almost everyone of any consequence who worked on the movie.

I hadn't started my research with any particular focus other than to try to examine and account for the public's fascination with the movie. But gradually, one event began irresistibly to dominate my interviews and my thinking about the project—Brandon's Lee's fatal accident.

My original purpose was certainly not to write a book that might be called *The Story Behind the Death of Brandon Lee.* But as my research developed, and I learned more and more about the making of the movie, I began to realize I had a responsibility far beyond simply writing a book about a film's production. I had to try to get the story of the accident right, to assemble as many facts as possible, and, for the first time, to put them all together in one place.

Once I had realized the extraordinary sensitivity of the actors and crew about Brandon's death, I was always careful in my interviews to move slowly toward the topic of the accident. I always offered my subjects the choice not to discuss it if they didn't want to. So, I was very surprised when many of them quickly introduced the topic themselves and often told me more than I ever dreamed I'd learn.

I have never taken this responsibility lightly and I believe that I have fairly represented the involvement in the film of all the people who spoke with me. Indeed, as each interview was completed, I began to understand that the story was really about the people. Not only about the cult status of the film or the Hollywood behind-the-scenes deals or the strange and unpredictable coincidences that ultimately led to Brandon Lee's death. No, it was about those many men and women who opened up their memories and often their hearts and souls to me.

As I spoke to people in bars, restaurants, offices, shopping malls, over the phone and in their homes, I realized that my interviews had a common thread. For all of them, except perhaps the studio executives or technical advisors who had no direct contact with the actual production, *The Crow* hit a personal chord. For some it was obviously more intense than for others. But everyone who worked on this movie was forever marked in some way by the experience.

As many of them told me in their own ways, *The Crow* was both the best and the worst experience of their lives.

Three decades later I discovered many cast and crew have moved on, some to become acclaimed filmmakers, while others have disappeared from public life or died. Some who still have declined to speak with me remain too traumatized by the experience and some do not want to revisit the past and potentially cast a negative shadow on their current career success. But of the many who have spoken to me for this new edition, their sense of pride and connection to *The Crow* is remarkable.

The story of *The Crow* comic sprang from a devastating personal tragedy that befell its creator, James O'Barr, just as he was beginning his adult life. O'Barr then exorcized this tragedy on the pages of his graphic novel. Then the novel became the movie. And the pain and torment that created *The Crow* came full circle, claiming the stunning instrument that gave it life onscreen.

It is again unexpected that the story of the making of *The Crow* has entered my life. With the collision of current events and the enduring appeal of *The Crow* story, it was clear an update of my book was merited.

Certainly, the reboot of the film finally becoming a reality after many years of Hollywood rights disputes and development hell has increased interest in the original film. Sadly, so has the tragic prop gun accident on the movie *Rust* in October of 2021 killing cinematographer Halyna Hutchins—the only on-set fatality similar to that of Brandon Lee's on *The Crow* in thirty years.

My goal is this new edition be a rich and accurate resource of the original production and touch on the legacy of the film's impact on both culture and Hollywood. This 2023 edition includes new anecdotes, and interviews though my original, extensive interviews done in 1999 form the backbone of the story of the making of the film. I have also made an effort to explain how filmmaking technology has changed since 1993, before the rise of ubiquitous digital effects and before many now-routine production innovations.

Since I wrote the first edition of the book released in 2000, six years after the release of the film in 1994, I have been sought out for an interview by a wide variety of international documentary series and news and biography programs. All have asked me to recount details, anecdotes, facts, and context to the film's production as well as insight into Brandon Lee's last performance and tragic death. Though always flattering to receive these calls, I have accepted only those inquiries that I felt genuinely wanted to focus on the story and the facts more than the conspiracies and sensational rumors.

Twenty-some years after my first edition was published, I find myself once again swept up in the enduring appeal of this classic film and epic story of love, revenge, and rebirth. As the author of the singular book about the making of this groundbreaking film, I'm honored to write this updated edition. My sincere wish is this book is enjoyable, insightful, and truthful and it honors the legacy of Brandon Lee and everyone else who gave their all making this film.

PROLOGUE

THE NIGHT OF THE LAST TUESDAY in March 1993 should have been just another long, intense session in the production schedule of the movie *The Crow*.

The cast and crew of the film assembled a little before 8:00 p.m. on sound stage number 4 at Carolco Studios in Wilmington, North Carolina, to begin day fifty of principal photography. In fact, day fifty was night fifty, since almost the entire schedule of the movie consisted of night shooting. But the end was now in sight, with only eight days of work left.

The major scene for the night was a flashback, in which Brandon Lee's Crow character—the hero of the movie, Eric Draven—is murdered by a group of hoodlums. It's a crucial scene in the movie, indeed *the* pivotal event of the story. But its dramatic importance did not give this particular evening a different feel from the previous forty-nine days of production.

Sometime after 11:00 p.m., the star of the movie, twenty-eight-year-old Brandon Lee, had arrived on the set, Eric Draven's loft apartment. Eric is a rocker with long hair who is dressed in a leather jacket, tight velvet pants, boots, and a T-shirt with "Hangman's Joke," the name of his band, written across it.

The director, Alex Proyas, took the cast and crew through two rehearsals of the scene. The atmosphere was friendly but tense, since they were all suffering from tremendous fatigue as a result of working twelve- to fourteen-hour days for two straight months.

Soon, the actors' moves were set, the lighting was finally adjusted, and the cameras' focus positions were marked. By midnight it was time to roll film. The prop master showed Michael Massee, the actor playing Funboy, that he had just loaded the .44 Magnum with which Funboy would shoot

Eric Draven with a single, full blank charge. This would produce the desired flash of flame from the end of the barrel.

The cameras and sound began rolling. The first assistant director, Steve Andrews, yelled "Action!"

In the scene, we find Funboy and his partner T-Bird, played by David Patrick Kelly, in the midst of a violent assault on Eric's fiancée, Shelly Webster. The front door opens, and Eric enters the loft, carrying a bag of groceries. Funboy spins around, gun in hand, sees Eric—and fires.

The blank went off. Bang! According to plan, the small explosive in the grocery bag detonated, exploding a milk container and ripping a hole in the bag. Eric grabbed his stomach, spun around, and then sank to the ground against the doorway. It had all happened almost exactly as it had been rehearsed.

Almost.

The action continued briefly, with Shelly and the thugs reacting to the shooting, screaming and yelling, while Eric lie there motionless. After enough time to get their reactions, Alex Proyas shouted "Cut!" The action stopped.

It took a few moments for the people on the crowded set to realize that something had gone terribly wrong.

It would take several more hours for them to realize that Brandon Lee had filmed his last shot on *The Crow* and that a tragic event had occurred, one that blurred the line between the real world and the world of movie making.

The lives of everyone present would never be the same again.

Origins of the Movie   1
The Comic

IT IS SCARCELY SURPRISING that a work as individual as *The Crow* comic springs from deeply felt personal experiences. What is surprising is just how exactly the story parallels the defining episode of its author's life.

Behind James O'Barr's gentle and shy manner is an active mind, which is no stranger to paranoia. He's a man who is more comfortable signing his autograph on his comic book than discussing why he was asked for the autograph in the first place. Though he is now in middle age and has seen his creation continue to capture loyal fans for more than three decades, at the time O'Barr conceived the idea for *The Crow*, he was a US Marine.

O'Barr was born in 1960 in Detroit. His early childhood is not a time he looked back on with any nostalgia. "I was raised in orphanages and foster care until I was seven. And it wasn't a very pleasant time," he remembered. "I got adopted when I was seven. And that was an even worse time."

As a child, O'Barr was an avid reader, escaping from an intolerable reality into a world of fantasy. Like many neglected and abused children, reading enabled him to have another secret, emotional life: "I didn't restrict myself to just comic books. Pretty much read everything I could get my hands on." He was also lucky enough to find another escape. "I had a difficult time communicating with people," he explained, "so I worked on other skills, writing and drawing, to get my ideas and things across that way." His ideas involved science fiction characters and monsters, but as yet he had no thought of creating an entire world and setting a story in it.

O'Barr claims that in his early teens his drawing style was inspired by an unlikely artist, Michelangelo. But by the time he was fifteen, his big influences were sword and sorcery paperbacks. Most notable among these were Robert E. Howard's breathtaking stories featuring Conan of Cimmeria, bearing covers by the legendary American artist Frank Frazetta, whose stunning oil paintings definitively portray the savage, barbarian pop culture icon.

The young O'Barr found little encouragement for his work until he was age fourteen. While attending a comic book convention, he met an artist who he admired, Vaughn Bode. Bode, he said, "was the first one ever to give me really positive feedback on my stuff." And O'Barr was impressed with Bode's style: "The way he portrayed violence, and just the way he laid out a scene, was really influential on me."

However, he met other artists whose reactions were not only negative but expressed in a manner that was a hurtful memory to the sensitive O'Barr: "There was this guy Dave Cockrum, he was like a big deal because he was drawing the X-Men at the time. He essentially told me I had no talent and I should take up truck driving!" Ironically, this luminary comic book superstar of the late 1970s, who was also known for his key "runs" on DC's *Legion of Superheroes* and Marvel's *Avengers*, would later go on to struggle with a growing fan distaste for his later artwork in the 1980s, towards the end of his career. And he happened to be dead wrong assessing O'Barr's talent, and the high levels of skill and mastery he would soon attain.

O'Barr readily admits that *The Crow* is directly autobiographical. The story is based on his own tragic, youthful romance. Just like the comic version he was to create, the real story started out very happily: "When I was sixteen, I met this girl, and she was the best thing that ever happened to me. Up until that point, my life kinda felt like an endurance test. And I felt like I finally got to the end of it, good things were finally gonna start happening to me. And so, I was with this girl for three years and we were engaged to get married when we graduated, and she was my whole world.

"A couple of weeks before her eighteenth birthday, she was killed by a drunk driver. That was just . . . completely devastating to me. I had no idea what to do with my life then. I was filled with such anger and frustration that I thought I was gonna just destroy myself. So, I carried this around for a couple of years and I just felt like I was full of this poison." The only way that O'Barr could work the tragedy out of his system was to draw and write about it, trying to "work out all that anger and frustration and bitterness towards God."

Although O'Barr claims that he is not religious, he felt "someone was responsible." His adoptive parents were Baptist, "but my girlfriend was Catholic. And so, I kinda came through the Catholic Church sideways.

. . . I liked a lot of the ideas and the imagery in the religion, but I don't particularly adhere to any one religion."

Unable to see a clear path ahead, shortly after his fiancée was killed, O'Barr joined the military. He signed on for three years, again looking for an escape. "I didn't wanna think any more. I wanted somebody to tell me what to do. I just wanted some direction. Put some structure back in my life. So, I made this horrible mistake in joining the Marines. And I was in Berlin for a little while, and basically that's where I came up with the idea [for *The Crow*], when I was over there, because that was a really isolating experience."

The Marines soon discovered that O'Barr had some artistic talent, and they put it to use, loaning him out to the Army to illustrate hand-to-hand combat manuals. "I was okay with that," O'Barr recalled. "It got me out of marching and doing drills and things."

In his spare time, O'Barr now began to work on the story that would change his life. Always a loner, *The Crow*'s themes of love, death, and retribution comforted him while he was doing a job he hated. He conceived the character of the Crow as a supernatural force, driven in equal parts by love and revenge: "One day I just began drawing *The Crow*. It came pouring out. My character Eric is able to return from the grave because some things just cannot be forgiven. And I believe that there could be a love so strong that it could transcend death, that it could refuse death, and this soul would not rest until it set things right."

This is almost a verbatim quote from Robert E. Howard's epic Conan story, *Queen of the Black Coast*, where Conan's murdered lover, the she-pirate Belit, transcending the bonds of her recent death, appears before him in battle as a ghostly, sword-wielding apparition, thereby saving her barbaric paramour from certain doom. This powerful influence cannot be underestimated and helps explain the timeless, primal, and powerful appeal of *The Crow*.

O'Barr continued with disarming frankness and admitted that, "Essentially, Eric was me. He doesn't physically resemble me, but all the emotional aspects were drawn from myself."

Almost every character in the story is based on a real person, some of them actual friends of O'Barr's. The names of the characters are names he copied from graffiti. The setting is his hometown of Detroit, using many actual places and specific buildings.

The Crow reflects O'Barr's bleak view of American cities: "They all kinda break down to all the same essential ingredient: there's good parts of town, the bad parts of town, and the ghetto. It's equal in every major city in the US. And there was this image of Detroit as the 'Murder Capital of the World' for a while, but now it's just an abandoned city. There are just empty skyscrapers everywhere and it just has more of a sense of sadness than danger."

His tour of duty done, O'Barr drifted back to the United States and worked in a car repair shop. Although he was taking *The Crow* more seriously, at this time he had no thought of selling it, or even showing it to anyone. "The process of writing and drawing it was painful," he said. "I could only do it in little increments. I thought it might be this cathartic experience . . . get all these negative emotions onto paper, but a lot of the time it was like picking a scab. It was just like cutting scars for myself."

Eventually, in the late 1980s, he decided to pitch what he had, about the first forty pages, to publishers. The response was negative. "They didn't get it. Or they missed the whole point entirely. Or the companies that did respond, they liked the violence, but they didn't like the moody scenes. 'That's too gloomy! You need to take out some of these rainy scenes and put more action in it.'" O'Barr felt that nobody understood his work and that they were trying to turn it into something more conventional. "They wanted to make it this *Death Wish* with zombies type thing."

Meanwhile, his regular life had to go on, but after several years of working on cars, he needed a change. "I was really bored. I kinda went through my whole life like that. I would learn something until I knew everything about it, and then I would just be totally bored and wanted to do something else." So O'Barr decided that he "wanted to do something really difficult. And I said, 'Well, medical school. It'll be difficult.' And I took the test for it. And I tested really well on it. And I got to skip a lot of the preliminary courses. And I did that for two years."

By now, O'Barr had pretty well given up on *The Crow*, feeling that it was a private creation that nobody else would ever understand. It sat on his shelf for a couple more years, by which time he was hanging around a Detroit comic bookstore, Comics Plus. Comics Plus was a mecca for local artists interested in comic books, and O'Barr and three or four others "all used to meet up there on Fridays when the new books came out." O'Barr began to work for Gary Reed, the store owner, using his artistic skills to paint T-shirts: "Anything to help pay for my [medical] books and things. And one day he asked me if I had done any comic strips, and I told him I started this one a few years ago. And he asked if he could see it, and I brought it in, and he liked it. He asked if he could publish it, and that was basically how Caliber Comics got started."

So, after all his rejections, just like that, O'Barr had found a publisher. This was just as well, because his medical school studies had hit a snag: "After two years the money ran out." He returned to working on cars, just as *The Crow* started to sell.

The Crow's first issue sold well, considering its limited distribution. O'Barr was not entirely surprised, because he had always been sure that there was an audience out there somewhere who would share his vision. "It wasn't like a typical comic book audience; it wasn't just thirteen-year-old males. Most of my readers were sixteen to twenty-five years old. Kinda like that fringe element deal, the alternative element. I knew they were out there, but I just didn't know if they would find it or not. But word of mouth . . . There were virtually no ads for it or anything. There was no promotion for it. And they just kinda found it."

In that first year, *The Crow* had four printings, but Caliber's financial woes prevented them from printing any further issues. This didn't really matter, because in 1989 another publisher, Tundra, acquired the rights from Caliber and continued to publish the installments until, by 1992, O'Barr had finally completed his story. Tundra published the complete story in three collections, grimly titled "Pain & Fear," "Irony/Despair," and "Death." In the last chapter O'Barr's alter ego, Eric Draven, accomplishes his mission, avenging his fiancée's brutal murder (also his own execution), and finally achieves peace through a real death. *The Crow* became the most successful story in Tundra's history, selling more than eighty thousand copies. The enormity of this success comes into focus once you realize that in today's marketplace, even the top publishers (Marvel & DC) struggle selling thirty thousand copies a month for most of their books.

Why did *The Crow* make such an impact? It was certainly different from existing comic books of the period. Although it did share a theme with some of them, a hero who is killed and returns to life to take revenge on his killers. At the time the stories and characters of other spectral avengers risen from the grave to pursue vengeance, like *Deadman* and *The Spectre*, were more mystical and colorfully psychedelic; they lacked *The Crow*'s gritty and grounded punk sensibilities. Its mood of despair, entwined with its final message of redemption, had a strong appeal to the new generation of readers.

Its visual style was strikingly different. Each black-and-white frame showed a strong cinematic influence. "I always thought of it as a little black-and-white film," said O'Barr, "and not really as a comic book series." The 1919 German Expressionist movie, *The Cabinet of Dr Caligari*, and 1940s film noir influenced him too: "I really like that stark black-and-white look, with the obscure camera angles."

The Crow was also not without its literary pretensions. In it O'Barr quotes from the French poets Georges Bataille, Antonin Artaud, and Arthur Rimbaud, as well as Lewis Carroll and Edgar Allan Poe.

Music was one of the biggest influences on O'Barr's work. He was a fan of punk and rock musicians Iggy Pop, Ian Curtis, and Robert Smith. In Germany he had seen "all the new wave artists. But you know that was like the end of the punk movement, and then it was kinda splintering up into the Gothic element. I saw a lot of those bands over in Berlin, like Bauhaus." In The Crow, O'Barr quotes from his music idols, such as rock poet Jim Carroll and The Cure's Robert Smith. Indeed, O'Barr dedicated the first issue of his comic to the lead singer of the art-punk band Joy Division, Ian Curtis. He was able to identify with Curtis, who had fought a losing battle against drug addiction, depression, and epilepsy, and then, at twenty-five, hanged himself.

The image of the crow seems to touch a chord in many people, and there has been much speculation about why O'Barr chose that particular bird to symbolize his leading character. Some aficionados claim that the choice was inspired by a Navaho Indian legend in which the crow is the messenger who takes the soul to its ancestors, while others have speculated that the crow legend comes from Greek mythology. According to the author himself though, the reasons for choosing a crow were much less grandiose: "I didn't wanna draw too many parallels to Edgar Allan Poe's The Raven. Poe was like a minor influence on me, and I didn't want people to mistake this for some kind of tribute to Poe. A crow is just a typical carrion bird, it wasn't anything special." Finally, adding to the many mysteries surrounding his work and the movie, he admitted, "I'm sure there must've been a reason for it in the beginning, but I'm not sure why I picked the crow."

O'Barr believes that The Crow has been very influential and began a movement that spawned a new trend in comics. "The black-and-white, violent, really stark camera angle, Gothic-looking book. With all these elements, it was really the first one like it."

HOLLYWOOD OPTIONS THE COMIC   2

THERE ARE MANY AND VARIED ROUTES by which literary works are turned into films. *The Crow*'s journey from comic book to film was typically convoluted. The details of exactly how Hollywood became interested in it are buried in several conflicting accounts.

James O'Barr's recollection is that a young producer, Rachel Talalay, heard about the comic and called him out of the blue. He remembers that Talalay offered him a deal that he didn't like. O'Barr said that before he could finally make his mind up about Talalay's offer, he got a call from Jeff Most and John Shirley, the same two men who Talalay claimed introduced her to the project.

Rachel Talalay's version is rather different. She recalls that a young wannabe producer, Jeff Most, and a friend of his, novelist John Shirley, approached her with *The Crow* while she was working on the production of *A Nightmare on Elm Street 4* (1988) at New Line Cinema. At the time, the *Nightmare on Elm Street* franchise was a big success for New Line, and they were looking for other horror writers and had talked with Shirley about his novels. Talalay thought that *The Crow* was "weird and dark" and was very unsure about it, so she decided to show it to a colleague at New Line, Mike De Luca: "I was a production person and he was a development person. He was 'Mr. Young Comic Book Head'!"

Although he is a comic book fan who shortly after brought other comic books to the screen, including *The Mask* (1994) and *Blade* (1998), De Luca's view was that, "It's so dark and there are a lot of better comic books out there, a lot more commercial comic books out there." So New Line passed on *The Crow*.

Talalay thought all along that *The Crow* could never be what the PG–13 audience for comic book movies wanted. She admits she was later surprised at the movie's success, but this merely goes to reinforce celebrated screenwriter William Goldman's old adage: "Nobody knows anything."

But to be fair, Talalay, now in her early sixties, has gone on to be a brilliantly respected TV director, perhaps best known for her dynamic and compelling work on the great British science-fantasy franchise *Dr. Who*, featuring Peter Capaldi's eccentric regeneration of The Doctor in such groundbreaking episodes as "Dark Water" and "Heaven Sent." She has also been tapped for directing the upcoming *Dr. Who 60th Anniversary Special*, scheduled to air in late 2023, which is notable not merely for the brand's longevity, but for actor David Tennant's return to the TARDIS, as arguably the well-traveled Time Lord's most-popular incarnation.

One can only imagine what a talent of her magnitude might have done with *The Crow*, back then, or today.

Whichever version is accurate, Jeff Most and John Shirley were about to change James O'Barr's life.

John Shirley had seen a lot of the less savory aspects of life but not lost his enthusiasm along the way. Along with his often brutally frank and sarcastic humor was a radical mind, not afraid to be politically incorrect. He started out as a singer-songwriter, notably having written twenty-three song lyrics recorded by the band Blue Oyster Cult. He also has become a successful novelist, publishing more than eighty-four books, including ten short-story collections. Shirley wrote the first screenplay of *The Crow*, and since he introduced the comic book to Jeff Most, he was instrumental in getting the movie made.

Jeff Most was ideally suited to be a movie producer. He had plenty of imagination, creativity, and persistence. His gravelly voice and mild New York accent conveyed a personable and persuasive manner. Most produced *The Crow* and went on to develop and make *The Crow* sequels. He created what Hollywood always dreams about—a franchise; a series of films that has a guaranteed core audience. Through the 2000s, Most continued efforts to keep *The Crow* franchise alive until he was shut out by the right's owner, Pressman Films, over personal and creative differences.

Beyond *The Crow*, Most has produced numerous films and series, including the CW TV Network's action-adventure 2022 series *Professionals* and the Emmy Award–winning TV movie *The Courageous Heart of Irena Sendler*. He also developed a project based on the graphic novel *Razor* created by Everette Hartsoe. Most describes the heroine as a sort of spinoff of *The Crow*: "A guardian angel instead of an avenging one like *The Crow*."

After graduating from New York University Film School in 1982, Jeff Most moved to Los Angeles where, by the time he was twenty-three, he was working as the producer of Columbia Pictures Television's daily syndicated show *Top 40 Videos*. Although he was a hot-shot success at *Top 40 Videos*, rising from production coordinator to associate producer to producer in only six months, Most's ultimate goal was to produce movies. He was already on the hunt for literary material that could be adapted for the big screen. It was this search that would bring him closer to John Shirley.

In Shirley, the wannabe producer had found a published writer who wanted to get into the movie industry and, more importantly, whose books were available to him. For his part, Shirley saw that Jeff Most was a young producer who was eager to option material and was serious about getting it sold. He gave Most "a cardboard box full of paperback originals I'd written, various kinds: horror novels, science fiction novels. He had an armful of them. . . . And like so many guys that start out as sort of cliff-hangers, he would talk you into doing it for a dollar! But I got paid for everything he made."

Most optioned one of Shirley's novels, *The Specialist*, and "got it set up at Limelight with commercials and video producer Simon Fields. He and I were the original producers, and then we got it set up at Warner Bros. That became the movie with Sylvester Stallone and Sharon Stone." But in 1988, that was still a long way in the future. At the time of the Warner Bros. deal, neither Most nor Shirley had made any significant money out of optioning *The Specialist*, and they were, in effect, back to square one.

Since Most was making no headway trying to set up other Shirley novels, he devised another very ingenious strategy. He had noticed that the studios were becoming increasingly interested in adapting comics for the screen. *Batman* and *Dick Tracy* were already in production, and studios were actively looking for other comics that could be turned into movies. So, Most's plan was to get John Shirley's books made as movies—by first turning them into comics: "I thought a way into getting a sale would be by creating a comic book off of this script which would also act as a storyboard for the movie." But none of these novel-to-screenplay-to-comic-to-movie plans ever came to fruition, so Most and Shirley were left still looking for projects.

This was the point at which they discovered *The Crow*.

One of Shirley's ideas had been rejected by O'Barr's publisher, Caliber Press. "They wrote to me and said, 'It sounds cool. We would like to do something with you, but *Angry Angel* is too much like something we already have—*The Crow*.'" When Shirley heard that, he naturally wanted to check out just exactly what *The Crow* was, because he was also "looking around for something that I might be able to option and might be a movie. I was deliberately looking at black-and-white comics, because I thought that I would be able to afford them if I optioned them. They're not gonna be big companies, black-and-white comics. Usually, it's not gonna be Marvel. You can't afford that. And I thought I could make a deal with some of the independents, and they would benefit, and I would benefit. And then I saw *The Crow* and I opened it, and I looked at three pages before I decided it was a movie."

In James O'Barr, Shirley had found a writer whose thematic interests coincided with his own. They were both fascinated by dark visions, in Shirley's case by "the dark avenger that comes at night . . . probably just my arrested adolescence and my background culturally."

Shirley saw that movies were a major influence on *The Crow*, which explained its very cinematic feel. "I know there's influence from samurai films on purpose. I mean he [O'Barr] loved them," Shirley remembered. "And Hong Kong films. Films like probably *Chinese Ghost Story*. Film noir influenced him. It was obvious. He knows all that stuff. He used to talk about it a lot. And so, you know it was a comic book that really was inseminated by some kind of wild, orgiastical coupling of unknown movies. From there, his cinematic influence becomes actualized in the way he draws things, and then people look at the cinematic inspiration, see that, and they think, 'That's a movie!'"

It was that specific cinematic quality that made Shirley immediately see *The Crow*'s movie possibilities: "It struck me as being—even just standing there reading in the comic book store—very archetypal, the bare bones of a movie, like something dark. It sprang out, full grown, almost in just a few pages, so that it doesn't require a lot of development, you can just see the bones of the story outright." He decided to abandon his own comic idea: "I said, 'The hell with *Angry Angel*. Maybe I can take *this* to somebody!'" The somebody was, of course, Jeff Most.

For his own reasons, Most found that *The Crow* touched a special chord in him. He had never really adjusted to the suburban, centerless sprawl of Los Angeles. The comic reminded him of "the lower East Side. The last place I'd had in New York was a loft on 2nd Street and Avenue B in the middle of Hell, with junkies standing outside my door and a shooting gallery next door. I'd have to wear a big overcoat 'cause I was going up to work at Rock Center, working at *Saturday Night Live*, and push them away from the door in the morning. It just brought me back to that hellish environment which, strange as it may sound, was very soothing to me."

As well as the look of *The Crow*, Most was immediately attracted to the lead character, Eric Draven: "I always had a particular affinity for the notion of romantic heroes." Most feels that, in the right circumstances, there's a hero in every one of us. "It's a reminder for me, in creating works of art that focus on these very strong emotional centers, that we are all good people who would save others ahead of ourselves, and of love being the greatest motivating element in anyone's life. I saw that in *The Crow*. There was a guy in such a prescient moment in his life, in love in a flourishing moment, [who] was tragically killed, and I thought that encompassed such a wealth of emotion."

Of course, Most also saw that *The Crow* was an "Adults Only" comic; that its very darkness meant it was destined for a very different audience from *Batman* or *Dick Tracy*. That difference was very attractive to both Shirley and Most. Shirley said that Most "liked the fact that it was very hip. I mean, so many action projects are just sort of like libertarian assholes with guns. . . . We felt like so many action movies had that feel."

The comic also attracted Shirley on a musical level: "It was also extremely 'rock culture' in its feel and very romantic in its flavor . . . and that romanticism of it, the deep romanticism, the Gothic romanticism of it, set it apart."

When Most got the first issue of *The Crow*, less than a thousand copies had been sold, so there was no public reaction to base a judgment on. But once he had read it, he knew that he wanted to devote all his energies to this one project. With no sense of irony, he admitted, "We figured this guy is young, he's good and he's probably cheap. We got a hold of *The Crow* . . . I want to make this movie."

Most was impressed by the style of *The Crow*, by the fact that O'Barr "told the story as if he was a film director sitting with a storyboard artist and these were storyboards. And it was reality—reality with a fantasy element."

Most got in touch with O'Barr and spent hours on the phone with him, discussing the storyline. The more they talked, the more he was compelled by it. Most offered James O'Barr a token one dollar for a two-year option, but Most said that he optioned the book for so little because "I made a good back-end deal for James. I told him I wanted his creative involvement. I pledged that I would not do what everyone else had done in Hollywood, which was to make a PG-13 comic book movie." In fact, financially Most had little choice, because "When I came along, I didn't have any money. I had left my job after five years of *Top 40 Videos*, and I was setting up *The Specialist* and living off of fairly paltry development money. I was staking my career on films."

The deal O'Barr wanted from Most and Shirley was that he would sell a two-year option, and that if the film was made into a movie, he would get a further $50,000, plus other fees down the road if sequels or television series were made. He was pleased that, "they agreed to it. I kept the publishing rights, and I could retain the copyright on the character."

Of course, Most couldn't just go out and sell the comics. He had to have a version of the project that Hollywood would understand, a "treatment." This formal version of the story (usually about twenty pages) would outline the narrative, present the characters, the atmosphere, and the uniqueness of the project. Many movie projects are sold on treatments alone. But O'Barr was still working on *The Crow*, and Shirley and Most needed to know what happened so that they could end the story. So, O'Barr gave them the final part verbally and in notes and drawings. Finally, Most and Shirley had an option on what they thought was a hot project and a treatment. All they had to do now was sell it.

Over the next two years, Jeff Most took his vision of *The Crow* all over Hollywood, both to studios and independent film companies. He had no real ammunition to get a production company interested in *The Crow*. He had no star or hot director attached. All he had was the first issue of the black-and-white underground comic, a treatment, and a vision.

Hawking a project around, getting rejection after rejection, is just a fact of life for wannabe producers, and the way they respond to it is a true test of their mettle. "This was a passion for me. I had already set up what was going to be a big commercial movie [*The Specialist*] at Warner Bros. And I had always had this plan," Most said, explaining how he was able to handle this process because of the philosophy he had developed for himself, "which was obviously always, 'Make money for the people you work for,' but also, 'Try to split your time between making blockbusters and things that are really heartfelt.' And this was a heartfelt one for me."

Most made contact with Pressman Films on the recommendation of a friend, Barbara Lieberman. Lieberman was Most's old producer from *Saturday Night Live* in New York, who had originally advised him to come out to Los Angeles and try to earn his stripes as a producer. She was now in Los Angeles herself, producing at Saban Entertainment. And for those of you not in the know, the company's owner, Haim Saban, was about to become not only a media powerhouse, but an influential and politically savvy billionaire philanthropist, through a strange confluence of unlikely events, where good timing, bad television, and exploitive merchandising yielded an empire. In reality, it boiled down to a pithy combination of four previously uncorrelated, little words: Mighty Morphin Power Rangers.

Most estimated that his effort to enlist Lieberman's interest was perhaps his forty-ninth try. *The Crow* was not for Saban, but Lieberman introduced Most to Caldecot Chubb, who was Pressman Films' head of development at the time.

Through Chubb, the project went to Ed Pressman, who expressed some interest. But Most's first two meetings at Pressman Films were with Chubb, not Pressman. Most said, "Comic books were not his interest." Chubb simply had different tastes, and he went on to produce the movies *Mallrats*, *Eve's Bayou*, and *Pootie Tang*. Most recalls that Chubb was baffled by Pressman's interest in *The Crow*. And Pressman was interested, but he wasn't prepared to buy an option until he was happy with where the project was heading. "But the treatment wasn't enough for Ed," continued Most. If they wanted to sell this project to Pressman, they had to come up with something better.

And Ed Pressman was very well worth spending the time on. He was a prolific and award-winning movie producer whose output included critical successes such as *Wall Street*, *Reversal of Fortune*, and cutting-edge independent films *Badlands* and *The Bad Lieutenant*.

And as the workings of Fate tend to produce unlikely coincidence, Pressman was also the executive producer on both *Conan the Barbarian* and *Conan the Destroyer*, two successful genre films, which made money, while launching Arnold Schwarzenegger's meteoric rise to stardom, but never came close to the quality of their literary source material, which so strongly influenced the young O'Barr.

Pressman also had a reputation for giving new producers and directors a chance to make movies. It's a truth of the industry: The unknowns work cheaper.

"It's not a surprise," Most recalled, "but when I finally counted up, I had fifty-one production companies and studios turn me down! And the fifty-second place I went was Ed Pressman. I was running out of time and it was very frustrating." Most's option with James O'Barr was in its second year, and Most felt as if he was getting nowhere. Pressman had shown more interest in *The Crow* than anyone else, so there was no choice but to work on the treatment again.

In writing the treatment, Most and John Shirley were not always on the same page. Most wanted to make the movie version "much more cinematic. John wanted to verbatim follow the comic, because he believed in the right of an author to have their work covered exactly in the same manner." That was exactly the view a writer would be expected to take and, unsurprisingly, O'Barr was also very happy about the idea of sticking strictly to his story. But they had to find a compromise that would suit them all, and more especially Pressman.

They produced two more drafts of the treatment by December 1990. It had been six months since Most had initially been introduced to Pressman, and he now had only two months left on his option with James O'Barr. Luckily, Pressman liked this third draft of the treatment and agreed to do a deal with Most as producer and to take up the option with O'Barr. Most insisted that Shirley be hired to write a draft of a screenplay, which would mean working closely with Chubb, a man who they already knew did not share their vision.

Meanwhile, the comic was still relatively unknown. The second issue had just hit stores and had sold only a couple of hundred copies, while the first issue had sold only twelve hundred copies. But, for the tiny distribution outlets available to small-time Caliber Comics, this was not a bad result. Most knew that O'Barr was getting fan mail through Caliber, and *The Crow* was actually developing an audience.

However, the Pressman deal did not mean that Most had found the money to make *The Crow* into a movie. This was simply a "development deal," under which Pressman would finance the writing of the screenplay. And after that, who knew what might happen . . .

WRITING THE SCREENPLAY 3

HOLLYWOOD IS A RENOWNED writer's graveyard, a place about which celebrated 1930s novelist and screenwriter Raymond Chandler famously said, "If my books had not been as good, I would not have been invited there. If they had been better, I would not have gone."

Even before work was started on the screenplay of *The Crow*, John Shirley knew, "There are no films in Hollywood which are just written by the writer, no matter what the credit says, because the nature of the business is collaborative, the nature of the artist is collaborative. Long after you think you have a finished script, if there's anything artistic about it at all, the director will be someone who'll bring to it his own sensibility, and that means he's going to kind of rewrite it in some way, according to his own instincts. . . . And even before that, producers have constant input all the time. Writers are always having to try to hold the line against their producers' impulses to put in 'just this' and take out 'this and that'! And they often ruin movies in Hollywood. In Jeff [Most]'s case I think he always was helpful. For the most part he gave good suggestions."

Shirley also had a very definite opinion about the current Hollywood system of buying a screenplay and then ruining it through "development." "Studios get really excited about a first draft of the movie and pay an enormous amount of money for it," he said. "And then they'll put it through all kinds of stuff—that's all kinds of notes and all kinds of input—so that it loses what it originally had that they were excited about, and they make some awful version later. I don't think that really happened with *The Crow*, but it was in danger of it. There were a lot of drafts that just got thrown away, and in some ways I think what finally ended up being shot was closer to the first draft than almost anything else."

John Shirley wrote the first draft, taking account of Jeff Most's ideas, while, he said, "James O'Barr gave input to everybody, and always has." Of course, he added, speaking from the heart as a writer himself, "What is the artist gonna do? He's gonna say, 'Stick to my story!'" And Most and Shirley did try to be faithful to the intentions of the comic. "For example, I tried to take things from the comic," said Shirley, "like the way the Crow moves as he speaks to his intended victims . . . He moves in a balletic sort of way, with a samurai sword. And he would move like a dancer with this sword, declaiming poetry he read, in the comics. Sort of a tragic figure. It was almost like a passion play or an opera. And I tried to bring that to it, because I thought it was beautiful the way O'Barr made that live. I put that in from the comics, and I kinda did my own spin on it. I think that I tried to modify the violence a bit. I wanted it to be a story with a lot of action and with that core of revenge happening, but I tried to modify it, because I just didn't want it to get lost in the morass of bloody movies out there."

One aspect of the comic that O'Barr had left vague was exactly what Eric Draven did for a living. Shirley and Most had the idea of making him a guitarist, thought Shirley, "because the guitar is the totem. It's not that far from a guitar to a rifle." O'Barr didn't much care for this, saying, "My idea was to make Eric a kind of Everyman not something special or, you know, not this hero type. In fact, when they said they were gonna make him this rock star musician in the film, I thought that was a really poor idea because it's elevated above everyone else." But Jeff Most had always been interested in music, and he remembered, "The first thing I said was, 'This is a music piece I know the audience will go after. I want to make him look cool,' because he had no job in the comics. So, I made him a guitarist, and the idea was [he was in] an underground band, a little indie label–type band. No rock star stuff. People always looked back and said, 'Oh he was a rock star,' but that never was the idea. He was supposed to be just a little indie guy. Well, we've never had a rock 'n' roll hero, know what I mean? We've never had a character, a dead rocker to boot, come back from the afterlife."

There was one deliberate change from the comic book Crow to the film version however. In his screenplay, Shirley was determined not to reproduce the Crow's use of drugs, because "I don't wanna encourage anybody to shoot up, but in the comics he did and it showed that he was part of an alternative to the mainstream culture, the street culture, the rock culture. He had sort of a hip criminal mentality or something." When he saw *Pulp Fiction* (1994), Shirley was disturbed by Quentin Tarantino's depiction of drug use: "One of the more likeable characters had to make a commercial for heroin even though he had to re-start some girl's heart, they made it somehow seem worth it."

Otherwise, John Shirley's first script was, said Jeff Most, "An exact duplicate of the comic's up to that point . . . We were satisfied with the first draft, it just needed more work."

As with any movie screenplay, everybody who read it had an opinion and wasn't shy about expressing it. So, when the first draft was delivered, Shirley thought that, "Some liked it and some didn't. It was pretty close to the comic book's, and that goes against their instincts, that's all. They like to screw with things more."

Of Ed Pressman himself, Shirley got the impression that he had little direct involvement. "Mostly, I think he let other people do it," Shirley said. "He had input too. I don't remember exactly what it was, but he had an Andy Warhol approach: sort of just walk through the factory and see the people working." But Pressman Films, like every studio and big company, had someone in charge of what is known as "development" in the movie industry. This job basically consists of collating opinions and trying to get the screenplay rewritten to match them. At Pressman, this person was Caldecot Chubb.

Chubb, a man who, by many accounts, felt that he was one of nature's aristocrats, was not an ideal collaborator for John Shirley. Chubb had a basic difference of social philosophy from Shirley, which was reflected in their differing opinions about *The Crow*. "Corporate types," Shirley believed, "are, you know, among the world's evilest. I think they kill people all the time, like covering up the toxicity they introduce to the environment." So, Shirley said, he wanted to, "Make the top villain one of these really powerful, ivory tower corporate slime balls, and Chubb of the 'Chubb Group' rejected the idea for some obscure reason. He felt that it was like vilifying white-collar guys. I remember him telling me he was sick of white-collar guys being vilified, and [Michael] Milken and all these guys being picked out as society's current Al Capone or something. So, we disagreed about that pretty sharply. . . .

"In a way, this is a class issue that developed in the writing of *The Crow*," Shirley continued. "I felt that my point of view was more working class and so is *The Crow*. His [Chubb's] point of view was more the upper classes which abuse street people as being the villains, and poor people as being the villains, and gangs being the ultimate villainy—rather than the corporate gangs that *really* run things."

This was to be a struggle that John Shirley would lose as the screenplay went through several more drafts. He believes that Pressman Films wanted the screenplay to be "more Hollywood. They wanted the Crow more sympathetic, and they wanted the bad guys to be more rounded or something.

"The second draft," Shirley acknowledged, "was somewhat disastrous because I was trying to please everybody. I think Chubb deliberately set me up to write a script that could not be made—because he wanted to get rid of me."

While not necessarily signing on to Shirley's conspiracy theory, Jeff Most agreed that Shirley wrote a second draft that in some ways took steps backwards. "This was because of the directives he was being given," Most said, "which were being overridden from what I was telling him to do." The rewrite notes came from Caldecot Chubb, of course, and he now seized the opportunity to get rid of Shirley. Most recalled, "Shirley got fired after the second draft, and I pleaded with Ed to keep him on and he wouldn't. I said, 'Look, I'll go up and work with John. You've got to give me eight weeks. I'll go live in his home and I will rewrite it with him. But you've got to give us an opportunity,' and he actually agreed not to hire anybody else while we did that."

Most now settled in to try to create the movie he really wanted to make: "During that third draft, I was starting to make substantial changes. I had fights with John Shirley about it because, again, he wanted to maintain exactly what was in the comic. Since we no longer had to worry, because we were on a free draft, about taking directives from people that didn't understand the material in my mind, I went kind of hog wild."

As he worked on the third draft, Most felt that although O'Barr's personal tragedy had inspired *The Crow*, many elements in the story weren't fully explained: "I would ask questions of logic, to which there wasn't always necessarily an answer." Most remembered that O'Barr would tell him, "'It was like . . . Well, Jeff, I didn't really think about that.'" Most understood O'Barr's problem. "You know, O'Barr started this in '81, and it didn't get published until '88, because everybody in the world turned it down. It was this dark, gruesome, cathartic experience that nobody wanted to publish," Most explained. "There was a lot of stuff that I had to kind of make sense of."

Most was primarily concerned about the resurrection of the Eric Draven character: "A person comes back from the dead and they don't have any memories, and the crow can sometimes take the soul back to the Earth, to put wrong things right. That's in the book. What I felt needed refinement was the notion that if you came back, why wouldn't you want to insert yourself into your life? Why wouldn't you just go, 'Hey, I don't want to go back anywhere, I don't want to be dead!'

"So, my notion was, well, you have to have a clean palette, and that a 'familiar,' the bird, could only take you on your 'mission' . . . So, I came up with two things. The first was the bird that you would follow and have the 'crow vision.'" This was a powerful visual concept, in which some of the movie's story would be seen from the bird's point of view. These shots would help to advance the story, as the audience gets an omniscient view of events.

Most's second concept was, he said, "To give the Crow empathic qualities, which he didn't have in the comic. He could touch people and things and use touch and position and place. Meaning the bird would take him to a place, [with the Crow] not knowing what he was doing [there]. He was just following this bird. If you come back from the dead, and this bird is around you, you'd follow it, and the bird would lead you. And only when the bird led you to places, gave you information, would you then start to put back the pieces of who you were, what happened to you, and what you needed to know to take care of the bad guys.

"I just needed to tie everything together. So, the idea of not only using thought to *get* memories, but of using empathic qualities to be able to *deliver* them. So that you could, like in the climax of *The Crow*, give the pain—which, for example, Shelly [Eric Draven's fiancée] suffered for forty hours in the hospital room—to another individual."

Most took the greatest pride in one particular idea he contributed. He had read that, for a decade, on the wild night before Halloween, gangs had torched buildings in poor neighborhoods in Detroit: "I came up with the thing about Devil's Night [the night before Halloween]. I said, 'Okay, why don't I put Devil's Night in, and give the bad guys something to do.'" This enabled Most to change the reason for, and the manner of, Shelly's and Eric's murders. "In the comic, they were killed out on a country road by popped-up guys on speed and crack and that kind of stuff."

Most's idea came from his concern with character motivation: "I needed a rationale other than, you know, drug sellers were after a diamond ring and wanted to screw this girl and have some fun with these people and fuck around with them." He also wanted to tie the motivation in with the location because, "El Rey is the district [in Detroit] that O'Barr actually lived in as a very poor artist who was [also] an auto mechanic." So Most came up with the idea that the villains worked for a slumlord. "The idea was that the fires of Devil's Night were actually an ongoing real estate ploy to clean out an entire neighborhood," Most explained. "And in the context of the clean-and-sweep, the tenants really were being pushed out. This was just their regular activity, to get buildings cleaned out so they could be sold. This was part of my experience of New York gentrification. So, I needed to combine everything into a place," Most continued, "and have a backdrop as to what these guys did as a very pervasive evil. You know that they were drug dealers, but they were also for-hire killers."

At this stage in the screenplay's development, much of what is seen in the final movie was laid down. "I made many other little changes," Jeff Most added. "I changed Albrecht from white to black because I felt it was Detroit and I wanted a sympathetic black character." Also, the little girl in the comic was nine, and had a similar name to Shelly, so Most made her older and changed her name to Sarah: "She was just kind of like this waif . . . Odd little stuff which I put in as a writer, which I'm proud of because they were all character bits that were ultimately important."

In spite of all Most's new ideas, all of which found their way into the completed movie, John Shirley acknowledged, "The next version of the screenplay was way too long. I was trying to respond to all these contradictory notes . . . trying to work in something for everybody according to the notes. And you know, I'd've done anything to stay on the project. They didn't give me the chance and I'm still bitter about it, frankly. I would've rewritten it a thousand ways to sundown and bled for it, but I did not get the opportunity."

Most was also unhappy about the way this went down. "When John and I sat and edited the script, we told Ed when we'd deliver," he said. "We were busting our asses. We had to start from scratch, rewrite the dialogue, reframe the entire picture in the script, and Ed was getting edgy. His head of development, Chubb, didn't believe we were ever gonna get there and do it." Most and Shirley delivered the third draft a day late and, Most said, "The day we were supposed to deliver and we didn't deliver, they hired a writer they had standing in the wings—David Schow. They were literally waiting to close the deal. They were going to do it anyway. So, David Schow came on and used all those things we came up with in the third draft, which were the changes from the comic." Schow went on to write the version of the screenplay on which the movie was based.

It was left to Most to give Shirley the bad news that he was off the movie. "It broke my heart, I remember," said Shirley. "I went into a deep depression for a while afterwards. I had to take antidepressants for like a year. I had a relapse. It was a drag." But Shirley's regrets are not only for himself: "It upsets me because I didn't get a chance to finish the project. If they hadn't changed anything major in this, Brandon Lee would still be alive . . . because I had a lot less violence in my script."

Ed Pressman was now looking for a director. Jeff Most had already thought that it would be a good idea to get a music video or commercials director, since they are usually very strong visually. His original candidate was a well-known music video director, Julien Temple, who he had worked with at Limelight on *The Specialist,* and who had directed the movie *Absolute Beginners* and the Janet Jackson *Control* video. However, at the same time, another director was suggested to Most, an Australian of Greek origin, born in Egypt, who was also a commercial and music video director: Alex Proyas. The fact that Proyas had been a cameraman also impressed Most: "He had started as a director of photography, so he had an incredible eye." Proyas' impressive credit list included commercials for American Express, Coca Cola, and Nike and music videos with Fleetwood Mac, Sting, and INXS. Proyas wanted to direct a Hollywood movie, and since his commercial work paid well, he had the financial freedom to wait for just the right one.

Most was immediately impressed by Proyas' work. They talked on the phone and got along very well. Most was certainly not deterred from offering Proyas what they thought was his first movie (in fact, Proyas had made one small film in Australia, *Spirits of the Air, Gremlins of the Clouds,* which he wrote, produced, and directed): "I saw this very much in music video terms and I felt that we needed someone young and fresh and with an eye. I saw Alex's reel with the kind of shadings and lighting schemes, in pools of darkness and desaturation, and an eye which is phenomenal, clearly in keeping with the design work of panels that James O'Barr had drawn."

Alex Proyas had a pleasant, if quiet and introverted, manner, which conceals his determination to do things his way. He was renowned for having an "eye"; for knowing when things look good and how to make them that way.

When, after Shirley's departure, Proyas was hired as *The Crow*'s director, he read Shirley's last draft and said to Most, "'Jesus, you're ninety percent there, and we just hired this other guy [Schow]!'" Screen credits are often the subject of fierce dispute in Hollywood (sometimes arbitrated by the Writers Guild), and it is certainly a mark of John Shirley's contribution that his name finally shared the "Screenplay by" credit with David Schow. Of the process of apportioning credit, Most said, "He [Shirley] wrote a stack of scripts. I remember . . . standing with Alex Proyas because we had issues over credit, and Alex didn't quite understand how the Writers Guild worked. But there was a stack this high of pages that David had written, and John's was about this high—it was substantial. I guess it was in the spring of '92, probably around May or June."

Shirley believed that "Alex wanted to stay with me, as I recall . . . or maybe he was just telling me that. Who knows? Who knows what the reality is in Hollywood? I think he wanted to stay with me because somehow I would've found a way to make it work. . . . Basically, Dave Schow plugged away and plugged away and plugged away. He did numerous drafts and he found a way to make it work, along with the director. A lot of stuff Dave did was thrown out, but he was persistent. Working closely with the director I think made a big difference. And that's exactly what I would've done had I been given the chance."

Most said that Schow was hired because, "We were actually trying to orient it to be a New Line movie and he was Mike De Luca's guy. He had been working with Mike De Luca, who was a rising senior VP [at New Line] at the time and we had heard good things about him. He had been a horror writer, a splatterpunk horror novelist, and he seemed like a good choice . . . he was a good writer."

Schow had moved from fantasy short stories and novels to movie screenplays, and his biggest credits at this point were *Leatherface: Texas Chainsaw Massacre III* and *A Nightmare on Elm Street: The Dream Child* (the fifth installment in the series). This could have been deduced from his appearance, which seems to have been designed to shock. It was easier to imagine Schow in an underground club than walking into a movie executive's office.

Schow used the work that Most and Shirley had already done to create a fourth draft, and then a fifth. Most recognized that "David Schow's dialogue was predominantly what was used in the picture," but added, "it was our structure, our story, our characters, with the exception of Bai Ling, who played Myca." Now working with Proyas and Jeff Most, Schow certainly made a contribution, coming up with an idea to make the chief villain (Top Dollar) more weird. He proposed that Top Dollar have an Asian half sister (their father was in Vietnam), Myca, who would be his incestuous lover. Top Dollar's motivation would be to punish the world for Myca's tragic life, and she would also replace the function of the soothsayer character in Most and Shirley's script, by recognizing the power of the crow.

However, David Schow was very different from John Shirley: a darker character, who brought his own dreams and nightmares to the screenplay, and, said Most, "David was going in a different direction than I had gone with John Shirley." There was a danger that the movie could become too negative, too depressing, and Most saw that there had to be a lighter side to the screenplay. For that reason, as he worked with Schow, he said, "A

sense of humor was something we were writing to include in the script
. . . I kept worrying that it was just a very, very dark tone. And working
with David Schow, I became more and more concerned it was gonna be
very bleak.

"I remember that a solution came up, for us to lay out index cards,
and we did a checkerboard. We said, 'Okay, after every really dark and
violent scene, we need a scene that's uplifting.' And during that process,
we realized we needed a character to almost have a sense of humor, [to
realize] how ironic it is that you find yourself in this position, coming back
to Earth. Would you be simply a tunnel-vision killer? Or would you be
somebody who goes, 'My God, this is kind of odd!'"

This may be the last context in which you'd expect to find a reference
to the classic Frank Capra movie *It's a Wonderful Life*, but at this point,
it was to that film that Most turned for inspiration: "I remember always
referencing Clarence, the angel in *It's a Wonderful Life*. . . . It was just, for
me, what I imagined. We saw the Jimmy Stewart character feeling the
depths of what life would have been like had he not been there, and you
have Clarence, this angel, who tried to bring him a bit of light and show
him what the strange world is all about.

"So, I really wanted to make sure the character was not just simply, 'I
am Terminator. I kill.' We would imagine any of ourselves up there on
the screen in this very awkward situation, finding humor and finding light,
at the same time as mourning the loss of the precious love of their life."

As Most, Schow, and Proyas worked on the script, they had more and
more complaints from Caldecot Chubb. According to Jeff Most, he would
tell them, "No, no, that's all wrong. I can see it now, it should be this
way." Most felt that Chubb's view was irrelevant because, he said, "He
didn't understand the fifteen- to twenty-five-year-old sensibility the way
Alex and I did. He would say things like, 'Let's have him put an apron
on and have him sweep in this scene.' We'd say, 'You got to be kidding!
The fifteen-year-old boys will be rolling in the aisle!'" But Chubb was
sure that Schow, Most, and Proyas were missing the point. He was getting
progressively more annoyed with them. Eventually, he had a dispute with
Ed Pressman over his involvement with *The Crow* and left the company,
although before he left, in typical Hollywood fashion, he did secure a
coproducer credit.

During the script development period, Jeff Most no doubt made some
compromises about the story he originally envisioned, but he didn't seem
to have any bitterness about not getting credit for his huge input into
developing the script. He was simply focused on getting the movie made:

"I was very passionate about making it something more, even than what was in the comics, because that was, to me, how you fashion a character that would withstand a franchise. I knew that, and that's what I pitched to Ed. And when we signed Brandon Lee, we signed him for three pictures."

By the time the screenplay was finished, Most felt extremely confident about his project. "I always believed that it would become one of those movies that there would be an audience [for] that would come back for more, and it would be financially successful, and this was a character that could stand the test of time."

With a producer, director, and screenwriter working on the project, Ed Pressman now needed a line producer, an experienced person who could handle all the setting up and day-to-day problems of a movie, and who would also have the respect of the finance companies that would invest in the movie.

Pressman's choice was Robert [Bob] Rosen. Rosen had been in the industry for forty years in 1993 and had worked with many great directors, including John Frankenheimer. His formidable list of credits included *Little Big Man*, *A Man Called Horse*, and *French Connection II*. He had a graying goatee and a professional, almost paternal manner befitting the man who was by far the oldest person to work on the movie. He easily adopted the role of the "boss" on the set of *The Crow*.

Rosen had met Ed Pressman on a John Frankenheimer movie, *Year of the Gun*, shot in Rome with Sharon Stone and Andrew McCarthy. This was a difficult shoot. "Physically, it was a nightmare," Rosen recalled, "because we went over there and the lira against the dollar went crazy. And suddenly, this movie that we [originally] had X amount of dollars to do, we [now] had sixty percent of that, and we had to figure out a way to do it on that. And this was happening while we were shooting! So, it was a very complicated, difficult movie for me. Somehow, we managed to get it together, to the end, and have a wrap party. And because of that, a relationship kind of stuck, and so when *The Crow* started being developed at the Pressman organization, he called me to get involved."

The level of experience of the person actually in charge of physical production is very important to financing companies. Rosen knew that "Jeff [Most] was inexperienced in terms of actually producing a film, and so I'm sure that's one of the reasons the studio deal, the completion bond deal, got made and Ed Pressman wanted me to get the ball." Darryl Levine, who had worked with Ed Pressman before, and would later be *The Crow*'s wardrobe supervisor, knew why Rosen was hired: "Bob's deal was money—getting the best movie out. Bob has done this for forty years. It wasn't 'amateur hour' and wasn't Bob being an 'evil man.' It was . . . you know, he was Pressman's lieutenant on the movie, with the mandate to 'deliver the best you can.' And they were already talking about a franchise at that time."

Ultimately though, Rosen was not to see exactly eye to eye with Jeff Most, who said, "I did not hire him. Ed Pressman had worked with him previously on a picture that had been shot in Europe that Frankenheimer was directing." For Rosen's part, a hint that he may not have taken Jeff Most as seriously as he might came in his remark: "I was involved from the very beginning and . . . I mean, I shouldn't say from the very beginning. Jeff Most had a big project and had made a deal with Ed to do the project."

By the end of July 1992, things were looking good for *The Crow*. The project had a producer, Jeff Most; a line producer (credited as an executive producer), Robert Rosen; a director, Alex Proyas; and a screenplay on which the money would be raised and the production planning would be based.

At this stage, Rosen had seen the screenplay and thought that it was promising, yet he had no clear vision of what the final movie was going to look like. Meeting Alex Proyas changed all that: "Certainly I could see what Ed [Pressman] felt about it. And if we were able to pull this off it could be a very intriguing movie. Something I hadn't seen before, per se. Until I met Alex, I didn't have a clear vision of what the end print of this picture was going to be. And he did. He did from the very beginning."

FINDING ERIC DRAVEN 4

T HE *CROW* MOVIE PROJECT now had all the executives it could handle. What it needed was a star.

Obviously, having a known name would make selling the finished film much easier and increase its chance of success. A number of names were discussed in those early stages, including Christian Slater, Johnny Depp, River Phoenix, and rock singer-guitarist Charlie Sexton. But no offers were made to these or any other well-known actors who were considered because, said Jeff Most, "By the time we finished the script process, the one, the only person we ever made an offer to was Brandon."

They still had reservations and they still wanted a star name, but when they saw Brandon Lee's previous movie, *Rapid Fire*, they saw that the actor was not only tough but, more importantly, he also had a vital quality of sensitivity. Most saw that, "He just really seemed to embody that wide range of talents that we required for the role. Not only did we need a good actor, but we needed somebody who wasn't something like a killing machine. We needed somebody who the audience would really care about."

As the script development process had gone on, getting the audience to care about the character of Eric Draven had become more important. In Brandon, Most felt that he had seen an actor who had that vital "sense of humor" and would not have the image of, "I am Terminator. I kill." They had also seen in him "a great martial artist and developing actor."

The actor's physical skill was necessary, again because of previous decisions about the screenplay: "One great thing that we had focused on is that the Crow would have the power of ten men. And his actual fighting style in the comics was almost acrobatic ballet. It was not martial arts. You'll see if you look in the comics, he does pirouettes and tumbles and things like that, and we needed an athlete."

So, who was Brandon Lee, and exactly how had he acquired the diverse qualities so necessary to fulfill the vision of the Crow character that the creators of the movie had in mind?

His father was, of course, Bruce Lee, the legendary Hong Kong martial artist who changed martial arts by developing and adapting the various disciplines, crossing the previously taboo boundaries that divided one style from another. Paul Maslak, a successful movie producer and martial arts expert, and a former editor of *Inside Kung Fu* magazine, explained Bruce Lee's contribution to the development of martial arts this way: "The traditional martial arts systems, for the most part, are based on very ritualized forms, which are sort of choreographed shadow boxing, that everybody has to learn. And the secrets of the style are contained within these choreographed shadow boxing routines. And what Bruce said was, 'That's like learning to swim without water,' because if you're doing a fighting art, the way to learn to fight is to fight. So, Bruce was the one who said, 'Let's get rid of these forms. They're very pretty, but let's not look at them as anything other than a piece of dance choreography with martial arts moves in it.' What he said you have to do if you wanna fight, is you have to do things based on sparring drills and fighting full-contact. And it was his influence that caused the sport of kickboxing to be created."

Jeff Imada, who studied Bruce Lee's method, and who would become the stunt coordinator on *The Crow*, defined Bruce's view as, "What would be good for me, would not necessarily be a good technique for you, because maybe somebody's flexibility is real good, so they'd have good, strong kicks, and somebody else with no flexibility might hurt themselves and couldn't kick. So, for them, learning the kicking part of it wouldn't necessarily be advantageous to them in fighting, so they'd be better at hands, and so he'd emphasize the hands for them."

Bruce Lee knew, said Jeff Imada, "It would be ridiculous for somebody who's six foot, to bob and weave under somebody's punch who's five foot four. It'd be crazy: 'How come your bobbing and weaving technique's no good?' 'Well, I'm six feet tall, I could just push you down instead of going underneath you.' So that's what the philosophy was, basically to use what is useful and disregard what is not useful to yourself. Very individualized." In this flexible approach, Bruce Lee differed from other, rigid, martial arts teachers.

Bruce was also renowned for rejecting the traditional martial arts hierarchy of belts. And Jeff Imada agreed wholeheartedly with that: "He felt that too much emphasis was being put on belts. Like, 'Oh, I'm a black belt.' Well, so what? You're a black belt from this system and that guy's a black belt from that system, but a guy who's a green belt [from another system] maybe could kick your ass." Imada quotes Bruce Lee's famous remark: "'Belts are for holding up your pants.'"

By chance, Bruce Lee was born in San Francisco, while his father, a comic actor with the Hong Kong Cantonese Opera, was there on tour. Fortuitously, he thus obtained dual nationality. Starting at the age of six, Bruce became a child actor, making more than twenty movies in Hong Kong. When he was on the losing end of a fight in school, at the age of thirteen, he began to learn traditional martial arts, *Wing Chun*. In a strange parallel activity, he also learned to dance. In his teens, he began to trade dance lessons for martial arts lessons in other styles, and by the age of eighteen was not only a formidable and original martial artist but, he had also won the Hong Kong Cha-cha-cha dance championship. But Bruce had an explosive temperament and was often in trouble. When he was nineteen, to escape police inquiries, he used his American citizenship to emigrate to San Francisco. There, he further developed his distinctive martial arts style and won many combat encounters. By 1963, he had moved to Seattle, where he started his first martial arts school and wrote a book on his philosophy of martial arts, *Chinese Gung Fu.* He also met his future wife, Linda Emery, in Seattle, and they were married in August 1964. Brandon was born on February 1, 1965.

Bruce Lee's life was dramatically changed when he was spotted by Beverly Hills hairdresser Jay Sebring at the Long Beach international Karate Championships. Sebring (later to be murdered by the Manson gang along with Sharon Tate in Roman Polanski's Benedict Canyon home in 1969) introduced Bruce to television producer William Dozier. Through this connection he met many Hollywood stars and became good friends with Steve McQueen and James Coburn. More importantly, Dozier put Bruce in his new television series, *The Green Hornet*. He also played a striking role in the James Garner movie *Marlowe* in 1969 and subsequently bought a house on Roscomare Road in Bel Air. With the money he might have spent on furniture, Bruce bought a red Porsche.

By this time, Bruce had a new martial arts school in Los Angeles, the China Town School. He had started to teach Brandon martial arts as soon as he could walk. In addition to the basic moves, he taught his son to be agile.

The success of *The Green Hornet* took Bruce Lee back to Hong Kong, where he and his family were astonished to discover that he was now a star. In his old hometown, while Brandon learned to speak Chinese, Bruce made some spectacularly successful movies, including *Fists of Fury* and *Return of the Dragon*. They were followed by the film that is considered to be his best, *Enter the Dragon*.

Bruce was preparing to make another movie (*Game of Death*) in Hong Kong when, on the night of July 20, 1973, he suddenly became ill. His death in the hospital shortly afterwards, at the age of thirty-two, is today still regarded with some suspicion. It was the beginning of a legend.

Bruce's unexpected sickness didn't begin at home, but in the apartment of a young Chinese actress, Betty Ting Pei, with whom he had clearly been having an affair. The fact that he took ill in Ting Pei's apartment, and that, possibly out of embarrassment or sympathy for the family, she delayed getting medical attention for Bruce, has helped to exaggerate the confusion and suspicion surrounding his death. In fact, there was so much suspicion, it was decided to hold an autopsy. It was conducted by a British professor of forensic medicine, who flew out from London, and by the clinical pathologist from Hong Kong's Queen Elizabeth Hospital, R. R. Lycette. The inquest concluded that Bruce had died from a rare and unusual reaction to a painkiller, Equagesic, found in his body. It was also concluded that the traces of cannabis found there were irrelevant to the cause of death. Several medical professionals disputed that view, and this simply added to the many and mysterious explanations for Bruce Lee's death, which ranged from murder by jealous traditional martial artists who believed that he had betrayed precious local secrets, to murder by the Triads, a notoriously brutal Chinese crime syndicate.

Brandon's mother retained her interest in martial arts and kept Bruce's ideas alive in his school. Eventually, Bruce Lee's protégé, Dan Inosanto, closed the China Town School and opened up another school in Torrance, California: the Kali Academy.

After his father's death, nine-year-old Brandon Lee became withdrawn and angry. When his mother moved the family back to California, he had difficulty adapting to the American way of life. It was symptomatic of his unsettled state that he attended and subsequently was asked to leave a number of Southern California schools.

Jeff Imada, who is a third-generation Japanese American, was born in Los Angeles. An accomplished martial artist, stuntman performer, and actor, Imada has performed in more than one hundred films. By the age of eighteen, Imada was already a big Bruce Lee fan: "I thought he was cool in *Green Hornet* and everything else, you know." So Imada, who had already been studying martial arts, was determined to get into the Kali Academy and learn the Bruce Lee martial arts style. The academy was very picky. "They screened people and wanted to find out about their background," Imada remembered. But nevertheless, he got into the school and found it, "very new to me and very eye-opening."

It wasn't long after the school opened that the nineteen-year-old Imada, then helping out in the children's class, first met Brandon. "Brandon was having a tough time," said Imada, "because his concentration wasn't as good, because of his dad." It was quickly apparent to Imada that the boy's father's death was weighing heavily on him: "The point is, he missed his dad. His dad had passed away and he came in to train and work out. I don't know if it was his idea or his mom's idea, but he came."

At first, having such a famous name naturally caused Brandon some problems with other students. Imada remembered, "They didn't go around saying, 'This is Bruce's kid.' We just sort of kept it low-profile. But it was very difficult for Brandon because there's pictures of his dad everywhere. Training equipment that his dad worked out on and things like that were all over the school. So, it was difficult for him." Imada added, "I saw Brandon go into the waiting room and sort of crying at one point. It was hard for him to be in the class and seeing all his dad's pictures." Within a couple of years, Brandon would become interested in soccer and less interested in martial arts, and Jeff Imada and Brandon gradually drifted apart.

At this time, Imada had no idea of the boy's potential, or that one day he himself would be the stunt coordinator on a movie in which Brandon would play the lead.

Brandon continued to have great difficulty with discipline in school and finally, in the spring of 1983, four months before his high school graduation, he was expelled for misbehavior from the Chadic School, a private high school in Palos Verdes, twenty miles south of Los Angeles. He later received his diploma from the nearby Miraleste High School. But by then he had decided he wanted to act, and after graduating he moved to New York and enrolled in the famed Lee Strasberg Actors' Studio. Shortly after, he continued his acting studies at Emerson College in Boston. Later, he joined the Eric Morris American Theater Company, making his stage début in Los Angeles, in *Full Fed Beast*, a play by John Lee Hancock.

It was inevitable, with Imada and Brandon's shared background, that their paths would cross again, and sure enough, in 1985 Brandon and Imada both worked on *Kung Fu: The Movie*. It was a movie-of-the-week spin-off from the 1970s CBS series, with Brandon portraying the long-lost son of Caine, played by David Carradine. This was an ironic twist, since the part of Caine in the *Kung Fu* television series had originally been written for and developed by Brandon's father, Bruce. Instead, Carradine was cast as the half-Chinese, half-Caucasian renegade monk. This casting change was blamed by many on Hollywood's then prejudice against Asian actors playing leading roles.

Imada knew that Brandon, then age twenty-one, had been reluctant to appear: "He didn't really want to do that show. They talked to him and said, 'This would be a great vehicle for you . . .' and blah blah blah, and so he ended up doing the show. But he wasn't too thrilled about doing the martial arts stuff. It was just sort of a hard thing to . . . I mean, imagine, you're the son of Bruce Lee. Everybody's gonna be looking at you under a magnifying glass and seeing if you're good or whatever. And he just didn't want to be in the shadow of his dad."

Shortly after, with some reluctance, the young Brandon appeared in an episode of the TV series *O'Hara*, playing the malevolent Japanese son of a Yakuza boss. Imada, who was the series' stunt coordinator, believed, "They all said he should do it. I don't know about his mom and stuff, I can't remember, but I know he wanted to be coming into the business as an actor, but everyone wanted to bring him into the business as 'Bruce Lee's son' . . . [He said,] 'Okay, great, now I can do more acting. I want to just do an acting thing.' They go, 'Oh no, you have to do more martial arts.' It was good for his career, I guess. And probably they said, 'You can do martial arts just to get in the door.'"

Brandon's next part in an American production was in another *Kung Fu* movie of the week, *Kung Fu: The Next Generation*. Only this time, he was cast as the grandson of Caine. This meant Brandon was playing his own son from the last movie of the week.

At about the same time, Brandon decided to do what his father had done, go to Hong Kong to appear in action movies, starting with the 1986 film *Legacy of Rage*. "The fact that Brandon's father was so famous," Paul Maslak reflected, "was both a plus and a minus. You know, when I first heard about Brandon, I talked with one of the directors who worked with him in Hong Kong. He said he was a spoiled brat. But that was when he was just starting. And a couple of years later he said, 'Boy, is he ever changed!' And everybody that talked about him said, 'Yeah, this is like the salt of the earth. This is just great.' So apparently, he had an identity crisis for a period of time, when he was just a teenager, and he was a bit sullen and he turned some people off, but by the time he blossomed into a man, then it all changed. So, I think it was a plus and a minus. Certainly, that he was the son of Bruce Lee helped him in the acting world. Helped him in the film business."

In his early twenties, after his time in Hong Kong, Brandon became very serious about his acting, and even about martial arts. He returned to the Kali Academy, which had by then been renamed the Inosanto Academy. Soon, Brandon had found a group of guys to work out with, one of whom, Chad Stahelski, became a good friend and later worked on *The Crow* as a stuntman and Brandon's stunt double. After *The Crow*, Stahelski's career took off. He became Keanu Reeves' stunt double and coordinator on the *Matrix* film series and then moved on to direct Reeves in *John Wick* (2014) and all three of the hit film's sequels.

Stahelski remembered that Bruce Lee's reputation was such that the Inosanto Academy warned a group of young men that Brandon would be showing up. They were told: "'Brandon is going to start working out here, that kind of thing.' I was like, 'Oh yeah, Bruce's kid.' No big deal or anything, but they did want to let us know. I don't know why they were telling us that. Maybe they didn't want anybody taking a crack shot at him or something. Especially if he's Bruce Lee's kid, you've got to be honest with him. But he came in and he was real low-key, just a cool guy."

Brandon was already highly skilled in different forms of martial arts and had, in fact, already been certified as a Thai kickboxer, passing the difficult tests of stamina and skill. "He was very good as a student there, very good as a martial artist," said Jeff Imada, who occasionally trained with Brandon at that time. "[He] worked really hard and didn't ask for any special treatment. Some people didn't even know who he was. He didn't want to be singled out. And a lot of the people did get to know him, found out that he was Bruce's son, and the guys were pretty respectful of it."

Unlike many martial arts schools that specialize in a particular style, Dan Inosanto had a very open-minded approach, which helped the students, including Brandon, to benefit from a wide range of influences. "Brandon liked the Thai kickboxing for the physical workout," Imada recalled. "He liked to work out and get a little physical and do some strong conditioning and make contact."

Brandon was already developing into a serious young man. According to Stahelski, "He wasn't out partying or anything like that. On his weekends, he was working out or he was with us in the gym or something. He wasn't one of those guys to wear the fancy clothes, go in and do a couple sets on the weights and go sit down and talk to the girls—there weren't many girls into kickboxing! Sometimes you see guys working out, you don't want to work out with them. But I mean, when it came to partner up, no one minded working with Brandon. He'd go twice as hard as anybody. Yeah, he took it real serious."

In fact, because of his background, Stahelski noted that Brandon Lee had great natural ability: "He had a pretty good background from his dad and, you know, you're Bruce Lee's kid, that's a big rep to live up to, especially in martial arts circles. So, he was always pretty decent, but then, I think he'd never really focused on one thing. Just my opinion of it, from what I saw. When he got in the academy, he really started focusing on the kind of stuff that they did there and the stuff that his dad had been really good at. And, being a good athlete, he picked it up, I would say, pretty quick.

"You could be a world-class kickboxer and still suck on film," Stahelski said, drawing a distinction between what martial arts really is, and what moviegoers *think* it is. "There's tricks you've gotta know. When you get into film, you've got to tweak your stuff. You know, you work on the higher, flashier kicks. You work on timing, where the camera is. You can cheat on so much stuff. You don't have to hit anybody, or for that matter get hit, which is cool."

Brandon was already thinking about the details of filmmaking. "Being Bruce's son," Stahelski recalled, "he'd have his idea of martial arts, what was cool and how to shoot it. So, on Sundays we'd all meet at the gym and he'd bring his video camera down, and he'd choreograph something and he'd shoot it, just to see how he'd look on film. It was like, 'Yeah, I've got nothing else to do on Sunday, let's go down and kick each other! Choreograph some stuff and play and just have a good time.'"

Though almost all of the young men Brandon tried out his movie fight choreography ideas on later became professional stuntmen, none of them applied themselves as rigorously to learning about filmmaking. Brandon ran and re-ran his father's films, analyzing them. "He'd break it down and see what shots made up the fight scene, what made the action fun," said Stahelski, "and then he'd come out and try to get a close shot. For the kick, he'd want to shoot the right angle . . . and just see his reaction and put a little acting into it."

Brandon did get work on other movies and gained a reputation for being an interesting young actor but, of course, he had been seen only in roles that required martial arts, like *Laser Mission* (1989), shot with Ernest Borgnine in Namibia, *Showdown in Little Tokyo* (1991) with Dolph Lundgren, and *Rapid Fire*, the 1992 movie he was in immediately before *The Crow*. Jeff Imada was the stunt coordinator on *Rapid Fire* and recalled that it was, "Quite heavy on stunts, a lot of gunplay, a lot of fight stuff, some car stuff, explosions, and quite a bit of it was action. With Brandon doing the action and with his physical ability, it was a dream, because Brandon was real talented. It was just easy to do things with Brandon."

By then it was clear to Imada just how much Brandon Lee had inherited from his father: "Like kickboxing. Even when he moved, and his gestures and his physical chest movements while he was fighting, were similar to his dad's. And people thought he was trying to copy his dad." Imada knew that Brandon wasn't, and he remembers that when Brandon saw the similarities, he would say, "'Wow, I wasn't even trying to do that.' And I'd go, 'Yeah.'" At the time, Brandon was just beginning to recognize the similarities himself. On one occasion, Imada and Brandon were in Brandon's trailer watching a videotape of the dailies on *Rapid Fire*. Imada recalled that Brandon wasn't particularly interested in the scene, until suddenly he said, "'Oh God, wait a second.' And he'd rewind it and go, 'Look at this!' And I go, 'What?' He goes, 'Oh wow! Did you see that?' I go, 'Yeah.' He goes, 'Who'd that look like?' I go, 'It looked like your dad.' And he goes, 'Yeah, I'll be damned.'" This was truly a revelation to Brandon, who said to Imada: "There's something to be said for genetics."

Chad Stahelski had recognized the physical similarities between father and son too: "There's certain mannerisms, I don't know about actual physical ability, but mannerisms, like the way Brandon warms up his neck and moves his shoulder, it might as well be his dad. I could show you things from *Enter the Dragon* and I could show you a clip from *Rapid Fire*, [and] you'd swear, he did this one little thing."

Of course, the major qualities Brandon had inherited from his father were less tangible but no less genetic: an instinctive physical ability that cannot be learned and a desire to experiment. So, was he naturally talented? "Talented is an understatement!" said Imada. "He would try things that he hadn't done before. I'd be setting up something and we'd be talking about it. I said, 'I want you to try and do this. Have you done it?' He goes, 'No, I haven't done that kind of kick before. Let me try it.' So, he'd do a jump-spin kick or something like that. He'd maybe do it once and then maybe the second time. By the second time he'd have it down [and] he goes, 'How was that?' And I'd go, 'Yeah, that was perfect.' So, he was just naturally talented, physically gifted that way. And mentally, he was sharp as a whip."

Despite Brandon's ability and inclination to do so, and unlike his father, Bruce Lee, who was renowned for doing all his own stunts and could boast that he'd been doubled in only three shots in his whole career, Brandon was often prevented from performing his own stunts. Bruce Lee's reputation had been gained in a different era of legal liability claims. For many years since, movie insurance companies had known that if something goes wrong, it's easier to replace a stuntman than an actor. So, when Brandon wanted to do all his own stunts on *Rapid Fire*, he wasn't allowed to.

Brandon's natural skill as a martial artist didn't mean that it had become his major interest. Far from it. He had already made an important personal discovery: What he really wanted to do was act. And he foresaw many of the problems that his martial arts skills might cause him. In spite of Imada's view that Brandon had "definitely put one hundred and twenty percent or more of himself into that film [*Rapid Fire*]," as they came to the end of the shoot, he frankly told Imada that he thought, "It'd be great to finish this film and not do any martial arts for a while. It takes its toll. You're making contact with people no matter what, and you're getting bruised up and not getting to heal up quite as well . . . and you're just physically tired from fighting all the time." When Brandon told Imada that he didn't love doing martial arts, Imada responded, "'You're damn good at it for something you don't like that much.' He said, 'Thanks buddy, [but] it's not something I'm totally in love with.'"

Brandon's natural physical ability was simply a part of his life that he took for granted. Physical activity was normal and necessary to him. Imada said, "Brandon liked to go to Joshua Tree [National Park] and climb rocks. Go to different places and ride his motorcycle and go mountain biking. He was always doing something physical. He loved training, working out." But there was not the slightest doubt in Imada's mind that: "Of anything, he enjoyed the acting the most. That was his first love."

Indeed, by now Brandon's real interests had spread far beyond the physical, and he had developed an interest in writing. "There were different times we were jotting down ideas for scripts, but I remember one time in particular, we were out in Joshua Tree camping with some of the guys, and we had stayed up all night. . . . And we were tossing around some things. I think at the time he was going to get together with the writer who did *Rapid Fire*, because they were looking for a sequel or something. He was jotting some stuff down for a story that he wanted to do." Brandon's idea was not for a martial arts film, but for an action film, and Imada remembered Brandon added some comic elements. But Brandon was never to complete any of his screenplay ideas.

With *Rapid Fire* finished but not yet released, Brandon was now searching for his next project. Imada thought Brandon could have easily had a future in movies as a fight coordinator like himself, but acting, and even directing and writing, had become his passion.

Many of Brandon's friends, including Chad Stahelski, knew about *The Crow* comic book: "Someone gave me a copy of *The Crow* just for a birthday present. But I started reading it. [I thought,] 'Actually, this is a pretty bitching comic book!' Me and my buddies used to joke, 'Yeah, what a great movie.' That's when we'd just started doing stunts." Then they got a surprise when they heard about their friend's next job: "Oh yeah, Brandon's doing *The Crow*. And we were all so jealous because, what a great movie to work on!"

As soon as Brandon heard that he might be doing the movie, he excitedly told his friend Jeff Imada about it, saying, "There's a couple things coming up, but one of them I really think is going to be great. It's from a comic book. This guy has got super-human strength, but yet, it'll be different, because the guy can't die." The project still wasn't green-lighted, but Brandon showed Imada the comic book. "I said, 'It's pretty dark,'" Imada recalled. "And he goes, 'Yeah, but we'll have some fun. We can do some things.' He said, 'It's not set yet.' But after Brandon made his deal, I got a call from Bob Rosen, the producer. And then I was on my way to Wilmington."

REFINING THE SCRIPT AND DOING A DEAL

5

I N THE FALL OF 1992, after Brandon Lee had returned to Los Angeles from doing publicity for *Rapid Fire*, he officially joined the group of people trying to get *The Crow* movie up and running.

The screenplay was still being worked on, and Brandon made sure that he contributed his own ideas to that process. Changes had been made to the screenplay since Brandon had agreed to do the movie. He talked first to Ed Pressman about it, and then to David Schow and Jeff Most. Most said, "Brandon coveted the comic and carried it around with him. He felt tremendous passion, and I remember him saying, 'You can do anything you want with this. This is the most important character I've ever played. I have some pointers.' And it was refreshing to me because we'd started getting into some areas that were more comic-like, but less emotionally involving. And he brought it back down to earth, and he had tremendous insight into the character and what this role should be. . . . So, when he left for location on 1 December 1992, Brandon had reinvigorated the focus on simplicity, on not adding more metaphysical characters, and that was a tremendous benefit."

Brandon Lee was also concerned with his dialogue. He relished the lyrical lines that had been written for his character, especially in dealing with the villains. But he didn't want the dialogue to spread aimlessly. According to Most, "He also felt that brevity and economy of words was effective, and his [the Crow's] words are very carefully chosen. He had a strong ear for the rhythm of dialogue, and he felt that in being succinct, he became more threatening."

There's no doubt that Brandon had a great influence on the development of the shooting script for *The Crow*, but Bob Rosen, who may be one of Alex Proyas' biggest fans, said, "The script, if I may say so, and with great deference to Ed and Jeff Most and everybody else involved, was totally Alex's. I think that the evolving of *The Crow*, from the original script that we had, became Alex's, and we contributed, helping Alex conceive of what he wanted to do and figure out a way to do it."

Brandon's contribution to the concept of the movie was by no means limited to his input on the screenplay. Brandon also had very clear ideas about how he wanted his character's physical nature to be realized. For the first time in his life, he was going to be able to combine his now considerable experience of both martial arts and moviemaking. This started as a collaborative venture with the producer, the screenwriter, and the director. They would meet on weekends at Alex Proyas' house in the Hollywood Hills and watch movies on laser disk, which they had rented in Los Angeles' Little Tokyo or Chinatown, looking out for interesting sequences. "We would dub them down to tape," Jeff Most recalled, "and then we would take some portion (we never copied anything into *The Crow*) perhaps some aspect of the design of a move, and then recreate it for Eric Draven. Not in its entirety but in pieces, so that what we were doing was actually grafting together action sequences in which Brandon knew he could perform various aspects of the moves, to arrive at something completely new and different."

By now, Brandon had convinced the team to hire Jeff Imada. Imada, of course, was enthusiastic about the idea of working with his gifted friend. His contribution was welcomed by the team because, Most said, "Jeff Imada knew so many of the great talents that Brandon possessed as an athlete and a martial artist, and his willingness to venture into areas that had never been performed on screen.

"During this time," Most recalled, "Brandon would tell me and Proyas and Schow stories of all the various types of moves he had been called upon to do and, in fact, accidents which had ensued in each of his productions. He prided himself on the fact that he took the risks, and there was no task he was ever asked [to perform] that was too great. In each case, in each production he had been involved with, he had gone to the hospital; he would say, 'I've gone to the hospital on every show I've ever done. I've broken this or broken that.' He certainly was willing to push the envelope on what a man's body could be put through."

Neither Imada nor Brandon wanted Eric Draven to do conventional martial arts moves. "Brandon felt that the type of moves indicated in *The Crow* comics were really of an acrobatic and even somewhat balletic nature," said Most. "As such he really wanted to have no formal martial arts portrayed on the screen. He imagined that Eric Draven, as a guitarist, was an artist and would perhaps not have been someone who was fully trained in the martial arts. To Brandon, it was the task of imagining a man with the strength of ten men, because Draven was an immortal, being able to perform acrobatic feats and stunts that no man could perform. Using his martial arts training as a backdrop, he would then move it into the area of a kind of newly created form of fighting. That was a great instinct Brandon had, and we followed through with it."

Part of Brandon's desire to use a "newly created form of fighting" was probably in order to distance himself from the stereotype of a martial artist. Even though the comic book featured martial arts, Imada said that "Brandon didn't want to get pigeonholed as a martial artist."

The discussions about what Eric Draven could and could not do were wide-ranging and affected how the action in the movie would be developed. The creative team worked out the character's limits, "Because he's dead but he came back, but yet there's certain limitations he should have," recalled Imada. "He shouldn't be able to fly through the air and things like that. He should have a certain amount of strength, but what level of strength and power should he have?"

Brandon the actor was as much at work in developing this aspect as Brandon the physical performer because he already understood the importance of character. He told Imada that he wanted to have "very powerful, raw, organic simplicity in movement, so that it came from deep within and it wasn't choreographed and didn't have that feeling of choreography, that it was something more emotionally driven. So, it came from within, from his character." At this early stage in pre-production, when the script was still taking shape, many of these moves and details of fight choreography were incorporated into the writing and would later be seen in the finished movie.

During this period, Proyas, Most, and Schow were getting to know Brandon, discovering the kind of man he was. Nothing illustrates this better than the first of many innocent practical jokes he was to play on them. "It was Saturday," Most remembered, "we were at Alex Proyas' house and we'd been watching Hong Kong laser disks, and we adjourned in the afternoon to Alex's terrace table. It was a Saturday night, Halloween. A number of people had come over after we had done our work, to hang out. And Brandon went into the bathroom and disappeared for like twenty-five, thirty minutes. About five-thirty, he came out of the bathroom. He looked just awful. He was sick and he was holding his stomach and looked like he was about to throw up all over us. He walks over and he starts to vomit and he throws up shaving cream all over us! He held the shaving cream in his mouth, came out, spat it out, it went flying all over the place, and [he shouts], 'Happy Halloween!' We had a lot of that."

With Ed Pressman's track record, getting initial interest in financing *The Crow* was not difficult. The producers were looking for around $14 million at a time when the average studio movie cost around $30 million, and low-budget movies were in the $1 million range. However, *The Crow*'s budget was by no means an extravagant sum for the kind of stylish and visually complex movie that was being proposed. It did not have any highly paid names in the cast or an expensive writer or director, but it still wasn't exactly rock-bottom cheap.

A combination of the screenplay and Alex Proyas' show reel were enough to excite the interest of the then-head of Paramount Pictures, Brandon Tartikoff. Tartikoff's tenure, as is typical of studio executives, was to be short, but while he was in the job he wanted to make *The Crow*. It was surprising that Tartikoff, who had made his name at NBC television, where he had green-lighted such sitcom comedy hits as *Friends*, would like an essentially dark project like *The Crow*. But James Janowitz, who was the attorney for *The Crow* (for which he received a co-producer credit), and who has been working with Pressman since the 1980s on virtually every film he has produced, nevertheless believed that Tartikoff had high hopes for the project. "This is not an Academy Award–winning script. The genius of the film is in the direction and the performance, and the strength of the underlying concept. Tartikoff understood that," recalled Janowitz. "And in fact, I remember there was a letter from Tartikoff saying something like, 'This is great, let's go punch a hole in the sky.' Then fairly soon thereafter, Tartikoff left Paramount, and Sherry Lansing took over from him."

Janowitz was a savvy, charming, and sophisticated New York lawyer who, at the time of production, was in his fifties. It was to fall to Janowitz and Bob Rosen to follow through on the details of the deal for the movie. Janowitz's own first response to the screenplay was very different from Tartikoff's: "I didn't like the script. I had trouble reading it. When I read a script, I like literary material, and there wasn't much to get out of this thing." But he had to handle the deal anyway. In any case, Paramount would not be putting up all the money for the film. In a sense, because this was a "negative pick-up" deal, they were in fact to put up no money at all!

Janowitz gave a detailed explanation of how this kind of financing works: "You go to the studio and say, 'We want to make this movie, will you pay for it?' They say, 'Yeah, we'll pay for it, you deliver the movie to us and we will pay you on delivery, we will "pick up" the negative of the film.' So, you go out and get a bank loan. The studio does not give you the funds to make a film. The bank loan . . . A lot of people wonder, 'Gee that sounds awfully risky. Why would a bank lend money to make a picture?' But it's a well-put-together way of dealing with it, where the bank looks to the commitment of the studio to pay for the film upon delivery. And you get a completion bond to make sure that if the film is *not* delivered to the bank, the completion bonder will pay the bank. So, the bank is fairly comfortable with this kind of a situation."

In 1992, the struggle was to put together a combination of financing involving a primary pick-up deal plus further money from the advance sale of foreign rights and a completion bond insurance to guarantee that the movie would actually be completed.

The foreign sales deal wasn't easy. "There was a lot of scrambling," said Janowitz, "and that's not so uncommon. Independent films are very tough to do. Ed [Pressman] is really a master and has done it more than almost anybody. But it isn't easy and there are often cliff-hangers." The agent they used to sell the foreign rights was a company called Pandora. But there may have been some misunderstandings because, said Janowitz, "We thought we had a deal with Pandora, in my opinion we had a deal with Pandora, but Pandora, I think, concluded that they couldn't sell the film as well as they wanted to and told us that we *didn't* have a deal with them." Janowitz's theory is that in October of 1992, Pandora went to MIFED (the film market that followed the Milan International Film Festival, which, until it folded in 2004, was a major market to sell foreign film rights). "They sort of tested the waters, you know, put their finger in the air and tried to figure out whether people were really interested in this movie, concluded that they weren't as interested as they wanted them to be, and decided not to go forward."

The collapse of the deal with Pandora was close enough to the start of the movie's production to count as one of Janowitz's "cliff-hangers." Pressman Films even contemplated suing Pandora, but in the end, Janowitz said, "They were able to make various foreign pre-sales. I think Japan, I do remember Germany, and I can't remember which other territories. It wasn't enough to cover the budget. Then we got a bank to step in to fill the gap, which again, I don't remember precisely, but I suspect that Pressman guaranteed the payment, because I don't think we had enough foreign sales to fully cover the $14 million budget."

At the same time, Bob Rosen was struggling with Paramount executives, "The nuts-and-bolts production guys who were saying, 'They can't do that.'" The "that" the executives thought those producing *The Crow* couldn't do was make the movie for the amount of money Rosen et al. wanted, which was a guarantee of $7 to $8 million dollars from Paramount for the American rights. Rosen did have his own doubts about the budget at first: "We had a very low budget on this movie. Nobody, initially including me, thought we could make the picture for this price." So, before he could convince Paramount and Film Finances, the completion guarantor, he had to be convinced himself, and Proyas was gradually persuading him. "Ultimately, I thought it could be done," said Rosen, "because I was spending hours with Alex in meetings, and I could hear and see where he was going and felt that we had a shot at doing it for this number." Even so, Rosen was still surprised that he did manage to convince Paramount and Film Finances that *The Crow*'s budget was realistic. "I'll be damned if I know [how he did it]," he said, shaking his head. "A lot of it was producing a budget, and a lot of it was convincing them that we were going to make the film within these limitations, no matter what happened.

"There was a given number . . . of what we had to make the film for, and between the completion bond company and the initial financial company, Paramount, nobody thought we could make the movie. I remember one of the ugliest meetings I ever had in my life was trying to convince Paramount that we were going to make the picture for this number. And people who were very bright, old friends of mine who were across the table from me, telling me that I had totally lost control of my senses, thinking that we were gonna do it for this price! And between Paramount and the completion bond company, it was a tough sweat to get the picture to a green light, because of the limited resources that we were going to have to make it, and how we were going to make it."

Of course, Film Finances also had to be convinced that the budget was realistic, because they were the people who would have to put up money to finish the film if it ran out of money before completion.

In all of this, a first-time director can play no part, since by definition there is no track record on which to judge someone's future behavior. So, on *The Crow*, the past records of the producer and the line producer were the crucial matters. "Alex [Proyas], who, as I say, I adore," said Rosen, "doesn't give great meetings. I don't really see that Alex, ever, in a meeting, swung the thing. It was based on a number of things relating to those people, the production department of Paramount and the completion bond company, but I think in a sense, and I have to say this, probably my track record of not going crazy on movies, together with Ed Pressman and everything, had something to do with that. Probably more than what Alex had to do with that.

"Alex's background, at that point, was pretty minimal. But I've had a long streak of not going over budget or going into bonds or going into completion bonds. . . . And just everybody sitting down, going through the script page by page in a meeting with Paramount, and me with the completion bond company [helped to convince them that the film would be made for the budget]. I don't think Alex ever really met anybody in production at Paramount or in the completion bond company prior to the start of principal photography."

James Janowitz explained very carefully that the most important thing in a pick-up deal is to make sure "the studio is *not able to reject the film*, in other words, when you make the film, and you deliver it to the studio. What you don't want is to have the studio look at the movie and say, 'Don't like it!' So that is not one of the conditions for rejecting delivery. Delivery can only be rejected on some very, very narrow grounds: technical imperfection, failure to shoot the script, failure to deliver the actor."

At this early stage, of course, as the deal was finally done to finance *The Crow*, it did not enter Janowitz's head that there might be a problem on any of those grounds. But in fact, a situation would eventually develop in which *The Crow* would fail to satisfy the studio on all of those grounds.

PRE-PRODUCTION IN LOS ANGELES

6

S INCE THE PARAMOUNT DEAL and financing were coming together, it was time to set up a pre-production office for *The Crow*. When Ed Pressman had hired Bob Rosen, he had been working on another project, intended to star Jack Nicholson, in offices on the corner of Santa Monica Boulevard and Sepulveda Boulevard in West Los Angeles, just south of Wilshire Boulevard, near UCLA. After the finance collapsed on the Nicholson project, Rosen took over those offices for *The Crow*.

Rosen brought Greg Gale, his previous associate producer, to work with him. Before *The Crow*, Rosen and Gale had completed *Sniper* (1993), shot in Australia and starring Tom Berenger and Billy Zane, for Barry Levinson's company, Baltimore Pictures. On *Sniper*, Gale worked his way up to associate producer and garnered a post-production supervisor credit, the same positions he would occupy on *The Crow* (though he is uncredited for the latter). Quick-minded, even-tempered, articulate, and well-organized, Gale was very well-suited to manage the complex production process required for completing *The Crow*.

While making *Sniper*, Rosen had also worked with production manager Grant Hill. "We hit it off," Rosen recalled, "and I felt he was a good guy for something like this." Rosen hired Hill as *The Crow*'s production manager/associate producer: "We collaborated on putting the crew together."

The Crow was a movie on which strange things were reputed to have happened. This started very early in the life of the project. Almost as soon as the Los Angeles office opened, an assistant received a threatening call, warning that, "This film should never be made," Rosen recalled. At that point, the news was out that Brandon Lee, the son of Bruce Lee, had been cast as the Crow. There was speculation that someone could have made the threatening call because of his father's so-called curse. Or could the dark nature of the comic book have attracted the attention of some unstable person?

In the meantime, Alex Proyas had no doubt about who he wanted as his director of photography (DP), a man whom he had worked with on several commercials. Jeff Most remembered that early in the hiring process, Proyas had only one answer when asked, "'Who would you like?' 'Derek [Dariusz] Wolski.' Derek had only done one feature, beautifully done." Wolski was born in Poland and studied cinematography at the famed Warsaw School. He and Proyas had worked together on a number of music videos and commercials, including those for Black Star Beer and Nike. Wolski had also just finished *Romeo Is Bleeding* (1993), his first movie, still respected to this day, featuring stunning performances by Gary Oldman and Lena Olin.

Before becoming a director, Alex Proyas had himself been a director of photography. The production team, Most, Rosen, and Hill, were easily sold on Proyas' choice of Wolski because, Most recalled, "Alex certainly had the experience and we had double genius DPs. They complemented each other." A dedicated artist with a brilliant flair for his job, Wolski tended to have an autocratic manner on *The Crow* set, which did not always sit well with the film crew. This may have been exacerbated by his experience with the typically smaller crews on big-budget commercials he'd worked with before. Regardless, many of the crew saw him as talented but a poor communicator.

Other than the DP, the other closest position to the director is the first assistant director. Steve Andrews, another man from "Down Under," was hired. Most of Andrews' work had been in his home country of Australia, working on movies from *Gallipoli* (1981) to *Mad Max Beyond Thunderdome* (1985). His calm voice and efficiency would prove a tremendous asset during production of *The Crow*. Like almost all the members of the creative team, before *The Crow*, Andrews had yet to become established in Hollywood, and like many of them after the film, he would move into the mainstream of big-budget Hollywood studio productions.

Andrews became one of the most successful first assistant directors in the business. His credits include *The English Patient* (1996), *The Talented Mr. Ripley* (1999), *Moulin Rouge!* (2001), *Thor, Ragnarok* (2017), and the hit TV series *Professionals* (2022), produced by *The Crow*'s founding producer, Jeff Most.

Production manager Grant Hill went on to become a spectacularly successful line producer on films such as *Titanic* (1997) and *The Thin Red Line*

(1998) and executive producer of *The Matrix* film sequels, as well as many other international film and TV successes.

Since *The Crow*, Wolski became a celebrated, Academy Award–nominated cinematographer. He went on to work with top directors, such as Ridley Scott, Tony Scott, Paul Greengrass, and Tim Burton, on such films as the *Pirates of the Caribbean* trilogy, *The Martian* (2015), *House of Gucci* (2021), *News of the World* (2020), and notably, five years after *The Crow*, *Dark City* (1998), working again with director Alex Proyas.

But *The Crow* came around before most of its creative team were ever heard of by Hollywood. In fact, that's exactly what Jeff Most and Alex Proyas were looking for, contemporaries who had big ideas but not necessarily big-time credits. "We had a mantra," said Most, "which was, we wanted thirty-year-olds with thirty years' experience. We were determined to have very quick, very stylish, very smart young department heads who had accomplished a great deal in a short time. We wanted risk-takers. We knew that straight up. We were going to make something that had never been on the screen before. And we were gonna push every aspect of what we could do to achieve that." But they didn't totally exclude gifted, established people. "We saw some that were a bit older," Most recalled, "and some that were fresh out of music and commercials as well. But the idea was [that] just because people had done studio movies, we didn't want to stay away from them. It wasn't that. It was the type of movies they'd done. We did not want anything that was not pushed to the max and wasn't fresh."

Because one of the few successful movies adapted from a comic book was *Batman* (1989), they considered hiring its art director, Nigel Phelps. But for Jeff Most, *Batman* didn't recommend Phelps: "We didn't want to be *Batman*. We ultimately regarded ourselves as the real *Batman*, in terms of what we were doing emotionally. For our age audiences, *this* was the real *Batman*. This isn't a gussied-up little comic book that was made pretty. This was gonna be edgy and real and hit the core of the spine."

The fact that *The Crow* was not a big-budget movie was something that obviously fit in well with the ethos of hiring a young team. But the experienced Bob Rosen, during the process of hiring a production designer, said he didn't consciously decide, "Let's go with somebody young and cheap. But probably somewhere along the line that was in the back of our minds. I mean, obviously we couldn't afford the top production designer in the film business at that point, and we had to come up with ideas that came from people whose background was working in low-budget movies and who knew what one could get away with."

"We saw a zillion production designers," said Most. "One of them was Alex McDowell, who had previously worked with Alex Proyas on commercials." McDowell started out in England as a graphic designer in the late 1970s and early 1980s, doing artwork for such bands as The Cure and Siouxsie and the Banshees. He had then moved to Los Angeles and been a production designer on big-budget commercials, working with Spike Lee on several Nike spots. He had also worked with David Fincher on Madonna's famed music video *Vogue* and with John Singleton on the Michael Jackson video *Remember the Time*. He had just finished his first feature, *Lawnmower Man* (1992), when he was considered for the production designer job on *The Crow*. "At this point, Alex McDowell was at Propaganda [the top commercial production company]," said Most. But, he continued, "I hadn't even heard his name. And I actually had been working at that point with Brett Leonard, the director of *Lawnmower Man*, who had praised Alex McDowell."

Jeff Most recalled that, ultimately, it wasn't just Alex McDowell's résumé and recommendations that got him the job: "Alex was determined to get the job, and kept coming back in, showing us exactly what he wanted to do, with his textbooks, reference books, and started doing design work from compiling photos and color Xeroxing . . . 'This is this, and this is that' . . . Alex had a very definite sense about what he wanted." After the third meeting, McDowell had created enough of an impression to get himself the job. His detailed renderings are artworks in themselves. One crew member later managed to keep one and has it framed on his wall. In dark greenish-gray tones, it depicts a cityscape, seen from the roof of the decaying buildings that come alive in the movie. It is impressive how accurately the vision in McDowell's paintings was realized on the screen.

Like many of his fellow leads on the creative team on *The Crow*, McDowell's career took off. He went on to work with legendary directors David Fincher, Steven Spielberg, Tim Burton, Terry Gilliam, and Anthony Minghella on films such as *Fight Club* (1999), *Minority Report* (2002), *Charlie and the Chocolate Factory* (2005), *Watchmen* (2009), and *Man of Steel* (2013).

McDowell's skill in expressing the look of *The Crow* was found in Peter Pound, an Australian storyboard artist and a colleague of Alex Proyas'. "Peter was one of the most detail-oriented illustrators that I had ever seen that they've ever hired," recalled associate producer Greg Gale. "Peter was in our office, he was doing storyboards even at that point in Los Angeles, before we got out to Wilmington. If you watch the film and look at the storyboards, they are so close to what he [McDowell] actually had envisioned and Proyas had actually had on film. It was just amazing."

At this stage in pre-production, Brandon was often at Pressman's office, keeping abreast of the film's progress. "We talked to Brandon about our department hires," recalled Jeff Most. "We took a lot from him. He actually discovered a costume designer for us, Arianne Phillips. She was somebody who we didn't even know of. She was an incredible find."

Arianne Phillips was a warm and spontaneous, high-energy person. She was businesslike and creative and knew how to get her artistic visions turned into reality. She was a free spirit, innately trendy, and one of those people who always knew what was next. Phillips met Brandon a year and a half before *The Crow* went into production, on a *GQ* magazine photo shoot. Phillips had just moved to Los Angeles from New York and was working as a stylist on music videos and fashion and celebrity photo shoots. Movie posters were the closest she had come to working in the movie business.

Phillips had, of course, heard of Bruce Lee: "Every little boy I knew was obsessed with Bruce Lee. Brandon was kind of the antithesis of what I would imagine Bruce Lee's son to be like. He was just this sweet, loveable, funny, super intellectual, and kind of a seeker. He had a spirituality about him that was really special. Kind of a hippy spirit. The thing about Brandon is, he was a guy's guy. He didn't have a lot of close girl friends. He was really close to his girlfriend, Eliza; they were best friends and boyfriend and girlfriend. And I think that he was very private."

Brandon and his girlfriend, Eliza Hutton, were then happily living together in a rented two-bedroom house on Benedict Canyon in Beverly Hills. Hutton was also in the movie business working at Stillwater Productions, Kiefer Sutherland's company, as a story editor. When the couple had met more than a year previously, she had been director Renny Harlin's assistant.

Phillips got a call from Brandon inviting her to his house, for what turned out to be a special occasion. "In the middle of the cocktail party, Brandon announced his engagement to Eliza," Phillips recalled. "He was really romantic. They had gone to Italy and he had proposed to her, and this was kind of his announcement to his friends and family. I felt really lucky to be there. . . . And at that party he was talking about this film he was gonna do and he was like, 'You've got to do the costumes. . . . You're perfect for it. It's really rock 'n' roll.'"

Phillips had by this time done only one very low-budget feature, and although she wanted to work on film, she had no interest in action movies.

But Brandon aroused her interest in *The Crow*: "He showed me all the comic books and I thought they were kind of Gothic, and things that were interesting about the comic to me initially. There were some quotes from bands from the '80s that I was really into, like Joy Division and The Cure, and so I knew that obviously the person that had written the comic, they had really created this whole kind of Gothic thing that I related to on the music end."

Although Brandon was insistent that Phillips call Alex Proyas, she didn't make the call. A week later, she said, "Brandon called me up and said, 'How come you haven't called him?' And I just felt awkward, like going in as the actor's friend. So, Brandon was like, 'You've gotta.' So that was the groundwork. I was really surprised. So, I called him [Proyas] up and they said, 'Look, Alex wants young people.'" When Phillips found out who the creative team was, she realized that Proyas was a director she had long wanted to work with: "I was really impressed because Alex came from the same world I came from. Then I found out before the meeting that Alex McDowell was the production designer. I'd been a fan of his work for ten years. Then I found out that Derek Wolski was the DP, and I thought, 'Wow, these are my people! These people come from the commercial video stylized world that is interesting to me.'"

Indeed, Phillips' career went on to great heights, much like the other newfound crew members on *The Crow*. In the music world, she became Madonna's personal and concert tour stylist, as well as styling other music industry icons, such as Lenny Kravitz, Courtney Love, and Justin Timberlake. Phillips became a sought-after film and stage costume designer, working on numerous critically acclaimed films and Broadway productions, gathering both Academy Award and Tony nominations.

At their meeting, Phillips and Proyas really hit it off. "I could immediately see how intelligent he was," Phillips said, "and his perspective, and why he decided to do this movie." However, before Phillips could be hired, Bob Rosen told her she had to accept one potentially awkward condition, that they intended to hire a more experienced person to supervise her. Usually, a costume designer will hire their own wardrobe supervisor, but because this was Phillips' first big movie, Rosen hired a supervisor he knew himself, Darryl Levine. "All my friends are like, 'Don't do it, you'll get screwed,'" Phillips remembered. "'You don't want to work with someone you don't know.'"

Levine had a friendly, humorous, and energetic manner with a seasoned depth of film industry experience. Rosen was a good friend of his father, who was also a movie costume designer. Darryl Levine had known Rosen for more than twenty years, and even though they had worked together only twice, Rosen knew he was the man for the job. "He called me and said they had a first-time costume designer and he wanted somebody with experience to help her run the show," Levine recalled. "I was hired before we had a conversation. It wasn't like, 'Do you want to do this?' Bob said, 'You're doing this.'"

To make sure they could work together, Phillips and Levine arranged to meet for lunch, and Phillips chose the Kings Road Cafe, a casual West Hollywood hangout for young artists and industry folk. She recalled that "Levine came in, and he said, 'I would never come to a place like this. I'm so not hip.'" But despite their different social sensibilities, they really hit it off on location. "Darryl really took care of me," Phillips said, "and he had a long working relationship with Bob Rosen. It was, I would say, one of the most pleasurable experiences I'd ever had, as far as being able to realize my designs."

The Crow's young creative team would be accompanied by a young cast. None of the characters who inhabit the world of *The Crow* are older than age forty. Most are meant to be contemporaries of Eric Draven, in their twenties. This was fortunate because the movie couldn't afford well-established actors or real stars. Bob Rosen budgeted that "double scale [the Screen Actors Guild minimum] was our high price on the movie." Most of the cast would be paid only scale, about fifteen hundred dollars a week.

Billy Hopkins, a well-known New York–based casting director, was hired. He had cast two other movies produced by Ed Pressman, Oliver Stone's *Wall Street* (1987) and *Blue Steel* (1990). But compared to the rest of Hopkins' résumé, *The Crow* was a small project. Hopkins had cast such big features as Oliver Stone's *Born on the Fourth of July* (1989) and *JFK* (1991) and *True Romance* (1993).

The Crow's second lead was Officer Albrecht, the down-and-out Detroit cop who helps Eric Draven complete his avenging mission. In casting this sympathetic role, Billy Hopkins called in Ernie Hudson, whose work he knew well. Ironically, he had cast him in several other movies in recent years, all as policemen. Hudson was a graduate of the prestigious Yale School of Drama. He was a handsome, tall actor with a commanding voice and a very independent mind.

When he was offered *The Crow*, Hudson's career was in high gear: "I was probably the only actor [in the cast] at that time who really had any sort of recognition. At that point, I had done the *Ghostbusters* [1984], other films and I think *The Hand That Rocks the Cradle* [1992]. I wasn't totally sure *The Crow* was something I wanted to do. I liked it, but I wasn't sure.

I was kind of at that stage in life where I wanted to be in movies, but I wanted them to want me in movies as much as I wanted to be in a movie. So, I wasn't totally committed." Hudson's career went on to flourish as both a supporting and lead actor appearing in a long list of top film and TV series, including *The Basketball Diaries* (1995), *Congo* (1995), *Miss Congeniality* (2000), *Ghostbusters: Afterlife* (2021), *Modern Family* (2012–2016), and *Grace and Frankie* (2018–2020).

Hudson became more interested after reading the script and having a couple of meetings with Alex Proyas, the first in New York and the second in Los Angeles. "I thought the script was kind of interesting and I liked Alex right away. I saw his demo reel, which was fascinating." Hudson was also intrigued by the idea of doing a movie based on a comic book: "I thought it was very creative, kind of neat. I never worked from a comic book before. And so that was cool."

To cast the rest of the main roles, Hopkins sent videotapes of many New York actors to Los Angeles, and then Proyas went to New York to see those whose work had interested him. Hopkins had "seen a zillion actors," Jeff Most recalled. "We were looking for great bad guys, real great character actors. He knew the New York scene quite well. We needed the grittiness in our bad guys." Ultimately, Top Dollar and his henchmen were all played by New York–based actors.

As Top Dollar, the chief villain who oversees the crime-ridden world of *The Crow*, Michael Wincott brought some celebrity to the cast. He was a classically trained actor, a graduate of Juilliard, who had been in the movies *The Doors* (1991) and *Robin Hood: Prince of Thieves* (1991). After *The Crow*, Wincott continued to star on Broadway and TV as well as in films such as *Strange Days* (1995) and *Alien: Resurrection* (1997).

Top Dollar's female co-conspirator, lover, and half sister, Myca, was to be played by Chinese actress Bai Ling. *The Crow* was her first movie in the United States. "It had opened doors for me," said Bai Ling. "The film brought me into this Hollywood world that people know there's a Bai Ling."

Remembering her first audition, Bai Ling admitted she knew almost no English at the time and had to use a dictionary to look up the words of the script and then memorize them. When Bai Ling arrived at the audition she recalled, "I thought I will never get the role because every girl had dark lips, purple hair, dressed kind of weird like the Crow character. I had no makeup. I had long hair, dressed in jeans and T-shirt. Like an innocent student come from a different world. Like I walked into the wrong room."

She was shocked when her agent took a cab to where she was staying in New York to tell her she had a callback. "I said, 'What is a callback?' I had no clue.

"So, I put on some makeup, I bought a dress for eighty dollars, which was very expensive at that time, very sexy. I walked in next time and Alex Proyas said 'Fantastic job! But I want to see if you have this magic power. We want her to have this magical power to manipulate people.' So I started reading it. Halfway through he said, 'Perfect!' Later I asked him, 'Why did you cast me?' He said, 'All the other girls looked like the character but you were the only one who had the power inside.' That's what he told me."

After *The Crow*, Bai Ling's career took off, with starring roles in *Nixon* (1995), *Red Corner* (1997), *Wild Wild West* (1999), *Anna and The King* (1999), and *Taxi 3* (2003). She also appeared in the hit TV series *Lost* (2002) and *Entourage* (2004).

If Myca was Top Dollar's left hand, Grange was his right. Tony Todd was cast in the small but important role as the assistant and enforcer of Top Dollar's will. Todd became a recognizable face when he starred in the title role, opposite Virginia Madsen, in the 1992 horror film *Candyman*. He had also appeared in Oliver Stone's *Platoon* (1986) and Clint Eastwood's *Bird* (1988), the story of jazz great Charlie Parker, and his presence lent some weight to the young and largely inexperienced cast recruited by Proyas. Todd's career continued in the hit TV series *Law & Order* and *Star Trek: Next Generation* as well as in films such as *The Rock* (1996).

Top Dollar's "soldiers," as he calls them, bring to mind the Four Horsemen of the Apocalypse: War, Pestilence, Famine, and Death. But in the world of *The Crow*, they are simply four punks, antisocial criminal minds who obediently carry out, as best they can, Top Dollar's edicts.

The leader of the four, and by far the most intelligent of the bunch, is T-Bird. He's a sadistic pyromaniac who likes to taunt his victims while his three underlings execute most of the violence. David Patrick Kelly was cast as T-Bird. He, too, was a classically trained theater actor, who had studied with Marcel Marceau's International School of Mime and was very active on the New York theater scene. Kelly's film credits dated from the 1979 teen hit *The Warriors* (1979), in which he played the lead. He had also appeared in *Wild at Heart* (1990) and *Malcolm X* (1992) and was a series regular on the hit TV show *Twin Peaks*. After *The Crow*, Kelly continued to appear in TV and film, including reprising his role in the 2017 revival of the 1990 hit show *Twin Peaks*.

Angel David, a New York actor of Cuban descent, was called in to read for the role of Skank, T-Bird's half-witted sidekick. Skank would be the last member of T-Bird's gang Eric Draven would kill, so the role would span more of the movie than those of his cohorts. When David auditioned, he was told that the script was in pieces and not yet completed. However, he read the comic book and the excerpted scenes that he was given, and said, "The thing that intrigued me most was the quotes that Eric did, [as] the character, the Crow. He would just kill people and just quote Edgar Allan Poe, which I thought was very cool." In the audition, David recalled what landed him the role: "They go, 'Okay, just be you, and we'll see if you're the part,' not, 'You're an actor, act the part.' So I think Billy [Hopkins] and his group, they're smart enough to know that there are actors that could come in and create things. And that's what I did. I came in and I was totally in character and made Alex laugh." David remembered that his "take" on the character of Skank, "Always ended up being to the extreme, but it was always [because] he was a total fuck-up." His "initial reaction was, this is gonna be a cool fuckin' film."

David's enthusiasm was shared by New York actor Laurence Mason. Mason, whose parents were from Trinidad, was a graduate of the famed High School for the Performing Arts, and he "really wanted to work with Brandon, 'cause I'm a big Bruce Lee fan, so that was like as close as I could come." Billy Hopkins had recently cast Mason in a small part in his first big movie, *True Romance*, starring Christian Slater and Patricia Arquette. So when Hopkins called Mason to audition for the role of the knife-throwing, psychotic Tin Tin (for which Alex Proyas had originally wanted musician and actor Lenny Kravitz, but he was unable to commit) his career was already on the upswing. "I think they called me because I'm a mean freaky motherfucker," said Mason, who had long dreadlocks and a deep, gravelly voice. Mason auditioned for Alex Proyas with the violent fight scene between himself and Eric Draven, where Tin Tin is killed. Here, Mason's instinct to take risks paid off: "I took some kung fu and stuff, so I was doing the moves there, like with the knives and shit. And he really got into it. I don't think I was wearing a shirt either. I went all out."

The fourth hoodlum is the punked-out drug addict Funboy. Cast in the role was Michael Massee, who had studied at the prestigious Actors' Studio. Massee's other major credit was as a transsexual in the 1991 movie *My Father Is Coming*, a role very different from the drug-crazed, macho-minded Funboy. Massee is a Method actor and would go on to approach his role with a deep level of seriousness on and off camera. He would also play a significant role in the off-screen drama to come.

In New York, they also cast what would become the pivotal role of Sarah. Hopkins' office called in the twelve-year-old Rochelle Davis. Davis had no prior acting experience and had never been to an audition. She had only recently been taken on by her actor uncle's manager, who, she said, "Set up two auditions in the same day. Nothing became of the first one. The second one was *The Crow*."

That day, armed with her first headshots and a blank résumé, the cute and feisty young actress took the train into New York from her grandmother's house in Philadelphia. The naturally outgoing Davis had planned that, "When I went into the audition, I'd do something weird to kinda spice up the mood." What she did was squeeze a small, squeaking, monkey doll belonging to her younger brother. "They started laughing," Davis recalled, "and I walked in and I said, 'Well, it's a tension breaker. It had to be done. Had to break the tension before I came in here. I'm not nervous!' And they thought that was kinda cute." Davis also recalled that "their questions didn't seem like the things you'd ask somebody on their first audition. But they did. And they asked me if I was afraid of heights. And if I knew how to ride a skateboard. If I was used to cold weather and rain, and stuff like that."

A couple of months and three callbacks later, Davis got the call: "At first I think my eyes rolled back into my head and my head started spinning in circles. I screamed at the top of my lungs. I remember my sister thought that somebody in the family must've died or something because I was screaming so loud. I don't think it went through my head for a couple of days and then I finally went, 'Wow! I'm going to film a movie!'" Davis recalled that a few months later, on the set, Proyas confided, "You know, you landed the part the first time you came in."

The Crow was also the second audition of Canadian-born pop singer Sofia Shinas' acting career. At the time, Shinas had just signed a recording contract with Warner Records. Though she was represented only as a musician by the prestigious William Morris Agency in Beverly Hills, it was agent Beth Holden who was interested in broadening her selling potential as an actress. At first, Shinas was reluctant to audition for the part: "I'd read the script and I just felt that the subject matter was so dark. In fact, my agent made me go in, and she just insisted. Because she said that Ed Pressman would be involved and he makes wonderful films."

In addition to Shinas' compelling talent, during the audition, Proyas and Shinas discovered they both spoke Greek. Conversing in their mother tongue, this bonding moment was timely. According to Jeff Most, casting director Billy Hopkins "was literally talking to actress Heather Graham's agent offering her the role and discussing the terms of the deal when Alex and I were meeting with Sofia and Alex just asked me, 'You know, can I just have this one.'" Graham's offer was quickly retracted.

After the audition, in an effort to convince Shinas to take the role of Shelly, the production team sent her a copy of *The Crow* comic. Shinas, whose only exposure to comic books came from reading *Spider-Man* and *Superman* as a child, said, "I fell in love with the character. It was great."

Looking back on her first role, playing Shelly, Eric Draven's fiancée, Shinas remarks, "What a film début!"

WHY SHOOT IN WILMINGTON, NORTH CAROLINA? **7**

WILMINGTON, NORTH CAROLINA, was an unlikely place to find a movie studio. It is a port town, near the mouth of the Cape Fear River, a few miles from the Atlantic coast. It developed in the eighteenth century as a shipbuilding center and then, at the height of the South's cotton boom, became the home of one of the world's largest cotton export companies. The town is listed in the National Register of Historic Places. Lining its streets are ornate Victorian, Georgian, Italianate, and antebellum mansions. Many have been fully restored, and many were converted into charming bed-and-breakfasts or museums.

In summer, the town is booming with vacationers who come for its local festivals and beautiful beaches. Close by is Wrightsville Beach, a typical summer resort with rows of bars and boats and summer homes and condos lining its beige, sandy shore. The gentle warm breeze of the Atlantic and the lower cost of living has always invited retirees and city folk from the North, but the COVID-19 pandemic helped lure even more urbanites to choose it as their new, remote work home.

In 1984 the legendary Italian producer Dino De Laurentiis, who produced more than 500 films, of which 38 were nominated for Academy Awards, decided to build a movie studio in Wilmington. The chief attraction was the fact that North Carolina was, and still is, a Right-to-Work state where workers are not required to join a union as a condition of employment. This meant that the cost of shooting a movie there would be lower than in other established, union-regulated entertainment production centers such as Los Angeles or New York City. At the time, Wilmington was a film frontier. Most of the fifty states are still Right-to-Work states, but since the early 2000s, the majority of productions in Wilmington elect to hire union employees.

De Laurentiis built his studio right next to the small Wilmington Airport, in the industrial area on North 23rd Street. The part-joke, part-truth was that he would be able to bring his Italian crews over and they'd go straight from the plane to the studio and start working. He called it the DEG Film Studios, a spin-off from his Los Angeles–based De Laurentiis Entertainment Group. The studio itself soon became the biggest film studio in the United States outside of Hollywood.

On his thirty-three acres on North 23rd Street, De Laurentiis built seven sound stages and, of equal importance, a three-block back lot of mock streets, which doubled for most major cities around the world. It was a full-service studio, with screening rooms, editing suites, facilities to build sets, and ample production office space.

As well as the low local labor costs, the area offered diverse locations: mountains, beaches, and small Southern towns well suited to contemporary or historical stories. The climate is generally mild and warm, apart from the occasional serious hurricane.

During De Laurentiis' reign, more than thirty feature films were made at the studio. *Firestarter* (1984) was the first movie filmed there, but many other hit films were to follow, including *The Bedroom Window* (1987), *Crimes of the Heart* (1986), *Year of the Dragon* (1985), *Raw Deal* (1986), and *Teenage Mutant Ninja Turtles* (1990). The studio also attracted other types of production, including movies for television and commercials.

Although many of his movies were mostly low budget, De Laurentiis' studio helped put North Carolina on the entertainment world map, behind only California and New York in US film production. But Dino De Laurentiis made few friends in North Carolina, where he was regarded as a stubborn and confrontational owner who was insensitive to the local community.

In 1988, after losing money and producing unprofitable films each year of its operation (in 1987–1988 alone, DEG had lost $69 million in operating costs) DEG filed for Chapter 11 bankruptcy. In April 1990, after eighteen months of bankruptcy proceedings, the US Bankruptcy Court sold the studios and other DEG assets for $30 million to the Hollywood-based Carolco Pictures Inc. The sale was a shot in the arm for Wilmington. Carolco was one of Hollywood's most successful independent film companies, producing big-budget box office hits. As the sale went through, the Julia Roberts' starrer *Sleeping with the Enemy* (1991) was in production at the studio for 20th Century Fox.

Carolco's production slate was optimistic. Despite the fact it had no big hits in the previous year, it planned to make four or five big-budget films a year, though not all in Wilmington. Carolco also intended to rent its newly acquired studio to other film companies. It immediately began advertising in the Hollywood trade magazines, *Variety* and *The Hollywood Reporter*, as a cheaper alternative to shooting in California or New York. Carolco's plan showed immediate results; in 1990 alone, the new studio poured $400 million into the local economy.

Carolco's Hollywood cachet created a sense of optimism among locals. Sylvester Stallone was on Carolco's board of directors and was one of the company's stockholders. It was thought the name value alone would bring other film companies to Wilmington. It did. One was Pressman Films with their $15 million film, *The Crow*.

Many remnants of previous movies remained at the studio in 1992. De Laurentiis had shot his 1976 remake of *King Kong*, with Jessica Lange playing the famed Faye Wray role from the original 1933 film, in Wilmington, and the top half of the Kong model was still sitting on the ground at the back of the studio. More importantly for *The Crow*, to protect its lower costs, the Wilmington studio also fiercely guarded its traditional non-union status. At the front gate, visitors were greeted by a large sign that warned that any attempt to unionize workers on the lot would not be tolerated.

The low cost of shooting in Wilmington was one of the chief attractions for those planning *The Crow*, but there were other important financial factors too. "We couldn't afford to do it in LA, union," said Jeff Most. "And North Carolina was starting to get a reputation as a hot place in production." Bob Rosen also knew about Wilmington. "In fact," he said, "I spent some time back there preparing something that never happened. And so consequently I had a little leg up on a few people, but it was a collaborative thing. It was totally about money. The studio in Wilmington, North Carolina, had a back lot, which is the only place at the time that made sense to shoot a non-union movie that needed so much back lot work.

"And also," Rosen continued, "at the time, they were renovating the dilapidated back lot and so there was a way for us to come in and tell them what we wanted. And the financial deal was incredible." Because Alex Proyas' and production designer Alex McDowell's vision of *The Crow* would require total control of an exterior street set to achieve their creative vision, the back lot in Wilmington was crucial. It was recommended to Jeff Most by Steve Barron, a fellow music video and commercials director who had directed the 1990 feature film *Teenage Mutant Ninja Turtles* and who knew *The Crow*'s financial restrictions. The back lot provided a perfect location to create the Detroit back streets from the comic book. "The biggest surprise to most people who've seen *The Crow*," said Jeff Most, "is that we shot this whole thing on the back lot, which is a block long, which again is a credit to Alex McDowell and Alex Proyas. But it gave us a place to shoot this movie that we had control of in dealing with the crow [the actual bird], among other things, and rain and fire, and all the other stuff that was inherent in this movie."

Added to the studio facilities themselves was the infrastructure that had developed in the area. Bob Rosen knew, "there was a pool of talent, a system in place there. There is a great caterer. There are certain things that exist in Wilmington that you just can't get any other place."

Vick Griffin, the local location manager, who was eventually hired for the movie, was a Southern native and family man in his thirties, with a pleasant but decisive manner. He was a professional who you would immediately trust to get the job done, or to tell you, point blank, it can't be done. In our interview in 2000 Griffin said, "Basically, the thing that draws the folks in Wilmington is the crew. There's a crew base of seven hundred technicians, craftsmen, artists, that's here. And that's an awful lot of people to draw from. We have five or six movies in at a time. And the fact that it's been a Right-to-Work state all this time has certainly made a difference."

But of course, it wasn't just that there were crews in Wilmington. Compared with big cities like Los Angeles and New York, working in Wilmington was *convenient*. Griffin said, "If you don't have to shoot your show in LA or New York and you need rural settings but, you need small towns, you've got sets that you'd like to build and you'd like to build them in something besides an old warehouse somewhere, and you want to be able to drive five minutes or walk two hundred feet to pick up your camera package and get all your rental stuff, you can do all that here."

Also, Wilmington is very used to filming. "It ain't nothing they've never seen before," Griffin said. "Although I would say that there are probably a few actors [and] actresses who may generate a little more buzz or excitement, though I'd be hard-pressed now to name anything like that in recent times. It's not an uncommon occurrence to be in a restaurant and for Jeremy Irons to come sit down two tables away from you."

The city of Wilmington also has another summer life, as a vacation center, but in early 1993 that was six months away. Jeff Most recalled, "It was phenomenal, because we were in the winter and we had the town at our disposal because it's mainly a golfing summer community, [a] beach community."

Of course, not being in a major movie center such as Los Angeles or New York City did have its problems. "You can't just pick up the phone if you've forgotten something and have it arrive tomorrow morning," said Bob Rosen. "And so consequently, whether it's equipment or anything else, that all had to be pretty clearly thought out. But even on a budget like what we were talking about, it happened anyway."

There was no doubt in Rosen's mind that even if the movie had to be more carefully planned than usual, "The pluses of Wilmington for this movie were the fact that it was the only place that I know on the face of the earth that had a back lot that we could make into our own, with total control."

Of course, as they would find out, nothing in a movie can be done with "total control."

When Griffin, a longtime comic book fan, first saw James O'Barr's comic, he found it, "very Gothic and black. Very dark. Didn't bother me. I thought it was a good opportunity as far as the job went." But, Griffin admitted, "For me, it's not so much about the script. For me it's usually about the people. If the people are easy to get along with, and nice and polite and not hung up on themselves, then that's the main thing for me." Griffin liked the team on *The Crow*.

When the production finally arrived at Wilmington Airport for the preliminary scout, they were met by Griffin. On this trip, the location manager found himself playing tour guide not only to Jeff Most, Bob Rosen, and Alex Proyas, but also, he recalled, "that was one of the few times Ed Pressman was ever there." The team started by getting the lay of the land, and Griffin found that they were no different from other movie teams: "Everybody wants to drive to the beach. That's one of the silly things. Everybody wants to see where they're going to live for five months. I'm serious! It happens every time."

In the town and the surrounding areas, Griffin showed them almost all the locations they might need even though, at the time, he didn't have a strong sense of the script. As part of the small group of location managers in the Wilmington area, he knew that, "As far as diamonds in the rough that you're uncovering, they don't exist [in the Wilmington area]. They're not here anymore. We know where everything is. The locations we're shooting on *The Crow* were things we've gone to time and time again. We just gussy 'em a little differently and it's another movie." In fact, there were only four or five locations total off the studio lot that were used strictly as interiors because "it was easier to rent an existing interior and dress it up than build a room from scratch in the sound stage."

For exteriors, the best and only solution was the studio's back lot. There they could re-create the decaying streets of urban Detroit without Griffin "having to get permits from the city and have Police and Fire on hand. Too much hassle." Even more importantly, Griffin knew that, "Because most scenes had rain, steam, and specific lighting, it was impossible to create on an actual street."

However, in 1993 the back lot was in far-from-perfect move-in condition for *The Crow*. Griffin recalled that when it was built in 1985 for *Year of the Dragon*, starring Mickey Rourke, "It was a dead ringer for Chinatown." But now, seven years and a few hurricanes later, it was in serious need of a face-lift. According to Jeff Most, "A quarter million dollars minimum of materials, under production designer Alex McDowell's direction, was added on top of our budget by the studio because they needed to repair the street and, as an enticement to get us in, they had it redone." McDowell had been to Detroit, where James O'Barr had shown him the neighborhood in which he had set the story of *The Crow*, and this trip helped McDowell to create, in a matter of weeks, a complete-looking city block and a full-scale Gothic graveyard. He also worked out that by shooting from different angles and re-dressing the street, a relatively small area could be made to look like an entire district.

Although the set was new, in order to convey the dingy and dark look of the film, it had to be "aged." The gaffer, Claudio Miranda, recalled, "Everything's painted dull. Nothing at all was pristine." Miranda found it especially humorous that, immediately before *The Crow*, the movie *The Hudsucker Proxy*, which had used a small portion of the back lot, had painted the streets bright and "happy" colors. Miranda said, "It was like Alex McDowell had to just tear it apart. Physically, it was going to be a dirty movie. You could see it. You could see it by walking around and seeing how they were going to dress the sets with all the trash."

From the start, Griffin knew that the general run-down condition of the back lot was, as he said, "Fine with us, because it was supposed to be a kind of post-apocalyptic Detroit. So all we did was bring in more junk to make it look even worse. There was a building downtown, an old icehouse that they were demolishing, and I remember [that] when we were downtown scouting and we happened to see it and Alex or somebody in the art department said, 'We need that rubble,' Griffin promptly bought it! It was old bricks, big honking pieces of the building, put in dump trucks and hauled down to the studio, because we used all that rubble for dressing making it look like it was torn down. And it was funny, here they are tearing down a building and we're like, 'We can use this. . . . This is great.' Only in Wilmington."

Another, much smaller scale set was also being constructed in Wilmington. "Purely by luck," recalled Bob Rosen, "there was a local guy in Wilmington who was this incredible miniature maker." The discovery of Gus Ramsden was, Rosen said, "Just incredible. What we were able to get for the dollar, with the guy making it in his garage, was extraordinary." To construct the miniature buildings, Ramsden worked from the production designer's renderings and sketches of the Detroit skyline. He also found other inspiration from nineteenth-century photographs taken by famous documentary photographer Eugène Atget of lonely urban streets and graveyards.

For many scenes, miniatures were the only practical solution. This was an area in which Alex Proyas and his longtime partner in his commercials company, Andrew Mason, had a great deal of experience. It was also the only way they could achieve the stylized image of Detroit they had envisioned and derived from O'Barr's comic. Miniatures would be used for the movie's signature shots, from the crow's point of view, which sweep over rooftops and between buildings. Even some of the more spectacular car-chase sequences were done in miniature because, according to Bob Rosen, "We didn't have enough money to do it any other way."

It was planned that later in post-production, under the guidance of Andrew Mason, the shots of the miniatures would be digitally composited with footage of full-size subjects. It might have seemed simpler to get movie shots of the right kind of neighborhood and composite those, but because Proyas and McDowell did not want a photo-realistic look, miniatures were necessary. And with miniatures, they were not limited by the real world; they could choose the shape, size, and relationship between buildings and then totally control the effects and action within it in a way that they never could with a real location.

Today, these miniatures would easily be replaced with CGI (computer-generated images). But in 1993, that technology was in its infancy, and it was certainly beyond *The Crow*'s budget of $15 million.

Three years after *The Crow* in 1995, Carolco filed for Chapter 11 bankruptcy reorganization. In 1996, the newly formed EUE/Screen Gems Studios bought the Wilmington facility as its first production hub. It thrived.

A few years after *The Crow*, the studio's back lot fell into disrepair and was demolished and replaced by state-of-the-art sound stages. Then in 2009, EUE/Screen Gems Studios in Wilmington built stage 10: the biggest sound stage and special-effects water tank east of Los Angeles. Such blockbusters as *Iron Man 3* (2013) and *The Conjuring* (2013) as well as numerous hit series have since shot at the studio.

Today, in addition to the Wilmington facilities, EUE/Screen Gems operates sprawling state-of-the-art production facilities in Atlanta, Georgia, and Miami, Florida.

Since *The Crow*, the Wilmington film industry has had its ups and downs. Though in 2021 Wilmington saw productions spend a record $315 million, the competition from many other states offering greater and greater incentives over the last two decades upended North Carolina's reign as the number three production hub in the United States after Los Angeles and New York City.

According to Johnny Griffin, the director of the Wilmington Regional Film Commission, the intense competition turned "our industry into a bidding war between the different states to try and get the project."

Wherever in this wide world you can find the biggest incentive, tax rebate, or non-union workforce, or a cheap cost of living, whether it's in Singapore or Quebec City, that's where you'll find Hollywood. In the business, top stars get paid (albeit grudgingly), moguls, studio execs, finance people, and top-tier producers always find a way to keep lavish fees, and everyone else must buckle down, tighten a thinning belt, and work from check to check (not an employee's paycheck, but an independent contractor's wage).

To say Hollywood runs on greed, really isn't fair. It also runs on ego.

WILMINGTON 8
Pre-production

CROWVISION WAS THE COMPANY established specifically to produce the movie for Pressman Films. It officially set up a production office at the studio in Wilmington on December 1, 1992, by which time the actual shooting budget was frozen at $15.1 million.

Grant Hill then hired a second assistant director, a much more important job on this movie than on many others, since from the beginning it was planned to have a lot of shooting done by a second unit. This "Key Second," Randy LaFollette, was recommended to Bob Rosen by producer Rick McCallum, who had been working on the George Lucas production *The Young Indiana Jones Chronicles* (1992), which had just wrapped in Wilmington. Rosen knew that McCallum was, in LaFollette's words, "a little crazy. So he knew if I could keep up with Rick, then I could pretty much keep up with anybody."

The patient and good-natured LaFollette had a keen eye for detail. *The Young Indiana Jones Chronicles* television series was a period piece and, according to LaFollette, good preparation for *The Crow*: "It's like mini-movies, back-to-back to back. So they knew I could deal with a movie, and [with] prepping the next movie at the same time, which is not that easy. And George Lucas is nuts about detail. If you have an extra that's supposed to be the mayor of Chicago and they send you a picture, you have to find someone that looks like the mayor of Chicago in 1920. Details."

LaFollette ultimately had a short and pleasant meeting with the first assistant director, Steve Andrews. He remembered being hired very early in pre-production, partly because he was more familiar than Andrews with Movie Magic, the industry-standard computer scheduling program used then: "So I would put all the schedules into the computer and did a lot of computer work and helped break things down. It was a very complicated script."

An assistant director (AD) isn't strictly a director's assistant. They have a different task from the director. The first assistant director's job is to run the set each day. As Randy LaFollette described, "He [Andrews] had to coordinate and run the set and do all the communications so that the director can concentrate on the creative aspects. That's part of our job, to filter and organize all that information flowing to him."

LaFollette recalled that the crew of *The Crow* was a mixture of people with good experience of moviemaking and newcomers. "There was a lot of people that had done a lot of features, but it was inter-strewn with people from Propaganda [the top commercials production company]. People were starting to break out from the commercials and music videos and such and do more features."

The next step was to hire the local crew. This is usually done by the production manager, Grant Hill, who would check out the local people and either interview them himself or refer them to the appropriate head of department. Out of courtesy, the director might also be involved. For example, the key grip, whose crew set up all the lights, was to be Chunky Huse. Hill would therefore have referred Huse to the two people who would be his immediate bosses, gaffer Claudio Miranda and the DP, Derek Wolski. Daniel Kuttner, the twenty-eight-year-old proposed prop master, would have been referred to the production designer, Alex McDowell. The choice having been made, the production manager would then make the deal with the individual crew member.

Many people on the crew were surprised that someone with such a slight résumé as Daniel Kuttner (his last job had been as an assistant on *Super Mario Bros.* (1993)) would be hired as the prop master on such a prop-heavy movie as *The Crow*. His hiring is partly explained by the fact that he had been recommended by Simon Murton, the art director, for whom he had worked on his previous movie. In turn, Kuttner then hired his girlfriend, Charlene Hamer, a former set dresser, as his assistant.

Some crew members felt that Kuttner was hired to save money because he was cheaper than a more experienced prop master and felt that this could lead to problems later on. Unfortunately, they were to be proved correct.

As production in Wilmington got into full swing, many of the department heads assembled at the studio for their first big production meeting. First, Alex Proyas screened his commercial reel to give everyone an idea of his style and where the look of the movie was headed. Line producer Bob

Rosen had made certain that "all the key department heads were problem-solvers and people who could make the low budget work. We had a saying on that movie, it's a saying I've used on a lot of movies, 'it's a great time for bad ideas.' And if anybody had any thoughts on how we were trying to accomplish what we were trying to accomplish, nobody poo-poo-ed it."

With the crew heads assembled for the first time, Clyde Baisey, the on-set medic, wanted to talk about safety, and about the weather and the working conditions they would face. A set medic's job description is very broad: anything to do with basic health conditions and basic safety on the set. Baisey did not get an enthusiastic response: "By that time, the meeting had been two hours long. Everybody's pretty much off in their own little tangents, thinking about getting this done and that done. Nobody ever actually heard anything I had to say. . . . It was irrelevant, because if it didn't deal with the actual filming process, then they were not gonna discuss it." But Baisey, an experienced paramedic, faced this challenge on every movie he'd worked on.

A North Carolina native, Baisey's experience, charm, and sense of humor made him the kind of man you'd like to have around if you had an accident. Baisey started working as a medic on movie sets in Wilmington by chance. *The Crow* was his second movie. His first was *Amos & Andrew* (1993), starring Nicolas Cage and Samuel L. Jackson. Shortly after, he was referred to Grant Hill by the production manager of the TV series *Matlock* (1986). Working on a set, especially one as heavy on special effects as *The Crow*, would be a learning experience for Baisey: "There's nowhere that you could actually go to school to be a set medic." Indeed, there were no real guidelines to getting hired as a set medic in North Carolina. Baisey would simply apply his paramedic training and basically improvise the rest.

The sets for the movie were now under construction. The crew was building a large churchyard on the back lot and working on the urban street. On the sound stages, they were constructing the huge Gothic church, several modular rooftops for the scene where Eric Draven runs across them, and the loft where Eric and Shelly live, complete with its distinctive round window.

It soon became apparent, says associate producer Greg Gale, that, "The art department was going terrifically over budget. Part of the reason was [that] Peter Pound's detailed storyboards were getting built exactly as they were drawn." A production accountant named Bill Rose was therefore hired specifically to audit the budget. Greg Gale recalled that "Alex Proyas wanted a vision and they [the art department] would draw [it] expensively, shall we say. Peter Pound was even talked to on the side, I believe, by Mr.

Rose: 'Don't draw up things as quite as elaborately as you've been doing sometimes, kind of "down-draw" them.'" This is the familiar battle in movies, between the director trying to realize the best possible version of his vision and accountants trying to keep to the agreed budget. "The art department," Gale thought, "tried every different which way we could to get Alex's vision. And I think it was accomplished very well."

"Preparing the special effects was also costly and time-consuming," recalled Bob Rosen. "And within the schedule, they were going to be difficult to deal with." They needed big explosions, fires, and an elaborate setup to create rain. To handle this, Rosen hired a longtime colleague and friend, JB Jones. They had worked together a few years before on *Porky's Revenge* (1985), in which, Jones recalled, they had successfully pulled off a very complicated special effect: "A boat going through a bridge, and we had to knock two stories off it."

Jones was an older, lean, and slow-talking Southerner who wasn't afraid to get his hands dirty or speak his mind. Jones learned how to work safely with explosives in the U.S. Army during the Korean War. From there, he said, it was a natural transition into special effects: "Common knowledge. You ain't gonna put something in your hand if it's gonna blow your hand off. It's the same difference. Testing special effects, testing and making sure it works in the beginning without hurting anybody, is where your basic intuition comes in."

Jones had almost forty years of experience with special effects, working on everything from the television shows *Flipper* (1964) and *Miami Vice* (1984) to the Robert De Niro movie *Cape Fear* (1991). He also had his own Miami-based movie rental company, supplying virtually everything but cameras. But on *The Crow*, Jones and his crew were hired solely to create the complex special effects, and the only equipment he rented to the movie were the guns: revolvers, shotguns, and semiautomatic weapons.

By December, Jones and his crew were ensconced in Wilmington. After meetings with Alex McDowell and seeing Alex Proyas' commercial reel, he had a clearer idea of exactly what had to be done. And he was very conscious of the difference between commercials and movies: "Commercials are like hand-painted pictures, and you got time to do them [that way]. But with a movie, you gotta move on or you're gonna lose your tail."

Jones was sure that "some of the effects Proyas wanted was just crazy stuff, like cold winds, and some effects that had to be done optically because there was no way we was gonna be able to do 'em realistically." He thought Proyas was no different from other directors: "He was demanding, you know what I mean? He kinda lived like most directors do, in a fantasy world. They think that they can have the world, but in reality it turns out that you just have to settle for what you can get." Nevertheless, Jones knew that Rosen trusted him to accomplish the special effects to the best of his ability. "He knew sometimes that it might cost a little bit more money, but I'd get it done anyway," Jones said, "because that's the way I am. Bob said from the very beginning, 'Now JB, if you have a problem with anything, come see me. We can straighten it out.'"

One of the most costly special effects was creating rain. Proyas wanted it in some form in every scene, outside on the back lot as well as inside on the sound stages. Even on interior sets, rain had to be seen falling outside the windows. Jones brought four of his crew from Miami and another ten or so were hired locally. No fewer than six were given full-time rain detail. Large fire hoses were run from a fire hydrant to a powerful water pump that was connected to special "rainheads" (similar to sprinklers), which were strung on cables across the street or across sound stages. Different size heads and a regulation valve on the pump would supply varying quantities of rain. After the long pre-production, Jones knew that he was ready to produce one of the most elaborate setups for rain ever built, with the ability to create five different types of rain, from heavy downpour, to light drizzle, to a fine mist.

Director of photography Derek Wolski hired his gaffer Claudio Miranda, a colleague he had worked with many times on numerous commercials in Los Angeles. Miranda had worked with both Alex Proyas and Wolski on Nike, American Express, and Black Star Beer commercial spots. As the gaffer, Miranda was the DP's right-hand man, in charge of setting the lights in accordance with his instructions. Miranda came out to Wilmington a few weeks early, assembled his equipment, and hired his local crew. He rented all the regular lights from local suppliers but also brought with him his own special lights, which he had designed and made.

Miranda wasn't impressed with the script, but once he saw Alex McDowell's drawings, he was certain that the visual style of *The Crow* was something he was very interested in creating. "He is an art director who is so conscientious on lighting," said Miranda, "and that's rare. And art direction where there are actually plans for places to put lights behind things . . . ! Alex is amazingly talented. Amazingly lens-oriented, too, in his design." Since *The Crow*, Miranda became a very successful cinematographer. His many films as DP include *The Curious Case of Benjamin Button* (2008), *Tron: Legacy* (2010), *Life of Pi* (2012) (for which he won an Academy Award), and *Top Gun: Maverick* (2022).

Derek Wolski also hired the man who would set up Miranda's lights and position the camera, the key grip, Charles Huse. He was a tall, thin man in his fifties, inexplicably nicknamed "Chunky," who was proud to announce he was half Gypsy, half Irish. He had already established himself in the English film industry but, with its limited size, decided to come to the United States in the 1970s, where he set down roots, became a grandfather, and acquired a long and accomplished résumé. Huse and his wife, Cornelia (Nini) Rogan, who would become *The Crow*'s script supervisor, had only just moved to Wilmington from New York when *The Crow* went into production. Rogan's maternal nature and fearless ability to speak her mind would become a very encouraging foundation for the young crew.

Although Rogan and Huse were both well established in the movie business, moving to Wilmington had offered a more relaxed way of life. Rogan recalled, "In the late eighties, producers were boycotting New York, so work was slim."

Huse brought his grip crew with him, a group of bikers, most of whom were from Wilmington or other areas of the Southeast. After reviewing the comic book and the drawings, Chunky assessed them: "Number one, it was going to be a black movie because it all took place at night. No day shots, all night. It was going to be rain and it was going to be dirty. And it was demoralizing." But he liked the look of the new group he was about to work with. "There wasn't the odd asshole in there like there normally is. Everybody was nice."

The night shooting could present safety hazards on the back lot, and medic Clyde Baisey was concerned about that: "It's not paved, just mostly dirt back there, mud holes." A week before shooting was to begin, Baisey carefully tagged areas that were not safe and clearly marked exits and entrances for the crew to get out in case of an emergency, such as a fire. "There's one way into the studio, there's one way out of the studio," Baisey said. "So I drew up maps so transportation [the movie department that deals with trucks and vans] and everybody else could find the quickest way out of the back lot."

Since the costume department had to make most of the supporting characters' costumes from scratch, it was imperative they establish a large, fully operational shop at the studio. For costume designer Arianne Phillips, this was not like working in Los Angeles, "It was like being on an island." Ironically, although Wilmington had historically been a large cotton port for the South, Phillips recalls, "There were no cotton fabrics. Everything's polyester, and the thrift store shopping is limited." Commercial sewing machines and fabrics had to be shipped in from New York or Los Angeles.

Phillips had completed her sketches and chosen fabric swatches earlier, so much of the fabric was purchased in Los Angeles.

Phillips' costume budget was approximately $130,000. "We had to keep reworking this budget," wardrobe supervisor Darryl Levine recalled, "to try to get to a number that the company was comfortable with. Meaning they always want more than you can deliver for the money they give you." Phillips was pleased she didn't have to go out and buy designer clothes off the rack but was instead able to bring her own costume designs to life. About 85 percent of the movie's costumes were not bought, but made, "Because" she said, "there's so much action and blood . . . it was great."

Because of the anticipated difficulty of working conditions, the constant rain and the extensive stunts, all the characters' costumes needed multiple copies. Darryl Levine recalled having many meetings with Jeff Imada, the stunt coordinator, and JB Jones, the special effects coordinator: "And that's when your budget changes. How many shots does the director want to get; does Alex want to have four takes of a high fall? Then we have to make sure we're covered on that wardrobe. Or four takes on a guy's chest blowing up. We have to make sure we have at least four shirts and have another two in case they get wet. Everything is logistical."

Arianne Phillips also had to coordinate with the production designer, Alex McDowell, in terms of colors: "If you think about the film, it has a real slim color palette, which creates this incredible style. We made strong choices about color, which gives it that really incredible look."

By the time Brandon came in for his first costume fitting, "The creative heads of the movie were speaking a language we all understood," Phillips recalled. "We have the outline of the comic, of what existed and then our film, and within that, the practicality of what looked good on Brandon and making it look right. Everything looked good on him . . . that helped my work, because we wanted to have a very slim, lithe silhouette because of the character of Eric Draven, the rock character." This was a very familiar world for Phillips, who had spent much of her career up until then dressing rock musicians such as Lenny Kravitz. "I sort of get really inspired. Usually when I'm sketching and working initially, I like to work to music and I'm really a music-oriented person. So I started to listen to Nick Cave and Iggy Pop and it started to inspire the feeling of the clothes."

Guided by Darryl Levine's practical experience, Phillips had to compromise and simplify some of her designs. Levine would explain: "It looks great here, but you can't get it on camera. . . . There are areas that you work on that don't matter, that the camera will never see." In some cases,

Phillips wanted to use fabrics that would not be "read" by the camera. Levine would "Suggest an alternative, as opposed to saying flat out, 'No.'"

In Los Angeles, a problem arose for Phillips when Brandon Lee insisted that Eric Draven would wear an expensive pair of leather pants: "And he goes, 'We've gotta have those real leather pants in the movie,' because they were right for the character." The leather pants Brandon wanted cost more than a thousand dollars each and their real silver buttons cost between sixty and eighty dollars, and they would need twenty-five pairs of those pants, in different states of disarray, as well as those for Brandon's stunt double. Darryl Levine's response was: "If we

Brandon posing for a continuity photo, around the middle of the film's shooting schedule.
Photo by Lance Anderson

do these pants, he gets no shirts and no jackets, I go right to the jugular now. It's not a $100 million movie where my wardrobe budget is [$]2.8 [million]. It doesn't happen." Levine had another rational argument against these tight leather trousers: They would not only inhibit the range of physical movement demanded of Brandon, but "they will stretch, number one. I need backup. You're not gonna look good. Now once you don't look good, the pants come off." His compromise was to make the twenty-five pairs of pants, but with some made out of leather and some made out of vinyl, because "If I'm shooting a movie at night, and exterior night, you can't tell the quality." As for the expensive silver buttons, Levine decided they would cast plastic replicas. He explained to Brandon, "Nobody's gonna get a close-up of your crotch. Really, it's not gonna happen in this particular film." But in the end, in a way, Brandon got what he wanted: Levine agreed to buy him one pair of the leather pants for himself.

Unlike the pants, Brandon's costume shirt as the Crow was low maintenance. It had to be an affordable, durable material that would hold its shape and remain tight when it got wet. It was a stretchy synthetic, much like the material used to make dance tights or leotards. "We get it out of a company in New York," Levine said. "[It's] the same fabric used for a character like Superman."

Of the six locals whom Levine hired as his costume crew, a couple didn't have much experience. "Because we were non-union, and because of the workforce at that time in Wilmington, it was thrown upon me to train the people." The good Southern folks Levine employed were deeply impressed by his blunt professionalism. Levine quickly taught them how to make costumes and maintain them on a movie set. He knew they had to be prepared to deal with scenes where there would be "fifteen, twenty stunt guys working in multiple outfits with bullet holes." Time was of the essence. "My local crew," Levine recalled, "wasn't used to somebody saying, 'We need this by tomorrow morning,' and it may be six o'clock at night. 'I need four of these by tomorrow at eight,' and they wanna go home for dinner, which just doesn't happen." Levine's explanation for the local crews' enthusiasm in putting in ungodly hours was that "They could feel as though, they made a pair of pants for this guy. 'Oh, cool, I'd do anything you want.' So it's that mystique. I think they had a part of that."

Compared to the costumes, the hairstyles in *The Crow* were relatively simple. Using the storyboards and the comic as reference sources, key hairstylist Michelle Johnson made sure that once a character established a particular style, it would remain consistent throughout the film. Johnson was a very experienced professional, an outspoken character who liked actors and the movie lifestyle. She was a single mother and would often bring her small baby to work with her. Johnson stayed true to the dark character of the movie, "pretty dark and rich colors," with the exception of the bleached hair of the character Funboy and his girlfriend Darla. Her hair designs were largely accepted by Proyas who, she was delighted to find, gave her "a great deal of creative freedom."

When it came to designing Eric Draven's hairstyle, the opinionated Johnson's idea differed wildly from the comic book: "It was like a black rock 'n' roll hairdo, an early '80s little spikes–Rod Stewart thing, but black. And I thought, 'Yuck! Not at all what I would put on somebody's head.' Some period piece or something." When *The Crow* started shooting, Brandon had been letting his naturally wavy hair grow. "It was almost like a bob. It was just above his shoulders." But Alex Proyas wanted Eric Draven's hair to have a longer, loose look, falling below his shoulders. Johnson's solution was to use hair extensions rather than a wig. In a daily, thirty-minute process, Johnson was able to place a series of clips holding longer pieces of hair, which matched Brandon's, in between pieces of his own hair. Once in place, these extensions held well until they were taken out at the end of the day. "He was so easy. He was like, 'Just get those things out. Good night. See ya.'"

Special makeup effects artist Lance Anderson was hired onto *The Crow* early in pre-production. His long list of credits included *The Serpent and the Rainbow* (1988) and *Pet Cemetery* (1989). He was a fit, middle-aged man with a gray-speckled mustache, a full head of long gray hair, and a quiet, soft-spoken manner. His work ranges from making bloody body parts and transforming actors physically, to creating entire animatronic creatures. His first profession as an electrician comes in handy when he is wiring the tiny servo motors that animate his creations. For *The Crow*, Anderson's most notable animatronic creations were a bird to be used in shooting the scene where the character of Myca has her eyes pecked out and a walking, talking corpse character called the Skull Cowboy, which was later cut from the final film.

In Los Angeles during pre-production, Anderson made a life cast of Brandon Lee's body to enable him to create latex molds that would conform perfectly to the actor. Some of the molds would incorporate the many bullet holes and wounds that Eric Draven receives during the course of the movie. The special effects crew would mount small explosives (squibs) into some of these rubber chest and back pieces to simulate bullet hits. From a cast of Brandon's hand, Anderson also created a puppet hand to be used when Funboy shoots Eric through his palm, leaving a visible hole that would appear to heal up on camera.

In the story, after his resurrection, Eric Draven paints his face, and Anderson wondered why he did so. The movie suggests that the idea comes to him suddenly when he sees the reflection in the makeup table mirror of the masks of Tragedy and Comedy hanging on the loft's wall. Although it might also seem logical to make a connection between the Crow makeup and the rock musician Alice Cooper or the band KISS, Crow creator James O'Barr insists they were never part of his inspiration. But Anderson found no real explanation either in the script or the comic book for the makeup. "I always read it as a fright factor," said Anderson. "That he did it to scare the be-Jesus out of these guys after he comes back." Another inexplicable feature of the Crow makeup was a scar across his nose. "I don't remember any justification for it," recalled Anderson, "other than it was in the comic book."

Because it was impossible for Brandon to spend long hours while Anderson fine-tuned the Crow makeup, a mold was made of his face. The mold was then made into a positive head cast. Using the comic book as a guide, Anderson would experiment on the face mold to find the right colors and lines that would turn Brandon into his character.

The molds of Brandon's face and body, made so innocently before the movie started shooting, would later assume a more somber significance.

In the comic book the Crow's makeup is a stark white and an equally stark black. But to complement the dark lighting and shadows of the movie, Anderson imaginatively added a touch of maroon to the black and the white, so that, "It wasn't so stark. There is a slight purple cast to the shadowing around the cheeks and the jaw." The mouth was dark, painted into an upturned smile. Anderson interpreted the lines around the eyes, he said, "Almost like cry lines . . . Sympathetic lines coming down from the eyes almost like crying." The eyes were also deeply shadowed "to get the deathlike, hollow look."

Anderson used regular grease makeup to create the Crow look. It can last for hours and is waterproof. "Fortunately," he recalled, "Brandon had very resilient skin. So I never had any problems with him breaking out or anything. I always washed him up and put moisturizer on and kept his skin toned up, so when I sent him out of the trailer he was always prepped for the next day." A couple of weeks before production started, Anderson tested his makeup design on Brandon under the various lighting conditions expected in the filming and carefully recorded each stage with Polaroid photographs.

Over the course of the twenty-four hours Eric Draven spends as the Crow, wreaking his revenge on the bad guys in the rain and cold, the makeup wears off. "So that by the end of the film," Lance Anderson recalled, "the lines are gone. The makeup deteriorated towards the end of the movie. It started out pristine when he did it, and then by the end of the movie it's almost all gone . . . wasted away." With no guidance from the comic book or the script, the experienced and creative Anderson made this character determination himself. "I just did it," he said. "I felt he had been through the rain, he had been through all of this, he's not going to run back and touch up his makeup."

The first day on set when Brandon was made up as his character, Greg Gale remembered that the actor started off with a joke: "He came in and just popped into people's offices and looked around the corner and no one knew he was going to be walking through the production offices doing that. He would just kind of slowly creep around the edge of someone's door and when he did it to me, I was . . . just like, 'Aaah!' . . . it was great!"

Brandon Lee's dedication to the movie extended into every area of his daily routine. In the weeks before shooting began, with great discipline and determination, Brandon molded his body into the image of Eric Draven. For *Rapid Fire* (1989) he had bulked up, but Imada recalled Brandon felt, "The guy's a rock star, so he shouldn't be bulky like that. So he stripped a lot of weight; put himself on a strict diet, to the point of weighing food. All the stuff he loved to eat, he couldn't." Costumer Roberta Bile recalled, "He purposely modeled the character after this guy from The Black Crowes, the singer [Chris Robinson]." Though he was not a "fitness freak," according to Jeff Imada, Brandon always kept very fit and muscular. For his workout, Brandon focused on cardiovascular exercises using a Stairmaster, replaced the heavier weights with lighter ones and did more repetitions to stretch and elongate his muscles. And to lose body fat he significantly increased his aerobic activity. This became a routine, which he continued in Wilmington and, indeed, would follow almost every day, even once the movie started shooting. "Brandon was religiously working out at a local gym called Wilmington Fitness Today," recalled Jeff Most.

Brandon didn't just want to look like a rocker, he also wanted to learn how to play the guitar. There were scenes in the script of the lithe young rock musician playing his guitar against the rooftops of decaying Detroit, and Brandon wanted to play the guitar well enough to play it himself on screen. So, once in Wilmington, with no previous musical experience or familiarity with the guitar, he began taking lessons from a local teacher, J. K. Loftin. He picked it up quickly and was soon able to perform a short guitar piece he wrote himself. "And you know," said Jeff Most, "he was very proud of that."

But Brandon Lee's major focus, for what he regarded as the most important role of his career, was on preparing himself emotionally to play Eric Draven. "We talked about how it would be if he put himself in that position," Imada recalled, "to the point of losing somebody very close to him and coming back." On *Rapid Fire*, Imada had seen Brandon cope with a similar acting challenge. In a pivotal scene, his character, Jake Lo, witnesses his father being run over and killed by a tank in Tiananmen Square during the 1989 student uprising. Although Brandon never spoke much about his own father and was struggling to show the world he was his own man, Imada recalled that before shooting this scene, "He brought to work a book that his dad had written, and so he used that to motivate some of the emotion from himself. He'd be reading it right before he'd actually come on the set." Imada thought that Brandon used similar personal influences to tap into Eric Draven. He doesn't know what they were, but assumes they were "more contemporary."

As the start date approached, many of the main actors began to arrive in Wilmington for rehearsals, which Angel David, who played Skank, recalled "were very, very strange." On many movies there are no rehearsals, but Alex Proyas wanted time with the actors, reading over and discussing the script before shooting, "To allow them to arrive in an artistic manner at what they would portray on the screen," recalled Jeff Most. This was to ensure that by the time they got on the set, "Alex was done with each character, and they were ready to take on the role."

Angel David, a native New Yorker, became enchanted with Wilmington's small-town flavor. "It's like going out into some beautiful section of the United States and making films. What's better than that? You have the beach if you want, the woods if you want." David was also struck by the anomalous nature of the studio. "In the middle of this beautiful community, there's this huge back lot, and I'm thinking, 'This doesn't belong here.'"

Laurence Mason was also thrilled to arrive in Wilmington a couple of weeks early: "It really turned me on, 'cause I'm from the old school." This was Mason's first trip to the Southern United States. Having been raised in New York but coming from a close-knit family with its roots in Trinidad, after three months in Wilmington, he realized to what degree he was "alien to this whole African–American thing. It was real educational."

While working with Alex Proyas, Mason began to realize, "He was pretty quiet through the whole thing. But you can always tell that there's something going on and wheels were turning." But Proyas' quiet talent was not Mason's first impression. "At first, I didn't think he could create that kind of a dark, scary thing, but it was there."

Mason had similar initial doubts about Brandon Lee's ability to carry this edgy movie. "When I first met him, I was like, 'God, this guy's so sweet. I can't believe this is Bruce Lee's son.'" But Mason's impression of Brandon changed in a single moment, during the first dinner for all the principal cast: "We're sitting at a long table, kinda like the Jesus table, the Last Supper kind of thing, and on one side is Brandon with his fiancée, on the other side was Michael Wincott [Top Dollar]. So it's the good guy and the bad guy. Michael said something kind of weird, kind of inappropriate, because there were ladies at the table, and so Brandon just kinda leaned forward, put a finger in his face and said, 'You gotta watch your mouth. There are ladies at the table.' And just the way he said that—I saw all the Lee Dragon shit; he said it real quiet, but it was so intense."

Proyas had carefully chosen his actors to fit the world of *The Crow*. They were all risk-takers and rebels. The rehearsals were to focus them. "I guess he was just trying to get us into the mood," recalled Mason. "Which, after a while, was not a problem."

Proyas spent a lot of time with the four thugs who had crucial scenes with Brandon, rehearsing the dialogue and blocking the extensive action and fight choreography. He walked the actors through the sets on the back lot. Angel David suggested that this was, "To make them more comfortable and familiarize us with the world and the look." Though he admitted, "It's not like it's Stanislavsky. It's not like these huge scenes where you sit down and talk to people. Basically you yell three or four things and you shoot somebody, but in a cool way. So the rehearsals were more like getting to know each other." After working with the final script for the first time, David thought, "This is going to be a hell of a lot of fun."

Ernie Hudson also arrived in Wilmington for rehearsal a few days before the cameras rolled. Hudson had worked in Wilmington before, appearing in *Weeds* (1987) with Nick Nolte and *Collision Course* (1989) with Jay Leno. He, his wife, and two small children had a rented condo on Wrightsville Beach. Hudson was fond of Wilmington, but his kids were perhaps even fonder. "For the longest time my kids talked about going on vacation to Wilmington. It's like a vacation spot for them." But while his kids were playing on the beach during the day, Hudson knew he would be sound asleep trying to regenerate his batteries for another long, cold night of shooting.

Michael Wincott did not get off to such a positive start in Wilmington when he took a very different view of his costume from Arianne Phillips. Although Phillips grew to like and respect Wincott immensely, their initial conversation was tense. "I think he was talking about Armani suits and I was trying to steer him in a different direction." Phillips was very protective of her ideas and, certainly on her first chance to design a movie, she wasn't "into buying designer clothes for anything, because, I am a designer." But Wincott had only read the script and not seen the stylish look that Phillips' costume sketches suggested. Fortunately, when he finally arrived for his actual fitting, "We immediately liked each other. We're both intense. We're both New Yorkers. And he really got it." Wincott's intense interest and concern sprang from his belief that his costume was extremely important in developing his character: "That, to me as a costume designer," said Phillips, "is the ultimate thing you can do for an actor. Help them with their character." Later, Phillips recalled, when she was designing the costumes for the movie *Tank Girl* (1995), Malcolm McDowell (an "anti-Method") actor, told her "an anecdote that actually has been my mantra: Laurence Olivier always said he started with his character by buying the shoes."

Michael Wincott had a problem with his hair too. He had expected his character's long, silky brown hair to be ready and waiting for him as planned. But he arrived in Michelle Johnson's chair only to discover that the production had neglected to tell him they decided there wasn't enough time or money to make his wig. "So he comes to the trailer," Johnson recalled, "'Where's my wig? You don't have a wig!' I think he was really flipped out." After a discussion with production staff, Wincott returned to Johnson, who had no choice but to improvise and find a way of getting him on the set in an hour. Luckily, Johnson had a large store of long, silky brown human hair extensions, exactly the look they had intended for the wig. "Michael was thrilled. 'It's great. It's just what I needed . . . Just what I wanted.'" He was ready for the scene. Johnson was also delighted that her original concept of Top Dollar's hair had been realized: "Long, silky, straight hair, so that when he's doing all the sword fighting it would just move and flow and be really pretty."

PRODUCTION BEGINS

9

THE LOOK AND ATMOSPHERE that Alex Proyas and Alex McDowell had decided on for *The Crow* meant that for the night shooting on the exterior back lot streets, the entire set would have to be continually soaked with fake movie rain. This might not have mattered in the summer, but they were shooting in February, and the studio back lot is notoriously cold and windy.

Clyde Baisey was not surprised when, on the first night of shooting, "The temperature was seventeen degrees [Fahrenheit] . . . wind blowing out of the northeast at ten to fifteen miles an hour, wind chill factor of about five or six degrees . . . Freezing!" Robert Zuckerman, the movie's still photographer, had worked on many films on which they had started shooting with the easier scenes, but this film was different. "This was just like, first night, boom!" he said. "Rain machines, freezing weather and that was it."

In a piece of extraordinary Method-acting preparation, a couple of days before shooting started, Brandon Lee had conducted an experiment with Jeff Imada. Brandon wanted to know how it would feel, being dead and coming back to life. "'If you're coming back from the dead,'" he told Imada, "'you'd be cold. You're not warm. You'd be sort of cold and shivering.'" Imada remembered, "He goes, 'I can imagine how it is. What about if we pack me in ice, and time it and see how long it takes, and see how my body is and how controllable?' He just wanted to see how he would be physically. Okay, fine. We went down to a liquor store and bought about . . . I forget how many bags of ice we bought . . . about ten or twelve bags. And we came back and we went on the back porch and we packed him in ice. 'Okay, time me!' And he's laying out there. It's already cold outside, windy and everything else. He goes, 'Okay, let's pull off the ice.' So we pull off the ice and he's shivering. He started walking around and totally getting into it."

Brandon was to learn that even this self-imposed experience with freezing temperatures would scarcely prepare him for the bitter cold he was to face on *The Crow*'s back lot. That first night it was below freezing and his costume, as Eric Draven returning from the dead, had already been decided with no thought to the conditions.

The crew, in contrast, was dressed for the cold weather. Jeff Imada said, "I never had so much winter clothes on. I had layers. That's when you got into the fleece and everything, trying to stay warm. And Brandon's out there barefooted, jeans on, that black cotton outfit that the character wore and that was it. And it was so cold. I said, 'Brandon, I don't think we need any ice tonight.' And he goes, 'No, I don't think so!'" This was the moment at which Brandon began to earn the crew's deep respect. The costumer, Roberta Bile, was astonished: "He's barefoot, naked except for his pants, and dripping wet, freezing cold in the middle of the night. And never complained once. Not once."

This first night's shooting consisted mostly of scenes of Eric Draven roaming through the streets immediately after he has been resurrected from the grave. It's the nature of filming that scenes must be shot from many different angles, and this meant that Brandon would be called on to repeat what he was doing many times. Jeff Imada remembered that "Alex would say, 'Let's do one more.' And Brandon'd come out and do it again and never complain. Other people were bundled up and freezing. They're going, 'God, he's nuts!'"

Every single person present was impressed by Brandon's attitude and his dedication. Lance Anderson, the special makeup effects artist, noted that, "He really dove into this project with his whole body and his whole heart. He never complained." Robert Zuckerman was experienced enough to see that a pattern was being set. "It was . . . just cold, bitter cold," he remembered, "and Brandon was out there with no shirt on and bare feet, walking in this rubble, in this twenty-degree weather. And that kinda set the tone for the whole production. It was just physically grueling and intense."

Naturally, everything was done to make Brandon as comfortable as possible in the conditions. Clyde Baisey sometimes "had an ambulance sitting just outside of the camera frame. As soon as it was over, he'd hop in the back, I'd wrap him up in a blanket, inside the ambulance." They were struggling to keep the ambulance warm, even with its heater going flat out.

"I think we were maintaining a 100–105, maybe 110 degrees [Fahrenheit] at the most," Baisey said. "And that's with the heater continuously blowing hot air. Then you open the back door of this ambulance and there goes all your warmth right out the door! So get him in there for ten or fifteen minutes, and I'm sweating, peeling clothes off, trying to stay cool because I'm just pouring sweat, and he's just getting warm!"

There was no question in Jeff Imada's mind that Brandon knew what he had agreed to do. "I think he just had a very strong mindset. He also didn't want to let anybody down. He didn't want to let people down that had put faith in him."

It wasn't simply that Brandon didn't complain; he was so pleased just to be doing his own movie that he was always very good-humored. Roberta Bile remembered him, "Telling stories . . . real stories of when he was younger, because I guess he grew up in the Hollywood scene 'cause of his dad . . . telling the stories to the people that were around him, actors that were around him, because he was so excited about this movie. So excited about getting into the mainstream."

This was also the first night that the birds would shoot on the movie. The five trained birds were to be directed by Larry Madrid, an experienced animal trainer, who was used to doing live shows at Universal Studios in Hollywood. They had not prepared him for the conditions on *The Crow*. He recalled that on that first night it was so cold that "the water was freezing as it was hitting the ground."

Madrid had to work on a shot where Brandon goes over to a dumpster and, as he's looking into it, the crow flies in next to him and then leads him off down to the alleyway. "The bird had to fly and sit there and then fly off," Madrid said, "and we did it one time, then we went to do a second take. And the bird flew in and I tried to get him to come off and fly to me and he wouldn't fly to me, wouldn't fly." Madrid was amazed to see that, "the bird's wings . . . had frozen over like an airplane. So he needed to be de-iced, otherwise he couldn't take off! So I went and picked him up, and we took him over to a trailer and let the water dry out. Just basically dry out on him. He was fine, because birds have a waterproof barrier, so it just beaded up on the outside and then froze. He had too much weight so he wouldn't try to fly because he knew it wasn't right. He's smart. So then we dried him off and we put him back and we did one more take. And he was fine!"

The first day of shooting on a movie is when relationships are established, and each crew member positions themselves in relation to the others. This is especially true for the still photographer. Robert Zuckerman was tenacious and self-motivated, but also sensitive and sympathetic. He was used to the freelance life of the movie still photographer, who is a part of the crew and gets to know the actors intimately yet remains strangely separate from the behind-the-scenes action. In order to get the shots that are needed for publicity, the photographer must be next to the movie camera, but also can't be in the way. Zuckerman said, "I just made it a point, the very first night of filming, just to walk right up, next to the movie camera and establish my position there. And you know, once you do that, it's kinda like people see that's where you're gonna be. It's accepted."

However, like any still photographer, there would be times when the crew thought Zuckerman was in the way. "A number of times, the director of photography, Derek [Wolski], he would think I was standing too close to one of his lights, or I was in the way of the lights, even though I was outside the edge of the light. A lot of it's just one inch in on a movie set. He'd come in and shove me out of the way. I'd crawl right back around there and get in again. It wasn't done with hostility, but it was just done because he's intense in his own work. And he's responsible for the whole look of the thing."

Zuckerman and his talent were beloved by a long list of celebrities he worked with on hit films such as *I Know What You Did Last Summer* (1997), *Training Day* (2001), *Terminator 3* (2003), and *National Treasure* (2004). In the 1980s, he co-produced the award-winning documentary *Video from Russia* and directed and produced the New York City portion of *Hands Across America*.

He published the award-winning book *Kindsight* (2005), a collection of photos and text illuminating the richness of everyday-life encounters and experiences. After being diagnosed with a rare degenerative disease, he continued to work to inspire and mentor young artists around the world before his death in 2022.

The first day of shooting on *The Crow* was not without its accidents. The pressure that the crew were to mention so frequently had already started building. "It was a very kind of hurry-up day," producer Jeff Most remembered. "'Let's get ready for the group. Gonna get our first shot today,' situation." During the day, a few hours before they shot the first take on the movie, James Martishius, a carpenter on the back lot, high up on a cherry picker, accidentally backed himself into live power cables. In the production office, Greg Gale noticed, "A little flinch in the power, and we heard about five minutes later that there had been an accident."

Only days before, during his safety check of the back lot, Clyde Baisey's attention had been drawn to the large power poles that lined the fake streets. His concern had been that they would be hard to see at night and that Chunky Huse's grips or JB Jones' crew could easily run into them when they were moving equipment. If the poles were not knocked down, at least they could be destabilized. This was a very serious consideration, because the back lot had been built directly underneath the main power supply coming from the state capital of Raleigh-Durham into Wilmington. The poles were carrying several hundred thousand volts.

The miracle was that James Martishius, in contact with thirty thousand volts, was not immediately killed. The arc in the power lines set his many layers of winter clothing furiously blazing, and he was trapped in the cherry picker's cage. "Where's he gonna go?" Baisey pointed out. "There's nowhere to drop down and roll over to put himself out. The guy's six foot two. He's standing inside of a jail." As soon as the ground crew realized what was happening, they switched the crane's controls to override and lowered him to the ground. But during the two or three minutes it took to get him down, he was engulfed in flames.

Not unusually, the production had not budgeted for their medic to be present during the day when the set-up crew was preparing the location. But by chance, another medic was at the studio, working on the set of the television series *Matlock*. "He heard about it and he rushed over," recalled Baisey. "Unfortunately, there was little he could do."

"Martishius was very badly injured, and we didn't think he was going to pull through," recalled Greg Gale, and, like the rest of the crew, Gale thought the carpenter was going to die. But, after a long period of treatment and rehabilitation, Martishius survived. He had second- and third-degree burns over 80 percent of his body, but eventually, he went back to work at the studio. Clyde Baisey said, "Martishius has the most outstanding personality of anybody you ever wanna see. He makes jokes about his physical condition. He lost his ears . . . 'Where did I leave my pencil? Because I don't have an ear to stick it behind.' I guess he looks at it like, it takes forty-two muscles to make a frown, it only takes three to make a smile."

This incident also meant legal trouble for Crowvision. An investigation by the North Carolina Occupational Health and Safety Division (OHSD) followed. And there was always the possibility of an expensive personal injury lawsuit. But ultimately, the only real damage the production suffered was the bad press generated by the accident. Associate producer Greg Gale recalled, "At the time the production was more concerned about his life. I mean, to hell with the lawsuit, you got insurance and things like that to cover that. . . . You concern yourself about the human side. To hell with production. Production is a movie. It's *only* a movie."

Unfortunately, fire became a theme of *The Crow*'s first night. In a totally unrelated incident, a brand-new equipment truck, belonging to key grip Chunky Huse, was gutted by flames. Having worked a long day preparing the night's work, Huse left his crew on set and went home to bed. At some point during the night, a crew member inside the truck had put a blanket over the door to keep out the cold. The blanket was later forgotten, and a light bulb mounted on the door then ignited it. "I got a phone call saying, 'You better come to work, your grip truck is on fire,'" Huse remembered. "I just said, 'Piss off! What are you waking me up for? That's not funny.' Well, it didn't burn to the ground, but it damaged a load of stuff inside." Smoke had severely damaged everything in the interior. The next day, Huse's grips salvaged what equipment they could and outfitted a new, rented truck, ready for the next night's shooting. Without hesitation, the production paid the cost to rebuild the interior of Huse's truck. It was finally delivered back to the set, ready for work, two days before the end of shooting!

The North Carolina Occupational Safety and Health Division's investigation into James Martishius' accident resulted in a mere $9,500 fine, and the unit production manager, Grant Hill, then decided to ask Clyde Baisey if he would be the safety coordinator on the film. Baisey suspected that this newly created job could be merely a way for the production to protect itself against future penalties. "I'd be the heat man for it," he says. "It'd take the monkey off their back and put it on mine. And I told him, 'No!' I wasn't interested in doing that. I'll just be the medic."

As the medic, Baisey's position didn't carry the responsibility of overseeing and enforcing all safety precautions, but perhaps the most important part of his job was "the coordination of all EMS [Emergency Medical Services] on the film." This meant that if an accident happened, he would provide immediate, basic medical attention while the local paramedics were en route. Nobody could have imagined what a crucial task this would later turn out to be.

However hellish the first night of shooting on *The Crow* may have been, the results on film were so successful that the process became acceptable. Jeff Most found that, "These were the moments that touched me. And I think the entire opening sequence is truly memorable. Brandon returning from the grave and then walking aimlessly through the streets, shivering, gathering clothing, having no idea what he's doing. It's almost like the Frankenstein monster being born, but at the same time this is not a monster, this is a human. The rebirth for me was very powerful."

Despite the accidents and harsh conditions, what appeared on film was a promising start.

THE BIRDS   10

E VEN THE MOST SYMPATHETIC PERSON would have difficulty believing all the supernatural tales told by and about those who worked
on *The Crow*. On the other hand, even the most skeptical person
would have to be impressed by something extraordinary that happened to
camera operator Ken Arlidge before the movie was shot. . . . In September 1993, Arlidge was having dinner in a restaurant on Melrose Avenue in
Los Angeles, where the manager had pretensions as a fortune-teller, using
Native American tarot cards. The very last card he laid out for Arlidge was,
he said, "My Future card . . . It was a picture of a raven and underneath
it said 'Magic.' That was about three months before I worked on the film.
So here I am working on *The Crow* with a raven called Magic! And Magic
was the bird that would always perform. There were a lot of good birds,
but Magic was our favorite. He was our star."

One of the most important elements in *The Crow* was always going to
be the crow—the bird, that is. The screenplay had completely ignored the
movie cliché "Never work with children or animals" and called for a child
actress as well as a multitude of difficult shots involving birds. This created
a realistic apprehension in the production team, even in the experienced
Bob Rosen: "One of the biggest reservations I had, which turned out to be
absolutely unfounded, was the amount of work that the crows had to do."

The birds on *The Crow* were not, in fact, crows, but ravens. Larry
Madrid, one of the animal trainers, explained: "The reason we used ravens
was because they're very, very intelligent and they're less flighty and less
wild than crows. They're more tamable."

One skeptic about their "tameness" and what they could be trained to
do was the director. It was clear to Madrid that when Alex Proyas read

the screenplay his reaction to the crow sequences was: "'How is this gonna happen?' And he was a little standoffish at first." But by the time they had finished the first scene and Proyas had seen what Madrid could do with the birds, his attitude completely reversed. "I felt that he and I were on the same page for the rest of the movie," said Madrid, "and he highly regarded the work and was very happy with it."

Bob Rosen was as surprised at the birds' skill as his director: "The crows were like wind-up dolls that did everything we wanted them to do. Flew at night, in the rain, through fire, and hit their marks. They were incredible."

Once Proyas realized the capability of the birds, he began to press harder and harder to get the results he had only hoped for. "He made it challenging and he made it really fun," said Madrid. The result was that they were able to shoot everything the screenplay had called for. Madrid was proud that "there was a scene where he [the crow] flies over the cockroach that runs across the ground, picks up the cockroach, flies out and eats it. That became a reality. All the flying-in-the-rain shots became a reality for him [Proyas], because he never figured the bird would fly in the rain. And the bird was wet all the time! I'd have to take time out to dry him out and stuff before he could go on working at night."

With Proyas prepared to spend time on it, they also managed to shoot all the shots that required the bird to sit on Brandon Lee's shoulder.

As with virtually everything on *The Crow*, Brandon was responsible for much of the success in filming the birds. Second assistant director Randy LaFollette said he knew, "They had to make sure that Brandon was comfortable with the birds and the birds were comfortable with him, because like any animal, if you're nervous around them they'll sense it right away and they'll bug off." LaFollette made sure that the shooting schedule allowed Brandon to spend time with the birds, and Madrid was very impressed, not only with Brandon's attitude, but his capability: "Brandon was fine with taking the time to spend with the birds, so that he understood what they were about. And that made a big difference for me, because with his confidence level . . . He's a very confident person and the birds picked up on that. As a trainer you have to have a very high confidence level, and with the right instructions to him, he was able to mimic a trainer's mentality. So the bird would pick up on that and be all right with him. So we were able to transfer that and turn it into sitting on his shoulder, flying in on his shoulder and stuff." To reinforce this behavior, as with most animal training, the bird would be given food as a reward, in this case, by Brandon.

Madrid was even more impressed at how cool and comfortable Brandon was in potentially dangerous situations with the birds: "He was an amazing person. He just took to it like he'd done it his whole life." The prudent Madrid actually had to stress to Brandon that in some situations, he could possibly be injured by the bird. "I mean, you have to tell them up front," said Madrid. "Still a wild animal, even though he's trained. There's nothing I can do, say, if something happens, [and] he [the crow] decides to poke him in the eye. I can't stop that if I'm fifty feet away. I mean, what am I gonna do?" Madrid told Brandon that one solution was for him to be in proximity to the bird for as short a time as possible, but he remembers Brandon replied, "'You know, I don't really care if I get my eye poked out. I've always wanted to wear a patch anyway and play a pirate!' That was his answer and he was so cool about it. So from there forward he had no problem with the birds."

The technique that movie animal trainers develop is being just out of the camera's view, to encourage and, in effect, direct the animal from off camera. As Madrid said, "The art of it is . . . just making it seem like the animal in the movie is doing his own thing. And yet behind the scenes the trainer's losing hair, losing sleep, working twenty-four hours a day, seven days a week and trying to communicate with the actors, the director, all the people involved in the movie, and yet act like they're not there. They make 'em perform in front of a camera. It's an amazing little trick that we perform, I think."

The Australian-born Ken Arlidge, a thoughtful, aspiring young moviemaker who worked as a camera operator on *The Crow* and would later work on *Babe* (1995), had originally wanted to become a veterinarian and to make wildlife documentaries for National Geographic. Arlidge knows that on a movie set, the crew must relate to the animal actors in a special way. "The fact is," he said, "that when you work with animals, the same with the pigs on *Babe*, you maintain a distance from them because you want the animal to interact only with the trainer. If it starts to bond with other people, then you could potentially divert its attention away from the trainer."

Madrid revealed his own understanding of the way the animals (birds in this case) think and how he tries to get the birds to regard the actors: "The bird's got other things on his mind, such as, 'When do I get to leave?' and 'When do I get food?' and 'What are you doing?' They pay more attention to *you* than to the actual person that they're [perched] on. So we try to teach them to treat that person more as a prop, as an entity, and yet at the same time we have to make sure that that person is comfortable."

Animal trainers always bring more than one animal to any shoot, and on *The Crow*, Larry Madrid brought five well-trained birds: Jay, Dart, Baby, and two birds he had raised himself, Omen and Magic.

All the birds were capable, but Magic became the crew's favorite. Arlidge observed, "He would always drop the ring in the hand. He would land on the tombstone and peck the tombstone in the right place. Larry would motion with his hand, 'Peck the stone! Peck the stone!' and sure enough Magic would bend down and peck a few times and look back up. He'd say, 'Peck it again. Peck it again!' and sure enough, the bird would peck it again, and then he would go up and he'd reward the bird with a bit of food. It's just remarkable, absolutely remarkable what these birds can do." Madrid agreed and said that he had recognized in training that Magic was special, "Because his brain capacity in school would be that of an 'A' student. So he was able to excel and move on and graduate and move into the next level of performing."

Although the other birds performed well, some had little idiosyncrasies that limited their behavior. "There was one that talked a lot," recalled LaFollette. "So you couldn't have it in the scene, because it was chatty."

On the other hand, Robert Zuckerman always found "the ravens were so well trained, that they'd have to be in a position for the motion picture camera, so it was real easy for me to go in and photograph them. They were professional ravens, you know."

The Crow, with its meticulous director and emphasis on the image of the crow, was obviously a difficult assignment for Larry Madrid. "Flying through the broken window was our biggest challenge," he said, referring to a window broken by Eric Draven to get into Gideon's pawnshop. Draven is then followed by the bird, which flies in through the window. "That was really hard," recalled Madrid, "because you have the bird flying in from outside, into me inside, where the cameras are. You have the glass breaking and falling, and yet the bird has to have enough confidence to go through there which is a very scary thing for any animal, especially a bird. Birds like to just fly away. They don't like to deal with things that are challenging to them or scary. They just wanna leave." But Madrid and Proyas talked about the scene and decided that they should try it. On the night, they got it on the first take! Madrid was justifiably extremely pleased with his bird: "To get to the focus and do the behavior. So that was pretty neat."

Like the movie crew, the birds also had to get used to working at night. The birds stayed with Madrid at all times, living in kennels in the garage at his rented condo. He had had ten weeks of preparation for the movie, but his first seemingly impossible task was to turn the birds' body clocks around. In fact, he said, "It was real simple. It's basically [that] when the sun's up, they're awake; the sun goes down, it gets dark, they go to sleep. Put them in a garage in their kennels and, during the daytime, you black out the garage, close up the garage and turn the lights out. It's nighttime. Six o'clock at night, you turn all the lights on, they wake up, you go out, you get your day started, you keep lights on them all the time. Take them in the van, you drive to the set, you pull up to the set and you get lights from your electricians and you set them up around your van and shine them into the van so it's daytime inside the van."

There was another skill the birds had learned, which Madrid had previously used for demonstrations in live shows, and that was flying, apparently static, into a wind machine. A movie wind machine is basically just a huge propeller with a cowling around the edge of it, but Madrid had the movie crew make a baffle as well, so that the usual circular blast of air from the propeller was turned into a relatively straight wind. Since 1982, Madrid had worked at Universal Studios in Los Angeles, doing shows there and he had, he said, "Developed the wind machine. I trained eagles and vultures and hawks to play in the wind machines, up in the show. And then when I trained Magic, I decided to train him to fly in the wind machine." This creates very impressive "static shots of the bird flying without going anywhere." Just what *The Crow* needed for its special effects shots of the crow apparently flying over the city.

Considering the tough schedule that the birds worked, with their body clocks out of whack, working in the same cold and rain that the human crew found so tiring, it would be natural to think that at the end of the shoot the birds would be exhausted. But Larry Madrid insisted, "It never showed in their performance. It never did. And my impression is, they're so smart, that when you get 'em and you teach 'em at a young age, that their life is working in the movies and in front of the camera, that's what they do. . . . They love that as much as they love flying. So it's like, as far as being free, they don't really understand it because they don't know it. But they know enough to know that flying around and stuff is really cool and it's fun. So when they go to work, it's not like they're doing something that's stressful to them, it's actually fun. So I don't think that they were stressed out at all."

In that respect, the birds differed somewhat from the human crew who worked on the movie.

TOUGH WEATHER, TOUGH DAYS

11

*T*HE *CROW* WAS ALWAYS GOING TO BE a difficult movie to shoot. It was an ambitious film for the amount of time and money that was available. And nobody was more aware of that than the most experienced person working on the film, Bob Rosen. "Every day was a challenge," he described. "Every sequence was a challenge. When you look at that movie, it's never two people talking in a room. It was very complicated. And once we had set a tone for the movie . . . Here's what we were doing: we were shooting nights; we were shooting in the rain or making rain when it didn't rain; we had loads of special effects; we were working with animals; we were working with a child a lot of the time. We were doing everything that makes filming difficult, and it was also cold and unpleasant. Brandon was working without a shirt in weather that was freezing. There was nothing easy about it."

Weather, both real and artificial, was a big factor in shooting *The Crow*. Part of the problem was the "artistic" need for rain and for the sets to look wet all the time. The pattern of much of the shooting had been set on that first night. Since even in low temperatures the water would evaporate, special effects coordinator JB Jones would find himself wetting the street down again and again: "They would want it wet every time they got ready to shoot, and if they hesitated before they shot, then we'd have to wet it down again." For Jones and his special effects crew, this was just part of the job. "The only problems we had were when we would stop at one o'clock [a.m.] for lunch, sometimes the hoses would freeze up. Then when we go back, I had this pumper which was such a gigantic force, we would just force that ice right on through everything."

Another of Jones' more difficult problems was creating steam, which was meant to emerge from the manhole covers and waft off the streets to turn the back lot into the urban wasteland of Detroit. In fact, in the freezing weather, the steam usually turned to ice.

A confusing factor in filmmaking is that the crew is often more experienced in shooting than the director. Directors spend a great deal of their time in the setting up and preparation of their films, and then a great deal of time in post-production, whereas crews simply shoot all the time. Alex Proyas, although an experienced director of commercials, was a first-time director on a major movie, and he was no exception to this contrast in experience. So JB Jones found that "Alex couldn't realize that the wind had a lot to do with the effect of the rain. He would want mist, but when you create a mist forty foot high and the wind came along and blew it, you didn't have no rain. So, then you'd have to bring it up a little bit. And sometimes he wouldn't be real happy with it, but there wasn't really nothing we could do."

For the cast and crew of *The Crow*, rain simply became a fact of life, but on a scale they had never before encountered. "I had done movies where we had a lot of night work and a lot of rain," said Chunky Huse, "but I had never done a whole movie that it was *all* night and *all* rain!"

On the second unit, Ken Arlidge found the conditions no fun, but it was just one of those times he felt when, "You just have to go into professional mode and just push forward, and you accomplish the day. And you look back on it and you say, 'Well, yes, I pulled through and delivered the goods.' But you don't look back at those specific parts of the shoot with fondness in your heart."

Even when they shot interiors, there was still rain! Robert Zuckerman said, "They built a big church rooftop scene, where Eric and the crow and Top Dollar have a big battle. There was water pipes, big rain machines, all across the top of the studio, so they had rain actually inside the sound stage for a good portion of that, and then, just pretty much wherever we went, there was always rain. That was part of the texture and the atmosphere of the film."

The interior rain created yet another problem for Jones: drainage. First, the sound stage floors had to be covered with tar paper and hot tar. Then a six-inch-high dam was created around the perimeter to tame the spread of the water and channel it into concave drains that led out through the doors. Still, the water needed to be pushed out by Jones' crew with large broom-like squeegees.

Like other crew members, Arlidge soon found that, "It was too difficult to move. You develop a wet suit rash. You go home and you scratch yourself with a hairbrush at the end of the day. And it's just difficult conditions. It's like Forrest Gump said, 'There was a rain that came at me sideways and rain that even came back up.'" And Brandon had to put up with it more than anyone. Rochelle Davis said, "I felt really bad for Brandon because he had to go barefoot and shirtless sometimes, in the freezing cold rain. And we made jokes a couple of times to Alex about, 'Can't we have hot rain?' And he said, 'People like Mel Gibson get hot rain.' And we said, 'Okay, fine. We'll stick with the cold then!'"

Everything was done to make Brandon comfortable, and he was kept warm off set until he was actually needed. And with good reason, thought Jones: "At first, I could not believe that this actor was gonna get through this picture the way he was working. I mean, here's a man without his clothes on at one o'clock in the morning, and it's zero degrees and it's raining. You can't get much worse than that. But he was a good strong man, and he was holding up."

Sandra Orsolyak, one of the assistant makeup artists and a friendly and hardworking former Brit with many opinions, believed that Brandon's resistance came from his martial arts training: "He could put himself into another mindset and just block it all out. And everybody that was on the set, I'll have to admit, was envious of the fact that this man could do that. Because we couldn't!"

Angel David was reminded of a song that was in the finished movie: "'It Can't Rain All the Time.' I love that song, it's a beautiful song. Yeah, it was rain, rain, and more rain, and darkness."

What compounded the rain, of course, was the unrelenting cold. "The biggest battle was cold," Jones thought. "It was *really* cold. I'm not kidding you. I'm a poor boy from Miami, Florida. Born and raised there. So you can imagine what cold did for me." One crew member even claims that the production crew put alcohol in the water to prevent the rain from freezing.

Arlidge marveled at how helpful JB Jones was: "JB's workload on the picture was huge. Here we are, second unit, coming and asking him for rain over in this part of the stage when he's having to make the whole street rain. And it was quite remarkable. The temperature dropped so much. It got down to thirty or below thirty [Fahrenheit]. The rain would fall, and we had icicles falling on the scaffold in the street itself where we had the camera mounted."

Cold and wet are not friends of the film movie cameras used on *The Crow*. Arlidge knew that "Invariably, no matter how well you protect the camera, you get a certain amount of moisture working its way into the electronics itself. And from time to time you'll have a glitch with the remote head, which is the multi-access head that the camera's mounted on. You're sitting back comfortably with the wheels, and there's the crane and the camera and the remote head stuck into the thick of it, with the wind and the rain and the freezing cold temperature." Every now and then there would be an equipment failure and then an hour or two would be lost while it was fixed.

One solution was, "Drying it off . . . Throw another camera body on it. If you look at films like *The Abyss* (1989) or a film I worked on, *Hard Rain* (1998), you work in a tank, four feet of water, that's two football fields in size with rain bars dropping rain on you ten or twelve hours a day. Eventually, water seeps into your plastic covering. The only way to really protect the camera is to put it in an underwater housing, but that's very limiting in getting access to the camera and working efficiently, and pulling focus, etcetera. Those conditions make it difficult to shoot, and invariably you have technical problems with video, lighting, and with the camera itself."

The combination of the rain and cold regularly produced another problem, ice. When they had to move the camera on its dolly, the gaffer Claudio Miranda remembered, "The grips had to heat the tracks, use blowtorches before they could make the move. Otherwise, when it rained, it hit the tracks and then it froze and then the move was really bumpy. It froze that quick. When the ice is around, you slip and fall, and that was mostly the hazard. But as far as water and the lights, we were always sort of protected against rain, and always put covers over lights."

The ice also affected the speed at which the movie progressed. The cranes that Miranda used were sensitive to cold: "The hydraulic fluid, when you get that cold, things don't perform quite correctly. Like, for the street scenes, they actually lift the lights up in the air. They would take half an hour just to get up to the height . . . When you test them in the daytime, they go right up."

And it wasn't only the equipment that froze. "When it rained and it hit your back, it actually turned to ice," said Miranda as he laughed. "If you took off your jacket carefully, you could set it down and it'd stand. If you hit it, that could shatter your jacket." These conditions meant that on *The Crow*, the costumer's job was more than just dressing the actors and maintaining their costumes. "You had the coats on the actors, and the hand warmers, and the towels and furry knee pads," said Roberta Bile, "and you'd be rubbing them to keep them warm. It was really quite an ordeal. Plus ourselves, we were all freezing. Going to the bathroom was a feat, because you had to take off ten layers of clothes."

The grip crew on a movie were notoriously tough, but even they complained to the gruff Chunky Huse. "So I called them over to the set, and I said, 'Take a look. You guys are bitching about how cold it is. Take a look at that man there. He's naked, he hasn't got any shoes on, he's out here in four inches of water in the pouring rain, walking through all that gash metal and broken bottles. And you have everything on you could possibly have to keep warm and you're bitching! Take a look at *him!*'" Of course, "that man" was Brandon.

The producers were certainly mindful of the crew's hardships. Jeff Most knew that their work conditions were "extremely stressful . . . We worked very long hours, six days a week. As production wore on, people were getting sick right and left." The movie was scheduled for eight weeks. "We had fifty-one days," said Most. "It was just very exacting work and we were in a non-union environment. So we were going fourteen, sixteen, eighteen hours a day. It was just very hard."

Some of the crew were used to those fifteen- or sixteen-hour days, like JB Jones: "That's normal for a coordinator like I was." Clyde Baisey said he couldn't believe the hours that Jones worked. "JB, I'll tell you, that man, I don't know how he did it, but he would work all day during the daytime, and he would be there all night at night sometimes. It's like the man never slept!"

There could be no letup in the hours because the movie was such an ambitious production in relation to its budget. Additionally, there was always the danger of falling behind, and the completion bond company would constantly be looking over the production's shoulder to monitor that possibility.

The bond company would also be keeping their eye on the production because it was the director's first experience on a big movie. "Alex Proyas came out of commercials," said Most, "and was used to a great deal more coverage [different shots of the same scene] in the commercial world than on a $15 million film of this complexity. And the line producer [Bob Rosen] got hold of the reins on the shooting schedule after it was clear in the first three weeks or so that we were doing an abundance of coverage that we couldn't afford on our schedule. We were falling behind in places."

The crew's long days and six-day weeks were made more exhausting because the days were actually nights. "We're not naturally nocturnal," Randy LaFollette pointed out. Working at night means sleeping in the daytime of course, so the crew, said LaFollette, "All got duvetyn, that black cloth, and we put it over the windows. Everyone did that, so that it would be dark so you could sleep."

Although Robert Zuckerman said that he enjoyed the night working schedule and that his body got completely adjusted to it, even he never got used to eating lunch at midnight. "And you have to go back to work for six hours. I don't know about other people, but when I eat a big meal in the middle of the day, I get tired afterwards. Fortunately, because it was really cold, it was brisk enough to keep you awake."

For many of the crew, the night shooting meant that they had to do their preparation in the daytime. Wardrobe supervisor Darryl Levine remembered, "I was probably at the department at about eight or nine a.m., and I wouldn't leave the studio until two or three the next morning. That was on a daily basis. We were constantly building and rebuilding clothes because of the action sequences."

As stunt coordinator, Jeff Imada would often be shooting all night and then have to stay in the morning to meet with the day crew, the set decorator, the costume department, or production designer Alex McDowell, to check on elements that were important for future stunts. He would then snatch a few hours of sleep, only to return to see dailies in the midafternoon.

Because of the tight schedule, Imada remembered having to simplify or condense certain stunts or parts of the action: "There was some compromising, yeah. But we'd start off choreographing something, and as we started shooting, we realized we're not going to have enough time to do the whole thing. So we'd condense it from there."

The thirteen-year-old Rochelle Davis was conscious that the production, "Never forced me to work longer hours than I wanted to. But usually what happened was, I would work my nine hours and they would say, 'Okay, we can either do this scene now, or you can go home.' And I would say, 'No, no, let's do more.'" Davis thought, "They were under a lot of pressure to get finished really quickly." But there was one day when she had worked for twelve hours, and it became too much for her. "I think Alex wanted to get a few more shots in, and this is when my aunt was staying with me, and I said, 'Look, I'm really tired. I worked twelve hours, I'd like to go home.' And he said, 'Well, can we just do this one last scene? We'll just do this one last scene, you'll be done.' And I said, 'Yeah, but one last scene means a lot of takes, and I'm tired. I wanna go home.' And he said, 'Oh, come on, just stick it out. It'll only be an hour. I'll get you out of here in an hour.' And my aunt walked up and said, 'No. She's going home now! She worked twelve hours. She's done.'"

Night working affects different people differently. Chunky Huse talked about his physical response to it, believing that for everyone there is a dead patch when exhaustion takes over: "For me it's two 'till three. And everybody's got it. That one hour, two 'till three. There is something about night work, you miss a beat, or your metabolism says, 'You shouldn't be here, you should be sleeping.'" Others, like Roberta Bile, had a more mystical response to the night shooting: "There was a very odd feeling that I had the whole time I was working on it. It was surreal, and I think it was because we were on nights. We were like in our own world, and I definitely had nightmares every single night I worked on the movie, or in the day when I was sleeping, about supernatural stuff, like the devil."

For local crew, like Huse, whose homes were actually in Wilmington, the problem with night shooting was that, as he said, "They would get home and their kids were getting up. They never saw their kids. They were working at home, and a lot of folks who work at home choose to work at home because of their families, and yet they were working at home in these situations. They got exhausted." They also had little family life on their one day off because they would use it to catch up on their sleep.

All film crews accept that when there are night exterior scenes in a movie, they will have to work at night. What puzzled the crew and actors of *The Crow* was that the production team insisted on shooting at night even when they were *inside* the studio. Although it made little logistical sense, Alex Proyas and Derek Wolski were determined to shoot the night interiors at night. "The reason they wanted to stay at night," Jeff Most said, "was because they had gotten into the groove and this was a night show. And it was difficult for the crew to do it, but they just felt that they were creating this world at night, and they loved it." Most may have been a relatively inexperienced producer at the time, but even he was aware of how strange this was: "Alex and Derek wanted to continue night work on the sound stage, which I surely never heard of." This scheme of shooting night interiors at night even baffled experienced crew members, like Huse: "Even when we were in the stages, we shot at night. We were shooting interior night, on stages at night, with rain. Inside the stages! Weird."

The production team's determination to continue shooting the night interiors at night did not sit well with the crew. "That's the thing that really sort of freaked people out. They were very tired," said script supervisor Nini Rogan. Like many crew members, she thought that money was the consideration, because to switch from day to night shooting would have lost a day, or meant paying a very expensive day's overtime: "Why were we shooting at night in a stage? Well, because the company didn't want to pay for the turnaround." Roberta Bile bought the artistic explanation, that "Alex being a perfectionist, he didn't want to compromise anything." But the experienced Ernie Hudson was not exactly in agreement with that analysis: "I think it's bullshit. I think it's money, but I don't know." And Hudson didn't even know that Chunky Huse's crew had even offered to forgo the day's pay the production would lose by turning the schedule back onto days: "We said, 'cause if it is [the reason], we are willing to waive that. Just don't want to be paid. Just turn us around. Let us come back on days, let us have a normal life.' And they said that, 'No, it's nothing to do with payment.' It's to do with the fact that the director and the artists, because quite a few of them were Method actors, felt like the 'right way' to do it was to do it at night."

One of the artists who was happy with nights was Michael Massee, who was to have a significant role in the drama that lay ahead. Huse, taking a practical view, thought that Massee was "a crazy Method actor. He was crazy to the point [that] he was really a pain in the ass."

In any event, whatever the crew or the actors thought, *The Crow* continued to shoot its night interiors at night. This was a challenge for the management as well, of course. They too had to work during the day and monitor the shooting progress at night. "It was horrendous," said Bob Rosen. "As I say, every day was a challenge, every sequence was a challenge. There was pressure from completion bond companies and what have you, so it was a challenge the whole way. . . . If we coughed, we were in trouble. What can go wrong on a movie that involves children, crows, rain and special effects, and that amount of shooting days? A lot can go wrong. There's a lot of pressure." Just how much pressure there was, and how much it contributed to what eventually happened on the movie, will never be known. But it became a factor in the life of every single person who worked on *The Crow*.

Looking back, Ken Arlidge sums up the conditions under which the movie was shot: "A very dangerous mix is long hours, potentially life-threatening stunts, weapons or explosives, combined with an over-exhausted technician who is handling more than one or two items at a time."

THE LOOK

12

A s *THE CROW* SETTLED INTO PRODUCTION and the members of the crew became acquainted, they also began to form opinions about each other. As the focus of any movie crew is the director, there were more opinions about Alex Proyas than anyone else.

Bob Rosen, the most experienced person on the movie, thought, "Proyas gets as close to (and I don't use this word lightly, as a matter of fact, I don't think I've ever used the word) as close to a genius as I've ever come across. He is extremely knowledgeable. A consummate filmmaker. A person with the vision, not only to make the picture, but to make the picture creatively." Rosen was clearly overwhelmed by Proyas. "I cannot say enough about him as it relates to getting this picture done. It's all about him." He repeated, "It's all about him."

The makeup department found that Proyas gave them the creative freedom to do what they wanted, so naturally they thought that he was easy to work with. "I guess, obviously, if they like what you do, they're not gonna tell you to change stuff," key hairstylist Michelle Johnson said. "So, I mean, that's always a good thing. And if they start sending actors back to the trailer to be changed, that's a problem, but he didn't. He was always really open and happy with whatever we did."

Proyas gave the costume designer, Arianne Phillips, similar creative freedom, and he got a similar response from her: "He lets you do your best work. There's a lot of people that second-guess your work and a lot of pushy, demonstrative directors and producers, but Alex is the kind of guy who was very secure with the people he hired, and he let us do our work. He really let us run wild and go all the way to the end, and he rarely ever, if ever, didn't like something." The wardrobe supervisor, Darryl Levine, saw that Phillips and Proyas worked extremely well together: "They hit it off in a strange, bizarre way, which is great."

Levine himself, who was much more experienced than Phillips, and whose experience was from movies rather than commercials, was not so close to Proyas, finding him a poor communicator. "Alex is very dark," he said, "very quiet, very private, very hard to figure out what he wants . . . You try to be able to read people, but I couldn't with him. I *think* he liked us. Very hard to tell." Levine felt some residue of irritation that, although the costumes looked great and were always ready, despite the difficulties and changes, Proyas was slow to express his approval: "Alex even became appreciative . . . but he certainly wasn't at the beginning. It wasn't in his nature to show it, whether he was . . . Yeah, it's a very common disease in our business."

Proyas' lack of communication skills also caused something of a problem for Nini Rogan, the script supervisor. A director and a script supervisor need an efficient working relationship, but in this case, they got off to a very bad start. Based on discussions with all the department heads and the director, a script supervisor makes a list (a "breakdown") of what is needed for each scene. However, on the first day of shooting, Rogan made what Proyas considered to be a terrible mistake. On a particular scene, Proyas clearly thought that he had asked for a "red nail polish" to be provided. "And I said, 'But Alex, you never told me that you wanted X or Y. And anyway, that's not my department.'" Rogan continued, "I showed him all my breakdowns, I showed him all the stuff and said, 'Nowhere here is red nail polish mentioned.'" She asserts that whatever the "red nail polish" was, "wardrobe, hair, makeup [departments], none of them knew. Somebody fucked up, but nobody told anybody. This person hadn't done it and hadn't told anybody else about it. And he [Proyas] came to me. And I said, 'I don't know what you're talking about. So sorry.' Which is a terrible, terrible thing to have happen on day one, in terms of his trust of me. But on the other hand, it was like, 'I'm sorry, I can't provide for things I know nothing about.'"

Now Bob Rosen became involved and wanted to know what the problem was. Rogan explained that nobody had told her about the "red nail polish": "Nobody said anything to me about it. I'm sorry. I can only do what I can do. I can't read people's minds." Rogan, a proud professional, was deeply upset that she was being blamed for something she was sure was not her fault. Both Rosen and Proyas could see that Rogan, who, like Darryl Levine, was much more experienced in movies than the director, was obviously telling the truth. Rogan thinks that Proyas learned a lesson from this: "He had to make a choice then. He was either going to keep me on and not trust me, or he was going to take my word for it and realize that I had not been communicated with. At that point he realized, and this is the joy of working for non-Hollywood people, he realized the mistake was partially his and he said, 'Okay, fine, you didn't know about it.'" After that initial episode, Rogan recalled, "The entire crew got along like houses on fire. Absolutely. The best crew I've ever been on."

Possibly as a result of this incident, Rosen saw that Proyas could have his problems with the crew: "His strongest suit is that he knows exactly what he wants. He has a vision going in and he's very stubborn about getting it. Sometimes Alex is not the greatest communicator in the world, and so the only difficulty that people had, I think, from day to day, was just getting inside Alex's head, or Alex trusting people enough to allow them to get inside his head in order to give him what he wanted."

After their problems, Nini Rogan certainly developed great respect for Proyas. Describing his manner, she said, "Does he schmooze? He does not. Absolutely does not. Does he have the social graces? Yes. 'Please,' 'thank you,' 'good afternoon,' 'nice to meet you,' yes, but very spare. He's not effusive. He keeps his own counsel. He's not Hollywood!"

Robert Zuckerman, the movie's still photographer, always in a position to observe what went on, judged that "Alex is kinda just internal. He's got a real good sense of humor, real easygoing, but he's not one of these really vocal people. He just kinda says what he wants and has his vision and he expresses it to the people he needs to express it to. But he's not one of these people who's really verbose and vocal on the set."

Perhaps the real issue was not that Proyas was not verbose, but that he was not verbal. Commercials had been Proyas' world. It's a discipline where typically everything is storyboarded, the entire thirty or sixty seconds laid out in a series of graphic illustrations, so that the agency creative people, their executives, and the executives of the client company could examine and discuss every frame of the whole commercial before a foot of film was shot. Consequently, it was much easier for a director who is visual rather than verbal to be successful. As Bob Rosen observed, "The storyboards, I think, were Alex's way of communicating in many cases with key crew. Much more than the verbal. Once you found out that's what it was, then it got easier." Rogan certainly found that the storyboards were very useful: "Absolutely. Because he really knew what he wanted. It wasn't necessarily clear to anybody else at the time, except the people who knew him."

The use of storyboards was a vital part of Alex Proyas' planning. "There was a young sketch artist, Peter Pound, [an] Australian," said Bob Rosen, "who Alex had a prior relationship with, that we brought in on this picture. He was a wonderful storyboard artist, by the way. But you pretty much knew what Alex wanted to do all the way down the line, because of the storyboards."

Jeff Most made an extravagant comparison to Proyas' planning: "Alex works a lot like Alfred Hitchcock, and everything is on the page." Certainly, Proyas spent a great deal of time working with Pound on the storyboards. "Him and Peter were always in meetings about, 'What's the look?'" said production manager Greg Gale. "And every once in a while, Peter would get frustrated because he'd do some drawings and he'd have to go change them. With Peter's drawings as extensive as they were, each one of his drawings, each storyboard frame, was a masterpiece in itself."

The only difficulty was that the storyboards were created in response to the developing situation of the detailed planning of the film, and consequently Rogan found that they came in fairly late most of the time. "They were being worked on and revised. As the locations are chosen and actually get nailed down, the storyboards can change."

The storyboards were so important to Alex Proyas that Randy LaFollette used to attach them to the "call sheet," the document issued to the crew each night detailing the work for the next day. Like so many others, LaFollette was aware of Proyas' vision: "His whole thing is the visual side of it, and he was very precise about it. And a lot of directors aren't exactly sure how they wanna get there, so they wanna go in a way that's gonna give them a lot of latitude, but it's gonna cost them really big bucks. . . . And he [Proyas] was like, 'No, we have a visual. We know what it is. We're living exactly by the storyboards and this is how it's gonna work.'"

Of course, Proyas didn't intend his plans for the movie to be set in stone before he started to shoot. He was aware that it had to develop as it went along, and that went for the storyboards, too, which were modified and redrawn as shooting progressed. But Ken Arlidge would still ultimately be struck by the similarity between the storyboards and the finished movie: "If you look at the stack of storyboards, which is the thickness of the Yellow Pages, and you look at the final film, there's very few scenes that were altered or changed." Now, of course, Arlidge's description seems unimaginable since most storyboards are no longer drawn but conceived digitally.

Another difference between commercials and movies in 1993 was that in commercials, an enormous amount of film was shot relative to the length of the finished result. "Alternatives" was a popular word in commercials, where the action was covered many times in many different ways. The result was that commercials directors were able to cover the story in a detail unknown in any but the most expensive and self-indulgent movies. And it was apparent to Jeff Most that Alex Proyas came from this commercials tradition: "Alex is a real perfectionist. So not only is he looking at performance issues, but the frame had to be perfect and he wanted even the movement to frame perfectly. Everybody was fantastic, but we didn't have a big-budget movie shooting an awful lot of coverage. That's what Alex was used to. He was used to working on big-budget commercials. That's where you get to move the camera just a little bit to the left, take it again. So we did an awful lot of shooting. Coming out of a superlative background in commercials, one gets to make certain that you have a great deal of coverage. So there were a variety of ways to cut things, and Alex wanted to make certain that the impact was there on screen."

However, Proyas was aware of the danger of so much coverage slowing filming down, so he shot a lot of material with more than one camera. Bob Rosen had seen that technique before: "If we could avail ourselves of a second camera and not have to do things more than once, that would make sense. Certain people can work with multiple cameras and certain people can't. For example, John Frankenheimer is a genius when it comes to multiple cameras. Maybe it's because of his background on *Playhouse 90* [an anthology TV drama series, 1956–1961], which is when he first started it, but he can utilize three cameras on a shot and when you actually see the answer print, all three shots will be in the picture. And Alex, because he knew exactly what he wanted, that lent itself to using multiple cameras. Plus, the fact that so much of this involved effects, stunts and birds flying around or something, that the more cameras the better. And he certainly utilized multiple cameras in practically everything we shot."

"The first camera was operated by Derek Wolski," Jeff Most recalled, "and Alex would be coming up with a strange B-camera angle, and it was not always stuff we'd even use. But he was playing very artful . . . he'd come up with something cool. He had been a [camera] operator, and sometimes, he would operate and come up with cool shots."

Wolski, the brilliant director of photography whose background was also in commercials, could also be hard for the crew to relate to. Among the frustrations encountered by the grip crew was the fact that, Chunky Huse found, "You could spend two hours lighting a set, getting it the way you wanted it, [then] somebody changed some of the action and that meant you've got to start all over again. Although it is the way of making movies and it happens to us all the time, we never quite get used to it or accept it. We go, 'Oh no, not again. No. All that work for nothing.' Really, all you should just say is, 'Fine. If you don't like it, sir, fine, we'll start again. Pull it out, boys. What do you want to do?' You can't. It's just human nature. They go, 'Nope, don't like it, we're going to have to change all this.'" At this point, to cool down his frustrated grips, Huse would send them away for a coffee break, which baffled Wolski, but Huse insists these were just normal frustrations on any movie set.

Great efforts were made by Proyas and Wolski to pre-plan their work and wherever possible to have the lights rigged during the day for the night's work. Huse was in favor of this way of working. "They just throw a switch," he said, "and it all lights up and everything is done, and your rigging crew is standing there and you just turn around and say, 'Well done, guys, that's terrific. Thank you very much. Go on, off you go, go on. Thank you.' And the DP turns around and says, 'Chunky, this is wonderful.'"

Huse always took trouble to thank his crew, but there was a feeling that the grips were not thanked by everyone concerned, and it rankled. Roberta Bile knew, "A lot of the electricians and grips were always frustrated with Derek [Wolski] because of the way he wanted to light things. . . . But I have a feeling that was more of a cultural difference, because he's Polish and these boys were mostly from the South. That for him to communicate . . . Sometimes it was just easier for him to do it, and they interpreted that as, 'He thinks I'm an idiot.' But I don't think that's what he meant at all." Bile thought there was an additional difficulty, again the difference between movies and commercials: "He also comes from commercials, you have a smaller crew on commercials. Here, these guys are all big film people, so there's the chain of command. It's like, 'Okay, you've got to tell the gaffer and then he tells the key grip and then he tells his guys to do it.'"

Ken Arlidge, in contrast, was very impressed with Wolski and said that he learned "a lot about lighting from Derek Wolski." The movie was being lit in a very particular style, with many of the scenes very dark, or "low-key." Arlidge added, "I was certainly taking in a lot of information about working on a limited exposure from Derek Wolski, and a lot of tips that I learned from Derek, I use to this day."

One of the most difficult things for movie cameramen is to light very dark, or low-key, scenes. The balance between what needs to be seen and what can fall away into the shadows is very delicate, and this was a style Wolski had already mastered. Arlidge noted that "Wolski was working on the threshold of exposure, and it was interesting because there will be a single low-key, soft [light] source coming from one direction, and his lighting was bold and the film has a very moody look, no doubt. Can it classify as 'dark'? It certainly has a very, very rich, dark, ominous look. That was hugely beneficial to the mood of the story."

Wolski's solution in lighting the very dark areas, the blacks, was to use a number of very small light sources: "In the exterior back lot scenes," Huse remembered, "we used fire, bonfires in the background. Which is a good trick in war movies and movies like *The Crow*."

For still photographer Robert Zuckerman, naturally using top-notch actual film camera equipment before the age of digital, taking stills in this dim light to capture the process of making *The Crow* for publicity was a challenge: "It was difficult, but it actually made for great photos. There's so much texture and stuff going on, and the lighting was good for it. I used a lot of high-speed films, both black and white, and color."

Zuckerman, who was an experienced stills man, also realized that his shots had a use other than publicity: "Sometimes, before I sent stills back for their [Paramount's] labeling and numbering, and their system of contact sheets, I would get the film processed locally and bring some of it in to show Alex pictures, and he came to really relish that. He'd kinda say, 'Robert, do you have my photos *du jour*?'" Zuckerman would bring his prints to the set every few days, and sometimes they gave Alex Proyas insight into his own movie. Zuckerman said, "I was an eye that was looking, observing the goings-on, and he was able to see things [in the stills] that he couldn't see otherwise, because he's so focused on getting the film done."

The source of light in a film is crucial, and at night it means finding streetlights, or light coming out of the windows of buildings. Chunky Huse and his grips constructed their own streetlights as a visible source, and then they swung powerful lights from rooftops to create the actual lighting effect. Huse recalled, "We wanted these lovely pools of light in the street. Black. Pool of light. Black. Pool of light." They also simulated the light from the light bars on top of police cars, getting the revolving effect by putting lamps on electric drills. "Very inexpensive," said Huse.

There were several lighting innovations on *The Crow*, none more important than the Deca light, invented by gaffer Claudio Miranda. This light had many small bulbs in it. Ken Arlidge liked them because, "They could be broken down into many sections. So they became an extremely useful tool and had a lot of applications, from bashing a huge amount of light down the streets, to creating a little bit of flicker light that resembled a burning flame in a barrel." He added, "The Deca lights created heavy shadows. It would just give you deep rich shadows, which helped create the ominous mood of the picture." These lights found great favor with Huse and his crew: "You didn't have to gel them [put sheets of tinted gelatin in front of the light to dim it down]. You didn't have to flag them [put up screens in front of them to cut down the amount of light]. You could pick up the whole thing and walk it. We had no problem."

For the flashback, the crucial scene before the murders that sets up the whole movie, Alex Proyas wanted a totally different look. Here, Derek Wolski used bright, vibrant colors using filters and lights to distinguish these scenes from the dark mood of the rest of the movie.

The end sequence (another flashback, which is running through the Crow's head as he's about to kill Top Dollar) had blue as its key color. "The other flashbacks are red, in the apartment," Ken Arlidge remembered, "which was a very unique look. So we applied that idea of the Lightning Strikes unit, which is a unit that flashes like a bolt of lightning. And Derek wanted me to use that device in the hospital scene, and we had a very blue-green palette in the hospital environment."

In all the creative process of making the movie, visual effects supervisor Andrew Mason, along with his old colleague Ken Arlidge, was a key collaborator for Alex Proyas. Mason, another Australian, was very approachable and a good communicator. "Andrew made a big contribution to this picture, I think," said Bob Rosen, "and because he had a relationship with Alex, was very helpful to me."

Second assistant director Randy LaFollette noted that "Andrew Mason allowed me to do my job as well as I did it because, in the practical way that the assistant directors buffered Alex Proyas, he did that in the creative way. And the fact is, his whole thing is figuring out how the visual effects work, how you're gonna take all the elements of the shot, like the crow, blue screen and the miniatures, and how you're gonna make all that blend and work. . . . He was very good at breaking that up." This also opened another channel of communication for LaFollette: "So that was another way, if you needed to get information sometimes from Alex, you could do it through Andrew too."

But working with the actors on a movie, the director is typically alone, dealing with an aspect of his work where nobody can help him. It was in the nature of Proyas' past work, as is generally the case with commercials directors, that working with actors had not been his specialty. This hadn't prevented him from having a vision of who the characters in *The Crow* were, and Bob Rosen found that "Alex was very definite with the actors." Rosen's view was that Proyas helped the actors enormously. "There was never a question when the actors were wondering who they were or where they should stand or what door they came in. He was very definite about everything, and any actor could relate to him."

The young Rochelle Davis had read the comic book before she arrived in Wilmington and had decided that the character of Sarah was, "kind of like me." But, as the most inexperienced actor on the whole movie, "Proyas didn't give me direction on how to do it," she found. "He just said, 'You know what you're doing. Go do it. Walk from here to there, say these lines, do it the way you do it and that's all I want from you.' So I did it that way and it worked fine."

Actress Bai Ling, who went on to work with other famous directors including Spike Lee, George Lucas, and Luc Besson, remembered the liberating experience she had working with Proyas. "I asked him what he wanted and he said, 'Do whatever you want. That's why I have hired you.' I could essentially be totally trusting."

Jeff Imada felt that the whole process of making this film was a collaboration, and that the way Proyas handled the actors was no exception to this: "Alex Proyas had a vision of how he wanted things to look. Alex McDowell had certain things that he thought would be cool for the look of things. And Brandon was very influential also, I think, with Alex." Recalled Robert Zuckerman, "Even when the director was satisfied, a lot of times Brandon'd come up and say, 'What if we tried this?' And the director sometimes said, 'No, I think we're okay.' But a good portion of times, he'd think about that and say, 'Okay.' And they'd try it with some other twist." Zuckerman admired Brandon's determination to do things better: "A lot of times he could've gone back to his trailer and just dried off or warmed up, because it was very cold and wet most of the time. But he would go for one more time, just to see if he could get something even better." Imada felt, "Brandon was very heavily involved. I'd say he helped shape that show quite a bit: character-wise, look-wise, a lot of things, wardrobe, different things. Alex had things that he had an idea of, or I'd have things, but Brandon also, he'd say, 'Well, I'd like it to be like this.'"

Ken Arlidge also saw Brandon and Proyas as a team. "They were very much in sync with making something special out of this film. And they certainly achieved that. I remember reading somewhere a negative comment on the internet, about Alex forcing Brandon to work in the cold, which is totally incorrect, because this was not a director pushing the actor. This was a director and actor one hundred percent in sync about making something special. Alex had to gain or lose as much as Brandon did, and they were both driving each other through the film."

Ernie Hudson also observed the collaboration of star and director: "He [Brandon] had a wonderful rapport with Alex, and all the things I talk about, it really wasn't on Alex. Alex was doing the best he could to try and direct the job and keep everybody happy, the production and the studio and everybody else. But as far as directing, Alex is right there and he and Brandon were very close."

Hudson's own working relationship with Proyas was highly satisfactory. "I always felt," he said, "that technically he's amazing. Even his demo reel. That's one of the reasons why I wanted to do the movie, after I saw his demo reel. I knew he could do that part well. He's sensitive, he's open, he listens and he doesn't get in the way, which is the most I can ask from a director. A bad director is somebody who has to assert himself when he doesn't know what the fuck he's talking about."

Angel David, playing the role of Skank, was very impressed with Alex Proyas: "Alex, to me, is as close to the perfect director that there is. Not only is he just a really nice guy, just a really nice person, but he's serious about filmmaking and he wants to get his vision done. Unlike a lot of directors that don't understand the acting process and then get insecure about it, he doesn't." There were specific things Proyas did that commanded David's respect. "One is that he described the world that I was gonna be in from shot to shot. He said, 'This is what it's going to be. It's going to be this, this, and this.' And the second thing he did was he let me live in the world as the character and then he would direct me in the world. Except his major direction was, 'Angel, you're too likable. We have to not like you and right now everybody is liking you!'" But even David recognized that Proyas had his limitations: "I don't think he totally understands the acting process, but he understands when actors are doing the right thing. And when they're not exactly doing what he wants, he guides them towards what he wants."

The actors were still conscious of the pressures that their director faced. In spite of the fact that, David said, "I never, ever felt like I couldn't take my time with the rehearsal or I couldn't have another take if I wanted one," the actors knew that though Proyas may have wanted to do more takes, he was under pressure to finish each day on time. And the pressure sometimes meant that things had to be slightly altered as the film progressed. "Certainly there was tension," said David, "and there were days that Alex was not happy because there was a lot of constraints on him and he was making a $50 million film for $15 million."

It may have been that Proyas' openness, which the crew and cast generally describe and liked so much, actually meant that there were many areas of the production where he simply did not have a clear and fixed vision. After all, there's nothing most actors or technicians like to hear more than "do it your own way." This was apparent in terms of the dialogue, where he frequently allowed the actors to improvise.

"I contributed something to the film which is the way my character died," recalled Bai Ling. "She's the evil one, right? They wanted [in the script] somebody to randomly shoot her. I told them, 'No, no, no. If you want my character to die, I want to die by the crow [the actual bird] because she connects to the power of the crow.' Basically, that's my idea and they changed it."

Certainly, Ernie Hudson was surprised that the screenplay was being rewritten during production and that "Alex was always open to rewrites." This baffled Hudson, who felt that the actors' job was to deal with what had been written. "You just sort of make it come alive. I don't know, I didn't see why he had to rewrite it, 'cause *I* didn't." Though, Hudson admitted, there were also advantages to this approach: "You know, they were always open to listen if there was a problem. I only complained if there was a problem. Something you've got to say and it doesn't make sense and the words don't come out right." But Hudson's preference was to stick to the script. "First off, I never consider myself a writer, so I don't like taking liberties unless I have to. Sometimes you just have to. But if I can make it work, my job is to give them what they want, which is why they hired me." So Hudson was puzzled by the constant presence on the set of screenwriter David Schow. "He was there. He was rewriting. Yeah, he was there. I don't know. He was there doing whatever."

Greg Gale also remembers seeing Schow on the set. "He was on the set quite a bit," Gale said. "He was hanging around a lot because he had been doing rewrites, but at that point he wasn't doing much in the way of rewrites, I believe. [He was] more or less hanging around the set. He was doing videos on the set and videotaping things all the time." Arianne Phillips pointed out, "This was really Schow's genre. He came from the whole sci-fi-comic book thing. He was there doing rewrites and making sure everything was happening. It's not uncommon to have a writer there. He was very involved, obviously cared immensely about the project. There was something kind of goofy and sympathetic about him. He was nice. He just reminded me of the comic book–sci-fi geeky guy you knew from high school." While Schow was there, he even managed to get into the movie during the boardroom shoot-out scene. "He had a cameo in the movie," recalled Phillips. "I dressed him."

To Laurence Mason, David Schow appeared to be far from a "geeky guy." "He was cool," Mason said. "He's a really cool guy. He's in that nice position where he really doesn't have to impress anybody or worry about what anybody thinks. He can just do his thing as long as the director likes it. Or the producer likes it. So he was pretty candid with me about his stuff. He also documented the whole thing. He's constantly shooting video. It was cool to have him always around, because he was involved, but you didn't have to worry about what you said to him because he was on a different payroll than you were."

There were also rumors that Ed Pressman or the production team, perhaps, brought in other writers who were never credited. Certain crew members, including Darryl Levine, believed this: "They also sent out for other people to rewrite a bunch of stuff. It wasn't just him [David Schow]. So we were always updating and changing. There were always script revisions."

However individual and original the production of *The Crow* was, the movie was apparently proceeding according to the famous dictum of *Lawrence of Arabia* (1962) producer Sam Spiegel: "Movies aren't written. They're re-written!"

THE ATMOSPHERE ON SET 13

A S IN MOST SITUATIONS where a group of people face adverse circumstances, the physical difficulties and the pressure of time in shooting *The Crow* developed a sense of unity in the crew. "People would get ill and we'd try to have cover for them," recalled Jeff Most. "We were beset by bad weather and accidents and things that all seemed to make the crew, if anything, come together as a more solid, unified team. We were really, I suppose, much like going to war. You're on the front lines, and we developed a bond that made us all stronger." Angel David said, "There were people there that were cold and wet and tired because they were working hard, but I always loved it. I love working! Like I said, I liked the people a lot and we were always joking around, and by the second or third week, people were quoting dialogue back at me. I loved that."

In film units, as with other groups, the team spirit comes from those at the top. Arianne Phillips not only thought, "The group was very collaborative, almost more so than any other project I've worked on since," but she also attributed much of that feeling to the director. "I think there was this enthusiasm Alex Proyas felt for his film. And there was a real enthusiasm to do the best work we could."

The star of a movie can also have a very powerful influence on the working atmosphere. "We all came together as a tight-knit family," Ken Arlidge felt, "and a lot of that was because we had a very amiable and determined actor at the helm, and everyone bonded with him."

The extent to which a random group of people can be brought together and feel a sense of team spirit depends on the choice of individuals. "All the way down the line," Bob Rosen felt, "in the key areas, we made the right decisions on who we chose." The management, the director, and the producers all promoted a feeling that they were willing to listen to suggestions from any quarter. Randy LaFollette found that, "People had an open mind about what we were doing creatively, and what Alex Proyas wanted to do creatively." This meant that there was an unusual exchange of ideas between people working on different aspects of the movie, as in the case of Arianne Phillips, who found that it was, "Not uncommon if Jeff Most would come back and see what was happening with the costumes, or I would go up and see what was happening with the music, and we all saw each other all the time."

The feeling that everyone was involved extended to the grips, often the least noticed members of a film crew. Chunky Huse's grips called themselves the "Bail Bondsmen," because they got everyone out of trouble: "Somewhere all the way through that movie, I guarantee you there isn't one department that hasn't come to us for something, and that's good because if you get people out of trouble, they always remember you."

There was, however, one predictable exception to the team spirit. The movie may have been a Pressman Films production, but Ed Pressman was mostly conspicuous by his absence. He did visit Wilmington but made no contact with anybody on the crew. Certainly, Arianne Phillips had no impression of Pressman: "I believe he was kind of like The Wizard in *The Wizard of Oz*. Ed Pressman, our version of a studio executive, the head of the studio, whatever, in LA. We were in Wilmington, and I think he came to the set once. He was quiet. In a suit. Those guys are always suits to me." Darryl Levine, with more experience in the industry, wasn't surprised that "Pressman would fly in and everybody would salute, and then he would leave."

On all movies, the makeup and wardrobe trailer is considered a refuge by many of the actors. On *The Crow*, it was a place of jokes and music and, above all, warmth. With the difficulties of the cold and wetness, Brandon Lee and the other actors could often be found there when they were not actually shooting. Makeup and hair personnel spend the first, early hours of their long day with the actors, getting them ready for work. Key hairstylist Michelle Johnson said, "When I have a great group of actors like that it makes my life easy." Added assistant makeup artist Sandra Orsolyak, "Most of the time, after we did our work of course, we'd laugh and joke and we had loud music playing all the time. It was just a lot of fun. Everybody clicked after a while when I got there and it was just this happy family."

Actress Bai Ling fondly recalled the makeup trailer as the place where an innocent misunderstanding between her and Brandon turned into a

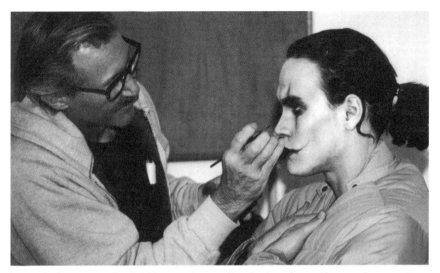

Lance Anderson puts the finishing touches on Brandon's makeup. These makeup sessions, conducted before the day's shooting, took around an hour and a half.
Photo by Lance Anderson

deeply bonding moment. "So every day we're two hours sitting next to each other doing makeup. He's teaching me how to play video games. And finally, one day he asks me, 'Bai Ling, I heard you're Chinese?' I say, 'Yeah, I'm Chinese.' He says, 'I'm Chinese.' And I say, 'No, no, no! You're this handsome white boy. You're just kidding.' He says, 'No, I'm Chinese. My father's Chinese actually. Really!' I say, 'What does he do?' Brandon says, 'He was a big movie star.' I asked, 'What's his name?' He said, 'His name's Bruce Lee.'" Bai Ling, whose English was still rudimentary at best, felt she had disappointed Brandon when she replied, "'I have never heard of him.' He could not believe me. He said, 'You never heard of him? Probably you're one of the first in the world to not know my father's name.'"

Later that day, Bai Ling called her friend in New York who spoke Chinese and recounted the story. "He said, 'He's a big star!' My friend was laughing. 'Bai Ling, it's Lee Jun-fan!' which is Bruce Lee's Chinese name. So next day, I told Brandon I learned who his father was. I did not know in English. He was so satisfied and happy."

Brandon had learned some Cantonese as a small child living in Hong Kong while his father was making movies, but he retained little with lack of practice. Additionally, Bai Ling's native tongue was Mandarin. Nevertheless, "The special experience found me with Brandon Lee. I think I reminded him of his father Bruce Lee come to Hollywood with no English when things were more racist. You know Asians and all of that. I think he had compassion for me."

But not everyone on *The Crow* was as initially welcoming. When Bai Ling first arrived, she recalled Michael Wincott's disapproval. "He was naughty. He told Alex Proyas, 'You cast the wrong girl.' Because I walked around in jeans and I followed people around. I understood nothing. I didn't. Then finally, I had all the makeup on and everything. I walked out with all the costume. I said, 'Hello!' Everybody was shocked. They said, 'What is this?' I suddenly transformed into my other world. This mysterious, powerful force of character."

Undoubtedly though, there were some communication problems. Maybe costumer Roberta Bile had a clue to them when she said, "I think a lot of people were afraid to ask questions, because they were afraid it would look like they really didn't know what they were doing. Then there was a strong element of unapproachability. Usually, when you work on a film or TV, whatever, there's some sort of continuity between people that know each other or people that were recommended. People that have worked together." On this film, she thought this "continuity" was lacking.

Tensions definitely developed between Jeff Most and Bob Rosen. On several occasions, crew members claim, Most and Rosen had screaming matches. Associate producer Greg Gale, who had worked with Rosen for years, recalled, "There was one time where they were going to kill each other. . . . I've never seen Bob Rosen's face turn red before. He was physically, physically angry with Jeff. I've never seen him get so mad at anybody." Ed Pressman was supposedly informed about this, but if he was, nothing was done until the situation had escalated beyond repair.

A couple of weeks before *The Crow* was scheduled to wrap, Most was banned from the set by Rosen. One crew member claims that this was because Most had seen the dailies of the scene where Eric is on the cathedral steps with Sarah. Most, who had not been present when this scene was shot, saw that Brandon's hair was constantly blowing in his face and obscuring his expressions and realized at once that it would have to be re-shot. The story goes that he sent the tape of the dailies to Pressman, who called Rosen a couple of days later and asked for the scene to be re-shot, saying that Most had drawn the problem to his attention. The scene was indeed re-shot.

The problem doesn't seem to have been one in Jeff Most's personality or behavior, because LaFollette's experience was that "Most was also very humble, in fact he was almost embarrassed about not knowing. And so you'd have to spend time sometimes [explaining], 'You can't walk on the set right now because there's explosives on the set.' You know what I mean—'Well, I'm the producer.' 'Well, no, we want you alive!'" LaFollette continued, "God bless his soul, but Jeff was clueless about some stuff . . . and you'd find yourself explaining what MOS [Mittout Sound, derived from a German-speaking technician's mispronunciation of "without"] means. I always felt that I had to really lay it out, like Film 101–type stuff."

Darryl Levine felt he knew where the problems had started. "Jeff's background was music, right?" he said. "And he has this movie about this hero, this supernatural comic book deal, and they turn it over to other people to carry out that idea. Well, we each have our own agendas, so the agenda to get the movie made by Ed Pressman was, 'Here's the best we can do money-wise, and we're gonna go and we're gonna do it. So Bob's gonna run the movie, and guide a bunch of people to do this movie for him.' [So] now Jeff is partnered in the movie, but what Jeff is concerned about, nobody else is." Robert Zuckerman said of Most's involvement in *The Crow*, "It was kind of a big deal for Most. But he was very enthusiastic and was just kinda bringing all the elements together, bringing the music people in."

According to Gale, this clash of agendas led to Most saying, "'The hell with you, Bob Rosen. I can kick you out of here just like nothing!' It didn't happen. He tried, I think, but it didn't happen." LaFollette thinks that there was an unavoidable conflict between the roles of the two men: "Bob was very much the money-organizing side of the producing realm. And Jeff had his vision, and he was there because he found this project and sat home and dreamed up what this was gonna be, and obviously fought hard to get it to the point where it was made." This resulted, in Levine's view, in political infighting: "Jeff's not allowed anywhere near the place, no matter what anyone ever tells you, he's not, because they don't want any part of him. Even though he came there, he was not treated well."

LaFollette said philosophically, "That happens a lot in Hollywood." Darryl Levine has a similar view: "It's very common for the guy who comes up with the movie, for it to be stripped from him. It's very common. This is a business that's driven by actors and directors. Unfortunately. The creator gets bowled right over. So I think those were the problems. The problems were politics and inexperience. Nobody wants to be told, 'Hey, I'm the producer. Come on, I have a title here!' Well, that didn't work. So I think those were the problems."

Bob Rosen was clear on how they got to that situation: "There was a period of time, about midway through the picture, where Alex and

Jeff weren't hitting it off, and Alex felt that he was being interfered with. Whatever Alex felt, I don't know, but that wasn't working." Jeff Most, of course, like any producer who has discovered and developed a movie project, was fighting to keep as much as possible of his original vision on the screen. However, Rosen took the view that "Jeff had never produced a movie before, and I thought that all I wanted to do was leave Alex to shoot the movie and not worry about all this other stuff. In order to keep putting out the film that we were doing, on a daily basis, I didn't want Alex to be dealing with this. In fairness to Jeff, maybe he took the brunt of that, but I could see we weren't gonna get to the other end here with that atmosphere on that set."

Greg Gale recalled that this created personal difficulties for him, "Because," he said, "I was the only liaison between Jeff and Bob because they wouldn't talk. 'Greg, go tell this to Bob.' Bob, he tells me, 'Go tell this to Jeff.' And it's like, 'Okay, I'm in the middle here. I don't like this, but I guess I gotta play it.' I was Bob's assistant, his associate producer and, mind you, I became friends with Jeff on the side, socially as well as on the production. And having worked with Bob for a long time, he's my bread and butter and I had to respect him. But Jeff had a lot of clout in the picture in his own way, so I was trying to respect that. But I knew the bottom line and had to listen to Mr. Rosen."

If there were tensions on the set, Robert Zuckerman was careful to stay out of them. "I didn't really see that," he said. "I don't know, for some reason you hear stuff on movie sets about, you know, affairs and about drugs and all that stuff, but I didn't see any of that myself. I just kinda don't . . . Like I said, I don't really pay much attention."

In many films, the leading players work only a percentage of the time, but Brandon Lee was on the set of *The Crow* every day. He would also get up long before his call time so that he could work out before filming started, determined to keep himself in the perfect shape to play his part. He felt that *The Crow* could be a turning point in his career, and this feeling undoubtedly helped to create his positive attitude, which was so helpful to the film's working atmosphere.

Ken Arlidge recognized that. "It felt like it was Brandon's vehicle," he said, "and he was there for it one hundred and ten percent, he really was. One hundred and twenty percent! The great thing is, with the difficult filming conditions, the rain and the cold, which makes it difficult, his attitude towards the crew always remained friendly and jovial." In fact, Brandon was even able to use the adverse conditions in his efforts to promote a good atmosphere, Rochelle Davis recalled. "Brandon always had funny things to do. Like he ran out in the middle of set one day while they were testing all the rain, and they were trying to get it to the right pressure or something, and we'd just been waiting for so long. And he finally just said, 'I have to do something to keep my blood going.' Made a comment and got up, threw off his blanket and ran out in the rain and started singing, 'Singin' in the Rain.' That woke everybody up a little! Made us all laugh because it was just very sudden."

Brandon's sense of humor was likely to pop up at any moment. "One night we were out in the back lot," Robert Zuckerman recalled, "and this opossum came through the set and Brandon just went over and grabbed it and was holding it up by the tail and was running around, you know, kinda taunting people with it." Randy LaFollette also remembered an instance when he and Brandon joked around with one of the wardrobe assistants, a rather shy girl named Amy. "Brandon would always kinda tease her, try to get her out of her shell, and he came up with the idea that we should make a sandwich out of her. So between Brandon and me, we kinda grabbed around her and kinda shook her and tried to make her get out of her shell."

Most of the crew members had worked with big-name actors before and had seen the usual movie star behavior, the way they would distance themselves from almost everybody working on the film. This attitude was summarized by Randy LaFollette: "The second you say, 'It's a wrap,' they're long gone!" Brandon's behavior was a startling contrast. "We'd wrap up and he'd wanna stay afterwards and help out," said LaFollette. "I'll tell ya, when the star hangs out and helps out and the crew is tired and whatever . . . they see that and it makes everything and everyone feel that much better about it."

While Alex Proyas was highly admired by the crew and well liked, he was a private person. "In a group," according to Jeff Most, "Brandon was lively and told the jokes and then he would, on a one-to-one level, be really interested in your personal life and in sharing experiences. He was just a warm, dear-hearted man who just loved life and cared about people." He added, "Brandon was at home hanging out, talking to the production assistants or the craft service person who was carrying coffee. Brandon would join us at meals and it was always like the most uplifting spirit. When someone is giving of themselves in that manner, to everyone, it really creates camaraderie and a buoyancy for morale."

But Brandon also had his moments alone. Michelle Johnson observed him taking time to himself. "Another favorite image of mine of Brandon was [when] they would turn the rain on and he'd have to go out there and get soaking wet before they could shoot anything, because it had to match," she said. "And he would walk out in the middle of that rain, with no shirt on. It's freezing cold, he had these wet leather pants, and he'd stretch his arms out and he'd tilt his head back and arch his back, until he looked like he was gonna do a back bend, or he'd look like he would almost fall over. And he'd just stand there, and never shiver or move. And it was freezing, and he's dripping wet. And it was a beautiful image."

The still photographer and Brandon had a unique relationship compared to the rest of the crew, as Zuckerman often worked one-on-one with Brandon. The photographer used the moody set and lighting to capture some key images: "I remember, one time I had him pose with his face lit by the flame of the garbage can, and that became one of the photos that got used a lot." Through Zuckerman's lens, Brandon shared some very intimate moments, and Zuckerman regularly showed him the stills he took: "And he really got off on 'em. He enjoyed them a lot. Yeah, he would always tell me, 'These pictures are capturing the mood and the feeling of this film.' So that was rewarding, to hear that from him."

However sweet and charming Brandon may have been, he was still the star of the movie and knew how to get his own way when it was necessary. If he was faced with what he regarded as too heavy a workload, he would go to Randy LaFollette and say, "That's a huge scene, is there any way we can switch that around?"

A makeup continuity photo of Brandon Lee, taken after shooting scene 96 in which, at the end of the movie, Eric Draven and Sarah say farewell in front of Shelly's grave.
Photo by Lance Anderson

Before the movie, Brandon was mostly known to the crew as Bruce Lee's son and a minor action star. They were to be surprised at what an excellent actor he was. LaFollette, who had seen many actors at work, realized, "He was a good actor. Everyone thought he was like his father, the martial arts and everything, which I think he was very good at. I'd think you'd have to be if you were Bruce Lee's son, but he was a *good* actor. He really had a promising future."

"He was very dedicated, very intelligent, very professional actor that I feel he was really treated as a professional not because [of] his father," recalled Bai Ling. "He was really humble and nice."

Clyde Baisey was impressed with the detail of his work: "It just had to have that special little something to it when he did it. He seemed so humble, yet gave to his character the point of what that particular scene was trying to portray." Even the thirteen-year-old Rochelle Davis was aware of this attention to detail: "It was like [when] he invented the idea of [having] the one boot flap down. It's kind of a weird thing, like if you look at his two feet, on one foot, the boot flap is down, but the whole top of it should fold it over or whatever. He came up with that. I don't know why, but it looked really cool."

Acting, real acting, was what Brandon was interested in and where he saw his future, and this was obvious to everyone who worked with him on *The Crow*. "Even though it was an action film," said Zuckerman, "there was still a lot of drama and acting to it, and that was something that was real important to him." Arianne Phillips concurred, "Brandon didn't want to be an action star, he really wanted to be an actor. And because of the nature of his family name, that was the obvious route for people to think of him in. And he was really looking forward to doing all the acting, you know, dialogue work and all his character work that was coming up."

Brandon's hair took more than an hour each day, particularly since he had to have extensions put in it and, on top of that, the Crow makeup was a meticulous one-hour process. But holding perfectly still for this long period of time was no problem for Brandon. While special makeup effects artist Lance Anderson's attention was on carefully transforming him into the Crow, Brandon would keep his head motionless, while his eyes would be glued to his small Game Boy, which he played tirelessly. "He wasn't talkative at all, but he had a wry sense of humor and when he would say something it was really funny. He could crack me up any time with one-liners."

When applying the Crow makeup, a rubber mask with slits cut through it (corresponding to the lines around the eyes and mouth) served as a helpful template, but Anderson still had to refer painstakingly to his continuity

Polaroid photographs to match the makeup exactly to the specific scene and the makeup's stage of deterioration. Anderson often thought, mistakenly, that Brandon was not conscious of what was going on. "I'd be doing his makeup, and thinking, 'He's not paying attention,' and he'd notice: 'See that line, it was a little darker yesterday,' or something like that." And Anderson would make a little quip: "Yeah, you're right. You *are* paying attention."

Spending hours making Brandon up and then accompanying him every night to the set, Anderson developed a very close bond with him. "He relayed to me that this was his big break. That this film was really going to go somewhere. This was the film that was really going to make him." The two men became friends and exchanged gifts. "I collect black panthers and leopards and things, so Brandon brought me little toys, leopards and stuffed animals."

Bob Rosen has worked with many great actors, but his lasting impression of Brandon was, "He was probably the most honest human being I ever met. He said exactly what he felt about everything and had absolutely no front. And there was a sweetness and innocence, almost naive. And that's not to say he wasn't bright, because he was a very bright guy, extremely bright guy, but there was such a simple innocence and an honesty about him that it was disarming."

The "enormous amount of crew camaraderie" on the set, which so amazed Nini Rogan, extended well beyond the long six-day shooting schedule. In their precious time off, an unusually active social network developed among the cast and crew of *The Crow*. "The only time we were apart was when we were sleeping," recalled Darryl Levine. He thinks that for a movie with such dark subject matter and, indeed, for any movie he has ever worked on, this social bonding was exceptional: "There were really no big stars, so we didn't have to put up with that crap, the star camp, and this camp and that camp. We all hung out."

There was one group who, understandably, did less socializing. As Chunky Huse, who has spent much of his life on movie locations all over the world, observed, "If you're all on location together, you tend to socialize. But half of these people were going home every morning." That half was the Wilmington locals, most of whom had families to take care of and bills to pay and lawns to mow.

But for the relatively young out-of-town crew, living on per diems, with no domestic obligations, a lively social world evolved. There were parties, dinners, and general exploration of what the small Southern town had to offer. The fact that, "The whole crew kinda inter-reacted, even on their day off," astonished Levine. "Every week, there was a big Sunday night meal, usually at one of the restaurants. Which is very rare. People didn't usually behave like that."

By day, a favorite excursion for some was a shopping spree at the local Wal-Mart. Roaming up and down the aisles, Rochelle Davis recalled that she and her mother would spend hours on end shopping because, "There wasn't much to do there." But Wilmington's small-town character was generally a welcome change for Davis, who was used to being a kid in the big city: "When I had my days off, I could walk on the beach. They had a little arcade, there was pool tables and things. It was fun. It was like a nice clean town. You could go out and play and not be afraid to have something happen to you. Different than if it was filmed in New York or LA or something."

The beach became a sanctuary for those who were living in the luxurious oceanfront accommodations rented by the production for low off-season rates. Robert Zuckerman recalled: "It would be nice to come home after a grueling night on the set, it was cold, having to wear multiple layers and being wet blah blah blah, and come back and kinda watch the sun rising over the Atlantic Ocean, just to go to sleep to that. That part of it was really nice."

Because the night schedule had reversed almost everyone's internal clock, social life off the set became almost exclusively a night life.

The local bowling alley stayed open late especially for the film crew, and Ken Arlidge recalled going there with Brandon's friend and stunt double, Jeff Cadiente, whom he described as, "A very likable person, a good bowler and an excellent stuntman." They were often joined by Brandon, who again demonstrated his physical coordination. "It just struck me he was one of these guys that anything he did physically, he'd be extremely good at it."

One of Brandon's other skills, and one that he was especially passionate about, was table tennis. He was determined to play while working on *The Crow*, and he rented a table that he put in his house in Wilmington. When he first arrived, the production had rented him a home on the exclusive Figure Eight Island, but a few weeks into filming, Brandon asked to move to reduce his travel time. With Eliza, he found a small, well-cared-for Victorian house, which was only minutes from the studio. One Sunday night, Randy LaFollette remembered, "They played Ping-Pong 'till four in the morning, just laughing and giggling and having a good time."

Such evenings were common, according to Jeff Imada, who recalled Brandon would "make up his own rules. It was agreed upon, but he'd say,

'How about if we use the walls? Bounce it off the wall and come off the table and come back down.'" Although Imada claims to be pretty good himself, Brandon, he said, "Beat everybody. He liked doing that. He liked beating everybody. He was very competitive."

In his precious hours off, Brandon was also able to show his superior billiards skill at the local pool hall. After finishing the long week's shooting on Sunday morning, then getting a few hours of rest, Arlidge said, "We'd all congregate at Stimmerman's Bar, Brandon included, for games of pool. Pretty much fifty percent of the crew would end up down there and have a good time, and we'd have a good fun night and release the tensions of the week."

Stimmerman's was an old bar located in downtown Wilmington, which contained a huge room with several pool tables and a foosball machine. There *The Crow* crowd was joined by a mix of locals, including college students from the nearby University of North Carolina and military personnel from the local Marine base, Fort Myers, the biggest in the country. "The place was huge," recalled Sandra Orsolyak. "They tolerated us because so many of the locals here are into the movie industry anyway." Stimmerman's became the unofficial home away from home for some of the out-of-towners. Actors Tony Todd, Angel David, and Laurence Mason took up residence in the nine-room inn above the bar. Originally booked into the Marriott, Mason had quickly realized, "All the cool people were living in Stimmerman's, right? Everybody's living down there." The party atmosphere was also thoroughly enjoyed by David, who liked the fact that, "You just drink all night and have a good time, and I'd go upstairs and go to sleep. Sometimes, on a good night, not alone."

After Stimmerman's closed, the party routinely ended up at British-born assistant makeup artist Orsolyak's house, "Because I had a hallway that was thirty-two feet long and ten feet wide and a huge apartment to boot. You could dance or play kickball or whatever down the bleeding hallway!" Orsolyak thought, like many others faced with the grueling conditions on *The Crow*, that this hectic social schedule was essential. "When you party all night and you're letting off steam, it's not like work. You can go back to work the following day."

Often joining *The Crow*'s nightlife was actor Michael Wincott. "He was really cool," Laurence Mason recalled. "He's a real cool guy. Very easygoing. Kinda superstar-ish. We're all wild cats there."

On the other end of the taste scale from Stimmerman's was the expensive Café Atlantic. "It was," said Claudio Miranda, "the only form of a good restaurant beyond, like, Hooters." His opinion was shared by the movie's production team, whose tendency to run up a high bill on the movie's tab was so valued by Café Atlantic's owner that he would open on Sunday specifically for their business.

The group regularly dining at Stimmerman's invariably included the creative elite: Alex Proyas with his girlfriend Kathy, Alex McDowell, Bob Rosen, Derek Wolski, and Brandon Lee. Eager to show his appreciation, many of these evenings were organized by Brandon. "Every week he would take different people out to dinner," Randy LaFollette recalled.

One Sunday, Ernie Hudson and his wife joined the group. It was near the end of filming, and many minds were beginning to turn away from *The Crow* and on to the future. "I was sort of complaining about my frustration in the industry," recalled Hudson, "and Brandon was very up tempo, because his career was really set, it seemed like he was set. We were talking about film deals all over the place. He was very upbeat, very excited about the movie. He was getting married and I'd met his fiancée and she was very cool. It was all positive."

Towards the end of March 1993, discussions of Brandon and Eliza's imminent wedding were inescapable. Bob Rosen recalled: "He and his fiancée were at my house for dinner, along with a lot of other people on the crew, and they were talking about his wedding and so forth." Nini Rogan, who knew the social ties that developed on *The Crow* were unusual, was especially touched by Bob Rosen's gesture of solidarity that evening: "It turned out to be quite an exceptional evening, because he was taking time out to thank a specific group of people, which I was shocked by. Never had it happened before or since. I thought it was an incredibly gracious and kind thing to do."

Naturally, when Eliza was in town, all of Brandon's free time revolved around her. Darryl Levine, who often socialized with the tight group of Jeff Imada, his brother Brian, and Brandon, felt that, compared to couples he knew, "They were together more than others." Imada recalled: "When Eliza was around, we'd hang out some, but he wanted to be with Eliza, so I'd give him a lot of space." Eliza was on the set for much of the production and was ultimately given a credit as "Assistant to Mr. Lee."

Even with his mind totally engrossed in making *The Crow*, Brandon had approached Robert Zuckerman about shooting some romantic photographs of him and Eliza in one of Wilmington's English-style gardens. Zuckerman recalled, "We kinda planned it and it got put off a couple of times, and then we were gonna definitely do this one day off, but he called me and he was too exhausted."

Brandon was particularly adamant about another, more offbeat, photography idea of his. Greg Gale, who was trying to coordinate the intended photo shoot, recalled, "He really wanted to go to the cemeteries that were around Wilmington, and there really are some great, great, spooky-looking cemeteries, just fantastic." There Zuckerman intended to shoot Brandon among "these old angel statues and everything." Zuckerman added, "But because it didn't look like there would be an opportunity during production, Brandon said, 'Look, I'm gonna stay here a couple of days after the film wraps.'" Those photographs were never taken.

STUNTS

14

TOGETHER, STUNT COORDINATOR Jeff Imada and Brandon Lee pre-planned almost all *The Crow*'s stunts and fight choreography. After studying the set floorplans and models, and discussing Alex Proyas' overall concept for a scene, Imada said that he and Brandon would often sit down at the computer: "We typed out a rough outline of things. Not specifically for moves. Sort of brainstormed."

Imada would often draw basic diagrams of the fight choreography: "Like, the Crow would dodge a bullet by Thug Number One. Number Two comes at him and does this, and the Crow knocks him back into a chair. And Number Three comes at him, and he does this, does that." Imada would then tell the set decorating and props departments what elements were needed for the scene, to make sure that if Brandon had to jump onto a table, it was strong enough to take his weight. Major stunts also required special equipment like decelerators, trampolines, or wires, which Imada would have to plan and organize weeks in advance. Then, when the sets were built, Imada would carefully check them out. This had to be done when the day crew arrived, after the shooting had wrapped for the night, and was the source of Imada's extremely long working days.

Despite all the careful planning, Imada also had to take into consideration that Proyas never wanted to finalize the stunt choreography until they were actually shooting the scene, "because Alex wanted to have some freedom too." However, this was not a problem for Imada, who was comfortable with improvising at the last minute and coming up with ideas. "And sometimes you come up with better stuff. You can be creative."

Getting stunt equipment was not an easy task in the small town of Wilmington. "In LA you can call up and say, 'I need five porta pits [a large gymnastics pad, approximately five by eight feet in size, with a thick twenty-four-inch cushion that breaks the fall] and three small eight-inch pads,' and different pieces of equipment. And somebody will bring them in and you can rent it from them." But because on his stunt budget Imada couldn't afford to have porta pits sent in, he had to make them himself. He ordered the thick plastic covers to be sent in but bought the foam locally. This seemed like a very thrifty idea, until "the foam came in and it was harder than the stuff we wanted, so we had to go in there and carve up the foam and make the pads softer." Even buying enough elbow and knee pads for the large cast of actors and stuntmen presented a challenge. Of the several sporting goods stores in Wilmington, each had only a few in stock. Ultimately, Imada had to ask cast or crew flying in to "pick up some extra pads for me and bring them in. It's a small town. So the things that you needed, you really had to think about ahead of time."

Imada also had to get creative with his tight budget when he booked the army of stuntmen needed to work on *The Crow*. First and foremost, he "wanted to make sure the guys got paid properly," but since the cost of flying them in and housing them quickly mounted up, Imada made sure the stuntmen were suitable to play several different roles. "For instance, Jon Polito's character had to do the thing where he gets blown out of this pawnshop into the wall, and he falls down and he's on fire. Well, I brought in somebody to double Jon [for that stunt] and then I kept him on to play 'himself' in another scene."

Working with Brandon was an exceptionally rewarding experience for Imada, who said, "There's other actors who are very physically talented that can do things, but with Brandon it was just like a dream, because he could do everything. Some of the stunt guys would comment, 'God, he'd be a great stunt guy. He's better than some of these other people we know.' Well, yeah, that's true. But that wasn't his thing. He quite easily could have been a great stuntman if he wanted to." The stuntmen were impressed by the fact that such a physically capable person was also such a good actor.

Brandon's abilities were also a challenge to the stuntmen. In the shots where they had to double him, they found it harder than their usual work, because they had to copy a man who was an exceptional, skilled athlete, and extremely graceful. One of them commented: "The guy was a good athlete. I mean he could *move*. He could run full pace, do a dive-roll up over something, get up, and not lose a beat!"

Brandon's ability was exciting to the producers as well. If the star can do his own stunts, a lot of time is saved because the action doesn't have to be repeated with stunt doubles, requiring cutting back and forth between the star and the double. In addition, the shots can be closer, because in many stunts the framing is chosen so that the audience can't see that it isn't the star swinging from that rope, it's his double. But of course, stunts are intrinsically dangerous. "This made me nervous as hell," Bob Rosen said, "but it was a help, I guess. First of all, he was so good at what he did, I can't imagine another person doing it."

Brandon didn't do all his own stunts because, despite his ability, there was a strict limit on what the production could allow him to do. Imada broke it down like this: "Where it's just regular stunts, car stunts, high falls, I would say, 'Okay, this is where you're going to do this much of the stunt, and your stunt double is gonna do the rest of it.' He was more interested in the scenes with him directly fighting or where there was a lot of movements involved."

Nevertheless, skilled as he was, Brandon wanted to do as many of his own stunts as possible. In one scene, there was a free fall from a fifty-foot-high rooftop, using no cables, only a pad disguised to look like a trash heap. But because of the level of danger involved with this stunt, Jeff Imada, as he often did, had to "talk him out of it" and let Brandon's stunt double, Jeff Cadiente, do the fall instead. "He was like, 'I can do this. Let me do this.' I go, 'I know you can do this. There's no doubt about the fact that you can do this, but the company is *not* going to want you to do this.' He goes, 'It'll look good on camera.' I said, 'It'll look great on camera, but if you happen to get hurt, even a little bit, then we're going to have to quit shooting because you're in almost every scene.' He goes, 'Oh yeah, that's true, but I won't get hurt.' I go, 'I know you won't get hurt, but maybe something might happen.' He goes, 'Oh yeah . . . Okay, but can I do it later?'"

Recalled Randy LaFollette, "The big falls and that kind of stuff were all Jeff [Cadiente], because we wouldn't allow our star to do that. But as far as all the hand-to-hand fighting, it was Brandon, which actually made it a lot easier because you don't have to bring in a double. You can shoot with two cameras or you can get close-ups right into that action." Though the movie's relentless six nights a week must have been taking its toll on an actor who was in every scene, Brandon would agree to let Cadiente double for him not because he wanted a break, but because he realized, according to Imada, "They're not gonna see me anyway, so let him do it."

There was one stunt on *The Crow* that Brandon was determined to do. This relatively dangerous stunt, an acrobatic piece of action, would be part of the movie's big car-chase sequence, involving Skank, T-Bird, the police, and the Crow. Brandon suggested that it be the last thing he would shoot, so that the production could avoid any major worries about insurance or losing him to an injury. The production team agreed to schedule it for one of the last days of shooting. Somewhat reluctantly, Jeff Most went along with Brandon's plea: "'Save the Big One for the last day, and that way the insurance won't have a problem, God forbid I did in some way injure myself!'" Most recalled, "That stunt involved a car coming at Brandon, in which we were going to use the Yugo driven by the character Skank, in which Brandon would literally leap straight into the air. He was actually working on a direct leap into the air, in which he would then somersault onto the top of the car with his two hands touching the top of the vehicle, and then spinning and thrusting off the top of the vehicle and spinning backwards to a standing position. And turn around and there he would be, smiling!" Unfortunately, Brandon was never to get the opportunity to perform the stunt.

Safety is always a consideration in shooting movie stunts. This isn't compassion from the wonderfully warm hearts of the producers. The brutal fact is that accidents slow down production and cost money. So for many reasons, safety was always in Jeff Imada's mind. "A lot of safety precautions were taken. Nothing lax there, I don't think. I don't feel like there was anything that wasn't done safely." As is the usual practice, Imada also worked closely with the special effects team, and JB Jones saw that Imada was "very conscious about safety . . . He makes double sure everything is right."

From the camera perspective, Ken Arlidge was well aware of the safety aspect: "Primarily, the trick with stunts is to play it safe. You don't need to take risks to deliver an effective shot with the stunt. Well-executed stunts are dynamic because of the stunt itself, but also because of camera angle, camera choice, camera dynamics."

But the fact is, there needs to be an element of recklessness in a stuntman's makeup. However many safety precautions are taken, there's always a risk, even if it's sometimes a small one. Clyde Baisey observed the stuntmen's temperament: "I had a stunt guy, Jeff Cadiente. Every time he did a jump, he hurt something. And most times he never complained. I can see him grabbing something, holding himself. Brandon was the same way. After each and every scene that he did involving gunfire, jumping, rolling, falls, whatever the case may be, I'd always ask, 'Are you okay?' Every time, every take, every scene, I asked him, 'Are you okay?'" Baisey soon found out that stuntmen will never admit to an injury: "They're always okay. And they were tired, after three and four weeks, of me asking. I mean it's like a recorded message asking the same question. Everybody's gonna be okay when they say it a hundred times!"

As part of his stunt duties, Jeff Imada had worked with many weapons on different movie sets. On *Rapid Fire*, many automatic weapons were used. And although he's not an armorer, he is always careful on set to make sure that weapons are used correctly: "We always make sure people aren't pointing right at each other and things like that, in conjunction with the prop people. But generally, that's always the [responsibility of the] prop department." Generally, but not always. "They'll bring in an armorer if they have automatic weapons or a lot of guns or something like that where they need extra help."

The decision about weapons, and who is to handle them, is a very critical one, as the production of *The Crow* would find out.

SHOOTING THE
IMPORTANT SCENES

15

A LTHOUGH SO MUCH WORK HAD BEEN DONE, and so much money spent, to transform the studio's back lot into the urban wasteland of *The Crow*, for some interior scenes, it was easier to shoot off the lot, on location.

Within the first week of shooting, the production team transformed an old, abandoned bakery in downtown Wilmington into the Pit Bar, the sleazy hangout for Top Dollar's low-life muscle. Angel David recalls that Alex Proyas had cast actors to play the four misfits who "were gonna *fill* that world . . . It wasn't just people loitering in the damn world." Each of the thugs would have a distinct personality, mannerisms, and look.

When David Patrick Kelly, who played the leader of the gang, T-Bird, arrived on the set, his character was "sorted out to a nutshell," recalled key hairstylist Michelle Johnson. "Him and Tommy Lee Jones—two of the only people that ever came in and really knew that character backwards and forwards." Starting with his physical appearance. Kelly wanted his hair to look like Julius Caesar: "It was a Julius Caesar–type thing towards his face. Really flat." Kelly also determined that underneath his macho, wise-cracking exterior, T-Bird was an insane pyromaniac and self-mutilator. Johnson recalled, "He was the one who said, 'Oh yeah, I would *burn* just to show how insane and tough I am.'" Assistant makeup artist Sandra Orsolyak placed scars on his face to suggest that he had put out cigars on it. Orsolyak also recalls putting "fake wooden dowels through his ear. He's a pre-punk rocker. Nowadays those things are fashionable . . . at the time it was quite bizarre."

Angel David also arrived with a clear idea of his character, Skank: "A big fucked-up kid. A lot of tattoos. In need of a serious bath." In the script, Skank was T-Bird's less intelligent sidekick, so David saw him as "a Lennie-type character to David [Patrick Kelly]'s George [in *Of Mice and Men*]. And I just kind of followed him around like a puppy dog, and he pointed and I went." Despite being the most blundering of the gang, Skank is the last of the bad guys to be caught and eliminated by Eric Draven, and when James O'Barr paid a visit to the set, David recalls he gave him a very helpful role model. "He said that, 'Your character is the Wile E. Coyote of the movie. It's like you can't kill him. You run him over, you shoot him, and you can't kill him.'" This encouraged Angel David to add a wacky humor to the pathetic, tobacco-spitting Skank. "Of all the bad guys, this guy was the funniest."

Angel David also had a clear idea of how his character should dress, and at his first costume fitting he presented Arianne Phillips with pictures he had clipped from magazines, but once he saw the sloppy leather outfit, clunky boots, and goofy wool hat Phillips had made for him, he thought, "This is brilliant, this is the character." Proyas saw Skank as a drug addict, a Speed-freak and, to remain true to the comic, at first wanted David to shave his head, but David had another idea: "I told him, I said, 'You know, with Arianne's costumes and this and that, I'm thinking kind of like this greasy, longish hair, with like this . . . not even a complete goatee kind of thing. And tattoos all over the place.' He went, 'Okay, that's it.'" This could be yet another example of Proyas' seemingly easygoing acceptance of an actor's suggestion, or perhaps it is another example of him *not* having a very specific concept of his own for the characters.

Although all the actors, with the exception of Brandon, wore hardly any actual facial makeup, Sandra Orsolyak had her hands full placing wounds and tattoos on the four thugs. "Angel [David] was extensive Mr. Tattoo Man," Sandra recalled. Among the ten tattoos placed on different parts of his body, she remembers that each night she had to hand-paint the words "Fuck You" across his knuckles and stencil a bat, a Grim Reaper, a skull, and the word "Saint" on his chest and arms. "What was really ironic though is that we put all these tattoos on him," recalled Orsolyak, "and they were seldom seen." Though each of the gang was intended to expose their skin, because of the extreme cold they were seldom able to remove their many layers of clothes. Nevertheless, every night Orsolyak painstakingly applied the tattoos with a product called Real Creations, which could also be used as fake blood.

The most memorable tattoo in the film is on the back of actress Bai Ling, playing Myca, simply because it's exposed when she enters the shower naked. The brightly colored, ornate design was hand-painted, not by the makeup crew, but by a local tattoo artist. "They were so smart. That's how they introduced my character. Showing my back," recalled Bai Ling. "I'm so proud about it. I looked so beautiful." Though pleased with the result, Bai Ling was not with the process: "Oh my god. It was extremely cold in North Carolina. I was laying on the big metal [makeup] table. One time I went to do the shot and they said, 'Stop!' I said, 'Why?' They said, 'Because we can see your goosebumps.' Then suddenly they have this big heater blow on me to get rid of my goosebumps. It was so cold and miserable."

It was unusually long hair, and not tattoos, that would become the most distinctive feature of expert knife thrower Tin Tin, played by Laurence Mason. When Mason arrived, his hair was in dreadlocks that fell to his shoulders, and though in the comic book, Tin Tin's hair was in a short Afro, Michelle Johnson made a more interesting choice: "I decided his existing dreadlocks would look so much better if they were really long." With human hair, Johnson created much longer dreads and wove them into his existing hair as permanent extensions. During his stay in Wilmington, Mason's impressive new hairstyle made a social splash. Johnson recalled that when he would travel to rave parties in other parts of North Carolina, Mason became so weary of answering questions about how long it had taken to grow them, that "he finally just started going, 'About seven years.'"

Initially, Mason thought the overall look designed for him was "too much." Aside from the hair, he was dubious about Phillips' idea of putting him in tight leather pants and leather vest, but he knew that this costume was an excellent way for him to play a heartless killer: "It was part of the job." However, Mason remembered his costume was often uncomfortable to work in. "It's cold, but it's sweaty."

Michael Massee's appearance as Funboy in the movie was designed to look surprisingly similar to the character in the comic book: a skinny morphine-junky with long, spiky blond hair. Because Massee's hair was actually very short and blond, it was decided early on that "we would have a lace-front wig tailor-made for him in New York." Johnson's only problem with the wig was keeping its front edge tightly glued to Massee's head, especially when he was exposed to the rain. On set, she would often look through the video monitor and even, she said, "Through the camera sometimes. When you have a lace-front wig or anything like that, you have to really watch the edges."

Like Tin Tin's fondness for knives, Funboy has a penchant for guns. He carries a shiny silver .44 Magnum and, recalled Orsolyak, "He has a huge tattoo of a gun on his stomach that went down his trousers." However, because Massee's skinny body was relatively hairy, Orsolyak had the nightly challenge of stenciling the tattoo onto his abdomen: "I'm trying to get this tattoo placed on top of the hair, it was quite amusing. I threatened to shave him at one point! I threatened to wax him, but I decided to leave his hair alone."

Facially, Funboy had very little makeup. Orsolyak applied just enough to suggest he was, "A heavy druggie who was very pale and nasty-looking, grungy-looking. We wanted him to look as yucky as possible and let those natural undertones come through. He has ruddy, dark circles under his eyes." The tattoos, sickly complexion, and messy blond hair transformed Massee into the dangerous and deranged Funboy.

His convincing look, combined with Michael Massee's tendency to remain in character between takes, was scary enough to frighten Rochelle Davis on her first night on the set: "He was all done up in his makeup for Funboy and I thought that's how he normally looked!" This was perhaps Davis' first exposure to Method actors. Before "Action!" was called, she said, "Massee kept making really mean faces at me and stuff, to make me afraid of him. And I was like, 'Whew, what's wrong with this guy!'" Later, Massee approached Davis: "And he goes, 'Did I scare you out there? I was just joking.' But I did the scene with him, and then once he got his makeup off that night and he came up to me again, he's like, 'See. Am I that scary looking?' And I was like, 'No.' But the first impression of him, I was really afraid."

At first, Rochelle Davis had a similar wariness of Tony Todd, who was cast to play Top Dollar's right-hand man, Grange, in the film: "He scared me to death when I first met him because I didn't realize that he was [the actor who played] Candyman!" Rochelle had seen Tony Todd's previous movie, *Candyman*, only a year before, in which he plays a deranged serial killer sprung from the macabre imagination of horror novelist Clive Barker. "When I finally did decide to come out of my dressing room and talk to him, he kinda laughed at me, and he's like, 'It's just a movie.' And I said, 'I know, but you're really scary. You're very tall.' He was such a sweet guy though."

In the scene at the Pit Bar, we see T-Bird, Skank, Tin Tin, and Funboy sitting around a table drinking tequila shots. They engage in a very dangerous game of Chicken, taking turns swallowing bullets. The situation then escalates when they squabble and draw their weapons on each other, each in turn around the table. As he often did, Kelly added a line that wasn't in the script to break the stalemate. Angel David recalled Kelly, in the character of T-Bird, yelling a rallying cry, hands waving above his head, "'Fire it up! Fire it up! Fire it up!' Which was improv'd. Came out of nowhere. We all just started doing it, and it was very cool." This line was so popular that throughout the movie it was regularly recited by the crew. David remembers one occasion when, "The four of us, four bad guys, were walking down the street like some bad Western, and the grips, Chunky's Gypsy Grips, they were great, they were walking up the block and they were going, 'Fire it up! Fire it up!' They're yelling at us, our lines, you know? And that happened like that throughout the whole movie."

Mason also made his own contribution to this locker-room atmosphere by deciding to "lick this waitress's [Darla's] arm. That *definitely* wasn't in the script!"

The success of the improvisations in this early part of the production would encourage some of the actors to take many more such liberties. Angel David recalled that Alex Proyas was so pleased with these inventions that he would often direct them to, "Do what you want to do." Weeks later, another memorable line added by David also became a hit with the crew. In Top Dollar's big meeting with his fellow crime bosses, David recalled, "Top Dollar grabs me and says, 'How do you feel?' I said, 'I feel like a little worm on a big fuckin' hook.' I improv'd that, too." In the car-chase sequence, when the old clunker Yugo that Skank drives in the scene turned out to be as unreliable in real life as it was meant to be in the movie, David quickly improvised yet another line. One of the Yugo's door handles came off unexpectedly and he commented, "'Foreign cars!' All that stuff was to make Alex laugh. It was all improv'd. I'm telling you, eighty percent of what I did was improv."

Ernie Hudson had arrived early for meetings and rehearsals and to settle in with his family. When he got there, he noticed the filmmakers were already edgy: "Alex seemed stressed and trying very hard. I felt that the studio was probably putting a lot of pressure on him to get it done." But his first night on the set wasn't until the beginning of the second week of shooting. The scene being shot was an exterior night at Maxi Dog, a grungy, greasy open-air hot dog stand, which looks like a remnant from the 1930s. Through the rain, we see Sarah ride up on her skateboard and seat herself on a stool to join Officer Albrecht. Since they first met a year ago, at the scene of Eric Draven's and Shelly Webster's murders, the two misfit characters have become friends.

Hudson was surprised by Davis' good instincts about her character. He knew from past experience, "When you get kids, sometimes they'll sort of reach too far, overdo it, but she was very natural, very comfortable." Davis said that her confidence in working with Hudson was partly because she felt that she understood Sarah: "On the outside, Sarah acted really tough, to make everybody believe that that's the way she was. But you know really deep down inside she's just a lost little girl."

An unusual technical problem arose in shooting the scene when Davis announced that she was unable to eat the hot dog that Albrecht buys Sarah because Davis is a vegetarian: "And Ernie kept making jokes to me about why I was a vegetarian. 'You're only thirteen. What are you doing being a vegetarian?' And things like that. Like, 'How can you not eat meat?' And I'm like, 'Oh, leave me alone.' But he was cool. We had fun together too." Davis got her a meatless hot dog, made from sauerkraut and ketchup.

Davis' only real difficulty with her role was learning to skateboard. She was given lessons on the smooth cement sound stage floors, "But," she recalled, "when it was time to shoot a scene on the jagged, holey pot-holes all over the back lot, I kept falling off of it." This was not a pleasant experience for Davis, who at one point fell off and sprained her ankle. Fortunately, the wide shots of Sarah riding the skateboard, jumping the curbs, and doing wheelies were done by her stunt double, a boy who was more skilled: "I felt bad for him. I made fun of him a lot. He had to wear fishnet stockings!"

The design of Sarah's costume at first confounded Arianne Phillips. She had never dressed a child before and had found little guidance from the comic book's depiction of this lost little girl. "I didn't have a vision about this little girl," she said. "How cool was she? Was she a girlie girl? Was she a tomboy girl? I tried all kinds of looks on her and I still wasn't feeling it. And I remember going to Alex with it." Phillips found his response very helpful: "'Play her real, play her real.' He was that kind of director. I don't think he ever shot anything down." Davis, though, was delighted, she said, with the "gazillion different clothes that they had out. I just felt like a Barbie doll for a day. I just had to keep going in and changing and going back and changing, and that was cool. We found a couple of good outfits that became Sarah's."

Nor had any particular style been determined for Sarah's hair, so the adventurous and opinionated Davis suggested her own. Her conservative father had joked with her before she left for the set, "'I hope you're not shaving your head again!' So, of course, to show him, I said to them, 'Well, what if we shaved the back of my head?' And they went, 'Oh, that's an idea. We can do it all the way up by your ears?' And I said, 'Yeah, that sounds good.' So they shaved it all the way up a little above my ear. And I was bald again in the back of my head and my dad was real happy about that one!" With the remaining hair, Michelle Johnson put "a few beads" in her ponytail. "Just really simple stuff." Davis' makeup was also simple: "A little bit of white all over my face, a little bit of darkness under my eyes, and I was pretty much done. There wasn't much makeup on me. So I did a lot of the dirt stuff."

Unsurprisingly, all through his first night on *The Crow*, the main thing occupying Ernie Hudson's mind was that he was extremely cold. "I got there, I was freezing, and I asked where the heaters were. They had no heaters, and I was going like, 'Wait a minute here!'" Hudson had worked in uncomfortable conditions on many movie sets, but this time he was totally shocked: "The little girl was there with her little summer outfit, and they didn't dress her for the winter. She was freezing and there was no place to warm up, and I thought, 'Man, this is ridiculous.' And they told me, 'Well, Brandon's been walking around in bare feet and no shirt on and he hasn't complained.' But I thought, 'Naw. Naw!'"

The reason for Brandon's willingness to suffer through the cold was apparent to Hudson. Hudson said, for him, "It was another movie. But for Brandon, I think it was his chance to step out from under his father's shadow." Hudson thought it was also a function of inexperience. "Sometimes you realize as you get older that if you want to continue getting older, you better say something, because they don't give a shit." Hudson knew that on *The Crow*, as on all movies, the main interest "is getting the shot" and saving as much money as possible along the way. But Hudson could not understand why the production would take huge chances by putting their star at such risk: "It's like killing the goose that laid the golden egg. But you want more eggs! Brandon was it, he was the movie. To take care of him was imperative. How do you not look out for him? And I didn't think they looked out for him very well."

More unpleasantly for Hudson, the cold caused him to injure himself on a movie set for the first time in his career. At the conclusion of the scene at the hot dog stand, Albrecht hears the explosion set by T-Bird and his gang at the nearby video arcade, a scene that was not in the final version of the movie. "I had to take off running at full speed," Hudson recalled, "and I took off and my hamstring just snapped. I was still able to work and do the movie, but somewhat restricted." Unfortunately for him during the shooting of *The Crow*, Hudson was never aware of Clyde Baisey's heated ambulance, in which Brandon sometimes sheltered. At any rate, Hudson was certain that if he had not demanded the production provide heaters on the back lot, "we would have done the whole movie in the cold." The next day, the heaters appeared.

A few weeks later, Hudson was very pleased not only to get out of the cold, but to film his character's most revealing scene. It's essentially an intimate conversation between Albrecht and Eric Draven at the cop's bachelor apartment. "Yeah," said Hudson, "the technology moved the movie and all the other stuff. But yeah, that scene was driven by what was happening on the screen, and that was nice."

The location had its own special meaning. Location manager Vick Griffin said, "We call it the *Blue Velvet* Apartment. It's the apartment where Dean Stockwell performed his lip sync version of 'In Dreams.'" Over the years, the sole function of this vacant top-floor apartment in a three-story building on Fourth Street in downtown Wilmington was as a movie location. The florist on the first floor, who owned the building, found it was more profitable occasionally renting it out for movies than to having a full-time, regular tenant.

In the scene, the un-dead Eric Draven makes his favorite entrance, through Albrecht's open window. He has come to acquire, through Albrecht's memories, a better understanding of what happened the night of his murder, the year before. As he enters, we see the lonely and out-of-shape Albrecht, wearing boxer shorts and his police cap, fumbling to get a beer out of the refrigerator. "I felt the character was, to me, a moral figure," Hudson said, "because the film was so dark that you needed that guy there, the guy who had a heart and the guy who cared."

Hudson was intrigued by the role because it was unlike any of the many police officer roles he had played before. "Here's a guy who really was not a very good policeman *because* he cared too much."

Though Hudson agreed with Proyas' interpretation of the psychological state of the character, he didn't agree on its consequences: "He wanted the character to be really overweight and asked if I'd wear a fat suit, which I totally refused to do because I felt I could *play* stress. I can play overweight without having to go to that extreme, so he kind of backed up on that. But he was always open." Their only other major creative difference came when Proyas insisted that "Albrecht be a stressed-out cigarette smoker, a chain-smoker, which I'm not. And I agreed to do it only if he agreed to, at least at the end of the movie, have me say, 'This really sucks and I'm going to quit.'" It was agreed that this change would be added to the climax of the movie: Albrecht, slumped on the stairwell to the church bell tower, bleeding from a bullet wound, renounces the deadly habit after Eric Draven offers him a smoke to calm his nerves.

Acting opposite *The Crow*'s star, Hudson discovered that "Brandon was very intuitive and he was very natural. He was very involved in the role.

When you get that committed to a role, the choices you make are good, unless you have a bad actor. He wasn't a bad actor. He was a good actor."

Brandon was even able to give acting advice to the less-experienced Rochelle Davis. Shooting Sarah's farewell scene with Eric Draven in the graveyard was an exciting learning process for the young and inexperienced actress. "That was when he had to break it to me that, 'You're not gonna see me again. I'm really dead.'" Davis recalled an embarrassing dilemma when "I couldn't remember one of the lines for the life of me." The frustrated Davis, who never had any previous problem remembering her lines, recalled that "Brandon sat down, he came over and sat down, Indian style, in front of me and he goes, 'I know what you're thinking . . . You can't remember something on there.' He said, 'Well, let's go over it a couple of times and you'll remember that line because you'll see the importance of it.' And I think that was probably the first time I'd ever really rehearsed a scene, because we just didn't usually do that."

Standing in front of Shelly's grave and saying goodbye to Eric, Sarah's surrogate father, Davis was also surprised that she became overwhelmed with emotion and "couldn't get myself to stop crying." (This phenomenon is not uncommon with inexperienced young actors, who often have difficulty leaving the emotion of the scene behind when the director calls "Cut.") "They'll yell 'Cut!' and they'll be looking for me to do it again, and I'll be around the corner wiping my eyes because I couldn't stop crying for some reason. It was very odd. A very emotional scene that I did with him. It was my favorite."

Laurence Mason also got a little professional advice from seasoned actor Jon Polito. In the scene, Tin Tin has come to Gideon's Pawn Shop to sell Shelly's stolen engagement ring. Because it was Mason's first time in front of the cameras for *The Crow* and there was no time for a rehearsal, he became somewhat apprehensive.

Between scenes, Brandon poses for a continuity photo in front of Shelly's grave.
Photo by Lance Anderson

But the more experienced Jon Polito reassured Mason in his gravelly voice, "'Don't worry about it.' And he was right. I just reacted to him. He was a big fat pig and that's what I reacted to. He played it well!" Stepping up to the plate against Jon Polito was very instructive for Mason. "He's like a powerhouse. If you're not on your toes, he'll eat the scenery and you with it! It was a little edgy at first, just getting everything down. After we got our rhythm, we got some great stuff."

Inevitably, most of the energy and resources on *The Crow* were spent on stunts and special effects.

Usually, in the fight sequences Brandon's physical skills were extremely valuable, but, oddly, Brandon's knowledge of martial arts made choreographing the big one-on-one fight between Eric Draven and Tin Tin more difficult. "We were working out the fight," recalled Imada, "and I go, 'How about this, this would be cool?' 'No, that's a martial arts move.' 'How about this?' 'Oh, now that looks like martial arts too.' We're going, 'This could be sort of difficult.'" After much thought, it was decided Brandon would do snappy regular punches and kicks, "but they would have the viciousness of raw power at the same time." This was amusing to kung fu student Laurence Mason, who admitted, "Any chance I get to do martial arts, I'll do it."

Tin Tin's fancy moves against Eric Draven weren't with his feet though, but with his many knives. Although Mason had "never picked up a knife in his life," in a matter of days, he had to learn how to twirl and throw them with some skill. Mason, whose fingers were more accustomed to playing the bass, said, "I found myself practicing morning, noon, and night. I was always twirling those things and figuring things out. I was obsessing. I didn't wanna look like I didn't know what I was doing." Mason became so skilled that when a shot was needed of him throwing a knife directly at the camera, he recalled, "I broke the lens like from ten feet away. I fuckin' nailed it!" Surprisingly, he hadn't even thrown a real blade, but a fake one. Mason was pleased with his newfound talent, but nevertheless thought, "That was weird . . . A lot of weird things happened on that set."

For the wider shots of Tin Tin, fake plastic knives were always used, but for close-ups, real knives with dulled blades were substituted. And, though those knives were the responsibility of the prop department, "They would be approved through me as stunt coordinator," Imada recalled, "or the director or somebody, to make sure that things weren't sharp."

In addition to the knives, there was a lot of hand-to-hand combat between Eric Draven and Tin Tin. Unlike Brandon, the idea of doing the entire fight sequence himself did not appeal to Laurence Mason. With the rain machines going, water inside his boots, his leather clothes feeling sweaty, his long hair extensions getting in his face, and the cumbersome weight of his bandoleer laden with several knives, Mason recalled that doing the action was "hard." The long, complicated scene demanded a lot of concentration, "to do dialogue, fight, dialogue, fight."

Mason was given ample padding, but when it came time for Eric Draven to tackle him into a muddy cold puddle, he was sure he wanted his stunt double to step in. Once the shot was ready, Mason recalls that he was told, "'What's gonna happen is you're gonna kick the trash can over, Brandon's gonna jump over, he's gonna rush you and just as he hits you we're gonna cut and then we'll use the stuntman.' But when we did the take, sure enough, Brandon threw *me* in the puddle!" Although Mason had total confidence in Alex Proyas and Brandon, he wasn't too happy about this incident: "That was one moment where I felt, 'Okay, the director and the lead are trying to get something and they're being sneaky about it.' I'm the kinda actor, I'll give you whatever you want, but you don't have to trick me into something." And Mason recalled another bit of unexpected improvisation that took place later. "Brandon gives me a little smack. So I spit on him. It was nice that the edge was there," Mason felt, "but you don't wanna get to a point where you don't trust each other."

Aside from this uncomfortable experience, Mason enjoyed working with Brandon, whose acting, he felt, "still had that glow and that enthusiasm about it." But Mason also thought, "Brandon hadn't learned all the pitfalls of acting, like the tricks, whereas me or David Patrick Kelly or Wincott, these guys have been around. You fall into stuff that you do well, comfortably. I don't think he found any of that stuff yet, so he was very fresh, and refreshing to work with."

The scene where Eric Draven kills Funboy may have been small in scale, but it called for graphic visuals and gunplay. It takes place in Funboy's apartment above the Pit Bar, for which an old run-down apartment in downtown Wilmington was used. As the scene opens, we see Funboy and his girlfriend, Darla, the waitress from the bar and Sarah's mother, shooting up. Darla was played by Anna Thomson, who also played the abused whore in Clint Eastwood's *Unforgiven* (1992). High as kites, Funboy and Darla are lying on the bed about to have sex when the Crow makes a surprise entrance through the open window.

The scene involved many special effects wounds. Ken Arlidge, who had arrived in Wilmington that day, remembered watching the scene. In part of the action, "Funboy's gun is fired at Brandon, placed on his palm," Arlidge said, "blows a hole in his palm, which heals." In the scene, Brandon peers through the hole in his hand made by Funboy's bullet. Of course, this was the puppet hand that Lance Anderson had made during pre-production. Its moving fingers were operated by Anderson as he sat below Brandon, out of the camera's view. Funboy fires many ineffective shots into Eric Draven, who then shoots Funboy in the leg. Eric later kills him with a lethal dose of morphine, injecting several syringes directly into his heart. This horrific dartboard for needle addicts was also a prosthetic constructed by Anderson, in the form of a latex chest-piece made for Michael Massee.

Later, Arlidge and the second unit would shoot a close-up of Funboy's hand pulling the trigger and the gun barrel revolving. These apparently routine shots would also later assume a disturbing significance.

For Jeff Most, the later portion of this "very eloquent" scene, in which Darla has the morphine evacuated from her arm by the Crow, is one of his favorites. The dark lighting and lack of makeup to conceal the blemishes and dark circles under her eyes turned the attractive Thomson into the haggard Darla. Anderson created a complete dummy arm and a latex shell to fit over Darla's arm, so that the effect of the morphine oozing out of her could be faked. Jeff Most remembered Eric Draven's moving words to Darla: "Mother is the name for God on the lips and hearts of children. Your daughter is out there, please take care of her." Darla is Sarah's delinquent mother, who until this cathartic scene, has destroyed her life with drug addiction. Draven inspires her to turn over a new leaf, give up drugs, and become a good mother.

In sharp contrast to the small, intimate scene between the Crow and Darla, only "big" could describe the explosion and fire at Gideon's Pawn Shop for special effects coordinator JB Jones. In a wide shot, Eric Draven steps out onto the street, turns around and fires a single rifle shot through the window, igniting the gasoline and ammunition inside. To protect Brandon's double, Jeff Cadiente, a dummy holding a dummy rifle was inserted right before Jones detonated the explosives. At the same time, Gideon's stunt double runs out of his shop, now engulfed in flames. The set medic, Clyde Baisey, was very pleased that the stuntman's fire-retardant clothes left the stuntman with, "No more than superficial burns, like you and I would get from starting a charcoal grill." In case of any injuries to the cast or crew, an ambulance was standing by, but the stunt went off without a hitch. Baisey recalled, "It was pretty much a totally safe shot." The creator of *The Crow*, James O'Barr, who was visiting the set that night, has a brief cameo as a looter stealing a television from the burning pawnshop.

The timing of the explosion was critical, because to do it again would have meant a "big remake" for Jones' crew. As predicted, the first take was a success. Jones said, "I made sure that we had enough in it not to have to go back and do it again." In fact, the two-story building had about thirty pounds of black powder explosive in it, enough to create a huge fireball and blow out all the first-story windows, which were made of breakaway glass. The elaborate chain of events included catapults, positioned to throw objects through the windows, and propane gas tanks on the roof, which threw large flames. Ken Arlidge, who was operating a camera on a crane looking down at the blaze, had a fireball envelope him and his camera. "We had protection on ourselves and on the camera. It was big! It was a big explosion. On a very cold night it warmed me up quite well!"

Jones admitted, "We did have a slight problem that night. I wasn't clear on how much fire Alex Proyas wanted. He wanted to carry through with all the shots with a gigantic fire." Gaffer Claudio Miranda recalled, "The stunt got a little out of hand when the building starts really catching on fire, which is not good." This was cause for great concern for Miranda, who had placed several of his Deca lights inside to simulate flames and illuminate the actors running out in the street: "The firemen come and they break out their hoses and they come in with axes and all my lights are in there! And they start chopping through the frames and they had some lights, knocked them on the ground. They're aiming their hoses at the lights and electricity, and I thought, 'God!'" The dread of losing so many of his lights was matched with joy when, miraculously, Miranda later discovered that every single one of them still worked.

Although the back lot had been successfully transformed into a decaying Detroit neighborhood, it was decided that Top Dollar's nightclub and lair would be shot at a place that location manager Vick Griffin described as "oppressive, so huge, so oppressive." About six miles out of Wilmington, off Blue Clay Road, is Ideal Cement. It had been abandoned at least ten years before and had since been used only as a movie location. "It's one of those places we'd shot at time and time again," recalled Griffin. "I know of over fifteen movies that have shot sequences there." Immediately before *The Crow*, *Super Mario Bros.* had used it as one of its primary locations. Enormous silos towered over the landscape. Griffin had been there many times, "But each time you pull up, it looks like something out of East Berlin. It's very austere, it's one color, kind of a gray-bone. If you took all of the cement that it took to build that plant and built a, I believe it's a four-foot-wide sidewalk, four inches thick, it would go from here to Miami, Florida."

Griffin recalled that when he first showed the plant to the production team of *The Crow* they said, "'This is fantastic! This is great.' They wanted something kind of post-apocalyptic, very dark, ominous. Just think of the music that was in the film. That's the kind of mood and setting that they wanted to do." Bob Rosen said, "It worked for us. Although it's a horrendous place to shoot, it was so unique and so perfect for what we wanted to do. It worked for two or three sequences in the picture. I mean we could not possibly have been able to create something with the look of that cement factory."

In the factory, huge lighting, rigging, stunts, and special effects were set up to successfully create the industrial hell of Top Dollar's world. And since the look of *The Crow* was the first priority for Alex Proyas and his team, the many difficulties and dangers presented by shooting at Ideal Cement would be tolerated or worked around. "It would take an earthquake to even rock that place, it's so thick with concrete and steel," recalled medic Clyde Baisey, "but it creates its own danger." The inside of the cavernous structure looked like an "obstacle course. A lot of machinery was torn out and left holes in the ground. There was a lot of overhead conduit pipes that were torn out, some pieces still hanging." For safety, areas had to be roped off and debris removed. JB Jones recalled, "There was some nightmares there in that place."

Although the location was fine from a creative point of view, it had no elevators and was a tough place for the crew to work. Bob Rosen remembered, "In order to get that sequence within the framework of our schedule, we shot very long hours at night." He knew the reality was that the crew had to carry the vast amount of equipment up the many stairs in the cold, damp factory. "Just the unpleasantness of that, together with the long hours, and lots of stunts and hundreds of bullet hits and bullet effects, and all those things." Making light of the difficult situation, Clyde Baisey remarked, "I got in pretty good shape there for a couple of weeks!"

It was early March when *The Crow* set up filming in the cement factory, and it would remain there for almost ten days. "It's spitting distance from the Northeast Cape Fear River and the wind that comes up off the river in March can be extremely cold, especially at night," recalled Griffin. "There's no way to heat all that cement. Even in the summertime, inside that place, it's cool, but in the dead of winter, it's freezing." Actor Ernie Hudson described it as "a damp freeze . . . It was the fuckin' worst— unreal." To generate some warmth, Griffin brought in space heaters, "And a humongous heating system that looked about the size of an airplane engine, and several hundred feet of ductwork." But in a matter of seconds the heat would escape through large open holes in the side and roof of the factory. As Baisey described it, "It was just like walking around Swiss cheese. It had openings everywhere, the wind was blowing through it."

In addition to the cold, the fine cement dust presented another hazard. It could "penetrate your lungs," according to stunt coordinator Jeff Imada. "So there's a lot of safety precautions that were taken." Masks to filter out the dust were issued to the cast and crew. But for costumer Roberta Bile it was hard, she said, "Trying to do stuff . . . It's hard to function with the masks on. . . . A lot of people wound up with bronchitis. We were working nights. We were like a bunch of vampires. It was like we were living in our own world because we were six-day weeks, six p.m. calls, sometimes we wouldn't be wrapped until eight a.m., and never got our turnarounds [union minimum breaks between shifts], ever. Turnarounds, they don't exist on location, non-union."

Because the location was miles from town and the scene to be shot at Top Dollar's nightspot, Club Trash, involved more than fifty extras, an ambulance was hired to stand by. Still, Clyde Baisey remembered an attitude of "safety last" on *The Crow* that was typical of out-of-town producers. But at the cement factory, the reality set in: "They finally get out to a place . . . 'Oh, wait a minute, we're a long ways from town. How quickly can you get a helicopter here?' There's no helicopter within 120 miles of here. No medical help. And they're not in LA. They're not in California. They're not in New York. We're still a small town in North Carolina. Most of the continental US is like that. Every hospital does not have a helicopter."

As if the crew didn't have enough problems to handle, while they were preparing the cement factory to shoot the scenes in Club Trash, an unexpected force of nature disrupted the filming. On March 13, what is still officially known as "The Storm of the Century" ripped through the North Carolina coast. In a forty-eight-hour period, its winds reached ninety miles an hour, as it destroyed beach communities from Florida to New England, killing more than two hundred people. Production on *The Crow* was shut down until the storm passed. "It was a wild day and night," recalled Jeff Most, who was living in a house on Figure Eight Island. "I saw shingles flying off the house. My backyard was the ocean." Some cast and crew members staying near the beach, including Jeff Most, had to evacuate their rentals. "We convened at the Hilton in downtown Wilmington, where they lost electricity," said Most. "I remember checking into it in the dark and needing a candle to go to my room. But it was one of many, many things that upset us." The Storm of the Century had special significance for gaffer Claudio Miranda. It was his birthday: "I stayed in my room because the wind was howling so hard. It was so freezing and there was no heat, and there was not enough light. I think that's gotta be the record worst birthday I ever had in my life!"

"It was a horrendous storm, a horrendous storm," recalled Bob Rosen. "Where it was eighty degrees and it snowed the same day. I thought the whole house was gonna blow down." Greg Gale, who was not required to evacuate his condo on Wrightsville Beach, recalled: "Oh God, it was the scariest thing I'd ever been through. I mean it was shaking like you wouldn't believe." Fortunately, his condo was undamaged, at least that year. When he returned to Wrightsville Beach three years later, in 1996, his roommate, production accountant Bill Rose, told Gale that, "Another storm had gone through and taken the complex off the ground. It was gone."

Not everyone on *The Crow* was traumatized by the storm. Perhaps utter fatigue spared costumer Roberta Bile, who slept straight through the worst of it. "I remember getting up one day," she said, "and it was kind of stormy and the lights were out at my house, but I've lived at the beach, so that's typical." She began to realize something was wrong when she arrived at the cement factory and found: "It was totally dark, it was so creepy."

The aftermath of the storm left buildings without their roofs, trees uprooted, and roads washed out. Claudio Miranda recalled that one of the notable landmarks in town, the local Hooters restaurant, was almost destroyed when the roof of the building next door blew off and came close to hitting it. More importantly for production on *The Crow*, the storm had caused significant damage to the studio's back lot, destroying the church cemetery set. Since the phones were out, it was impossible for the production office to notify the crew that the day's work had been scrapped.

The next day, shooting had to resume at the cement factory. Unusually, the scene at Club Trash was scheduled to shoot during the hours of daylight. To block up the outside light that poured through the huge holes in the factory's roof and walls, Huse's crew had spent hours hanging large black curtains. The huge winds blew down all the curtains, and they were faced with the dispiriting task of re-hanging them.

Once the Club Trash set was repaired, the crew assembled at the location. More than fifty local extras, mostly between the ages of eighteen and twenty-five, were used to fill the huge mosh pit below the stage where the live bands played. "We all pretty much dressed ourselves into the scene and that was really fun," recalled Roberta Bile, who, like many crew members, also joined in to create the rave-like atmosphere. "A bunch of people did stage dives and that was fun. That was probably one of the funniest times. It was at the cement factory, but still, we were rocking in there. It was like a party." This was a safety concern for Baisey. "You got that many teenagers out there that are 'rocking all night long.' I'm sure some of them were doing some *real* partying." Luckily, most of his job that day was treating flu and cold. "I gave out more Advil, Tylenol, sinus medication, cough drops, throat lozenges . . . there's no way even to calculate the number of medications I gave out. Everybody was sick."

Two bands had been booked to appear in this scene as themselves, playing at Club Trash: one, Medicine, was an all-girl band who would perform their song "Time Baby II" on the soundtrack; the other was Trent Reznor and his band Nine Inch Nails. Jeff Most was, he said, "A huge Nine Inch Nails fan and just alternative music in general, but Reznor was somebody that I felt was the perfect artist to bring into the movie." Indeed, Reznor was the first music artist Most approached. He sent Reznor, who had never written a song for a movie, the comic and the script. "When we met, he was then living in Benedict Canyon, I believe in Sharon Tate's old home—which is no longer there—which was just kind of eerie."

Reznor agreed to appear in *The Crow* with his band. But according to Most, reliability is not the strongest suit of rock bands: "Shortly before filming, Trent let a member of his band, a guitarist, go, and did not have someone new hired at that point to be rehearsed. He did not wanna go on stage with someone that he'd not worked with for a good deal of time." At the last minute, Most found another band, My Life with the Thrill Kill Kult. The band had appeared in one previous movie, *Cool World* (1992). This time, they were excited about the chance to be a part of something that sounded "more meaningful, more dark."

"They wrote a couple of different songs which I was not pleased with," said Most. "And then they came up with the backing track 'After the Flesh,' which I did approve. Alex Proyas and I listened to it over the phone, and we had literally less than a day before they were scheduled [to] go on camera." On the plane en route to Wilmington, on the night before they were scheduled to perform at Club Trash, the Kult's lead vocalist, Groovie Mann (Frankie Nardiello), and lead guitarist, Mars (Buzz McCoy), grabbed an airplane napkin and wrote out the lyrics to the song they would sing.

To appear in the scene at Club Trash, the band would need to mime to their own music, which had not yet been recorded! Jeff Most recalled, "We went into a recording studio in North Carolina, we stayed there until about six a.m. and they went on camera at two p.m." The studio was exclusively in the business of recording Christian music. Lead vocalist Groovie Mann said, with some relish, "Here we are in this Christian music studio, and I'm smoking a joint and the room is filled with smoke, Buzz has this big honkin' drink he made for himself because he knew we were going to be there for a while, and we're screaming "things of the flesh do it slow, do it slow!" Ironically, the song had an alternative title: "Nervous Christians." That afternoon, My Life with the Thrill Kill Kult went to the cement factory and performed to their brand-new recording.

During the scene, Skank and T-Bird make their way through the crowd en route to see Top Dollar in his office above the club. As on so many other occasions, unplanned action and improvisations became lasting elements of the scene. Angel David remembered, "So, in character, I kind of said, 'What are you gonna do?' even before we started the shooting. I was still in character, asking T-Bird what we were going to do just to get myself all revved up. He goes, 'Just follow me.' And I went, 'Okay.' And they yelled 'Action!' and there was hundreds of extras and he just barreled through these extras. It was a mosh pit and he was barging through. And they didn't know they were going to do that. It wasn't like he wasn't hurting people. He was moshing with them. He landed on the floor and I'm pushing people away, and it was like this big free-for-all. It was amazing. While we were filming!"

This was all the work of Alex Proyas, according to Randy LaFollette: "I don't mean to keep going back to Propaganda [the music video and commercials company Proyas had worked for], but [it was] that kind of mentality, which I think that Alex Proyas felt very comfortable in. Kind of like that rock 'n' roll . . . not rock 'n' roll, but sort of Nine Inch Nails–type of visions."

Director of photography Derek Wolski, gaffer Claudio Miranda, and key grip Chunky Huse had used a complicated combination of spinning and flashing lights, operated from a central lighting board, to transform the huge, abandoned factory into Club Trash. Strobe lights were placed high up in the building's shafts and pointed down at the crowd, "Like disco effects," Miranda said, "they simulate lightning." From above, production designer Alex McDowell hung spinning cages with siren lights inside. Miranda and McDowell also designed a new light specifically for this scene, which created a big shaft of light that looked like aircraft landing lights. They were, "Like the barrel of a revolver," as Miranda described them. "Like a six-shooter. Imagine, six chambers, so if you imagine that in that pattern." They then made another light, with six globes in a circle: "A six-sided mirror barrel, it's about six feet wide, two feet in diameter, and there's six mirrors." Miranda said, "It was a big, huge shaft of lights. It was pretty gigantic." This light was hung from a stairway and moved around on the crowd like a spotlight.

A great deal of *The Crow*'s construction budget was spent at the cement factory. A few floors above Club Trash, another elaborate set was being constructed for the most complex action scene in the movie. A large cement room was transformed into the imposing boardroom and living quarters of Top Dollar. Alex McDowell had contracted a local industrial metal art craftsman to make huge, bizarre metal furniture pieces.

Most of the set was lit through the windows, with some additional lighting positioned outside, in the large center area of the cement factory. The spot, with its flashing and spinning lights, would shine in through the windows of Top Dollar's boardroom, giving the illusion that Top Dollar was perched above his club, able to observe its goings-on. Inside, the six-globe lights that Miranda had designed hung in a row above the large boardroom table as part of the interior design. Miranda recalled, "The only other [light] source actually in the office was Top Dollar's sword cabinet." During the big shoot-out between Eric Draven and the entire gang of Top Dollar's thugs, Miranda created dramatic effects with his large, spinning light: "Alex [Proyas], when he put the music in there, it really kinda looked great. And when he's [the Crow] on the table and Skank is below, before he does the knife through the table."

In the scene, Top Dollar rallies a large group of his underbosses to discuss their yearly arson spree. When the superhuman Eric Draven crashes the meeting, a huge firefight ensues. Stunt coordinator Jeff Imada said, "The shoot-out was pretty cool. The shoot-out was pretty fun to do. Brandon was doing acrobatics, he was doing the sword play, he did gun stuff." Brandon was easily able to do his acrobatic stunts in the scene, but his long coat made it risky, because it could get caught up or get stuck over his head. So, for the flip over the big table, Imada brought in a stuntman: "His name was Bob Brown, and Bob played himself in the shoot-out and then doubled Brandon. That was, again, the case of bringing somebody in specifically for two different things."

Imada was confident going into this huge scene that the twenty stuntmen he hired "were all good guys and very helpful, so I didn't have to explain every little thing to them because they were all experienced people." Nevertheless, Imada said that blocking this scene was "hectic." Some of the action was planned ahead of time, but because of the tight schedule and budget limitations, stuntmen arrived on the set with little time to prepare. Imada recalled, "By the time they'd come in, I'd show

Alex everything we were going to do and then he'd say, 'Oh that's cool.' And then we'd make the adjustments and then we'd start shooting."

At the climax of the scene, Eric Draven, guns in both hands, jumps onto the boardroom table and the entire room opens fire. "We had one set there that we had hundreds of bullet hits," said Imada, "and we had 'em all on the walls, lined up. That was a shot!" This gun battle was the big moment for JB Jones and his special effects crew. Explosive charges mounted in the walls, in the furniture, and on people's bodies were detonated to simulate bullet hits.

The stunts were challenging, but the most dangerous part of the scene was the large arsenal of automatic weapons. Although they were loaded with blanks, Clyde Baisey remembered the guns were very real: "Machine guns, AK-47s. I mean multitudes of ammo being fired at one time, plus you got special effects, those guys, and they're shooting spark balls and dust balls and everything else all at the same time. The multiple camera angles involved was incredible."

All the weapons on *The Crow* may have been owned by Jones' company but, Jones said, "The only thing that we handled or even messed with was when they have automatics on the set, because the fact is that it takes a special license for the automatics." According to his routine, Jones brought in licensed armorers to care for the high-maintenance guns that are, he said, "A pain in the neck to work. They work sometimes, they don't work sometimes. So they was tearing 'em up, tearing 'em down, and cleaning them and doing all of that." From Miami, Jones brought in a specialist named John Patterson, while the production department hired its own specialist, Jim Moyer, a local Wilmington ex–police officer.

Automatic weapons must be altered to shoot blanks, otherwise the vacuum a real bullet creates, which loads the next round, is absent. But blanks may still be dangerous. The weapons experts' job was to make sure the blank rounds fired correctly and to clean the guns when they jammed. Safety precautions were carefully observed to make sure no one got too close to the weapons that discharged the cardboard wadding from the blanks at high speed and could easily put out an eye, or even cause wounds.

Angel David had to be exceptionally careful in this scene. Without a weapon, his character Skank, he said, "Had to run into one gun, and the other gun's shooting, so I run in the other direction and there's guns shooting in that direction, so it was pandemonium. I had worked with guns before, so I knew that just because it was a film, done with blanks, doesn't mean that you could get in front of it. It projects, I understood that."

The scene astonished medic Clyde Baisey: "I bet you can take a dumpster and fill it with shells, just from that one night! Standing off to the sidelines, just out of sight of camera frame and when all the firing took place, you could actually feel the percussion against your skin from all the guns going off at the same time. It was a really strange feeling." The noise and potential eardrum damage was a major concern for Baisey, who made sure everyone working on the scene was wearing earplugs. "It's like standing out at the airport when the jet just flies by," Baisey said. "You could feel the rumble of percussion of the sound that it was making. You feel it in your chest." Yet, with all the stunts and use of weapons, Baisey recalled, "There were no real injuries. This was without question one of the most potentially dangerous scenes in the movie." Only one of the stuntmen, ironically Jeff Imada, who had choreographed the complex action, received a minor burn on the side of his face from hot shells being discharged from one of the guns.

In this scene, Jeff Imada made his cameo appearance in the movie as Braeden, one of the underbosses, and screenwriter David Schow played a role as a silent casualty. Ken Arlidge remembered, "David was so excited about getting blown away in that scene, and I would hear about it for days before. And eventually there we were, and we took out the writer in that scene, which was just a very funny thing at the time. I remember howling when he got shot."

It took ten of JB Jones' special effects crew no less than two weeks of hard work to ready the set for the extensive special effects. In addition to the gun battle, there were stunts that needed vast amounts of breakaway glass: "We had to mount them, put them in the wall, put them in the windows, and we had to have more glass for the windows and frames. So in case the take didn't work, we had to be able to put it back in again. One of them didn't work and so we had to re-do the whole thing!"

As stuntmen were thrown through the glass, they would be seen falling several stories down into the screaming club crowd below. In this case, the professional confidence between Imada and Jones was vital: "Jeff, very capable man. Very conscious about safety. He makes double-sure everything is right. And it was between me and him, it was up to us to make sure that everything was right when we get ready to do the shot." A free fall is perhaps one of the most dangerous things a stuntman does. "It was one of the more time-consuming stunts," recalled Jeff Imada, "because of the tests and making sure. It could be a dangerous thing." It's a time when the stuntman is completely dependent on a single cable suspended from a device called a decelerator. The cable system of a decelerator is controlled by an air cylinder that, at a pre-determined point in the free fall, kicks in and slows down the harnessed stuntman, arresting his fall. Imada described it as "free-falling without any assistance. The cable is just going along for the ride until the last ten or fifteen feet, and then the cylinder will decelerate your speed before you hit the ground."

Although they had been invented years before by stuntman and actor Dar Robinson, who used them on such films as Burt Reynolds' *Stick* (1985), in 1993 decelerators were relatively new to most movie sets. On *The Crow*, the legendary stuntman Kenny Bates, who has coordinated and performed groundbreaking stunts in hundreds of Hollywood's biggest movies over the last four decades, brought his own decelerator and set it up.

Angel David heard that a stuntman was going to do his fall when Eric Draven tosses Skank out of the window: "I went up to Alex and I said, 'Alex, I want to do this. I want to go out the window.' And he thought I was kidding and he laughed. And I said, 'No, I'm serious, Alex. I want to do this stunt.' And he just kind of stopped and he looked at me and said, 'Do you really want to do this?' And I said, 'Yeah.' He said, 'Because if you do this, I don't have to cut away, I can do the entire scene in one take and follow you out the window.' And I said, 'Let's do it!'" With one successful rehearsal completed, Jones put in the breakaway window glass and David, harnessed to the decelerator, was ready to go: "What he [Brandon] did was, he physically grabbed me, and then he made the motion to throw me out, but I jumped out myself, headfirst." David nailed it on the first take. "It was amazing. The adrenaline rush was amazing. Alex sort of looked at me to assess whether he thought I'd be able to do it or not. And the stunt double was there just in case I did back out, which I didn't. And it was all very, very safe."

Ken Arlidge was operating one of the many cameras filming the falls. "We were one of the high cameras on that, looking down as he fell into the decelerator. And I had never worked with that particular rig before. It's quite unnerving and it's quite remarkable to see someone just throw themselves off and completely put their safety into a rig that's going to slow them down."

The free-fall sequences, with the various stuntmen and Angel David, would need to be completed later with shots of the actors on a green background. In post-production, both shots would be digitally combined into one. The second unit's Ken Arlidge, on a sound stage, would shoot the actors against a background of a forty-by-forty-foot green screen mounted near the ceiling: "If you put the camera directly underneath the actor, of course the cable and the hole in the screen is hidden directly behind him as he is pulled up and away from you. So we shot them being pulled up and away from us, and the film was reversed. Or we just dropped him down towards the camera and stopped just before he hit the camera."

The same technique was used for Top Dollar's death scene. Michael Wincott is actually being pulled up, away from the camera, when he falls to his death from the church roof. Notes Arlidge, "Where Michael is falling [down] towards the gargoyle, he's actually being pulled up towards the ceiling, and I don't think you'd notice, but his hair is actually hanging down towards the camera. It looks like the wind is blowing it forward as he's falling away from you."

There was one stunt at the cement factory that Brandon insisted on doing himself, which key hairstylist Michelle Johnson did not feel was done with safety in mind: "He was up on a ledge five stories up, and he was walking on this ledge, and also, you know, Brandon didn't wanna wear padding, ever. Also the design of the shirt, it was skintight." Johnson was disturbed when "Brandon said, 'Oh no, I don't need mats, I don't need anything down below.' You should've seen the shot, it was insane." No one objected, but in Johnson's opinion, "It was sheer stupidity. Nobody looked after his safety."

Automatic weapons, dangerous stunts, complex choreography; Brandon was very familiar with all this from his past action movies. But in all the excitement and action, Robert Zuckerman remembered, "A couple of times Brandon came up to me and said, 'Man, I can't wait 'til all this action shit is done and I can get into some real acting.'"

The last big action scene to be shot was the climax, where Top Dollar gets his just deserts and is impaled on a gargoyle. The scene comes right after Eric and Sarah have their (supposed) farewell meeting in the graveyard, in front of Shelly's grave. Eric is saying goodbye to Sarah, because he believes his work is done, having gotten his revenge by killing all the bad guys. Now at peace, he can return to the world of the dead and be with his love, Shelly.

Somehow knowing Eric Draven's whereabouts, Top Dollar has come to the church with his henchman Grange and his half sister Myca to have a showdown. Top Dollar is not only a sadistic, ruthless crime lord, he is also a shrewd businessman and sees the superhuman Eric Draven as a major threat to his underworld empire. His goal is to kill Eric by first killing the crow, thus robbing him of his superhuman powers. To lure Eric and the crow from the graveyard, Grange kidnaps Sarah as bait and takes her inside the contained environment of the church.

"The classic story of production design on *The Crow*," recalled Bob Rosen, "was that when we built the interior of the church, by that time we were at the very end of the schedule and at the very end of what was available for the budget. That church was built and eighty percent of it didn't have any walls! It just went to black." At first, Bob Rosen admitted, "When you walked on the stage you went, 'Oh shit! Are we going to get away with this?' Now we did, and we did because Alex McDowell and Derek Wolski have backgrounds in low-budget pictures, and Alex Proyas had a vision of what he could do and what we could get away with. Different people in those positions, certain positions would say, 'What do you mean, we're going to build a set with no walls?'" By carefully choosing camera angles and using dark lighting and black curtains, the few church pews, the altar, and gallery were made to look like the interior of a huge, dilapidated church. This also presented a challenge in choreographing the action. Jeff Imada recalled, "We could only shoot in certain directions. We had to move sets around and different things to make it work. We only had one wall!"

A major undertaking for Huse's rigging crew was hanging the huge black curtains that covered the forty-foot walls and entire ceiling of the sound stage. They are professionally known as "theatrical blacks": huge, thick black pieces of material that are mostly used in live theater productions. Even on night interiors, some light could enter and ruin the low-lighting effects that dominate the movie.

The distinctive beams of moonlight shining into the cathedral were created by Claudio Miranda's inventive use of a ring of aircraft landing lights. "These lights," Ken Arlidge pointed out, "are very expensive. They would only have a couple hours of burning time, perhaps even less than that. So they would be turned on just prior to rolling." At times color was added to this light, but naturally it shed a cool glow. This slightly soft but direct beam made a perfect shaft of moonlight, according to Ken Arlidge, because it had an "incredible amount of punch to it."

When they started shooting the major fight scene in the church between Top Dollar, Grange, Myca, Eric, and Albrecht, Ernie Hudson remembered the crew was running on empty: "When we got to this fight sequence, the crew had, in my opinion, been working those long hours and they were pretty stressed out. We all were. We just wanted to get it done."

In one section of the scene, Albrecht is wounded and Grange is fatally shot in an exchange of gunfire in the bell tower stairwell. During a take, Hudson's revolver, loaded with blanks, jammed. This was not a surprise to assistant makeup artist Sandra Orsolyak, who recalled, "Those guns had been used. We had used them everywhere." A trained armorer was on set that night, checking the guns, according to Hudson: "If it jams in the scene, you just have to play it out because everything is set up, and then the experts come in and they'll do whatever they do. In the movies, guns shoot and shoot and shoot and shoot. The reality is, they do jam up." In the cold sound stage with fake rain coming down in sheets, Orsolyak remembered many in the crew thought it was very funny. "We kept laughing and thought the gun might've been waterlogged." However, key hairstylist Michelle Johnson did not find it amusing. Having some knowledge of weapons, she was very concerned at what she saw. According to another member of the crew, "They tried to un-jam it by simply opening and closing it and pulling the trigger." That night, Johnson said, "I went up to the First AD and I said, 'Do you know what? These guys don't know jack shit about weapons.' I've been around them since I was six years old, and I said, 'I'm not gonna be on set.'" Indeed, Johnson promptly left the set.

The jammed gun was of little consequence to Hudson. What concerned him more was almost getting injured by an exploding squib. "We were shooting and they have these little squibs that they'd planted around to make the sparks. So I'm hiding behind the bench, but nobody told me the thing was going to be popping off in my face." But Hudson saw this as simply a small hazard possible during any production, and said, "The special effects crew were real professionals."

Michael Wincott's experience with weapons showed during the shooting of this scene. Johnson, who was on the set to make sure Wincott's hair extensions were not noticeable when they became wet in the rain during the rooftop section of the scene, remembered, "The first time they yelled 'Cut!' he just stood there with the sword up there in the air until somebody collected it. And I went, 'Now there's a pro!'"

Because it was so late in the schedule and time was getting short, Ken Arlidge recalled that the second unit filmed much of the movie's climax: "We did a lot of the wide shots there, the stunts, the sword fight. And that was obviously Jeff Cadiente and Michael Wincott's stand-in. So we had rain, we had a big dolly shot, we had crane shots, we had lightning, we had them sliding down the roof, and we had Sarah fall in through the roof."

At its peak, the roof of the church was more than twenty-five feet off the ground, with the huge, buttress-like areas that extended out to the gargoyles and the bell tower. Both cranes and dollies on the ground were used to shoot up at the church roof, while high cranes captured shots moving across it. The scene was entirely shot inside the sound stage, in the fake rain made by Jones' extensive rigging. The camera body was covered but, in order to avoid seeing drops running down the lens, a spinning piece of glass known as a rain deflector was placed in front of it. Because it rotates at extremely high speed, it is invisible on film.

For Jones, supplying the rain for this scene "was like a never-ending battle. Every day they would say, 'All right, we're gonna do this over on this side now tomorrow.' And then what I'd have to do is, while everybody else was sleeping, we would go back over and re-do it to make it work again." This was a time when Jones knew that Alex Proyas' artistic vision was technically impossible to realize. "When they were fighting on top of the church, with all this rain, they wanted the swords to flash. You can't do it in the rain." Jones remembered suggesting that the effect would only work if, "We could back it off and let the rain be in the foreground. But, no, he [Proyas] didn't want to do that. He just said, 'No, no, I gotta have the rain.' I said, 'Well, we won't duplicate it.' He got mad at me about that. He had something smart to say." To avoid a confrontation with the director who, like the proverbial customer, is always right, Jones said he, "Didn't give no answer. Well, I did tell him that everybody had an opinion, and whoever's opinion it is, that it isn't necessarily right. I turned around and walked off. But me and him never did really ever hit it off real good. Although I thought he was very professional all the way through."

The steeply pitched, slippery, rain-soaked roof was very precarious to shoot on. Jeff Imada knew that in terms of safety and practicality, for the sword battle between Eric Draven and Top Dollar, "The angle of the roof was . . . maxed out. To be able to stand up there and do fighting and stuff like that you came off the tip of the apex of the rooftop and you went off to the side two feet and you would slide all the way down. There's no way you could stand up there. You just couldn't do it." Because of this difficulty and the danger it presented for the actors, a copy of the roof was built closer to the ground, making the close-ups of Brandon and Michael Wincott much easier to shoot. But for the sweeping wide shots of the sword fight, the stunt doubles would still have to work on the full-size pitched roof. "Brandon did jump in there a little bit," recalled Imada. "Alex wanted Brandon to do it, because he could tell the difference in the movement." However, Ken Arlidge remembered shooting most of the more dangerous choreography with the stunt doubles: "There's a point there where they both ultimately fall and slip down the rooftop, which is part of the sequence, of course. From time to time, one of the stuntmen

Brandon poses for a publicity photo on the church set toward the end of the shooting schedule.
Photo by Lance Anderson

would lose his footing during the scene, and he would slide down the rooftop and climb back up. And then we'd continue."

Ironically, a stuntman doubling as Michael Wincott lost his footing and broke a couple of ribs, not while performing a move, but trying to help medic Clyde Baisey. Baisey was trying to get to the particular area of the roof where they were shooting in order to be on hand if any injury did occur. To get there, he had to slide down part of the pitch. But when the stuntman went to help him break his slide and get into position, Baisey recalled, "He kinda caught his arm wrong and some of the woodwork hit him right in the chest." Baisey called an ambulance, but because of a studio regulation that mystified everyone on the crew requiring any unauthorized vehicle to first get clearance from the studio manager, the ambulance was unable to get through the gate. "He's in quite a bit of pain. It hurt. I kept listening to his lung sounds and my biggest fear was he might develop a punctured lung," Baisey said. "Basically, I told them, 'If I come out here and an ambulance is getting dispatched out here and you got the [gate] arm down, you'll be buying a new arm tomorrow!'"

In the movie, this climactic sword fight concludes as Eric Draven pushes Top Dollar off the church roof to his death. The manner of Top Dollar's demise was another special effects extravaganza, and one that the crew had little time to plan. In mid-March, a couple of weeks before the scene was scheduled to shoot, Alex Proyas decided that he wanted a very graphic shot showing Top Dollar being impaled on a gargoyle. This presented a significant challenge for Lance Anderson. In a very short time, he would have to take a full-body cast of Michael Wincott and manufacture a convincing dummy, which would have to spurt blood from the chest and mouth on cue as the horns of the gargoyle pierced through his back. Once the dummy was successfully built, it became Jones' responsibility to turn the water gushing through the rain gutter into "blood." According to Ken Arlidge, part of the difficulty was, "You have low-key lighting, you have rain and you have dark, and you're trying to have red blood." Thankfully, after much trial and error, Jones finally found a paint substance that would mix with water while retaining the color and consistency of blood.

In the church scene Myca also comes to her long-deserved demise when, having had her eyes pecked out by the crow, she falls to her death down the inside of the church bell tower. A stunt double for Bai Ling was used to shoot this somewhat risky scene. Animal trainer Larry Madrid recalled, "I gave 'em a real bird. I had a custom mask made to fit her [the stunt double], an acrylic mask that the beak couldn't poke through, and then we shot it from behind her, with her holding the bird in front of her face and the bird thrashing and pecking and poking at her face. And then cut back to a shot of the real actress from behind the bird, and used the animatronic bird, constructed by Lance Anderson, for a shot of the two of them together, because you didn't wanna do that with the real actor."

An enormous amount of care had been taken with the big shoot-out and all the other action sequences at the cement factory and on the church roof. The remaining scenes on the schedule were simple compared to what had already been shot: few sets, special effects, or stunts. So with the last big action scene of the movie completed, Ernie Hudson thought, "Once we got past that, it seemed like everything else would be fine." Unfortunately, the same standard of care was not to be maintained for the rest of the filming.

Sofia Shinas, the actress playing the female romantic lead Shelly, was not needed on the set of *The Crow* until near the end of production, for the scene in the final minutes of the movie where she appears to Eric as an angelic vision in the graveyard, calling him back with her to the world of the dead. Initially, Shinas was only flown in to shoot this one short scene and then was flown back to Los Angeles. When she arrived in Wilmington, she was dismayed by the atmosphere, which was, she said, "Very intense. I felt the pressure the minute I arrived." She was also annoyed that she had been flown in for a scene where she didn't even have any dialogue. "So that was even more maddening. They were behind schedule as well," recalled Shinas. "I sensed tremendous anxiety. . . . People were very high in anxiety and everybody kept saying how tired they were."

In contrast to her first impression of the movie set, her first encounter with Brandon was very positive: "He had this huge smile. Great energy, wonderful, wonderful intense energy. I just thought, 'Wow, this is great. I'm really happy I decided to take this role.'" Oddly, Shinas had never auditioned opposite Brandon, something filmmakers regularly do when casting romantic characters who need to convey an on-screen chemistry. Shinas always thought this was "so bizarre," but says she was delighted when Brandon told her, "'I saw your audition tape. I heard your music. It's really good.' He had done his research work. . . . Brandon was so sweet. He was so lovely. 'They put you up in a nice place? Are you sure you're staying in a great place?' It was so odd." Shinas' working relationship with Brandon did turn out to be a positive one. "He was always happy. Clowning around constantly. He was just a happy person. Jokes, jokes, and more jokes, and more cigarettes. He was like a little boy. He was always like, flirting with me. He would never call me Sofia, he always called me Shelly."

The villain Top Dollar is impaled on a gargoyle after being thrown from the church roof by the Crow during their final confrontation. This life-sized dummy was rigged to move and gush blood to dramatize the gruesome demise.
Photo by Lance Anderson

A couple of weeks after shooting the graveyard scene, Shinas was booked to return to Wilmington to shoot the many flashback scenes in the loft with Brandon. "I came in. I was flown in. It was bizarre. It was like something you'd experience in a dream. Surreal." When Shinas returned to Wilmington, almost all her working time was spent on the set of Shelly and Eric's home, the loft set built on sound stage 4. Many days were spent on the loft set, with Shinas and Brandon shooting intimate scenes, including the couple cooking together, decorating the loft, Eric's proposal, and a love scene. Of all the romantic and emotional scenes that Shinas did with Brandon, she said, "My favorite was where we're having fun. The cooking scene was fun, when we're in the kitchen cooking. That was really fun. That was a great day!" In fact, several dialogue scenes between Shelly and Eric were actually shot, but some do not appear in the final film, or were merely used in flash-cut flashbacks.

Although the original script called for a lot of nudity in the scenes between Shelly and Eric, Shinas recalled, "They took the nude scenes out, which was great. Yeah, because they realized that they didn't really need it." It wasn't only Shinas who had been intimidated at the prospect of nudity. She understood that "Brandon was nervous about it as well, because here he's getting married, and he has a fiancée who was very uptight. Someone told me, he [Brandon] didn't speak to me directly, about it . . . about the whole nudity factor. I mean, he was so relieved when they decided to eliminate a lot of the topless scenes and the lovemaking scenes and all that." But even with the nudity removed, Shinas recalled that shooting the love scene still made both Brandon and her uncomfortable: "We just wanted to get it over with. We were so nervous. It was the first time I'd ever done anything like that. He was nervous. . . . He was getting married in three weeks. I could understand. He was so in love. They were so in love."

Though Brandon was dedicated to making the chemistry between him and Shinas work, it distressed the inexperienced actress that Brandon was never able to rehearse their scenes before it was time to shoot them. "We would meet on set. What happened an hour before we film [was] we rehearsed a little bit." It was suspected by some that Brandon's real-life fiancée, Eliza Hutton, wasn't comfortable with the idea of Brandon rehearsing with the attractive Shinas beyond the normal long work hours, but considering Brandon's profound commitment to the role, it seems unlikely he would do anything to jeopardize his performance.

In the two weeks Shinas spent working with Brandon, there was one aspect of his behavior that she didn't find endearing, but it was a cause for concern, the way he constantly pretended to injure himself. "He would fake hurting himself. I told him he was gonna get hurt actually. I said, 'You're gonna get hurt. Something tells me, on this movie set, that you're going to get hurt.'"

During the shooting, Shinas enjoyed moments with Alex Proyas chatting about their Greek heritage in their shared language. "That was fun. Yeah. Absolutely. That man was under so much pressure, I couldn't believe it."

In rehearsal, Brandon and Alex Proyas both liked to improvise scenes. This was disconcerting for Shinas, who didn't like changing lines on the spot. "It was all improv. We improv'd all of that. We changed lines and I hated that. He [Proyas] was the one who wanted to do it like that. The whole movie was improv'd, I swear."

By contrast, improvising was a welcome liberty to David Patrick Kelly as T-Bird. Before shooting the scene where T-Bird and his thugs rape and kill Shelly, Kelly and Alex Proyas decided he would add a poetic touch to his character's taunting of Shelly. He reads a powerful quote from the epic poem *Paradise Lost*: "the devil stood and felt how awful goodness is. Saw virtue in her shape, how lovely." T-Bird also reprises the line when he is about to die at the hands of Eric Draven. Before the rape scene, Proyas encouraged the bad guys and Shelly to become more comfortable with the scene by discussing it. "That's what I found so bizarre, was I had this relationship with the bad guys," recalled Shinas.

Aside from Brandon's lighthearted, almost foolhardy goodwill, Shinas found the atmosphere on the set of *The Crow* extremely tense. "I can't explain it to you. I guess it was the nature of the film. I guess it was the story as well. It's this young, hip, sort of adolescent thing, and I guess a lot of people that we're working with . . . I mean we have a young group, everybody's first time, so people barely know what they're doing . . . So it's inexperience. I think that's what it is. I'm not psychic by any means," added Shinas, "but I kept telling Jeff Imada that something bad was gonna happen on set. I felt it. Because there's too much chaos, too much negativity on set. When you make a record, it's all one big team. And I walked into this and it was like, I didn't like it. It was scary to me. The whole thing was really intimidating. It's like, nasty attitudes, bad energy, bad deal."

A FINE LINE   16

TUESDAY, MARCH 30, 1993, should have been just another long, intense night in the production schedule of the movie *The Crow*. According to Greg Gale, at this point the shoot had proceeded roughly according to plan: "We were probably somewhere in the vicinity of about eight days over."

As usual, Brandon Lee, like many of the cast and crew, woke up in the late afternoon. He had been lucky enough to have a relatively normal amount of sleep, as much as seven or eight hours. After he had eaten some breakfast and looked over his work for the evening, he went to the local gym, Wilmington Fitness Today, and worked out. One of the gym staff recalled that he was chatting enthusiastically about his wedding in three weeks' time and about the fact that he had only another few days of shooting left.

The cast and crew of the main unit of the film gradually assembled a little before 8:00 p.m. on sound stage 4 to begin day fifty of principal photography. The feeling among the crew, as they rushed around getting the set ready, was somewhat different from Brandon's upbeat attitude. Many of them felt under pressure to complete the last few days of shooting. Also, a number of scenes were planned for what promised to be a long night.

From his trailer, Brandon called his mother in Idaho. He often called her before the night's filming began. That evening, he shared with her his excitement about his upcoming wedding. He also told her that he was glad because it was the last night that guns would be used on the set. Signing off, he said, "Bye Momzo. I love you."

In the makeup trailer, Lance Anderson did Brandon's makeup as usual. But since there was no white face or continuity to worry about, just a light base was added to Brandon's natural complexion. This was because for this scene, he was to be Eric Draven, the living, healthy young man. Brandon's hair that night was also different from most of the previous filming. It wasn't the usual wet-down, unruly style he wore as the Crow, but was neatly combed. This made Michelle Johnson's work on Brandon's hair quite different that night. Looking back, she found that of significance too. "It was the first time I didn't put his extensions on," she said. "That was something that was really odd, because his hair finally grew to the right length. And he didn't need them anymore." When Sofia Shinas saw him later that night, she thought that Brandon came onto the set looking refreshed and surprisingly rested.

The major scene scheduled to be filmed that night by the main unit was the flashback in which Eric Draven is murdered and his fiancée, Shelly Webster, is raped and killed by Top Dollar's thugs. It's a crucial scene in the movie. Indeed, it is the pivotal event of the whole story.

The second unit, directed by Andrew Mason, and with Ken Arlidge on camera, was also on call, due to shoot several scenes on the church roof set, including one with Rochelle Davis, who played Sarah.

At about 11:00 p.m., the second unit was ready to shoot the section of the scene where Sarah has been taken hostage by Top Dollar and brought to the church roof. When the Crow follows Top Dollar to the roof to rescue Sarah, Top Dollar allows her to fall. She slides down the steeply pitched roof and ends up crashing through a hole. She grabs at a decaying beam and, as a fight develops between Eric and Top Dollar, she hangs there, apparently ready to fall to her death at any second. The scene, with the thirteen-year-old actress precariously hanging from the decaying church rafters, would be shot against a green screen. The completed shot would then be added to the church roof fight scene (most of which had already been filmed) at the end of the finished movie. But the second unit had a problem. They were unable to find the harness in which Rochelle Davis was to be suspended from the church roof.

The section of the scene scheduled for the main unit that night would show T-Bird and his cohorts, Funboy, Skank, and Tin Tin, breaking into the loft. Initially they confront Shelly with the petition that she and Eric were trying to get their fellow tenants to sign asking that the decaying apartments be cleaned up. In response to their campaign, slumlord Top Dollar has sent his thugs to get rid of Shelly because of the trouble she is making. In the loft, the thugs taunt her by reading the petition, citing "code violations, safety hazards, and relocation fees for tenants." Then, as they are about to rape Shelly, Eric Draven walks in on them.

The upcoming scene in which Eric would be killed was certainly violent, but in comparison with other scenes that had already been shot, it was not an especially difficult scene to stage or to photograph. Consequently, nobody working on the movie had any expectation that the night's work would prove to be anything special or unusual.

For Arianne Phillips, March 30th was always going to be an especially significant day: It was her last working day on *The Crow*. Her friend, actress Darryl Hannah, had asked her to design the costumes for her next project, the 1993 HBO TV movie *Attack of the 50 Ft. Woman*. This was going to be shot back in Los Angeles, and Phillips had been released from the remainder of her commitment to *The Crow*. She was predictably excited: "I was like, boom! My second movie." As well as getting permission to leave from the producers and Alex Proyas, Arianne said that she "had also asked Brandon, out of courtesy, because I was leaving to go do another project, and he did get me the movie and I was really grateful. So everything was set, and I had spent the better part of that day kind of packing up. Brandon had asked me for a few things from the extras wardrobe that he had liked, as gifts for Eliza. He had seen clothes on extras from the party scene [at Club Trash] and would say, 'Oh, Eliza would look great in that dress.' He was always thinking of her."

Phillips, who was very close to Brandon, had another reason to be excited at this particular time. There was a big change coming in Brandon's life and she felt as if she were a part of it: "Brandon was supposed to get married on April 17th and Giorgio Armani had sent us a tuxedo for his wedding and, the day before, I had fit him in his tux for his wedding. And I had been helping and advising Eliza on her wedding dress. I was really involved in the wedding plans and we were really excited, because the movie was going to be over and a week later we were all going to be going over to Mexico for Brandon and Eliza's wedding. It was really exciting, and it was at the end of all this depressing night action shooting, and Brandon was doing his acting part and he was really excited."

As well as leaving the gifts she had selected for Brandon in his trailer, Phillips also "wrote him a note. And I was never really that sentimental with him or that mushy or anything like that. I took the opportunity in this note to tell him how much I appreciated him for believing in me and getting me the job. And I had bought him a couple presents and I told him I loved him and I said, the last thing in my letter was, 'Next time I see you, I will be drinking tequila at your wedding.'" The letter remained in his dressing room and Brandon Lee never saw it.

Looking back on that evening, many people would remember apparently trivial details that, with hindsight, in the light of what was about to happen, have since taken on a deeper, symbolic meaning for them. Some have even remembered things that happened before and now seem significant: "The night before the accident, I didn't sleep as well," said Sofia Shinas, "because I had a nightmare that something bad was going to happen. And I told Jeff Imada too. I said, 'Something bad's going to happen, Jeff. Tomorrow.' He was like, 'What!'"

As usual, that evening a meal was provided for the crew by the movie production department before they started work. At one end of the studio some long tables had been set up as a cafeteria. Greg Gale, encountering Brandon at one of those tables, certainly remembered something different about that evening. It would have been unusual for Brandon to join him and other crew members to eat because he usually ate in his trailer, but there was more than that. Gale knew that Brandon didn't like to talk about his father: "Everybody said, 'Don't ever mention anything about his father. Just don't say it in front of him and don't even talk about it!' *He's not gonna ever talk about it, so none of us would even talk about it.*" But that night, Brandon did talk about his father. It wasn't until later that this seemed significant to Gale. "The next day, I said, 'God, that was strange!' You kind of reflect back what happened through that evening and that's just one of the things that kind of stuck in my head that I do remember. He did talk about his father."

Jeff Most was sitting in his office that evening as Brandon walked past on his way into work. Most was on the phone, but he saw Brandon through his glass office window. "He waved to me," said Most. "He was all dressed in white, almost like an Indian white, a hundred percent cotton shirt. Nothing he was wearing as a character costume. He waved, and it had a different connotation of a wave than I expected, and I waved back at Brandon and I said to the person on the phone, 'That's strange, he's waving at me like he's saying goodbye. Maybe he forgot he's shooting for two more days.' That was just an offhanded comment, but I just remember reflecting on it, because there was something. Maybe the mind plays tricks, and your last memory is something different than how it went down, but there was an ethereal quality to that wave, and my seeing him that last time."

A little later, at about 11:00 p.m., on the church roof set, Rochelle Davis was still waiting for the crew to prepare the scene. But nobody had yet been able to find the safety harness that would keep her from falling off the roof. The young actress was asked if they could stage the scene another way: "They said, 'Will it be all right if you go up there and just hang on to the thing and we'll try to put something underneath you in case you fall?' Or, 'Somebody will wait underneath you to make sure you don't fall and if you do they'll try to catch you.' And I was kinda like, 'I don't think I wanna get up on that building without a harness.'"

Rochelle's mother soon got involved in this conversation. "'No,' she said. 'You're not putting my daughter up there without a cable holding her. That's too dangerous. Its thirty feet up there! It's raining. How do you think she's gonna be able to hold on for a full scene without falling?'" Continued Rochelle, "So they were like, 'Oh, she'll be fine.' And Mom said, 'No. She'll be fine when she has a harness on. We'll be in our dressing room when you find it.'" Rochelle herself was quite determined about this: "You're not gonna endanger me and my safety to get this done on time."

Jeff Imada, who was on the loft set with the main unit, was then called back to the church set to assess the situation. He too determined that the shot could not be done safely without the harness. So, Rochelle Davis returned to her dressing room to wait. "I took off all my clothes and changed back into my sweats because I was cold and I knew they weren't gonna find that thing anytime soon. So, I laid in my little dressing room and listened to some music and read a magazine."

Back on stage 4, Jeff Imada was getting ready to choreograph the simple action of Michael Massee shooting Brandon with a single bullet, and Greg Gale recalled, "It was the last day scheduled to have a firearm on the set."

As with almost everything on *The Crow*, the final decision about exactly how Eric Draven and Shelly were to be killed by Top Dollar's thugs in this flashback scene is remembered differently by different people. The original script called for Brandon to be stabbed then shot once, fall to the ground, and then be shot several more times and ultimately tossed out the window. But since the writer, David Schow, was on hand doing rewrites and since the storyboards were frequently altered, it may be that Alex Proyas changed what was to happen to Eric Draven as the movie schedule progressed. Sofia Shinas, however, is sure that when she went to the set that night it was news to her that Shelly was going to be shot too. She thought she was simply going to be raped and beaten to death. Arianne Phillips also remembers that it was decided on the night that Shelly "was going to get shot."

What is certain is that there was a lot of confusion among key cast and crew directly involved with filming this important scene, and particularly about what was to become its most critical element: Brandon Lee was to be shot in this first portion of the scene before the rape.

Lance Anderson says that he had constructed a special harness for Brandon some weeks before: "I was under the impression that he wasn't gonna get shot, that he was gonna get stabbed. He's gonna get a knife thrown at him. And I built a harness to fit on the shoulder. The knife would be embedded in him, in the harness." When they were getting close to the scene, Anderson ran back to his trailer to get the harness and the fake knife. "I showed it to Alex and I said, 'I gotta get this on him for the scene.' And he said, 'No, no, we've changed it. He's getting shot!'" But Lance Anderson also admitted, "I never received a script change deleting the knife from the scene," and he had understood that the knife would only wound Eric Draven initially, and he would be shot later in the scene.

Alex Proyas' decision was that when Draven walks into his loft, he is carrying a grocery bag, and when he gets shot, he is shot through the grocery bag, exploding its contents. There was a squib with a blood bag at the back of the bag to make it look as if a bullet had gone through the bag and hit Draven, knocking him down but not killing him. The idea was that then the badly wounded Draven would have to watch the thugs beating and raping Shelly before they finally kill them both. When it was clear Brandon would be shot through the grocery bag, Anderson didn't need to put any special effects makeup blood directly on him for that scene, and he also abandoned his knife harness.

A "squib" is a small explosive charge, which is generally used with a bag of fake blood. It will usually be hidden in the actor's clothing, then, at an agreed moment, the special effects person detonates it, either directly by wire or sometimes by radio control. Ideally, this will be at the precise moment that another actor fires a gun loaded with blanks. The explosive goes off, the bag of fake blood is burst, and the resulting effect is as if the actor has been shot as the "blood" bursts from his clothing. In this scene, of course, the squib was not on Brandon Lee at all, but in the grocery bag he was carrying. In this instance, unusually, Brandon would detonate the squib in the bag himself by pressing a small hidden trigger, well concealed behind the bag. This would make the timing of the bag exploding coincide better with the gunshot.

Part of the original safety plans for the production had involved Brandon wearing a bulletproof vest for scenes that needed it. The big shoot-out at Top Dollar's was the only time when Imada recalled Brandon wearing a bulletproof vest, but on that occasion, Brandon "had tons of squibs. A whole bunch. More than forty." However, nobody thought that the action in the scene they were about to shoot in the loft merited that kind of protection. Jeff Imada believed, "It was very safe. Normal squibs. There was no need for him to wear a vest that night, really."

However, Jeff Most heard a totally different story about the bulletproof vest. The events that led up to Most hearing the story were very traumatic for him. Having been banished several days before, he was not on the set, but he heard from Sofia Shinas a story about the events in the wardrobe trailer that night.

He was naturally upset about being banned from the set of the movie he had originated, but with only a few more days of shooting left, he had decided to accept the ban. At about midnight, a tired Jeff Most left his office for home. He had been there since 9:00 a.m., feverishly working on "putting the music together for the soundtrack album and preparing the music for the assembly of the film, so that the music could be dropped in immediately." And, importantly, he needed to be at the studio early the next morning to have an important call with the completion bond company, which was concerned that they were over budget and schedule. The other producers were worried that they might even take over control of production.

Most never went back to the set although, on the evening of March 30th, he was asked by Sofia Shinas to be on set, who might have felt more comfortable with a friend and ally present. An inexperienced actress, Shinas was certainly apprehensive about shooting the flashback scene, where she would have to face rough and humiliating treatment from Top Dollar's thugs.

There was some question that night about whether Brandon Lee would wear a bulletproof vest. A day or so later, Shinas would give Most her version of a discussion about it in the wardrobe trailer that night. Shortly before the scene was to be shot, Shinas said, Alex Proyas changed his mind twice about how Eric Draven and Shelly Webster were to lose their lives. At first, Proyas decided that Shinas would be shot. She then put on her bulletproof vest. Most said, "The next day Sofia Shinas related to me that, while she was in makeup, getting final touches, the wardrobe supervisor came in and said, 'Well, Alex's gone back to the original shot. I need the suit vest and the armor protection to be taken off it, to be given to Brandon,' who said in front of Sofia Shinas that he wasn't going to put the vest on. He didn't want it to be seen in the shot. The wardrobe supervisor showed him it wouldn't be, but Brandon said, 'I'm not putting it on. If it's my time to go, it's my time to go.' And he went ahead and did the scene without the armament vest on."

In hindsight, Most thought that a different decision could have been enforced that night: "I believe that an experienced armor expert probably would've insisted, if for no other reason than a dummy wadding [from a blank] still comes at you with great force. I am unclear as to whose final responsibility it would've been, but I would imagine that the armor expert would've more than likely been involved in that decision as to whether or not Brandon were to wear that vest. Would I have insisted he wear it?" Most reflected. "Absolutely!"

But the wardrobe supervisor, Darryl Levine, recalled *none* of Shinas' version of events and said that he doesn't "remember any of those conversations. Which doesn't mean they didn't happen. Because I'm certainly in there. See, I was there, so I'm not gonna say they didn't happen. But I'm also gonna say that these guys, Imada and Brandon, and even our effects guys, they were not new at what they were doing. They looked at this, and they prepared people the way they should've been prepared. We didn't put a bulletproof vest on people for a revolver being shot." Levine was insistent on this point and repeated it many times during my interviews: "No, we never did that kinda stuff. Bulletproof vest? Excuse me. What are you, crazy? The only time you ever use that protective [clothing], is if somebody in a shot comes up to you with a gun, point-blank, because a blank with powder can still affect you. Then we put on a bulletproof vest. We were halfway across the room. There was no reason. We would not have done that. That would not have been in the cards." The stunt coordinator also agreed with Levine that a vest was totally unnecessary in this scene. "There was no squib on him at all," said Jeff Imada. "It was in a bag pointing away from him. So there was no reason to have a vest on." Indeed, Brandon was more than the required safe distance from the gun.

Nevertheless, looking back, Darryl Levine recalled that Alex Proyas did frequently change his mind. "Things were always changing," said Levine. "It was changing. Always changing." And he thought he knew why that was: "It was one of those shows where we were constantly trying to—I'm gonna give him the benefit of the doubt—they were always trying to make it better. There's a fine line."

That night, the line was to be very fine indeed.

The Gunshot

17

THE SCENE THAT SOFIA SHINAS regarded with apprehension certainly would be a violent one. Laurence Mason was well aware of what had to be done to her: "We had to beat her up and throw her on the bed, and we're tearing that place to shreds and they had to keep putting it back together again after every take. Destroying their house. He [Proyas] really wanted a sense of chaos."

The loft set was based on the loft pictured in the comic book, which was in turn based on an actual building in a rough neighborhood in Detroit, which had caught James O'Barr's eye. The set had a large round window and high ceilings and was in desperate need of repair, thus the reason why the young couple, Eric and Shelly, were actively trying to fix it up. So that the windows in the loft set could be used for stunts, the set itself had been built on a platform.

Judging from his own height of six feet, Randy LaFollette described it as, "at least, maybe, eight feet. You can walk underneath it and not duck. And there's a couple of little stairways that go up to the one door that goes in. There's a little hallway outside that goes into the set." All the cast and crew had to enter the loft from the little hallway through the door, which was used both as the door in the movie and as the only real way onto the set. Later that night, having only one single entrance was to cause some difficulties.

As the moment of filming Eric Draven's arrival drew closer, the set became more crowded. When Clyde Baisey arrived, script supervisor Nini Rogan was pleased to see him and told him to sit next to her. He was glad to do that, because he knew that she would be careful not to get in the way of the shooting, and because her job required that she sit somewhere

where she had a good view. Baisey recalled that he thought, "If it was safe for her to be there, I can pretty much sit in the same area. She was great to get along with." They were sitting at the dining room table on the set, about ten to fifteen feet away from the camera, so they had an excellent view of everything that happened.

Arianne Phillips had already packed her belongings and was ready to catch an early plane to Los Angeles on the morning of March 31. "I was leaving at seven a.m. from the airport across the street," she recalled, "so I decided my last night on the set, I was just gonna basically walk across the street and get on the plane." Until now, Phillips had not spent an entire night on the set. Usually, she had to leave at around 3:00 a.m., because, unlike some of the crew, she would have to work the next morning in the costume workshop. She entered the set just as the rehearsal was about to begin, and the first assistant director, Steve Andrews, "Kinda kicked my butt," she said. "People used to tease me because I wasn't on set all the time. . . . It was a very friendly group of people, very familial-like. And I walked by Brandon and he was about to enter the scene. We were on the set on the stage and he [Andrews] said, 'Hurry, take your place. Take your place!' So the only place for me to stand was right by Derek Wolski, over where it was very crowded."

Since this was a flashback to the living Eric Draven, Brandon was of course dressed in color, not the solid black of the Crow character. Brandon, Phillips said, "Was wearing the T-shirt with the name of his band, Hangman's Joke, on it and a leather jacket, an open, kind of floral shirt, 'vintage,' and a pair of dark blue velvet pants, and boots. So, it was a very kind of rock 'n' roll outfit." Darryl Levine thought this costume was more "fun" than the costume Brandon wore for the rest of the film. Maybe that was because it was less trouble in terms of continuity.

Makeup artist Sharon Ilson and her assistant, Sandra Orsolyak, were also there to monitor the makeup on the ensemble actors, while Lance Anderson was looking after Brandon's makeup. Michelle Johnson was on set to manage the actors' hair. Johnson was especially keeping an eye on Michael Massee's messy, long blond wig to make sure that it stayed in place while his character, Funboy, was engaged in the action of raping Shelly and trashing the loft.

As the scene was being rehearsed, in a bizarre contrast to the mayhem the actors were playing out, Michelle Johnson and Sharon Ilson were sitting quietly on the loft set's couch. This struck Johnson, she said, "As really odd . . . And then something funny was me and Sharon Ilson were learning to crochet. Lance Anderson's wife was teaching us to crochet because she crochets beautifully. She crocheted my daughter a sweater."

Not unusually, Alex Proyas had decided to shoot this multicharacter scene with two cameras, to save time and to see the scene from two different points of view (POV). Jeff Most recalled, "They were doing the master shot and a second unit shot at the same time because there was just so much they had to catch up on that night." The master shot was a wide shot, showing all the action: In the foreground it showed the thugs holding Shelly in the chair, while over the thugs' shoulders, including, crucially, Massee's shoulder, it showed the front door of the loft, where Brandon would enter. The other shot was a tighter shot on Massee, showing the gun in profile.

After the long last couple of months of filming, Laurence Mason was ready to go home, and the prospect of this violent scene was not a pleasant one: "It was very hard to wake up and go to that. It's not fun . . . I was ready to go. It was really harsh." Sofia Shinas had told Jeff Most that she was uncomfortable with this scene, and this didn't surprise Mason, playing Tin Tin, who said, "She had four guys running around, attacking her. I can't imagine. So that was definitely weird."

Chunky Huse, sitting outside in the walkway, outside the front door of the loft set, had noticed something in the planned playing of the scene that didn't make sense, the kind of thing that is usually the director's job to notice: "I was sitting on an apple box outside the door, talking to Brandon. And I just said to him, I said, 'Brandon.' He said, 'What?' I said, 'You've been out, right, in this scene, you've been out.' I said, 'You come back and these four guys are in there raping your girlfriend.' He went, 'Yeah.' I said, 'But when you come up the stairs, surely, aren't you gonna hear all that? You're not just gonna walk through the door?' He went, 'You're right. Hang on a minute,' he said. 'Thank you very, very much.' And off he wandered. And he went in and saw Alex, and he came back out and he said, 'Thank you, Chunky.' He said, 'I've got the answer.' I said, 'What's that?' He said, 'I'm going to wear a Walkman. I'm out there, I'm going to rock and roll.' I went, 'Terrific!'"

The plan was that when Eric Draven walked in, he would find the gang wrecking his apartment and beating and taunting Shelly while they hold her in a chair. Clyde Baisey, watching from the table, had no particular expectations that, although this was going to *look* like a violent scene in the movie, it would actually be a physically taxing scene for the actors. "This one was relatively minor," he said, "compared to any of the rest of them we had shot." Angel David, playing Skank, was, said Huse, "The

Brandon Lee as The Crow, arisen from the dead and meeting his crow guide.
Cinematic Collection / Alamy Stock Photo

Bai Ling as Myca, sitting in Top Dollar's lair.
Buena Vista Pictures/Photofest ©Buena Vista Pictures

Brandon Lee in costume, warming his hands on the freezing back lot street set.
Miramax Films/Photofest ©Miramax Films

Michael Massee as Funboy and Laurence Mason as Tin Tin, at Top Dollar's gang meeting in the Pit Bar.
Miramax Films/Photofest ©Miramax Films

Tony Todd as Grange, Michael Wincott as Top Dollar, and Bai Ling as Myca in Top Dollar's lair.
Buena Vista Pictures/Photofest ©Buena Vista Pictures

Sofia Shinas as Shelly Webster and Rochelle Davis as Sarah in the loft apartment as Shelly tries on her wedding dress.
Miramax Films/Photofest ©Miramax Films

Ernie Hudson as Officer Albrecht, investigating Shelly and Eric's murder scene.
Miramax Films/Photofest ©Miramax Films

Rochelle Davis as Sarah, placing flowers on Shelly and Eric's graves.
Miramax Films/Photofest ©Miramax Films

The Crow during
the boardroom
shoot-out scene
in Top Dollar's
lair.
Miramax Films/
Photofest
©Miramax Films

Brandon Lee and
director Alex
Proyas on the
back lot street set.
Miramax Films/
Photofest
©Miramax Films

Rochelle Davis as
Sarah and Ernie
Hudson as Officer
Albrecht at the
Maxi Dog hot
dog stand.
Miramax Films/
Photofest
©Miramax Films

Brandon Lee as The Crow finds Shelly's engagement ring on the pawn shop set.
Buena Vista Pictures/Photofest ©Buena Vista Pictures

Brandon Lee on set with a guitar, in the rain.
Miramax Films/Photofest ©Miramax Films

Brandon Lee saying goodbye to Sarah (Rochelle Davis) in the graveyard.
Miramax Films/Photofest ©Miramax Films

Brandon Lee, as The Crow, exacting his revenge on Laurence Mason as Tin Tin.
kpa Publicity Stills / Alamy Stock Photo

Jon Polito as Gideon describing his encounter with The Crow to Tony Todd as Grange and
Bai Ling as Myca at Top Dollar's lair.
Buena Vista Pictures/Photofest ©Buena Vista Pictures

Brandon Lee on the freezing, rain-drenched back lot set.
Miramax Films/Photofest ©Miramax Films

Brandon Lee as The Crow, at Shelly's grave.
Miramax Films/Photofest ©Miramax Films

Brandon Lee as The Crow with his crow guide on the church set before killing Top Dollar and rescuing Sarah.
Miramax Films/Photofest ©Miramax Films

Brandon Lee as The Crow, in full makeup.
Cinematic Collection / Alamy Stock Photo

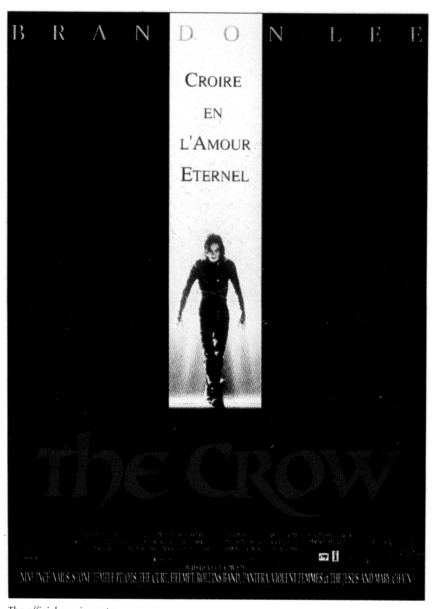

The official movie poster.
Miramax Films/Photofest ©Miramax Films

one holding Shelly, and Tin Tin is . . . I think he was to the left and he's throwing stuff around, and Funboy's over here in front of the chair to the left."

At this point, Jeff Imada was on the other stage, where the second unit was preparing to shoot the green-screen rooftop scene with Rochelle Davis. He had already been back to stage 4 a few times, checking on the action there. "They were calling for me in both sets and it was very busy," he recalled. "Whenever there was any action, I said I had to be there. And nobody ever said, 'We're going to do it without you.'" Shooting with both units at the same time also meant that the second assistant director, Randy LaFollette, like Jeff Imada, would be working on both sets and moving back and forth between the two.

After the earlier discussion about whether Eric Draven was to be shot or knifed, Alex Proyas' next decision was, which thug would pull the trigger? Actors playing bad guys in movies will often define their character by the particular kind of violence they hand out. Laurence Mason had firmly established in his own mind that guns were not his character's specialty: "And now we're trying to decide who's gonna shoot him, and Alex said . . . I think he'd wanted me to shoot him and I was like, 'I'm the knife guy, I can't shoot him!' I was just pissed off because I'm the knife guy. Why am I all of a sudden gonna use a gun? Just doesn't make any sense. I stood by that." So Alex Proyas chose Massee as the shooter. This did make sense, because Funboy often uses a gun in the movie. But to Laurence Mason, who was concerned principally with himself, the choice of Massee seemed random: "I guess he was just standing next to me or something, I don't know."

Huse was still sitting outside the door, trying not to be in the way on the crowded set, but nevertheless, keeping his eye on things. "Nini's in there, and I'm sitting outside the door, so every time they open up the door, I'm looking through the door and I'm looking at Dariusz [Wolski] and I'm going, 'Are you alright I'm here? I'm sitting right here.' And I was right outside the door."

The main unit was now ready to rehearse and then shoot the scene. They were late and now they were again delayed, waiting on Jeff Imada to get there.

Before they shot the scene, Sofia Shinas had a long conversation with Brandon, ranging over both of their careers and lives. He told her that he had been offered a movie with Dolph Lundgren and wasn't sure if he would do it. "And he says, 'What *am* I gonna do next?' And I say, 'Get married.' And he laughs! And he says, 'If I make it out of here alive.' And then I said, 'Yeah, at the rate you're going.' I said, 'Don't you think about these things? I heard that you're not even wearing a vest right now!' And he says, 'No, I'm not.' And he says, 'Hmm . . .' I said, 'Aren't you paranoid?' And he said, 'No.' And I said, 'Why not?' And he said, 'Because if it's my time, it's my time.' And that's a direct quote."

Jeff Imada wasn't too worried about the rehearsal and the exact blocking of Brandon's response to being shot because he had already worked on it with him: "They called me on the radio and said, 'Brandon's getting ready for this,' and I said, 'Brandon knows what to do because they're just going to block it.' Because Brandon and I had talked about it, as far as him falling to his knees. So, when I got there it had already been more or less worked out. Blocked, and the cameras were set, more or less. But I basically came in, checked everything out, we rehearsed it one or two more times for camera."

Angel David was certain of what Brandon's action would be: "We were doing the scene. We rehearsed it a couple of times and the thing I remember vividly was Jeff [Imada] talking to Brandon and telling Brandon, 'Okay, when you get hit, you drop the stuff and you fall forward,' and he said, 'Yeah, okay.'" There was simply no doubt in anyone's mind that Brandon was going to fall forward.

When there's any kind of explosion or gunshot in the course of shooting a movie, the implications of it must be explained to all present. Clyde Baisey described the first assistant director following the proper procedure: "The First AD would always gather all the information from the perspective of each group and put it all together and make the announcement, all at one time." The assembled company was told that there would be one blank fired from the gun, Funboy's .44 Magnum with a white handle, but that it would be very loud. It would be very loud because of the amount of explosive in the gun.

The decision about how much explosive to put in a weapon that will fire blanks in a movie depends on the desired effect. In this case, the director had decided that he wanted to see not only a realistic recoil from the weapon, but also some smoke and a flash of flame from the barrel. So the gun was to be loaded with a full charge, the equivalent amount of gunpowder contained in a real bullet, with the bullet tip replaced by wadding. This apparently inconsequential decision to have a full charge in the gun would turn out to be a fateful one.

The next major decision was also of paramount importance, and it was about where the gun should be aimed. This is a matter that involves not only the director of a movie, but also the stunt coordinator. Jeff Imada spoke directly to Michael Massee, Funboy, about this, and said that they "went over all the safety things, as far as aiming away from Brandon. Right before we rolled, as they were rolling cameras, I stepped on the set, 'Where are you gonna aim?' He says, 'Over there, on that spot against the white wall.' I said, 'Over here?' He goes, 'Yeah.'" Others in the crew heard Imada's instructions. For example, Michelle Johnson said, "I know Jeff told Michael Massee not to point it at him." And Angel David also heard Imada tell Massee not to fire at Brandon.

However, Lance Anderson remembered this conversation differently. His recollection is that to get the shot, Massee *had* to point the gun at Brandon: "The way I understood it was, they had to have been aiming the gun at Brandon [otherwise], because of the camera angle, it would look obvious he wasn't pointing it at him."

Clyde Baisey remembered things with yet a different slant. He remembered Imada and Massee's conversation, but that Massee was having a problem with pointing the gun away. Watching the rehearsals closely, Baisey understood that what had been rehearsed was that Funboy "whips around with a pistol. He aims at Brandon, fires the gun, because from the camera angle it would look like he was aiming directly at Brandon, whether or not he was aimed at him." Then, Baisey's recollection of events is that, "The actor with the gun was told, 'Do not aim directly at Brandon with the pistol.' Which he did. Was told not to do it, but he determined that it would look more real to him if he aimed directly at the actor." Baisey was also sure that before the scene was shot, everyone on the set was of the understanding that Massee would "shoot 'off to the side.' But I guess they didn't have control over this."

The exact angle at which Massee was to fire the gun would later become a highly critical matter.

As the shot was set up, the main camera would show Massee as he turned around to see Brandon entering the door to the loft. The shot was relatively wide, with Brandon as the point of focus. Massee was standing several feet away from Brandon, which Imada had decided was "more than a safe distance away. It's very safe, as far as distance-wise, for the blank."

The special effects man on the set that night and in charge of the squib was Bruce Merlin. By all accounts, he was a fully experienced special effects technician, whom JB Jones had worked with many times before.

Finally, the actors were all in their costumes, the props were all set, the action had been finalized, and Jeff Imada was on hand. The assistant prop master, Charlene Hamer, had gotten the gun from the prop truck parked outside the stage. Everything was at last ready for the cast and crew to rehearse the scene.

Laurence Mason recalled, "We ran it a couple of times and it was fine. The action is: He [Eric] walks in, says, 'blahdy, blahdy,' [we] shoot him and we all laugh as he drops to the ground. And we ran it a couple of times, without any rounds or anything, and it was fine."

During the rehearsal period, still photographer Robert Zuckerman shot photographs of the scene standing just a few feet away from the motion picture camera, where he would remain to continue taking stills when the camera actually rolled.

Once the crew was finished rehearsing, they were ready to roll film.

Then, in front of Massee, the prop master, Daniel Kuttner, took the gun, opened the chamber, loaded one single full blank into the chamber, closed it, and handed it to Massee. After the company was warned that the full-load blank would produce a load bang, Sandra Orsolyak, concerned for Brandon's safety, offered him earplugs. She had some trouble getting his attention. "He was la-la-la-ing to this song, and finally he looked down at me, because he's extremely tall, I think he had like a two-inch heel on or something, he's still tall, I'm looking up somewhat and I said, 'Brandon!' Finally he looks down and he says, 'What?' I said, 'What are you listening to?' 'Oh, nothing. It's in my head.' I said, 'You need earplugs?' 'No, I got a headset on. I'm fine.'"

There was now nothing to prevent the scene from being filmed. All proper precautions seemed to have been taken. Clyde Baisey said, "Everything had been checked, double-checked pretty much."

The camera and sound began rolling. The first assistant director, Steve Andrews, yelled "Action!" Funboy and his partner T-Bird began their taunting of Shelly, while Skank and Tin Tin held her in the chair.

Brandon Lee had been ready in his position outside the door of the set, and Chunky Huse may have been the last person to speak to him in the moments before he made his entrance. "Because me and him were just sitting outside the door shooting the shit really, that's what we were doing. And he went, 'Da da da,' and they said, 'Get ready,' and he looked at me and he said, 'Here we go.' I said, 'Yup, here we go. Good luck, mate!' and I was sitting with my back against the wall. And there's the door, 'Action!' . . . Open the door, in he went."

Brandon entered and attempted to get out his first line, but none of the crew later remembered hearing it. Funboy spun around, gun in hand, saw Eric and fired. The blank went off with a very loud bang. The rigged grocery bag detonated, exploding the milk container and a blood pack, ripping a hole in the paper bag. Eric fell to the floor. After a few seconds, Huse, from where he was sitting outside the door, heard Alex Proyas yell "Cut!"

Huse had no idea what had just happened on the other side of that door. But then, neither did anybody who was actually on the set.

CONFUSION 18

THINKING BACK TO WHAT EXACTLY did happen, Angel David recalled, "Brandon walked in, and I'm holding Shelly and dealing with her. I was looking at her. I wasn't looking at the situation, and things were flying around, stuff was going on. Just like we rehearsed it. You heard the bang, Brandon fell, and then there was a little pause and 'Cut!'"

As rehearsed, Michael Massee had waved the .44 Magnum around and fired a single shot. But before Alex Proyas had called "Cut!" the actors playing the thugs had to react for a few seconds to Eric Draven's wounded body. "It was just a continuation of what we were doing," David thought, "and I think the characters were getting a kick out of what happened, and the fact that we were all improvising in character. It was a few seconds before 'Cut!' because Alex wanted to get that." Laurence Mason said, "We laughed as he's on his back. They yelled, 'Cut!' Everybody milled about. I noticed he didn't get up."

Robert Zuckerman saw the whole scene through a wide-angle lens on his still camera. He noticed only that "Brandon fell in a different way than he did during the rehearsal. And my eye, through my viewfinder, remained on Funboy because he had dialogue in the opposite direction. It wasn't until they yelled, 'Cut!' that Brandon didn't get up. That was maybe like, five or ten seconds later."

Arianne Phillips, looking to see how her costume played in the scene, heard, "This sound that those guns make, that fake guns . . . it was like a pop sound, and Brandon went down, and I thought it was acting. It was the longest second in the world, it was like one of those things where everything just stops around you and you are in this weird space and he goes down and all of a sudden I realize."

Lance Anderson's view was that "Brandon was just acting and everybody thought he was just acting." Certainly Sofia Shinas thought this was simply a terrific piece of acting, as she saw him fall: "Like a little puppet when someone drops the strings . . . It's like a marionette when they drop the strings. It just slowly goes like that. I'd never seen anything like it. I just remember thinking, 'Wow, what a great actor. This is so theatrical.'"

At first, some people thought that Brandon had changed the action and was fooling around. David remembered, "Turning and seeing Brandon—he didn't fall forward, he fell backwards. In rehearsal it was forward. And then there was kind of a pause. After every take, people do what they have to do to reset and all that, and Brandon hadn't gotten up and I think people thought he was kidding around."

Michelle Johnson was still learning to crochet, with her blue yarn, and had completed about six inches of it. "I was just sitting there, frozen. We were sitting on the couch part of the set and when that happened, with our needles and our yarn, and I mean just . . . you just kinda froze." Although Johnson was not watching that closely, she instantly sensed that there was something wrong with the way Brandon fell. "It was like in slow motion. I mean, he was trying to say something, and it was just like, he's not acting, there's something wrong."

Robert Zuckerman heard other people say, "They noticed, which I didn't notice, but they said *they* noticed, Brandon making a hand gesture across his throat, like Cut! Cut! and then fell down after that. I think he must've lost consciousness right then."

Michele Johnson heard that "People were already saying stuff like, 'No! There's something wrong, stop it.' So some people did notice."

Clyde Baisey was conscious of the moment when everything seemed to go wrong: "Everything was just like it should have been. But the only difference was when Brandon fell backwards, he said, 'Cut.' It wasn't, 'Cut!' it was like, 'Cuuuut.'"

Brandon had ended up against the wall, on the floor. This was not remotely like the position arranged in the blocking, or the position he had fallen in during the rehearsals. Lance Anderson noted, "He went down in almost like a sitting position. He was sitting. And that's where he stayed."

Immediately after Alex Proyas called "Cut!" Jeff Imada went over to Brandon because he had seen straightaway that, "This was different than what we had rehearsed and talked about. And I thought, 'Okay, Brandon has been known to change things on the spur of the moment and do something different because the character maybe changes.' He ended up doing a little spin and coming down on the ground. We had rehearsed him falling to his knees and falling forward. And he ended up sitting up against the wall. And I thought, 'Okay, he's fooling around, 'cause he'll do that for a take or two or for rehearsal, and he'll start cracking up.' My initial reaction was he was fooling around and so I started talking to him, 'Hey Brandon, that was different.' And then I went, 'Something's wrong here!'"

Angel David saw it almost as a movie: "It all became, sort of like slow motion after that."

Brandon's reputation for kidding was such that although he had fallen in a strange way, even medic Clyde Baisey couldn't be sure that something really was wrong with him. But he went over to check anyway, "Just like I had done so many times before. 'Brandon, are you okay?' And most of the time I got a snide remark. 'Leave me alone. Go away,' or whatever the case may be . . . This time he just had a stare off into space and didn't say anything. And I asked him again if he was okay, and he still didn't say anything. I reached up and shook him a little bit, in case he was dazed from hitting the wall when he went backwards."

Clyde Baisey's initial concern was with Brandon's injury. "It was more from his fall backwards, more than it was with the actual gunshot." What was interesting about Baisey's close proximity to the accident was that he had information not usually available to paramedics, who see only the results of an accident but have no real details about what exactly has happened. Baisey was highly conscious of this problem from previous work as a paramedic: "The one thing you do not get a chance to see in the aftermath of the car accident or fall or whatever the case may be, is exactly what the mechanism of injury is. A lot of times, a person's injury is threefold. A person gets hit by a car. Not only do they sustain the injury from the impact of the vehicle to the body, but then again when they bounce off the windshield of the vehicle and then when they hit the ground again, so they're actually injured three times, not just one time. And in the hospital care you do not get to see that. You only see the aftermath of a person with broken legs, busted ribs, head injury, whatever the case may be." But the extraordinary thing was that despite being so close to the accident and seeing everything that had happened on the set, the correct explanation was the last one to occur to Baisey or anyone else there.

Once Jeff Imada realized that Brandon was somehow injured, his initial thought was, "Maybe he hit his head or something, against the wall. We didn't know what happened. I don't know how much detail I want to go into, but the medic and I worked on him. I remember seeing people just totally frozen in their places while we were working on him. And we were trying to find out what was wrong. We didn't know if something went wrong with the squib in the bag."

Arianne Phillips said, "Everyone wasn't sure at first . . . there was a moment of not being sure and then there was some commotion and I was just standing there, and then we realized something was wrong. You know, the paramedic was there initially, and they start, 'Everyone out of the room. Everyone out of the room.' And I didn't move, it was like my feet were glued, and I was just staring at him."

Baisey went through the usual routine in cases of this kind: "First I shook him . . . I tried it with the verbal stimulation. Nothing worked. Then I tried with the painful stimulation, which would be a sternum rub or a pinch or anything like that, is what it amounts to. Didn't elicit any kind of response, verbally or with motion. He didn't flinch back from it or anything like that." Imada remembered, "Brandon was unconscious the whole time. Just heavy breathing." Baisey now knew that Brandon Lee was unconscious and in some kind of serious trouble.

The set medic continued his examination of Brandon, laying him down on the floor, first trying to see if there was something wrong with his neck. "He was in a sitting position laid back in the corner. So my first intuition, thought, was his injury that he had sustained at that time did not result from the squib. It didn't result from the gun, but as a result of the fall. Possible cervical injury or spinal injury or head injury from hitting his head on the wall. Unlikely, but it could have happened. So I was more inclined to go that route and then rule out once I found anything different. We stabilized his cervical spine, got him on the floor, and started pulling clothes."

Once Baisey had established that Brandon was unresponsive, he began to evaluate his vital signs. At first, he found, "He had a regular pulse, I knew without even actually taking the blood pressure." But Brandon's pulse was to degenerate rapidly and alarmingly. "Within two or three minutes," Baisey found, "when I checked it again, it was absent." Baisey's checks revealed that, "His initial blood pressure was way, way low. Very scary low. *Fatally* low, let's put it that way." But Baisey was still unsure of the significance of the low blood pressure. "I still suspected a spinal injury, because a lot of times, with a spinal injury you can develop what's called 'spinal shock,' which is: no blood pressure, plenty of volume. There's plenty of blood in the system. It's just, because of the damage to the nerve vessels themselves, the body doesn't react the way it normally should. It's more or less like the pump is going bad rather than the volume not being there, as in a bleeding wound. The bleeding wound, the heart is still pumping, but there's nothing to pump." But at this point Baisey couldn't tell if the heart was working or not. And what Baisey *did* know of Brandon's condition at this point was completely perplexing.

One of the major reasons that nobody suspected the true cause of Brandon's condition was that he was not apparently bleeding anywhere. Furthermore, there was the fake blood from the squibbed bag to add to the confusion. Imada was as puzzled as everyone else because, he said, "The squib was in the bag and the costume had blood on it already, so it would be revealed when he dropped the bag. People at first were saying, 'Oh, there's blood here.' I go, 'No, it's the fake blood. That was from before.'"

Baisey said, "there was nothing to demonstrate that he was bleeding out. There wasn't an open wound anywhere for anybody to see that he was bleeding out. So, we started removing his clothes and that's when we found the T-shirt had a hole in it. He had a T-shirt on underneath his jacket and his pants. But wardrobe was standing outside: 'Is this hole in his T-shirt supposed to be here?' There was no blood on it or anything. It's just a hole. Darryl said, 'No, the T-shirt was perfectly fine, there was nothing wrong with it.'" Lance Anderson watched as they opened Brandon's shirt. "There was just a tiny little . . . looked like a tiny little slit. No blood came out or anything. It looked like a little scratch. No blood, no nothing. Right in the sternum area." Baisey had found "about an eight-to-ten-millimeter-size-diameter hole in his mid-abdomen about one inch below his umbilicus, or below his navel. There's no bleeding there." Again, nobody drew the obvious conclusion about the source of Brandon's injuries.

Jeff Imada didn't think it was obviously a projectile. "We didn't know what it was at first, and then we thought, 'Well maybe there was something,' but we didn't know how it happened, from the bag or where." Similarly, Lance Anderson figured that the problem had to be with the squib. "I think the first impression was that the squib in the bag . . . the impact of the squib in the bag blew against him. Instead of blowing out, blew the wrong way or something. That's what I thought. And I never dreamed that it came from the gun. I thought that it came from the bag."

Clyde Baisey had finally come to a very surprising conclusion: "I determined that what we had was not a cervical injury but more of a . . . possibly a gunshot wound. Still not sure that's what it was, but it was leading more toward that having occurred because it was a round hole. There was no powder burns or burn around the entrance hole, so that eliminated the squib, because if there had been a squib he would have had a burn right there, in that area. So, I determined that it wasn't a squib burn. It had to be something else that caused the puncture."

Angel David was looking at Baisey's expression: "You could just tell on his face that it was very serious, and he told them, 'Get an ambulance here, now, and clear the set!'" Robert Zuckerman also heard, when Baisey finally made a pronouncement, "He just said, 'He has an abdominal wound. Call 911.' That's the first words that were said. That part I remember very clearly." The watching crew members were stunned.

Arianne Phillips remembered, "They were ripping his clothes off of him and checking his vital signs and his stomach was . . . Well, I later found out that he was internally hemorrhaging, but his stomach blew up." After Baisey's announcement, Phillips said, "Alex Proyas just kind of slumped on the floor. Everyone had gone out of the room and Alex had just kind of slumped on the floor, and Nini, the script supervisor, had slumped next to him with her arm around him. And I was in shock. I couldn't move. And someone . . . Nini, took my arm and pulled me down on the ground. And by then if I had tried to get out I would have been obstructing the view. I was in total disbelief."

Outside the set, Chunky Huse knew that something had gone seriously wrong: "All of a sudden the ADs were getting everybody out of the room and as I came out and I went, 'What's going on?' They said, 'He's been hurt.' I said, 'Right, get everybody out of the stage. Get the doors open. Get the ambulance.'"

A message was now sent to the production office, summoning Greg Gale and Bob Rosen to the set. Gale, who had only just left the set, was on his way back to the production office when he heard on a walkie-talkie that the crew had a problem. He went into Rosen's office and told him, "'I think we should get down there.' And we had no idea what it was at that point, no idea . . . We were walking down there, you know, like something happened, not like there was anything life-threatening."

Randy LaFollette, on the second unit (shooting part of the church roof fight scene), also got a message: "Steve [Andrews] called me on the walkie and said, 'Get over here now. Get over here and you've gotta stop doing what you're doing.' So I just said, 'Guys, break!' and I ran over."

The news was slow to spread around the studio. Costumer Roberta Bile was in the wardrobe trailer, dressing extras for the church roof scene, when she heard the ambulance being called on the radio: "They were saying he was going into shock and that's when I knew it was something really serious."

Back on the set, as soon as Baisey announced that something was seriously wrong, the special effects technician in charge of the squibs, Bruce Merlin, checked that the explosive charge he had set in the bag had detonated correctly, so that it blew *outwards*, rather than blowing back into Brandon. Merlin found that everything was indeed correct.

At this point, Brandon's abdomen was continuing to swell, which confirmed Baisey's fear of internal bleeding. "Once I saw that hole, and I saw the large bowel had obstructed . . . I got away from the idea of spinal shock, to more of a condition like an internal bleed. Even though there was no visible signs of blood, the abdomen was starting to get more rigid as the blood was pooling underneath, making it harder. You take a balloon and fill it full of water and it's pretty hard. The abdomen responds the same way."

Baisey looked around and saw that many crew members had stayed around to see what had happened to Brandon. "Some were up on the catwalks looking down onto the set, like some of the electricians, grips . . . Couldn't tell exactly who was there, who wasn't there. They were all pretty much in shock that something had occurred and for the most part they were all relatively quiet."

Larry Madrid, the animal trainer, assumed the worst about Brandon's condition: "Everybody was freaking out because they just couldn't handle it. They just didn't know what was going on and they were just . . . people were panicking. And I was watching what was going on and watching Brandon laying there dead and the medic came in and immediately started life-saving techniques, that means, dead."

Greg Gale arrived on the set with Bob Rosen and quickly realized that this was not a routine situation: "Brandon was actually laying on the floor next to the door and he was unconscious."

Gale found that the crew was, not surprisingly, confused. "We had our lead actor down," Gale said. "Something we just . . . he's our pride and joy of the picture, as well as being a human. You know, he comes first here!" They wanted to make as much room as possible for the medic to work and for the paramedics when they arrived, and since Brandon was almost blocking the only door in and out of the set, the remaining crew members were told to stay where they were. To Gale's frustration, he found it was difficult to get everybody's attention: "They were all milling around the door to see what was happening, so I just had like . . . nobody was really wanting to listen. Finally it was just, and I don't yell a lot, but I just said, 'Get the hell out of the way! Clear this area! Stay on the side!'"

Randy LaFollette, more accustomed to commanding the group than Gale, was told by Bob Rosen to clear everyone off the set, and the crew members slowly left. By this time there were probably about thirty crew members still on the set itself, plus all the people outside the set, the sound people and all the grips and electricians and prop people. LaFollette did his best to shift as many as possible out of the way and then ran out to the studio main gate to make sure the ambulance could get in.

Among the few who stayed was Michelle Johnson. "For some reason . . . they said, 'Everybody get off set, get off set!' So, a lot of people left except for Nini and Alex and me . . . and the First AD and a couple of other people." Johnson wanted to leave the set, but that meant walking past Brandon's inert body. "You had to walk by him to go out the door," she said. "And I just didn't wanna go over there." She was also very concerned about Michael Massee. By now he had realized that something was wrong with the shot that he had fired, and it appeared to have been the cause of Brandon's very serious injuries. He was sitting on the bed, dazed. "And finally I asked Nini to go sit by Michael, because Michael was just in a state of shock. And so I asked Nini to go there and I said, 'Please look at Michael. Somebody's gotta help him.' So Nini, being the mother of all mothers as she is, she's great, she went over and sat with Michael on the bed, while Clyde did all his stuff."

A combination of concern and curiosity kept everyone hanging around outside the sound stage, to see what had happened, and what would happen, to their star. Angel David said, "We left the set, but we didn't leave. . . . The set was in the back lot and we didn't leave the back lot. We were all outside of the sound stage." The crew's recollections show how confused, demoralized, and anxious they were. "Everybody just all over the place," Laurence Mason recalled. "We were trying to keep everybody away. Get air. And it took forever for the ambulance to get there."

On the set, the remaining crew members watched with horror as Brandon's condition deteriorated. For Darryl Levine, this was a harrowing moment, seeing the young man he had come to like so much apparently ebbing away. "To be there that night, and to be a part of it, and the impact that it had on my life, with only knowing him for four months." Lance Anderson was in disbelief, "He never bled . . . never bled. He looked like he was in shock. His eyes were open for a little while, then they closed and then he was just in shock. He was paralyzed, just stiff. Not moving at all." Anderson was also noting the time: "It seemed like ten to fifteen minutes before the paramedics got there."

Clyde Baisey was disturbed to observe, "He was getting pale and his lips were getting blue. He wasn't doing any spontaneous breathing." In order to give Brandon some chance of breathing, Baisey had decided to give him a tracheotomy, closely watched by Darryl Levine, who saw, "At that point you know what, I was there he had already started cutting his neck. . . . We both saw his face. I mean, I know we both saw his face being gray, because we both said it, Imada and I, and there was never a doubt in my mind that he was dead. There was never a doubt in my mind." Although Chunky Huse was still not in a position to see what was happening on the set, he later also heard from his wife that Brandon had died. "I never saw, I only know what Nini tells me. She said that she thought that Brandon had died twice and Clyde brought him back." Nini Rogan was convinced that "Clyde was responsible for saving his life."

While Clyde Baisey was giving the tracheotomy to Brandon, the crew members still on the set were astonished by a strange sound from the next set: gunfire. The sound they heard was the gun that Michael Massee had used in the scene being test-fired. Michelle Johnson was incredulous: "I couldn't believe on top of what had already happened they went and did that. Especially while this guy's getting a tracheotomy!" Johnson had no doubt about why the gun was being fired: "I'm sure to get themselves off the hook because they were terrified that, oh my God, they're the ones that put the blank in the gun. I'm sure they immediately freaked about, 'Oh my God, we're gonna get in trouble for this. Somebody's gonna blame us.'" Johnson was certainly outraged by this test firing, but amazingly, it didn't remain in her memory. "Even in the police reports . . . when they [police] came when we all went to the hospital and we were waiting to find out what was happening with him, and the cop came around and he was taking all our statements . . . even I forgot about that second shot then. I don't think it was on my statement."

There was another potential problem for the crew to deal with: getting the ambulance onto the lot. Baisey remembered that they had the same problem before. "With the stunt guys, anything else that happened, we always got faced with that proverbial gate being down and nobody comes in until we get Keith Wally's permission. He was the general manager of the studio for Carolco at the time." Chunky Huse had also been involved on a previous occasion when an ambulance had difficulty getting into the studio and is still disturbed by the incident. On that occasion, at three o'clock in the morning, one of the grips had injured his back, and when an ambulance had arrived at the studio gate, the security guard wouldn't let it in until he got permission from the studio manager. Huse had certainly learned from that experience. He made sure that his grips went to the front gate to ensure that this time it would be open.

Of course, any delay would be crucial and could have threatened the chances of saving Brandon, so Baisey didn't mince words, saying, "'Tell them, "Leave the fucking gate open! Don't shut the son of a bitch. If it's shut, they're tearing it down when they come through it." Make sure you tell them that verbally word for word.' And needless to say, when the EMS crew got there, and it was a crew that I worked with a lot, they said that when they pulled up the gate was open and nobody was standing nowhere near, and there were folks all the way down pointing to go this way." Randy LaFollette was also determined that there would not be any delays, "So I went up there and I said, 'You're letting this ambulance in now. And I don't care if you get fired. You can tell them it's my fault, but if this ambulance does not come through here now and you slow him down at all, I'm physically gonna rip this thing down.' And so we got the ambulance in there."

Meanwhile, Baisey observed that Brandon's condition had not improved. In fact, Brandon had not recovered consciousness at all. "He had no pulse to this point and that is very serious."

When the paramedics arrived with the ambulance, they asked Baisey what he had done until that point. He explained the tests he'd done and then suggested, "'Go ahead and set up a couple of IV lines. I'll get him intubated,' which is running a tube in his lung. I said, 'We can hook him directly to an air control system and you can go ahead and give him one hundred percent oxygen.'" This would radically increase his chances of survival.

Some crew members who were still on the set recalled that by now Baisey had hooked up a heart monitor to Brandon. But they were to get no reassurance from it, and indeed, they saw it flatline on two occasions. "I gotta admit," said Baisey, "when we were bagging him, [we'd] got him on a heart monitor, and at that time he initially displayed what is called EMD, which is electromechanical dissociation. Now it's referred to as pulseless electrical activity, PEA, which in a trauma situation does not have a very great success rate." Pulseless electrical activity means that though the brain is sending electrical impulses to the heart telling it to beat, the heart is unable to do so because there is no blood circulating through the veins and arteries. In Brandon Lee's case, the low level of blood in his circulatory system was a result of internal bleeding. In the ambulance with Brandon, in spite of six IVs pumping him full of fluids, trying to replace what had been lost through his internal bleeding, Baisey and the paramedics could feel no pulse, though the monitors showed that he had a normal heart rate. In fact, his heart was still working, but without enough blood coursing through it. Clyde Baisey explained this in car mechanic terms: "It's like your radiator had a hole and you're trying to drain water out of it. Well, the engine is still running just like it normally should, but the water pump's not pumping any water anywhere. And the reason for that, in a heart, your heart shuts down, basically. I mean, the last three things that die in a body, the heart, the brain, and the lungs, they are the three major organs. You lose one of them three, the other two gonna die. That's what it amounts to."

Jeff Imada was impressed with Baisey's cool, professional manner. "Baisey stayed with Brandon the whole time, at his side, from the time he was down, to the time the paramedics were there. I helped the paramedics and medic on set. The medic on set was very cool and calm, very efficient. The paramedics came, took over and assisted. They knew each other because the guy [Baisey] was also a paramedic. I did whatever I could to help them out. So, I was with him [Brandon] all the way to the point where they loaded him into the ambulance and it drove away."

Only Daniel Kuttner and Bruce Merlin, Greg Gale, Robert Zuckerman, and a distraught Jeff Imada were involved in these initial attempts to see what had happened and also to preserve the scene and the film.

Jeff Most, of course, had not been allowed on the set that evening. He left for his house, about a thirty-minute drive from the studio on Figure Eight Island, at 11:45 p.m., planning to get some rest before a daunting conference call he, Bob Rosen, Steve Andrews, and Ed Pressman were scheduled to have first thing the next morning with the bond company. "The big concern was that since we are so far behind the bond company could take over." Indeed, the film was on a fifty-one-day shooting schedule and now was moved to fifty-nine, nearly 15 percent over, a hugely expensive amount based on *The Crow*'s already stretched budget.

The stunning visuals in *The Crow* were a significant part of what caused the production schedule overage. The original fifty-one days planned only for routine coverage, but Alex Proyas' frequent moving of camera to capture different angles in a scene cumulatively added to the schedule. This was a fact the production team had been hesitant to proactively admit to the bond company or the higher-ups at Pressman Films.

When he walked in the door, Most said the house phone was ringing. "Grant Hill was on the line. And he told me not to worry. 'Everything's fine. But Brandon had the wind knocked out of him. If there's anything to worry about, I will certainly call you.'"

However, at that stage of the night, Grant Hill had no firsthand knowledge of what took place since he was not on the set himself at the time of the accident nor knew how extensive Brandon's injuries were.

Most admitted he was nervous about the morning's call. "I'd never had a call with a bond company at that point in my career to worry about. I was not in charge of running the day-to-day but I was the lead producer, the creative producer. And nonetheless, I was responsible ultimately for what was going on."

Shortly after Brandon was taken to the hospital, the movie crew had been formally told that the working session was finished, or "wrapped." By this time, news was getting around the studio about what had happened.

Ken Arlidge, on the second unit, shooting the rooftop fight sequence with Jeff Cadiente and Michael Wincott's stunt double, was told about Brandon's accident. "We heard that we should stop filming," Arlidge said, "that there'd been an accident on the set where the main unit were filming, and as we were dealt information, there was the confusion initially about what had happened, but that Brandon had been rushed off to the hospital and that he was being given CPR [cardiopulmonary resuscitation] as he was being carried to the ambulance."

Once the ambulance had left, Randy LaFollette thought it would be a good idea to give the crew some food. On a film set, the middle meal of a working session is quaintly known as "lunch," at whatever time it's eaten. LaFollette said, "We pulled everyone together and we were like, an hour away from lunch, and we said, 'Okay, the caterer's there.' Told the caterer to get ready to serve." Of course, the group's first concern was not their meal break. "Everyone wanted to know what was going on," LaFollette recalled, "and everyone wanted to know how Brandon was doing. We had to tell everyone to go home, and that we would be calling them." LaFollette himself was still stunned: "All I remember is that Steve Andrews and I went and sat in the office, silent. Hardly said a word to each other, just sat there in shock."

Arianne Phillips also hung around and found that the atmosphere was one of "chaotic tension. People weren't sure what was going on and they were trying to keep everyone real calm, the producers."

Larry Madrid's attitude was typical of the many concerned crew members who remained on stage 4: "Basically I watched, waited and watched the whole time, until the paramedics came in and put him on the stretcher, and then wheeled him down and out the stage door, in the ambulance and away. And then we just all kinda sat outside there, then kinda went, 'What did we just see? What's going on?' And after about an hour of contemplation, decided to go to the hospital."

Although most of the crew did go to the hospital, LaFollette did not do so. "There's nothing that I could do if I did go physically, to help Brandon."

Bob Rosen, as executive producer and the man in charge of the movie on the set, had already gone to the hospital but would be calling into the production office with news.

Determined to find out what had really happened, Jeff Imada had returned to the set as soon as the ambulance left the studio for the hospital, and said, "I got together with the prop guy and the effects guy and tried to figure out if anything else went wrong." According to Greg Gale, "They looked around and investigated the bag and everything. Jeff [Imada] was beside himself at that point. It was like, him and Brandon were very good friends. I mean, it's our accident. It's the emotion that was bothering him . . . what the hell happened!?"

Imada looked at the video recorded by the main camera over Michael Massee's shoulder, onto Brandon. One of the first things he looked for was where Massee had aimed the gun. To Imada, "It didn't seem like it was aimed directly at him. It didn't seem like it was intentional, like an aim, directly at the door, it was more like a waver across and he [Brandon] got shot. Because he [Massee] was playing like he was high or drunk or whatever." Imada also noted that Massee had always been extremely careful with the gun: "Massee was always very concerned about being safe. Even from the scenes before where he used the gun, he wanted to make sure everything was safe, everybody was comfortable. He was not like a hot dog or anything like that. Even if he was using the gun with a blank in it and aimed it at him, he was more than a safe distance away. It's very safe, as far as distance-wise, for the blank." After he had looked at the video, Jeff Imada said, "They took the videotape and the film footage and took it away, to lock it up."

The movie's management had already realized that, since some disastrous accident had happened to their star, they would have to do something about protecting the set physically, because although it may not have been a crime scene, it was certainly an accident scene. Rosen gave no instructions on what to do before he left, and Greg Gale now locked the set: "There had been an accident going on here and whatever might occur, you know, the evidence . . . We weren't even quite sure what had occurred. There was a crowd . . . a bullet? At that point there had been wild talk that had already started."

One of their first concerns was to examine the grocery bag with the squibs in it. Like everyone else, they thought at first that somehow the small explosive charges in the grocery bag had gone wrong and injured Brandon. So, they knew that bag had to be looked after. Gale made sure, "It was the first thing I locked down, the bag with the groceries in it that had the squib in it. But we had examined the bag. It didn't seem like anything was wrong with the bag. We investigated it for a little while and there was a little crease." He later realized that little crease was "like the bullet had actually sprayed across the bottom of the bag or the edge of the corner of the bag."

The film from the camera was also a crucial matter at this stage because it would presumably show exactly what had happened to Brandon. According to Gale, "Grant Hill, the production manager, finally took charge of the film and locked it up. I think it actually stayed on the set 'till the investigators came out, and at that point he stayed there for a couple hours, waiting for the investigators to come out."

As well as the film in the camera, of course, one of the most useful items in studying what had happened was the cassette in the video playback system. This system recorded through the camera lens, showing exactly what the main camera photographed on film. Before digital cameras, this allowed the director and his crew a way to immediately re-play the action of a take once it had been shot.

Robert Zuckerman was asked to take photos of the set, to document the layout of the scene and any specific piece of evidence: "I documented the squibbed grocery bag and the room and took . . . the evidence photographs, which I also gave to the production." Zuckerman was also aware that the production confiscated everything, including his film. "I never saw it, and I guess there were a couple of moments in the confusion, in the aftermath, they wanted me to process and bring it to them the next morning. And then a few minutes later they amended it and said, 'No, just give me the film out of your cameras.'" Bob Rosen also recalled this, and explained that there were no sinister motives for it, especially concerning the video cassette: "It was the first take and there had been video of the scene, what happened . . . But we wanted to be sure that went to the proper authorities. Certainly, nobody was going to attempt to put that in the movie or anything."

The first Wilmington police officer to arrive at the studio was Detective Rodney Simmons, who was soon joined by Detective Brian Pettus. Brian Pettus was, at first glance, a friendly and unthreatening man, but behind his personable manner was a shrewd and seasoned police officer.

Pettus, who was to take over the investigation of Brandon Lee's shooting, had had no previous dealings with the movie industry in Wilmington. Indeed, he had never even been to the studio. What's more, he said, "I had no idea about *The Crow* or who Brandon Lee even was, until I was called that night."

The police were shown what had happened by the prop master and the special effects technician. Pettus said, "When we got there, it was Kuttner and Bruce Merlin who stood by the set. That's who was there. That's who walked us through what had happened."

When JB Jones was woken up and told of the accident, he immediately went to the studio: "When they told me at home, when I was laying in the bed, I knew that there's no way that squib could do that to that man. And I knew it. But I said, 'Okay. So, I come back in the meantime.' What happens is, when you're on the set doing something like that, you always have a second sitting by, so that if the first take don't work, you got the second take to do it with."

Not surprisingly, Jones was anxious to show the police that his special effects could not have been responsible for Brandon's injuries. "I waited for the detectives, and everybody came, and I said, 'Okay, we're gonna explain to you the effects department did not do anything wrong here. What we're gonna do is, we're gonna re-do that shot for you just like it was before.' And they said, 'Okay, good.'"

Brian Pettus recalled that he was shown a grocery bag. "The bag had a squib in it that had exploded, simulating the grocery bag being shot through and the milk exploding out the bag." Jones was pleased with the effect of his demonstration: "So my man that works on the set [Merlin], he actually did [Brandon's part], walked in the door with the bag. We did a bang, and I shot the thing, and it blew up, and did it just like it had been done before. But it was okay. There was nothing wrong." He was right. Brian Pettus was convinced that, "Because there was no hole in the back of the bag, nothing had gone through the bag. And the bag was in front of him when he was shot, so something had to go under the bag, and nothing went through the bag from the squib."

Through this process of elimination, Pettus had quickly deduced that a bullet was fired into Brandon from the .44 Magnum: "We concluded, just from what we saw, that there had to be a bullet fired out of the gun. So, we took possession of it and everything that was there." During this part of the investigation, Pettus noticed that there was a marked difference in the attitude of the prop master, Kuttner, and the special effects technician,

Merlin. "Merlin was professional. Kuttner had worked on one movie as an assistant prop master before that and all of a sudden he's thrust into this."

Pettus knew that Brandon was in the hospital and that most of the crew had gone to the hospital. "So, we did our crime scene management–type thing. Had gone through and looked for other bullet holes and anything that might've been standing out. Couldn't find anything out of the ordinary. So, we just grabbed what we had, took some photographs of the set, and went out to the hospital."

There was as yet no news of Brandon's condition.

AT THE HOSPITAL 19

SOON AFTER BRANDON HAD ARRIVED at the Emergency Room of the
New Hanover Medical Center, the routine procedures revealed
beyond any doubt exactly what had caused his injuries. Clyde Baisey
had remained with Brandon, and he remembered, "They placed him on
a couple of units of blood, did an X-ray of his abdomen and everything
else. That's when the X-ray came back and they saw the projectile sitting
next to the spine."

Despite this discovery, the most serious aspect of Brandon's condition
continued to be the lack of blood circulation. One possible remedy for
this was to put pressure pants on him. These are inflated tightly around the
legs in the hope that the pressure will push the blood upwards through the
system, towards the heart. Baisey knew that, "To survive, Brandon didn't
need all the organs, but you gotta have the heart, and the lungs and brain.
So what you're trying to do is shove the blood from the lower half of the
body up to the upper part of the body."

However, the pressure pants, the units of blood, and the IVs could only
do so much to counteract Brandon's internal bleeding. The only remedy
left was surgery.

Fortunately, in the middle of that particular night, a surgeon just happened to be at the New Hanover Medical Center. The first task for surgeon Warren McMurry was to get Brandon's blood pressure stabilized, and
that was quickly done in the Emergency Room, where he was to undergo
no less than twelve hours of intermittent surgery. The medical team continued to give Brandon blood, because until they repaired the artery that
had been damaged by the gunshot, blood would continue to leak into his
lower body.

Gradually, members of the cast and crew arrived at the hospital, among them Robert Zuckerman, who noted, "At least fifty people were there that I could remember." Angel David said, "We sat in the waiting room the whole night and we just kinda talked with each other. Most people went to the hospital. It was very crowded and it was very sad. And people obviously in their own way praying and hoping and crying and comforting each other. And then we were there for hours and hours and hours." Laurence Mason recalled, "I felt strange, being there still in costume. It was weird." As soon as Jeff Imada had done everything he could at the studio, "Then I went to the hospital. I picked up my equipment, my gear and stuff, put it in the car."

But there was at least one person working on the movie, who had enormous affection for Brandon Lee, who *still* did not know what had happened. Rochelle Davis had been waiting in her trailer for the second unit to find the harness in which she was to hang from the church rooftop in the scene they were to shoot. Consequently, she didn't find out about Brandon's accident until after he had already been taken to the hospital. Davis was not happy about the way this happened. "Pauline [White], the costume lady at the time, came in. She was so sweet. She came in and said, 'What are you doing here?' And I'm like, 'Well, I'm waiting to go back on stage.' And she said, 'Nobody's going back on stage! Brandon got shot. Didn't you hear about this?'"

Although Davis had no idea how serious Brandon's injuries were, she got the impression that he was going to be in the hospital for some time, so she got a ride home to change into some more comfortable clothes. What she found at the hospital made a vivid impression on the thirteen-year-old. "There were so many people in that room," she said. "It was the biggest waiting room I ever saw in a hospital. It must've been made for a film crew. It was huge. Everybody was sitting on the floor, laying down on the floor or just waiting, just waiting to see what happens. We all kinda planned the idea that he was not gonna die. We were all kinda like, 'Okay, well, when he gets better . . .' Because we knew he liked Game Boy and he didn't have one, we were gonna go and buy him a Game Boy and bring it in, so when he was recovering he'd have something to do."

Greg Gale arrived at the hospital. When he saw the crew there, "It was," he thought, "the most touching thing. If Brandon had ever known, I think he would have been very touched by how much the crew really loved him."

About an hour and a half after Brandon was rushed to hospital, Jeff Imada decided that he would speak to Brandon's fiancée, Eliza Hutton, himself. "I called her to see how she was doing." Hutton had already returned to Los Angeles from Wilmington to make preparations for her wedding to Brandon. Imada had known her for a couple of years and felt that he, "Knew her fairly well, just from Brandon—from the time they started dating until they moved in together and then got engaged."

When Imada called Eliza Hutton, he assumed she had already been contacted by someone on the movie. "They said they were going to take care of it, and I just felt like I needed to talk to her because this is some-body that you're close to, you want to talk. But she had not been notified yet." So he spoke to Eliza in all innocence, telling her, "'There's been an accident' and she should get on a plane, and she goes, 'What are you talk-ing about?' I go, 'Well, Brandon's hurt and I think you should catch the next plane over here.' She goes, 'Is this an April Fool's joke? Did Brandon put you up to this?' I said, 'No, you should get over here.' She goes, 'How bad is it?' I said, 'You should definitely get on a plane.' And she caught the last plane. I guess she told the cab driver and the cab driver just broke every speed limit to get to the airport and she barely made the last flight over."

As the senior executive producer, Bob Rosen had made himself responsible for passing on the news of Brandon's condition to the people who were not there. "I was getting some information from time to time," Rosen said, "and passing it on to Brandon's fiancée, and to Ed [Pressman] and Janowitz [Pressman's personal lawyer], and all the people that were involved at that point. I don't know if I was in charge of anything. The person that was in charge was the surgeon, but I was in the outer room with everybody else, getting the information."

As the crew waited for news of Brandon's condition, there was natu-rally a lot of speculation about what exactly had happened to him. From what he had heard, like many others, Ken Arlidge had initially assumed that the injuries had been caused by the squib: "But when we heard about the bullet thing on the X-ray, we all started to question how the hell that got there." Jeff Most recalled, "It wasn't until he was in surgery that we found out that in fact it was not wadding, but a bullet fragment that had entered his abdomen." Jeff Imada had heard something similar, that the medical team, "noticed there was something lodged in his body." Arlidge said that the crew was given the news by the doctor that, "It looked as if there was a bullet lodged in Brandon's spine. Brandon lost a lot of blood and they had to replace a lot of blood and there was potential of many other things . . . brain damage and paralysis. The aorta [the major artery taking oxygenated blood from the heart to the rest of the body] had been severed as well."

In fact, Brandon had been hit in an extraordinarily critical spot. At the back of the body, near the lower spine, the major artery forks to supply blood to each leg. The bullet had entered Brandon's front abdomen, just below his belly button. It then had enough power to easily rip through all the organs and cut directly through the center of the fork of the artery. Finally, it hit his spine and stopped. If the bullet had been the slightest centimeter to the right or the left, his chances of survival would have been dramatically improved.

According to Chunky Huse, while waiting at the hospital, Daniel Kuttner made an astonishing admission: He had never cleaned the gun. "Daniel told me," said Huse, "in a flood of tears, that if anything happened to Brandon, 'I've killed him. I didn't check the gun. I didn't check the gun. I didn't check it.' And I went, 'What are you talking about?' He said, 'Second unit had the gun.' And I said, 'How long ago was that?' He said, 'Two weeks ago.' I said, 'Two weeks ago?!' I said, 'Two weeks and you haven't checked it?!' Oh God! Total incompetence."

Whether due to exhaustion from the long hours of production, lack of experience, or both, Imada pointed out this unfortunately fatal mistake was out of character for Kuttner. Imada recalled he had made a point to carefully observe Kuttner for the first several weeks of production to make sure he was handling weapons responsibly. "He was always very anal about it." Imada always observed him following the correct protocols and cleaning the weapons, but in the fateful scene, "He didn't check the barrel."

Bob Rosen was totally baffled by the accident, which bore no relationship to anything in his long experience of working on movies. Rosen had worked on many films, including Westerns, which had involved weapons of all kinds. In fact, just before *The Crow*, he had produced *Year of the Gun* (1991) and *Sniper* (1993): "If you'd been around as many action movies as I have, and cowboy movies and war movies and all those things, an accident has never, ever happened to my knowledge."

So they all sat around, talking about what could have possibly happened, and finally, Rosen said, "The prop man [Daniel Kuttner] came up with The Theory at four or five o'clock in the morning. And he came up to me, and . . . I said, 'Gee, that seems pretty far-fetched.' I said, 'We'll have to look into that, but I can't believe that that's how it happened.' And it turned out he was right!"

In his own way, Ken Arlidge, too, was beginning to work out how Brandon could possibly have been shot by a gun loaded only with blanks: "We started talking about the gun, and then we started talking about where the gun had worked last, that it was on set, and then that last time when it was used, it was used for second unit."

JB Jones and his crew were also at the hospital. They may have proved that their squib had not injured Brandon, but nevertheless, he was injured, and they were very distressed about it. Jones said, "We all naturally, everybody, felt terrible. Here's a situation where the man's laying there and he's dying and there's really nothing you can do about it. I mean, they're trying their best. They've given him I forget how many pints of blood." For some of the crew, Jones recalled, it was a time to turn to their faith in a higher power. "We had a sound man that was really religious, and we had prayer, and we did all we could really do for the whole thing. It was really a sad situation and it was a shame that it had to happen, but accidents happen."

The two policemen, Pettus and Simmons, had seen everything they needed at the studio, and it wasn't long before they arrived at the hospital. Detective Pettus remembered, "we talked to a couple of nurses and they said it was a gunshot. They had done an X-ray and the bullet was lodged in his spine. So, from that point you work your way back, trying to figure out how the bullet got in the gun. And talking to more and more people."

Pettus went straight to the man who had fired the gun, actor Michael Massee, and the man in charge of the weapon, Daniel Kuttner. Pettus remembers Massee told him, "He fired the gun and he didn't realize it was loaded. He said he didn't check to see if there was anything like rounds in the gun. And Daniel Kuttner said, 'I'd put blanks in the gun.' Nothing out of the ordinary." Charlene Hamer, Kuttner's assistant, told them "nothing of interest," according to Pettus. But Detective Pettus knew that this was only the beginning of a massive amount of work to discover the details of what had happened. "This was four to six months of investigation."

At about 4:00 a.m., someone from the production office called Brandon's mother, Linda Lee Caldwell, in Boise, Idaho. Until this point Brandon's mother had not been told of the seriousness of Brandon's injury. Now the news was that Brandon had gotten out of surgery and that the doctors were able to stop the bleeding and had repaired his aorta. The production office told Linda that she and Brandon's sister, Shannon, should come to North Carolina immediately. Linda, in Boise, and Shannon, in Los Angeles, jumped on the first planes they could find and headed for Wilmington. They changed planes several times and each time called in for updates.

Jeff Imada was close to Eliza, and he felt that it was right for him to do something for her. "And we were at the hospital, and I think Bob came over to me and said, 'We heard Eliza's on her way over here. I was wondering if you'd want to meet her at her layover to her connecting flight. We'll fly you over there.' I said, 'Sure, I'll go.'" Eliza called Arianne Phillips directly from the airport. "Eliza was freaking out because the plane she was getting onto didn't have a phone," Phillips remembered. "It was horrible, but I was trying to calm her down because I really didn't think it was going to be that bad. I didn't realize . . . I had no idea." Imada added, "At that point, they were operating on Brandon. I didn't want to leave, but at the same time they said, 'There's nothing different with his vital signs.' They were operating or just finished operating, and so I jumped on a plane, met Eliza and came back."

After the surgery, towards morning, the doctor announced that Brandon's condition didn't look good. Angel David recalled, "We kept getting little updates about how he was doing. And none of them were good." Lance Anderson was very depressed to hear, "There was nothing they could do. Yeah, he was dying. And I guess we all left. I don't know whether they told us he died then or . . . or we found out later. I mean, we knew he was gonna die." Ken Arlidge remembered the shock: "All of the crew members were there and a lot of us that developed a rapport with Brandon. Some were very close to Brandon, others of us had come to like him. And we then heard that he had died, very early in the morning, very difficult moment. So, we went home." The crew was overcome by a sense of despair, but once they had been told that Brandon was beyond medical help, they knew they could do no good by remaining at the hospital. Robert Zuckerman's feeling was typical: "When we left the hospital, he was still alive, but we were told the chances didn't look good, but they had done all they could."

For Laurence Mason, this had started out as a special day, and it was also ending as a special day, but not in a way he could have wanted, or could have anticipated. "That was my last night of shooting. I was done. I was wrapped. Mentally I'd been waiting to get out of there. We were there all night. Some people went to the chapel to pray. It was harsh. The sun started coming out, and my mom was a registered nurse and she's lost patients and I've seen her deal with that, and so something inside of me was like, it's time that I go back to the hotel. There's nothing else we can do."

Mason had left the hospital earlier than many others and went back to his room above Stimmerman's Bar to get some sleep. "I don't know if anybody else did, but I left. Took a cab back to the hotel. Once again, I'll say I'm not a superstitious person, but I think I saw his ghost that night. It scared the shit out of me. I'm laying down in the bed, I could've sworn I saw him in the corner for like five seconds. And I laid back down and I turn the radio on and sure enough they were reporting that he'd passed away."

At his home, Jeff Most finally heard the bad news: "I received a call from Grant Hill about it. I don't remember exactly the time, it was five, five-thirty in the morning, and I was told that . . . he had died on the operating table. And then I jumped in my car and met everyone at the office." Most was stunned by the loss of his friend and star. "We were all in shock. First off, we didn't allow our minds to go to the place that this was something life-threatening. I don't think any of us were prepared for the fact that it was anything more than a dummy wad that hit him."

Most recalled, "Initially, right away, I believed this was not in fact a gunshot wound, that had occurred . . . the wadding in the gun had been placed there [and] had in fact grazed the skin, knocked the wind out of Brandon. And that it was possible that along with the wadding, some sort of possible fragment from the box of groceries he was carrying that included cat food, which was sticking out of the bag originally hit that possibly grazed Brandon." It was not until later that morning, Most concluded, "I started to find out that there was a fragment in him, and the first words I heard was that it was internal bleeding."

When Jeff Imada left the hospital to meet Eliza, the news had not been so grim. "I think before I left they weren't sure. I don't think they said he was likely to die at that point. I think I found out when I got back." Now the news Imada heard was, "His body's playing catch-up to the damage." When they arrived at the hospital, the only people apart from Imada the doctors allowed in to see Brandon were Eliza and Brandon's stunt double and longtime friend, Jeff Cadiente. "When we got there he was still breathing," said Imada. "And we saw him first and then the doctor called us over. They called us in the other room, and during that time the doctor told her [Eliza] that it wasn't likely he was going to make it. And then they called the doctor out of the office. Because they said, 'Doctor, we need to see you.' So he just left. He said, 'I'll be back.'" As the three sat in the hospital waiting room, they were unaware that Doctor Warren McMurry was engaged in the final attempt to save Brandon's life.

When exactly Brandon Lee died seemed to be matter of interpretation by the crew. It was later learned that Brandon Lee had died several times in the hospital but had been resuscitated. This could have happened as his body went into shock. The doctors continued to replenish his hemorrhaging body with blood and fluid.

Shortly after they saw Brandon for the last time, at approximately 1:00 p.m. on March 31, he was pronounced dead. Eliza, accompanied by Brandon's two best friends on the movie, received this news from the doctor. "Eliza was understandably a wreck," Jeff Imada recalled. "So I was pretty much with her, right by her side."

For Linda Lee Caldwell and Shannon Lee, this was to be an even more harrowing experience. Due to the difficulties of getting flights and the different time zones, their journey had taken almost a day, and when the two women stepped off the plane in Wilmington, they were not expecting the worst. There had been talk about sending a driver to meet them, but Imada felt, "Somebody should go meet them. And she [Eliza] said, 'Well, I'll go with you, we'll go.' And so, we went and met them when they came off the plane." Somehow, due to the confusion and their many plane changes, Brandon's mother and sister had never been informed of just how serious Brandon's condition really was. Now, the news of his death came as a total shock.

Later that day, Clyde Baisey, who had tried so hard to save Brandon on the set, looked back, with the two paramedics who had been called to the studio, on what had happened at the hospital. "We all sat down," Baisey described. "We completely went through the whole call in our own minds. We discussed between the three of us what had transpired, what we did, what steps we took, what happened when we got to the Emergency Room. And we went through everything we had done, and there's not a single thing I could've done different, they could've done different, the Emergency Room staff could've done different, or anybody on the surgical staff could've done different. I mean, everything was done that could possibly be done." Baisey was sure that his colleagues and his city had done as well by the injured young movie star as was humanly possible. "Yes, in Wilmington, we're a relatively small town. We're third in the nation in the film industry. We do a lot of different things here. But as far as the level of care that Brandon received or anybody else received on the set during the filming, I do not believe they could've gotten any better anywhere else."

FIRST REACTIONS   20

AFTER BRANDON HAD DIED, the movie production office made arrangements to inform everyone who was working on the film. The office notified the department heads, who were then expected to call their crews.

The news hit people hard. Randy LaFollette said, "You can't figure out why this has happened, and you're physically tired and emotionally tired without this. And then this happens and it's just the worst feeling." Like many others, LaFollette was overwhelmed by the unreasoning nature of Brandon Lee's death. "He was the type of person that you just loved, and was just such a good-hearted person, that out of anybody for something to happen to, why was it Brandon?"

It was the bizarre nature of what had happened that struck Chunky Huse. "We pull out guns, we shoot people, they fall on the ground in a pool of blood, somebody says, 'Cut!' And they get up, wipe the blood off, and say, 'How was that?' and 'You want to do it again?' And when they don't get up."

"The news," Jeff Imada felt, "devastated everybody. Total shock. People were in shock and just felt it was like a bad dream and couldn't believe that he was gone, that this all happened, how it happened."

Earlier on the morning of March 31, Arianne Phillips had caught her plane back to Los Angeles as scheduled. Everyone had encouraged her to go, telling her, "He's fine. You gotta get on the plane. You gotta go." Anxious to hear how Brandon was doing, Phillips called the production office as soon as she got off the plane in Los Angeles, "Because he would have been out of surgery by then, and they said, 'He's fine, everything's fine.'" Later, she heard about Brandon's death in an unexpected and unpleasant way. She called a mutual friend of hers and Eliza's in New York, to warn her that Brandon had been seriously injured and that Eliza would need all the support they could give her, but her friend told her that she had already spoken to Eliza. "So, I called the production office," Phillips continued, "and they said he was fine and that's all they said, and it was someone I knew at the production office. And then I called my friend in New York and she was hysterical, and I said, 'He's fine. I just called the production office.' And she was going, 'He's dead. He's dead. He's dead!'" This was so unexpected that the stunned Phillips fainted at the airport.

When Greg Gale heard that Brandon had died, he was at the end of a very long day. He went back to his apartment in Wrightsville Beach to tell his roommate, production accountant Bill Rose, what had happened. "Rose was asleep through this whole thing, because he works days. And I had come home: 'I have some bad news for you.' He thought I was kidding with him, and we'd usually joke around and things, but it was just like, 'I'm not kidding with you!' I had to grab him and say, 'No, I'm not kidding with you, this really happened.'"

Ernie Hudson had gone to Minnesota for the funeral of his brother-in-law and, in that already stressful situation, learned of Brandon's death just as he and his wife were facing up to their personal bereavement: "We heard that Brandon had been shot, and that just didn't seem possible. I mean, I had done a lot of movies and nobody really gets hurt to that extent. I heard about it from a friend in LA who called and asked me, 'What's up with your boy, Brandon?' I think [that] was the way he put it. And I had no idea. He had, I guess, heard the news, but I hadn't heard. So, for the longest time it seemed really . . . it just didn't seem like it was possible. Then you go into the anger and you go into, 'How could this happen?' and, 'Somebody has to be to blame.'"

Somehow, Sofia Shinas was left off the list of people to be told of Brandon's death, and finally, she said, "I called production and I said, 'What happened?' They said, 'We lost him.' They said, 'Unfortunately, Brandon is no longer with us.'"

"Then it was mass hysteria," recalled Jeff Most. "I mean, the outpouring of emotion is never anything that I'd been party to in my life. I never in my adult life then lost anyone as close to me as Brandon Lee. We had a very young crew. I don't think, to my recollection, anyone had lost a parent, brother, sister . . . I don't know. For all of us it was one of the most tragic moments in any one of our lives. We literally . . . a hundred people were in tears for three days or more."

Bob Rosen and Alex Proyas met at the studio, where after some discussion, Rosen said, "We swore that we would not try to finish the picture and that we wanted no part of anybody trying to finish the movie or cash in on anything. And both of us, and it was a highly emotional, *highly* emotional meeting for both of us, we said, 'We're just not going to be a part of that.'"

After hearing of Brandon's death, Rochelle Davis recalled that a group of the actors went to a local restaurant and talked about whether they wanted to finish the movie: "We were trying to decide, because the crew and the director and everybody didn't know what they were gonna do about the situation, if they were gonna finish filming. And we all got together and decided to at least put our part in and say to Alex, 'You know, Brandon really cherished this role. He really was very excited about it. Even though he died, I'm sure he would want his name to live on. And this is something he was really proud of himself for doing. And it should be released so that people can see how great he was, and how good he did that job.'" With actor David Patrick Kelly as their spokesman, they went to the studio and asked to see Proyas and Rosen.

"What they said was we had to finish the picture," remembered Rosen, "because we had seen dailies every night, and we knew how good Brandon was in this movie, and this was his legacy. And that in order for the rest of the world to know that this was his legacy, we had to finish the picture. And voices sounding remarkably like Alex's and mine said, 'Yeah, you're absolutely right.' Just after, two minutes before, saying we weren't going to do it! And I think that argument was the only argument that saw us through the next six months: for the world to know who Brandon Lee really was, we had to show them and finish this movie. Boy, during the darkest of the darkest times, you had to fall back on that the whole way or I don't think we could have gone through with it."

Jeff Most didn't want to put any pressure on Alex Proyas. "By no means did anyone wish to ask him to complete it. The attorneys were into it. The insurance company acted like an angel and said, 'You can put this on the shelf, it never has to be released. We'll pay everything off that has to be paid off. Or if you want, we'll give you whatever it takes to finish it. It's totally your decision.' It was amazing."

That very day, Robert Zuckerman, wanting, he said, "To put some words to the moment . . . to help allay the shock and the despair of people around the set and the office, to put some perspective on it" wrote a poem, expressing his feelings about Brandon Lee's death:

And he has left us,
Yet in his absence,
His presence is
And shall be
Stronger than ever.
For he is
Everywhere now,
And he is
Inside of us.
We, who witnessed
The brilliance
Of his flame
And were warmed
By its heat;
We, who heard
The chimes
Of his churchbell laughter
Ring the plains
Of starry dawns;
We, who stand
In the pure rain
Of his divine
And noble spirit
Are now its
Blessed, honored keepers.
Within and through us
He shall live on
And our lives
Shall ever be enriched
By him
In ways
Wondrous and untold.
Fly high, dear friend.

Robert Zuckerman
31 March 1993

His poem was well received by his colleagues.

The disoriented crew and cast, so many of them away from home, began to call Nini Rogan and ask her where they could meet, since they didn't want to spend this distressing time in their rented apartments. The warmhearted Rogan instantly invited everyone to her house. Slowly, crew and cast members gathered there.

When those at Rogan's house realized that nobody had called Michael Wincott, who had already finished shooting and had left Wilmington, they desperately tried to reach him before he heard the news from some cold-blooded source. But they were too late, he had already been told. Nevertheless, Rogan remembered, "Probably twenty of us talked to him. It was extraordinary. The neighbors were letting us use their phones so that people could call their families. It was unbelievable."

Talking to Wincott had a profound effect on Michelle Johnson. "I lost it. It just kinda hit me. It's when I heard Michael's voice. And I don't know why it took Michael's voice to sort of do that to me. Maybe it was just because he was one of my favorite people on that whole show."

At Nini's house, the group bonded as never before: "Suddenly the men were taking care of getting the ice and the coolers and the beer and whatever," said Rogan. "Setting up in the backyard, doing all that stuff. And the women brought food and started cooking. I mean it was just like a wake. None of this was set up. This all just happened on its own when word got around that you come to Nini's and Chunky's. They did."

Chunky Huse was even surprised at the response of his neighbors. "People were out in the street. The house was not big enough and everybody was in the street. And my neighbors even opened up their homes for the bathrooms for people."

By chance, Rochelle Davis' grandmother, who was acting as her guardian on the movie, was a professional counselor. That evening, according to Rogan, "She actually sat everybody down in the living room at one point and said, 'Okay, anybody wanna tell me how you feel? Anybody wanna say anything?' Well, that started it!" It was a chance, as Huse recalled, "For us all to talk about it, get it out, let everybody have a good cry or whatever they wanted to do."

A very disturbed Massee also showed up at Huse's house. "He was crying his eyes out," recalled Huse. "He was in a bad way, because he was told not to point the gun at him." From Huse's house, Massee called his brother to tell him about the accident, and to Michelle Johnson's amazement his brother joked, "'Well, you know, that's no way to get a leading part, just to shoot your leading man.' He said something really insane like that!" But Johnson felt that this bad-taste joke was, "The only thing that saved him. I mean, the guy was in shock. I've seen people even from accidents being in shock. You know what I mean? These people that have been injured. And he was in such shock, it was unbelievable. Poor guy."

The entire crew was concerned for Massee because whatever had happened, they were sure that the accident was not his fault. But they also had no idea how to console him. "Nobody knew what to do," said Darryl Levine. "There's no book for that." Even the young Rochelle Davis was mindful of the pressure on Michael Massee. "I think he had it the worst. He was really a mess. A total mess. And I felt horrible because it wasn't his fault. And it had to have felt like it was. I mean, when you pull a trigger and somebody dies from it, even though you didn't know it was going to happen, you still feel responsible for that. And I think that's how he felt. And I thought that was really unfair."

But after learning the news of Brandon's death, not everyone wanted to get together and share their pain. Laurence Mason left as soon as he could: "I called the production and I said, 'I gotta get out of here. You gotta release me. You gotta let me go.' And they did. They were really cool about it. They got me on a plane that night." Mason went to the airport and caught the first flight he could, which turned out to be the most nerve-wracking flight of his life back to New York. "I took a little two-propeller plane, in this huge storm, sitting in the window seat, scared. Lightning, it was like the movie. Scary!"

Michelle Johnson remembered that many people were in disbelief because there was no body, no physical evidence that the young man who had been the focus of their attention and affection for so many weeks was really gone. "There's something about that, seeing is believing. Or at least, even if you don't see the body, even if there's just a funeral service, it's kinda like it's an ending. It puts all that craziness to an end. You can sort of put it away and go, 'Okay, it's all right.' You know, people for months and years just didn't deal with his death and had no way of dealing with it. And part of it, I think, [is] if they would've just simply had some kind of a service or something. And I think a lot of those rituals for funerals come from that. It's just hard for your mind to believe that that person is no longer there."

The media was very quickly onto the story of Brandon Lee's shooting. There's always money to be made from selling such a story, and the theory among the crew was that one of the extras had made such a sale. But since the media had obtained a list of all the crew and their phone numbers, it seems more likely that the culprit would have been someone from the production department.

For most people on the crew, it was their first direct contact with a full media onslaught, and they were astonished and outraged by it. "It was unbelievable," Chunky Huse thought. "Geraldo [Rivera] was on the phone to me! It was unbelievable. Everybody was phoned. Somebody on that crew had leaked to the media a crew list with *everybody's* phone numbers." When journalists and camera crews came to Huse's house, they got a very hostile reception: "My grip crew threatened that they were going to break their legs if they didn't turn around and go away. The media took one look at them and they left. My crew are bikers."

But it was a hot story, and the media continued to hound many crew members. Darryl Levine was, "Getting calls. I mean, 'Stop it! You're not gonna get any information out of me that you wanna hear.' They wanna know the cause. They wanna know who's to blame. They wanna know this, they wanna know that. 'What was it really like? You were there. Tell us who was there.'" Levine was offered a lot of money for his story. "But," he said, "it wasn't something you wanted to deliver. You just wanted to get on with this. I just wanted to finish it."

At the studio, they quickly realized that the media was chasing the story. Jeff Most recalled, "All of a sudden the phone starts ringing off the hook from the press. There are camera crews outside the gate. And on top of all the grief we were sharing, we were all of a sudden the focus of a great deal of attention that was very disruptive."

When Greg Gale returned to the studio in the early afternoon, the media had already started to arrive, and with them the proliferation of wild theories about Brandon Lee's death, many of which persist to this day. "We had heard reports from the production office about New York papers or New York media thinking that there was ninjas in the rafters of the stage. . . . The curse of his father . . . I mean, the Chinese Mafia, etcetera." Bob Rosen heard that it was, "A Red-Chinese plot. Lots of things had happened, and it was the same people that killed Bruce Lee. . . . And it was all nonsense. So, everybody had their own theory. They still do. I mean, I still hear stories about the real insight into that incident. The idea that Brandon was playing a character who dies and comes back to life and so forth, and then this accident occurred. It's extraordinary."

Greg Gale heard that, "A couple of reporters had gotten successfully onto the lot. One that I could remember, that had actually gotten into the production office, I'm sure through one of the back doors, and started asking questions, and I realized who she was. And you know, she was invited to leave. Myself, I was not chased down by the media. I guess I was one of the fortunate ones."

Bob Rosen suddenly found himself, "In an office where there's helicopters flying outside the window, in Wilmington! . . . and news people at the gate and so forth. And we were always concerned about the security of the editing rooms. We didn't want to get any film stolen."

Ironically, that morning IATSE Union reps from New York, who had flown in the evening before, were planning to picket outside the front gate and rally support to unionize the non-union studio. The tragedy naturally upended their plans.

The next day, Ed Pressman arrived in Wilmington and, with Rosen and Alex Proyas, held a meeting to announce that the insurance company had told them that they could abandon the film, or if they wanted to finish it, the company would support them. They explained that they had been talking to Brandon's family, and that they were going to leave the decision to them.

Nini Rogan recalled that Proyas felt that he had to say something, however difficult it was for him. "Proyas said how deeply . . . how distraught he was." Rogan knew that, "Alex was not at the best of times able to communicate that strongly. There was no one who blamed him for that, because he was in total shock and pain. He'd become very close to Brandon during all the time they spent together prior to shooting, which had been a very long time, months. And I think they had kindred spirits."

A few days later, Greg Gale found himself, "Locking this thing up and shutting it down and going on a hiatus. And we didn't know if we were going to come back and do it or not, but we were going on a hiatus to see what we had got."

INVESTIGATIONS   21

A LTHOUGH IT WAS NOT KNOWN at the time, there were two simultaneous investigations of the shooting of Brandon Lee. In addition to the one carried out by the Wilmington Police Department, Ed Pressman's personal lawyer, James Janowitz, conducted his own inquiries.

It was natural that Pressman would call Janowitz as soon as he heard of the accident, at which point Brandon was still alive. As soon as Janowitz got to Wilmington, it was apparent to him that, "Nobody knew what had happened." So his first move was to go to the set. "I looked at where people were. Had the scene re-enacted . . . My investigation went faster than the police. I checked the sight lines. I mean, there were wild thoughts. I checked to see whether it *could* have been a sniper. Walked the set, picked up pieces of debris. I've done some criminal work. Not a lot. I represented Sid Vicious after the murder of his girlfriend [Nancy Spungen]. Anyway, I did my investigation and interviewed the members of the crew, which was difficult also. Some people didn't want to talk to me. They were getting lawyers. They were afraid for potential liability."

Janowitz heard all the rumors, "about it being a supernatural event and the curse of Bruce Lee, all of that." He did little, he said, "To dissuade anyone who might've been heading in that direction. Because from the liability perspective, if it had been caused by the supernatural, it was a better situation for us." But soon, Janowitz said, "During the course of one interview, somebody told me about a rumor, and that turned out to be the most important information. It explained what happened."

Janowitz listened to what everyone said and, after a couple of days, he admitted, "I figured out rather quickly the reasonable hypothesis of what had gone wrong, which I shared with Ed."

At the same time, the police were proceeding with their own investigation. In dealing with Brandon's death, Detective Brian Pettus said they "treated it as a homicide until we knew differently." But establishing whether it was a homicide was going to be a complex process, because the chain of events that led to Brandon's death was tangled.

The police had started by talking to people at the hospital, including Michael Massee, who they now knew had fired what had proved to be a fatal shot. "He said he fired the gun and he didn't realize it was loaded." People kept asking Pettus, since he knew who had fired the shot, why Massee was not charged with anything. But Pettus already knew that Massee was not responsible for Brandon Lee's death. "Massee knew absolutely nothing," said Pettus. "The guy put the gun in his hand. Yeah, maybe he has a responsibility to check the gun, but if he has no knowledge of guns, he's trusting this guy to be safe. That's what an actor does. He trusts some people to do their job." Pettus felt sorry for the actor's situation. "I didn't fault him at all for anything. He was very remorseful at the hospital. He had the weight of the world on his shoulders."

A later conversation only served to make Massee's total innocence clearer in Pettus' mind. "Massee said, 'Nobody ever told me not to point the gun at him [Brandon].' And if you watch the film, him getting shot by that gun would be like me pointing my finger across there and shooting you. It was just a freak thing. He was just waving the gun around. Just waving around and pulled the trigger. It was just, randomly. It was an unlucky shot." Indeed, it did seem to be the case that while waving the gun around, by an awful chance, Massee had pulled the trigger at the precise instant when it was pointing at the part of Brandon's body where it could do the most damage.

But this still left a major puzzle: How had someone been fatally shot by a gun that everybody was sure was loaded with a blank?

JB Jones, who had supplied the gun, said he knew, "There couldn't be anything wrong with the weapons, because of the fact that a .44 Magnum is a .44 Magnum. I mean, that's the simplest weapon that you could possibly have!" Although Jones had supplied the guns, it was the responsibility of the property department to look after them. Jones recognized the limitations of the prop staff, and he had helped them out when he had time: "They weren't experienced . . . They did their jobs like they were supposed to, but they didn't do some of the things. They didn't take very good care of the weapons. And I'd go in there and look at 'em and I'd clean them myself, because a gun that's not clean won't work." At that point, Jones' concern was purely that, "I didn't want to wind up with a bunch of rust. Rust is hard to bring back home!" It had not occurred to anyone that safety was an issue.

Pettus continued with his interviews, and within the next two days he got some "anonymous information" that, "There may have been some rounds that were made. So we went and asked them [Merlin, the special effects technician in charge of the squibs, and Daniel Kuttner, the prop master] about it. And then the whole story came out." What Pettus was told was to be the key to understanding how Brandon had been shot: Some members of the crew had made blank and dummy rounds from real bullets.

In the meantime, Pettus had talked to Wilmington's Assistant District Attorney, John Carricker, who had sent the fatal bullet over to the State Bureau Investigations Department in Raleigh. They came back with some very interesting information for Carricker: "They found black powder. That's right. Significance is, it's *black* powder. The only way black powder could have been on the back of the bullet was, black powder fired the bullet out. The only way *black* powder could've fired the bullet out is if they had a *blank* in there." Black powder is used in blanks instead of the usual explosive, because it produces the flash flame from the end of the barrel that moviegoers like to see.

Pettus now had to discover where the gun had been before the fatal shot and when it had last been used. Daniel Kuttner told Pettus, "The gun had been 'secure' in his truck since the second unit had used it for filming. That was a surprise to us. Number one, they never told us anyone had used the gun. As far as we knew this [the scene when Brandon was shot] is the first time this gun had been used."

Now that Pettus knew that the gun *had* previously been used by the second unit, he went to question second unit director Andrew Mason, while general manager of the studios for Carolco, Keith Wally, questioned the production's other lawyer. "We asked them who was on the second unit. And their answer to that was, 'What's the second unit?' We already had the names of the people who were on the second unit and we knew what had been heard or what had transpired and their answer was, 'What's the second unit? We'll have to check and see if there was a second unit.'" This irritated Pettus, who not only had a list of who was on the second unit but had already talked to them all. As he observed, philosophically, "Thing about police work, you don't ask questions you don't know the answers to." Pettus said he then asked Grant Hill, "If he had knowledge of a second unit doing any filming with any weapons? Hill said he did not, and Mr. Wally said that he had heard nothing about that either. And this was on the sixth [of April]." Pettus had to wonder if they were being deliberately obstructive. "You had a lot of people who were scrounging around trying to salvage their careers," he decided. "They've been attached to this movie, and they had so many mishaps and now there's a death. They were trying to distance themselves from it."

Randy LaFollette felt that one of the problems was that the police simply didn't understand, "When you set up a film production company, that people have different responsibilities in different companies. It depends on how they want to set their company up. They [the police] thought it was all clean-cut. On some shows you have an armorer all the way through, some shows the prop guys handle the weapons, some shows, the special effects people. It just depends how you choose to set that up. And they didn't understand that."

Pettus decided to go back and talk to Kuttner again on April 6. Kuttner, Pettus said, told him that, "He had a conversation with Ken Arlidge, and Arlidge had told him about the sound he heard when the weapon was being fired [the last time the second unit had used the gun]. And that's when we went back and talked to Arlidge later on."

Ken Arlidge had completely forgotten about the sound he had heard until the afternoon of March 31, the day Brandon had died. Arlidge had gone for a walk on the beach that day, trying to make his own peace with Brandon's death, when a disturbing recollection came to him. This was about something that had happened a couple of weeks earlier, when the second unit was shooting a close-up of bullets being loaded into the chamber of the Magnum. When the gun was fired, "I remembered hearing this cap sound [a bullet's primer detonating]," Arlidge said. "And for some reason, at that time, my mind jumped back to the one time I had been to a gun range in the past, and I had fired a .44 Magnum revolver, which was, I believe, very similar to the one that we were using. And I remember pulling the trigger and the bullet didn't fire. And I eventually took it back up to the guy at the front desk and he said, 'Oh no. Just put it back in and pull the trigger a few more times on it. It's a faulty primer.' And sure enough, I did; I pulled it a couple more times and eventually the bullet fired into the target."

Dummy bullets had been used for shooting the second unit close-up. Usually dummy bullets are just that: bullet cases with no explosive or primer, so they can't possibly detonate. But at the hospital the morning after the shooting, Arlidge had heard for the first time that the dummy bullets they had filmed had been made from *real* bullets. Afterwards he had remembered hearing that "cap sound" (the sound of a bullet's primer detonating) as they filmed the Magnum's chamber. For the first time, he realized what that sound was: As they had filmed the gun, one of the dummy bullets in the chamber had detonated. Arlidge then put two and two together.

Hearing all this, Pettus had to find out why the dummy bullets were made by the crew from real bullets. The usual practice on movies is to *buy* dummy bullets, which are cheap, and since real bullets are strictly prohibited on all movie sets.

"We found out," Pettus said, "that when they dressed the set up for one of the scenes, they rented a bunch of items from a local business. They go in, they just cleared out the room, they rented or they might've bought them." A set decorator, Marthe Pineau, had bought a box of live ammunition totally by chance, and that box had then been innocently placed among all the objects on the pawnshop set. "They didn't look to see what was in the box," Pettus said. "It was a real box of bullets, and they looked real. But Imada saw it and I guess he was curious, and he looked and he saw the live rounds inside of it. So, he got upset about it and had them taken off the set. And he put them in the trunk of his car, to get 'em off the set! Well, couple of weeks go by. Nobody could give us a time, exact date that they found them [the real bullets], and nobody could give us the exact date that they made them [the blank and dummy bullets]." Pettus went through the movie's schedule and talked to crew members, but he never could figure out the exact dates of all this. But at least he knew where the real bullets came from.

Next Pettus had to find out when dummy bullets had first been needed. He soon learned that for the scene at the Pit Bar, in which Top Dollar's bad guys sit around pretending to swallow live bullets, the crew had needed both candy bullets and dummy bullets. He was told, "They put the candy bullet in their mouth. This is a little bit of deception. They had the real [dummy] bullet in their hands, but then they turned off and put the candy bullet in their mouth."

But why were the dummy bullets made, and not bought, in the usual way? Pettus believes that the dummy bullets had not been obtained in advance by the prop crew and now they were needed quickly. Now an element enters Pettus' account that is not corroborated on the record: He believes that the crew was under severe time pressure. Pettus said that he was "told by some of the people who were working on the set," that the completion bond company was in Wilmington, "to make sure that it [the movie] is gonna be completed on time, it was gonna be completed on budget." But Pettus was never able to get an admission from the production that a completion bond executive was ever in town. "That was a kinda crossroads in the investigations, because if we could've gotten Grant Hill or Keith Wally or Pressman or Rosen to say, 'Yeah, completion bond company was here, yeah, we were over budget and, yeah, we were behind time,' *that* would've been a good element as far as criminal proceedings, because then you're gonna rush, and that would be your reason for cutting lines. But they would never admit there was a completion bond company in town. They would never admit it."

Pettus' sources were "the guys that know what's going on. The workers, they know what's going on." But, Pettus added, "They didn't wanna go on record, because it was their butts if they got caught telling us. But they were coming forth and telling us these things. They're usually the people who had no knowledge what went on, but when asked about the case they would tell us, 'There were these guys in town. They wanna make sure.' We said, 'What kinda guys?' The completion bond company. And they would tell us about it."

The only corroboration of this possible pressure comes from Jeff Most, who acknowledged that, "We did cause concern to the bond company. *That* I remember. There was a bond company representative that we would see on location. I don't remember if he was physically there when the tragedy occurred, but I mean, we had run into concern because we were running through our contingency; the monies that are allowed, ten percent of your production budget, which are there for the purpose of allowing for poor weather, things falling behind etcetera."

Pettus talked to a local gun dealer about dummy bullets and was told, "We could've gotten 'em in town overnight for about twenty dollars." But, as Pettus understands it, the crew were under pressure: "They had to improvise, instead of waiting and filming some other scene. They could've gone to another scene, in my opinion. Or they could've just waited. They were pushing for time. They couldn't stall the scene. They didn't wanna spend the money on bullets, because they were running behind. And Bruce Merlin was gonna be a trouper and say, 'I can save this money and I can save us time. Let's just make them!'"

In fact, although typically dummy bullets are bought from a gun dealer, to ensure their quality, Bruce Merlin's experience as a special effects technician did qualify him to make the dummy bullets from the real ones. So, knowing they needed dummies for the bullet-swallowing scene, Merlin told Pettus that he said, "'We can make some.' So, they went back and made the dummy bullets in the back of Kuttner's truck. While they're doing this, [Merlin says,] 'You're gonna need some full-load blanks, so just go ahead and make those too.' Kuttner says, 'You know, I'm real uneasy about this whole thing.'" Kuttner was uneasy because what they were doing was pulling the bullet apart with pliers, emptying out the explosive powder and then detonating the primer. Pettus said, "They didn't have the proper tools. All they had was a pair of pliers. And they just pull them out, like you pull a tooth out." Kuttner was concerned that doing this clumsily could have caused an explosion.

Whether it was pressure from the completion bond company's presence or not, the fact is that dummy bullets and blanks *were* made by the crew from real bullets. The dummies were made by pulling the lead tip off, emptying out the explosive [the powder], and detonating the firing cap [the primer] at the base of the bullet, which can be simply done by hitting it with a hammer. The lead tip would then be put back on, creating an object that looks like a real bullet, but which is completely safe. The blanks were made by emptying out the explosive and replacing it with black powder for the visual flash, but *not* detonating the primer, because it would be needed to ignite the powder. And of course, the lead tip was not re-attached, while a piece of wadding was stuffed into the tip.

Pettus' theory of the beginning of the fatal error is that the dummy bullets and the blanks became mixed up, possibly at some point during the process of converting the real bullets into dummies and blanks. As a result, one of the blanks, a "quarter-load blank" with very little explosive in it, was mistaken for a dummy, and its lead tip was re-attached. This would have created a bullet that looked like a dummy bullet, but which could eject its tip, albeit at very low velocity and enough to lodge it in the barrel of a gun. Pettus is very clear on this: "When they made the dummy bullet, they put a lead tip back into a quarter-load blank. That was a screwup. That was the bullet that went into the gun." This was the same gun that would later go into Funboy's hand and which was the one the second unit had been using to shoot the close-up of the Magnum's chamber revolving.

Pettus said that what happened then was, "They got the picture of the six bullets in the cylinder, the dummy bullets, and they're shooting down the barrel and watching the cylinder turn in a close-up. That's when the pop and fizz went off." This was the "cap sound" that Ken Arlidge heard but thought nothing of at the time. The problem was that nobody who heard that "pop and fizz" at the time really knew what it was. "At that time, one of the guys opens up the cylinder, [and] looks at it," Pettus recounts. "Had no idea what he's looking at really. He's looking at it, he sees all the caps in there, and he's thinking, 'Well, it looks okay to me.' But if they turned it over, looked the other way, they'd have seen one of the bullets missing [its lead tip] out of one of the cartridges. But they didn't think to look, 'cause they didn't know what they were doing. On the second unit, they had nobody that knew anything about handguns. I mean, they're just passing this gun all over the place to people who don't know what to do with it. Which is negligent."

It was that "pop" that Ken Arlidge remembered on his lonely walk on the beach. When he put that together with his other experience with a Magnum, he knew what had happened: that the "pop" had been the primer exploding. It had then ignited the quarter-load blank that they all thought was a dummy, with only enough energy to push its lead tip into the barrel of the gun. But tragically, it remained there, unnoticed, until after it had been shot, by the full-load blank, which contained enough explosive to propel the lead tip much farther and faster than the quarter-load blank had, and into Brandon. As he worked this out, Arlidge said, he was so shocked that he collapsed on the beach: "I fell to my knees and dry retched a couple of times."

Pettus now knew how the lead bullet tip that had killed Brandon had found its way into the gun barrel. But how had it remained there undiscovered?

He interviewed Merlin and Kuttner once again and was disappointed because, "Unless you asked 'em a specific question, you weren't gonna get a specific answer." So, he did ask them specific questions, and he found out a little bit more about who had done what: "Once the bullets are made, Merlin's out of it. Kuttner supplied the gun and the dummy rounds to the second unit for that [Magnum chamber close-up] scene. Then the gun goes back on the truck and is locked up for a couple of weeks."

Kuttner remained in Wilmington while this was investigated. In any event, Pettus knew where he lived. "Lived in Virginia. We had his home number and address and everything. We could've talked to him. He wasn't trying to hide anything, I don't believe. In fact, out of all the people, as culpable as he was in the whole thing, he was probably the most honest about what happened, to the best of his knowledge.

"He really didn't know what he was doing when it came to a gun. In one interview, we showed him a photograph of a gun, in fact the gun that was used, and said would he name the part of the gun? He points to that part of the gun and . . . he had no idea what we were talking about. And Charlene [Hamer, the assistant prop master] was the same way. They had no knowledge of weapons whatsoever. But they were in charge of them." So Pettus was not surprised that when Hamer went to get the Magnum from the prop truck for the scene of Eric Draven's shooting, "She didn't think to check it. The gun was not checked before it was taken to the set. Nobody looked at it." Pettus remained sympathetic to them. "I just think they wanna make it right. They really didn't know enough to hide anything."

So now we have the gun, with the lead tip that had been lodged in the barrel during the second unit close-up, heading for the set, for its fatal rendezvous with the movie's star.

The real .44 Magnum was used for the rehearsals, but it wasn't loaded. After the rehearsals, Daniel Kuttner showed Michael Massee that he was putting a blank in the gun, a full-load blank as requested by Alex Proyas, who wanted to see as much fire come out of the barrel as possible. This was perfectly normal filming practice. As Pettus said, "That's a director's call. If there hadn't been a bullet [tip] in the gun, lodged in the barrel, it wouldn't've been a problem."

Then the gun was fired, with fatal consequences, when the full-load blank exploded the bullet tip from where it was lodged in the barrel.

This was precisely the scenario that James Janowitz had come up with. And the police confirmed their theory with the results from the laboratory at State Bureau Investigations Department in Raleigh. Pettus remembered, "They sent the gun off. We said, 'This is how they made 'em, this is what we think happened, see if it can happen.' They did the testing. The guy made a quarter-load blank, just like they said they made. He fired it in the gun, the bullet lodged halfway up the barrel . . . wouldn't come out. See, you gotta have enough gas to force the bullet through the barrel, just force it through. And if you don't have enough, it's not gonna come out. So, it lodged in there." The first half of the story was proved. The second part was just as easy: "He made a full-load blank, fired it [the Magnum used on the movie]. They shot into a gelatin pack which is equivalent to your body. It went right in."

The Assistant District Attorney, Carricker, pinpointed the two occasions on which routine cleaning would have saved Brandon: "If someone had cleaned the weapon after that [second unit] shooting, just simply put a rod down the barrel, nothing would've happened. When they started to use the weapon in the scene in which he was shot, if they had cleaned it then, or looked down the barrel, nothing would've happened."

Looking back on the tragedy of Brandon Lee's death, Ken Arlidge thought that it could have been avoided by making sure that, "The people who are handling potentially life-threatening tools, whether it be weapons or explosives or the design of the stunt, the people handling those have to be focused only on that particular event. That should be their point of focus. They should not be juggling props as well and worrying about whether a chair is sitting right in the corner of the room, when they have a weapon on the set."

Detective Pettus' final judgment on Daniel Kuttner was, "He was very up front, and very honest about it. I don't fault Kuttner, I fault him for getting a little bit over his head in something that he couldn't do. But then you gotta put the blame on people that hired him. They knew what his qualifications were and put that much responsibility on him. Whatever reason he got the job, that falls back on them. If somebody came and offered you a great job, would you turn it down just because you didn't know everything about the job, or would you say, 'Well, I can learn'? You can't fault him. For the amount of money he was making, it was obscene."

According to *Variety*, in July 1993 Jerry Spivey, District Attorney for North Carolina's Fifth Prosecutorial District, which includes Wilmington, decided not to bring criminal charges against crew members. He said they were apparently careless, but not sufficiently so to warrant charges. Some weeks later a follow-up article reported Spivey stating that he had found no evidence of the "willful and wanton" negligence that would have been required to prosecute Crowvision separately on charges of negligent homicide. No criminal charges were pressed.

But Brandon's death was also investigated by the North Carolina Occupational Safety and Health Administration. They decided to fine Crowvision $84,000, as of 1993, the largest fine ever levied in the administration's history. The penalty included: $70,000 for having live ammunition on the set; $7,000 for not checking the gun before it was fired; and $7,000 for the gun being aimed directly at Brandon. Crowvision appealed the fine and ultimately, it was reduced to $55,000.

Once the police had decided that there would be no prosecution, Crowvision settled the civil lawsuit that Linda Lee Caldwell had brought against the production. After two days of negotiation, a "confidential, but substantial" sum was paid in full settlement of Brandon's death.

While the investigation went on, the production had naturally been worried about the actual footage shot of Brandon being hit.

Grant Hill and Bob Rosen kept the film under wraps for a couple of days, and then they sent Greg Gale back to Los Angeles to the film laboratory with it. There was very strict security there. "Everybody at Deluxe labs," said Gale, "was instructed at that point, to stay clear of this film when it is running on the projector after being developed. I mean, I had to walk through the darkroom, the developing room, watch it going through all the washes in the baths, and we had to have one other person as a safety with me. It was Mr. Pressman's assistant, Chris, at that point. Chris was a very young guy, but he had a very clean, very sharp-looking haircut and everything. I got him prepped up and let Deluxe labs know we were coming over with this film; we need special treatment and everything. They thought he was an FBI agent!"

The reason for the tight security was explained by Rosen: "First of all, we wanted to develop this scene so that we could learn anything from it. On the other hand, we didn't want this to get in the wrong hands and be on *Entertainment Tonight*."

A difficulty was that the lab technicians were asked not to look at the film, so they were unable to check their own work. The unenviable task of checking the shot of Brandon being killed finally fell to Greg Gale. In the event, the police looked at it, as did the various lawyers now involved in the case, and they all found there was nothing to be learned from it.

Given the affection they had for Brandon, nobody else involved in *The Crow* wanted to see the footage. Bob Rosen didn't look at it: "I don't know of anybody that was there that wanted to see the film or has ever seen the film. I would imagine Janowitz has, but there was nobody that was connected with the film that saw it. I don't think Alex saw it." Jeff Most's response was typical, that he cared too much about Brandon. "I did not wanna have that image of Brandon etched in my head, [with] so many other wonderful times with him and things to reflect upon. I myself didn't wanna partake of ever seeing the footage."

THE EMOTIONAL AFTERMATH

22

THE FACT AND MANNER of Brandon Lee's death left the cast and crew devastated.

No one could make sense of what had happened.

They were all making a film in which death was commonplace, and now suddenly they had to deal with the reality of death itself. Ken Arlidge found, "It's very strange to be on the set of a film where you're creating make-believe, you're creating a fantasy world that is going to be shown to an audience. And the reality of death and loss of life that is not a part of filmmaking at all, enters your world and rocks your world and just rips it apart."

Darryl Levine had encountered death, but that hadn't prepared him for this experience. "I'd seen people die," he admitted, "but never in a way like this. This was not a disease killing you slowly, this was not even a heart attack, this was something we didn't even know. What? And I was not even forty-one yet. And I'd experienced all the stuff. I was a drug addict for like, years. I sobered up. So, I've been through hell and shit."

Sandra Orsolyak found it impossible to adjust to what had happened. "I was having nightmares," she said. "I was an emotional wreck, crying all the time. I even went to see a trauma psychologist."

The production did eventually arrange counseling for the crew members in Wilmington.

For Clyde Baisey, stress debriefing was part of his job: "After about four hours of very intense therapy by myself, I was in there with the whole group of emergency medical staff. They made me go through every tiny minute step, relive it all in my head, all over again. And at that point I was allowed, I myself allowed, my emotions to come out."

While the production decided if they would continue with the film, the crew members who didn't live in Wilmington were anxious to get out of town as soon as they could. Randy LaFollette said, "I just needed to get away. People from *Hard Copy* and all these idiots were calling and bugging me. It's just that you felt that you were in a closed chamber of people bugging you, and I just needed to get away from it all." Ken Arlidge also felt, "This was now a horrible experience in my life. I just wanted to get out of there. I was thinking a lot about the 'what-ifs?' of the situation. What if we had noticed this? What if we noticed that? This wouldn't've happened."

Arianne Phillips was working on a film in Los Angeles and began her first day. "Other than that, I didn't answer my phone, I got all kinds of inquiries from press people, from different tabloids, people trying to find out what happened and, you know."

Darryl Levine, who had been faced with the sad task of packing Brandon's costumes and shipping them to Los Angeles, went home and spoke to no one for a few days. Lance Anderson said he went into a slump. "When I came home, I didn't wanna work anymore. I wanted to veg out. I was like, in some sort of shock. I think it made me re-assess my relationship with my own son and spend more time with him. More family oriented." It made Anderson, like anyone who has an encounter with sudden death, "realize how fragile life is."

Sandra Orsolyak lived in Wilmington, and for the moment she stayed home. Then, after a couple of weeks, her dog was killed in a hit-and-run accident. She confessed, "I totally lost it, on the side of the street, and was just standing there screaming. Went out there somewhere in la-la-land and just finally broke down. I said, 'I have to get out of here. I have to get out of here!'" She went to Maui alone, and on the second day she was there, while learning to scuba dive, she blew out her eardrum.

Then she had, what she considers, a mystical experience. On a street trader's stall she saw a small pendant in the form of a dagger. That night she dreamed: "Brandon was in the dream and there was a battle, and he handed it to me as the sword to use. I woke up the next morning and I went, 'Ha! I think I need that little pendant thing, my crossy dagger thing, wherever it is.' And I went in search of it. It took me two days to find it." She bought the little dagger and wore it regularly.

The memorial service for Brandon Lee was held on the afternoon of April 4, 1993, at the home of legendary actress Polly Bergen, in Beverly Hills. There were many of Brandon's friends there, including Lou Diamond Phillips, Kiefer Sutherland, David Hasselhoff, and Steven Seagal. Melissa Etheridge, who was close to Brandon, sang. "I flew back to LA for the service at Polly Bergen's house," Bob Rosen remembered. "I remember going to that, but I don't remember going to anything in Wilmington."

A handful of crew members were present at the service, including Darryl Levine and Arianne Phillips, for whom it was a shocking experience: "I just lost it, and it was like, you know, they had all been together and were processing everything, and I had been alone, I had started another project. I was a mess." Part of the reason she was shocked was that Brandon's fiancée, Eliza Hutton, had decided to wear her wedding dress to the memorial service. Eliza had bought the dress in Los Angeles and Arianne Phillips had given her advice in choosing it. But the sight of it was especially poignant since it was only two weeks before the original wedding date for which it had been bought.

The media had not let up its pressure, and they showed up at the memorial service, congregating at the foot of Polly Bergen's driveway. Not surprisingly, nobody at the memorial wanted to speak to them.

Brandon's funeral was a family-only affair in Seattle, where he was to be buried next to his father, Bruce, in Lakeview Cemetery. From *The Crow*, Jeff Imada, Bob Rosen, and Alex Proyas were there. With mixed emotions, Jeff Most didn't go. After all the tensions of the last two weeks of filming, when he had been banned from the set, he was still not speaking to Bob Rosen or Alex Proyas.

Most decided that he didn't want to bring those tensions to the funeral, but he now regrets not going, saying, "It's a decision that's haunted me."

HIATUS   23
Planning to Complete the Film

ANY FACTORS INFLUENCED the decision about finishing *The Crow*, but the chief factor was always financial. If the financial equation had been unbalanced, then the movie never could have been finished.

Jeff Most thought that the crucial opinion should be the director's. He was, he said, "A strong believer in allowing Alex Proyas the room to make the decision. As was Ed Pressman . . . Having been given the opportunity by the insurance company to either complete or put the film on the shelf."

Initially, Alex Proyas had no desire to finish the picture. He told gaffer Claudio Miranda that "enough is enough." Miranda also thought that Proyas felt, "like he killed someone, almost. He felt responsible."

During the hiatus, the production had agreed to keep Claudio Miranda on a half-rate retainer to try to keep him available when or if they were able to finish shooting. Miranda says this was exceptional for any movie, let alone a non-union one. "They did that for the crew too. The local crew. It was amazing. I never heard of that before."

Among the key crew members kept on a retainer was Darryl Levine: "Bob [Rosen] said to me, 'Don't leave. Don't take anything.'" Levine, a shrewd observer of the industry over many years, thought, "First of all, we were only eight or nine days away from finishing. This is the movie business! This is not a business [where they'd say], 'We'll say we'll write off $15 million, don't worry about it!' Oh, we knew that they were doing it. I never had a doubt. They were trying to figure out the way to do it."

The experience of other crew members pointed in the same direction. JB Jones figured, "They weren't gonna put all that much money in a picture and not finish it. Because I've been on pictures before that they had shot, like over in the islands, and they had problems and they come back to the States, and finally they wound up with the insurance company. They would show the insurance company that they were worthy and they could make money, and so the insurance company went along with them and they went ahead and did it. That's the same thing that happened with this one."

Bob Rosen, a man who dealt in practicalities, was well aware of the financial reality he was dealing with: "We had spent, I can't say how much, but say twelve million at that point, and if we had all walked away from it there would be a twelve million loss that would have to be dealt with by completion bonds and insurance companies and what have you. Certainly, they were delighted to hear that we wanted to finish and were trying to figure out a way, although at that point we didn't know how, to finish the picture. I mean, if I was them, I would be tickled to death."

Others, possibly more sentimental, like Randy LaFollette, believed that it was, "Basically left up to the family. Whatever the family wanted. If they wanted to do it for Brandon's sake, for us to finish. And basically everyone said, 'For Brandon's sake, we will be back and we will finish this thing.'"

Before anything could be decided, the production team had to cut together everything they had shot and look at it to see just where they were. They had already booked post-production offices and editing facilities in a light industrial section of West Los Angeles, where there are many facilities, including George Lucas' special effects studio, Industrial Light & Magic. Now, they simply moved into their space earlier than planned.

They were still concerned about security and worried that the scene of Brandon being shot might be stolen because it could be sold for a huge amount of money. Greg Gale said, "You're always wary about the *National Enquirer*. Anybody wanting to get their hands on something to make something out of nothing." So, once they got the film back to their new cutting room, they decided, "To keep a night guard for at least one week, a week and a half, that we had hired, to sit with the film all night long in the editing building."

It was significant that Jeff Most did not have an office in the post-production facility. Some people claim there was simply no room for him, others believe that the reason was that he had never managed to make peace with Alex Proyas or Bob Rosen. Instead, he busied himself working on the movie soundtrack with Jolene Cherry, the music supervisor.

It is common practice in the industry to have an editor on location, roughly cutting the scenes together as they are shot, so that the production team can get an idea of how the shooting is progressing. In Wilmington,

Scott Smith had been working on *The Crow* in this way, and now, back in Los Angeles, he spent three weeks putting the whole movie together roughly. He was, Greg Gale said, "Sweating to make something, a little creatively to just actually say, 'This is what we have.' I know there was some differences that came with Scott and Alex through the editing process." Indeed, Scott Smith would eventually be replaced by another editor.

Finally, all the film that had been shot was assembled in order and could be screened. In many ways, this screening was painful for those who attended it, among whom was the gaffer, Claudio Miranda, seeing it so that he could have a sense of what still needed to be shot. "It was like, no music, and it wasn't timed [color balanced] or anything. I just thought, 'Wow! This thing is awful.'" Greg Gale recalled, "There was a sense of quiet, a sadness at that point. But the discussions went on out of the screening room about what value we have there, 'Can we go on? What do we need to do? Can we do it?' to make a story out of this. We have so much of our story we hadn't filmed, dialogue we hadn't filmed."

They now commenced the process of comparing the cut film with the screenplay to see what was missing, how important the missing scenes were, and what could be done about it. Bob Rosen found this process, "The most painful experience known to man. To get up every morning and go look at pictures of Brandon. So much of that movie which was about death and everything else, and you're dealing with somebody that you know was involved in this accident. Just was horrendous."

Randy LaFollette was brought in to help figure out some of the practicalities of finishing the film: "This is what we need to fill in. This shot here goes up to here. This is where the people were. We need a transitional shot that goes here. However, we had to adjust to finish the story, because of the lack of Brandon."

So, what was left over, un-shot from the original screenplay and the remaining planned eight days of shooting? Of course, the scene of Eric Draven's death, during the shooting of which Brandon had been killed, was a major hole in the movie. In addition to that scene, Bob Rosen said, "Most of what was left [to film] was intimate dialogue between the girl and Brandon and the girlfriend. And a lot of exposition about the movie came out in these sequences."

Some of the intimate sequences had been among the most important in the movie to Brandon Lee. "Brandon was unable to complete a lot of his acting stuff, without the makeup," Jeff Imada recalled. "He [Eric] was supposed to be alive, and he was looking forward to doing a lot of that. Get out of the makeup, get away from doing the action, and be a normal person. It would have shown the audience, and he was really looking forward to that, because he got to act and not just be the Crow and beat up people." Sofia Shinas knew, "The scenes were important to Brandon . . . so he wouldn't end the film on a dark note. There's all these happy moments in his mind. Plus, he wanted to do it all at once, so he wouldn't have to put the makeup on, take the makeup off."

Among the scenes she had with Brandon that were never shot, Shinas said, "There was a scene when he and I were painting. I think it's in the comic book. There were a few scenes of him and her in the bathroom, we were decorating. At the beach, there was a beach scene." Shinas, who felt that all her scenes with Brandon embodied the humanity of the Eric Draven character, was very disappointed when a decision was ultimately taken to turn these scenes into a montage, using the small amount of material for them that already existed.

At the time when the production team had first seen Scott Smith's rough cut of the film, no one, said Bob Rosen, knew how to finish the film. "It was just a question of throwing a lot of ideas out, and a lot of people threw a lot of ideas out. And again, ultimately, it was Alex that in his own mind felt that he could work with this part, and part of this, and part of that. So, we storyboarded and went back."

Alex Proyas spent several tough weeks working with David Schow until he was satisfied that the screenplay could be revised so that the movie could be finished to a standard that would satisfy him, and that would have satisfied Brandon. It was by now clear to everyone that they would have to shoot some material with doubles, that some scenes would have to use CGI [computer-generated imagery], and that narration would have to carry some of the story points that were originally intended to be in dialogue that had not been shot.

When Jeff Imada was shown how these story points were to be gone over, using Rochelle Davis' narration, he was impressed: "I thought it was very smart, very creative how they used Sarah to do the voice-over and a lot of the things that Brandon's character would [have explained in] his dialogue."

Imada became involved with the process, trying to work out how they were going to shoot the remaining scenes, and had to discuss it with Alex. "I know they were going to do some CGI work," Imada said, "and [work out] how much we really wanted to see, facially, of the doubles, to give Alex enough to do what he needed to do. But also knowing that they were going to have to pay for CGI work, if they're gonna have to superimpose Brandon's face."

In 1993, digital effects were new, crude, and expensive. Though they seem ubiquitous today, usually only big-budget films could afford them, and they were far less sophisticated or believable by modern standards.

One decision that was made fairly quickly was to cut out a character called the Skull Cowboy, a larger-than-life decaying corpse with a crow on his shoulder. This role had been played by an actor named Michael Berryman, and some material had been shot with this character at the beginning of the schedule, leaving the remainder of his appearances until the end. "Scenes had been shot with Brandon and Michael Berryman," Jeff Most explained, "but only a master [shot] and no close-up. That required the scene to be shot in close-up. There's very little coverage from the work that the Skull Cowboy did with Brandon. Particularly missing was, you know, the interplay between the two." Greg Gale said he was told, "It was too much unfinished with Skull Cowboy having any kind of dialogue with Brandon, which was his purpose in the script. Without having that dialogue, you can't really do too much." The Skull Cowboy vanished.

It was now apparent that it was going to be impossible to finish *The Crow* for the original projected cost, and James Janowitz dealt with the insurance and bond companies: "There was an initial estimate given to the insurance company of what it would cost to complete. I don't remember what it was, but I do remember that it was at least a couple of million short of where we wound up, and of course, that did make them nervous." The reason the figure was inaccurate was that the production team was still trying to work out the technical details of how they *could* finish the film. There could even have been some legitimate doubt that it could be finished at all without its star.

Janowitz's job was, "To make sure that everybody believed in the integrity of the process. That they had the information, that they understood what we were doing and that it would appear to be, in fact was, a careful, honest, responsible effort to complete the film." In all of this, Janowitz had the total support of Ed Pressman. "It was pure guts, what Ed did," he said. "This is right up there with the true high-wire acts of making film. Because it would've been a very easy thing to just call it quits and move on with your life."

An additional pressure on Pressman would be the difficulty of controlling the cost of finishing the film. Although Janowitz struggled to, "Make sure that we were never spending more money than we were getting from the insurance company, we did, and Ed got pretty deeply in the hole, and it was tough, but he was very committed. He saw the film, he understood what he had, he believed in it, and he really put himself at great risk. But I think his judgment was a hundred percent right."

There was one more matter to resolve. Janowitz, dealing with Brandon's family through their lawyer, said, "I made it clear that we would not finish or distribute the film if Linda Lee didn't want us to. We thought it was a terrific film, that Brandon's performance was terrific, that it would mean something to her and to his fans and to his memory to have this film distributed rather than have it just abandoned, and we approached her on that basis, and she agreed."

A satisfactory financial arrangement was worked out and agreed with the insurance company and the completion bond company. And Alex Proyas, David Schow, Ed Pressman, and Bob Rosen had agreed on a revised screenplay and on how it could be shot. The production team made a decision. They would finish the movie; they would return to Wilmington.

Most of the crew were pleased by the decision to finish the movie and wanted to be involved in the final shooting. Chunky Huse expressed the feelings of the rank-and-file crew members: "It was my movie. I'm not gonna let anybody else do it, because no matter how much a director will tell you it's his movie, it's our movie too. Our names are on it as well. So, yes, it was a matter of pride and it was a matter of finishing it, really for Brandon, as far as we were concerned." Jeff Imada also wanted to keep up the quality. "I wanted," he says, "to keep it consistent with the way we had been doing the film. Keep everything consistent and make sure it wasn't being done in poor taste."

Bob Rosen was touched by the number of people who made themselves available. "There was such a period of time between the death and the time that we actually came back to shoot. Everybody wanted to finish it. Everybody seemed to feel that this might help with the closure."

One of the people who had been most affected by Brandon's death, Lance Anderson, admitted he was glad, "The hierarchy had decided to go ahead and finish it. I guess they could've put it on the shelf."

There were also people with mixed feelings, like Ken Arlidge: "We certainly didn't want to go back to a place that represented a very black space in our lives, a very dark space in our lives. But the ability to finish something and let it be a tribute to Brandon was certainly the driving force for most of us." As a measure of his feeling for Brandon Lee, Arlidge did go back to that "dark space."

Others were more reluctant. Sofia Shinas did not want to go back to what had been a bad experience for her. "I met some really great people

but, as a whole, working on the set was not the best experience for me."
But the production knew that Shinas was needed to complete the movie.
"They said, 'It's important for Brandon that we finish this movie.' I said,
'Okay, what would you like me to do?' They said, 'Do you object to com-
ing back?' I said, 'No.' I wasn't really okay with it, but I did it anyway. . . .
To me, it was sort of like, not the postscript, but just finishing it, burying
the hatchet with the whole thing. I wanted to go back and finish things
and make sure it was done."

Ernie Hudson was as reluctant as Shinas, but his mind was changed
by another member of the crew. "I was not in favor of it, but I got a call
from Lance [Anderson], who was the special makeup effects. Lance felt
that Brandon worked hard on this and that it was important to him, and
that we owed it to him to finish it." Hudson did return to Wilmington,
but he had already committed to make another movie in Australia, so he
managed to squeeze *The Crow* re-shoot in just before he left for Sydney
directly from North Carolina.

Although Lance Anderson had managed to persuade Hudson, he knew
that not everyone was willing to go back: "Some people felt just opposite
of me. They felt like they never wanted to be back on the set again. They
were done. They were through. They weren't coming back."

Among those who were not coming back were Arianne Phillips,
Michelle Johnson, and Sandra Orsolyak. Phillips wanted to do whatever
Eliza or the family thought was appropriate, and she knew that they
wanted to finish the film in homage to Brandon, "So that was the line that
I took, in support of the family, but there was no way in hell that I was
going to go back there. I was so traumatized from the experience, there
was nothing that you could have done to make me go back there." Phillips
felt that Alex Proyas and the rest of the team would understand how she
felt. Michelle Johnson was hired shortly after *The Crow* went on hiatus by
actor Dennis Hopper (with whom she had worked on *Super Mario Bros.*)
to work in Wilmington on his movie *Chasers*. This saved her from working on *The Crow*, although she was a single mother and needed the work.
"But I just couldn't go back. Well, thank God, Dennis Hopper called and
he was doing a film so, he was like, 'You wanna do it?' I go, 'God, thank
you.'" Sandra Orsolyak was called and asked to take over makeup on *The
Crow*, but it was too traumatic for her as well.

The feelings could hardly have contrasted more strongly with those of
Clyde Baisey, who knew how important the movie had been to Brandon.
"This movie had violence, it had love, it had anger, it had compassion, and
every emotion that every human being experiences. And he was that good

in all his capacities. And he wanted to portray himself as something other than a kung fu fighter. He didn't wanna be another version of his dad."

Randy LaFollette had returned to his hometown of Seattle but, hoping the decision would be taken to finish the movie, left his car in Wilmington. While LaFollette was in Los Angeles, working on the planning of the re-shoot, *Dragon* (the 1993 biopic about Bruce Lee), ironically, was released in theaters. In *Dragon*, there is a sequence at the end where the small boy (Brandon Lee) is pursued by a figure of Death. It made a great impression on LaFollette when he saw the film. "That whole thing about the ghost comes back to haunt the spirit or something like that, the curse or whatever."

Ernie Hudson also saw *Dragon* around the same time, and he too, was struck by, "This demon that sort of pursues Bruce Lee throughout the movie, and then at the very end of the movie, the demon turns around and he sees Brandon and he goes after Brandon. Brandon was just a little kid. And there's something about that whole thing. And that happened. It was too weird. Too odd. Too screwed up."

Before Randy LaFollette left his Seattle home to head back to Los Angeles, he went to pay his respects at Brandon's fresh grave. There, he had another striking experience: "He's buried right next to Bruce. And when I was there, a crow flew right nearby and stopped right when I got there. It was the weirdest thing. Not on the headstone, but the crow flew right behind it. And his gravestone was near a road that goes through the cemetery, and it sat kind of behind it, right on this little lip from the road. He was perched there. Just as I got there. And then a couple minutes later all these people come up and start taking pictures of the graves, which I thought was really weird. Tourists."

BACK TO WILMINGTON   24

THE CREW RETURNED to Wilmington to begin re-shooting *The Crow* on May 26, 1993, in a very different season and to a very different atmosphere. Warmer weather had arrived and now Wrightsville Beach was mobbed with summer vacationers, mostly from the north. Robert Zuckerman's luxurious beachfront condo, which they had rented for $900 a month in the winter, was now $4,000.

The out-of-towners quickly settled in and joined the local crew, both old and new, for a dinner with Alex Proyas. It was their first meeting as a group since Brandon Lee's death, and Proyas wanted to re-engage with the crew members and actors and to make sure that they were all of one mind about finishing the movie. He told them that he had seen all the footage they had shot and that he was convinced they were going to make a fine movie and one that Brandon would have been proud of. Actor Angel David thought, "If two or three of the people would've said, 'No, I don't think I can go on with this,' that would've been it." Since everybody who was at the dinner had already decided that they wanted to finish the film, there was little likelihood of that.

But the meeting may have had another significance because, said Ernie Hudson, "For the first time after the accident, Alex came in and he took total control. And I told him it's too bad he didn't do that from day one. Really, I believe that the accident is what made the movie. I think Alex really committed in a way that he maybe wouldn't have committed otherwise. I mean, I don't know that for sure, but it's sort of a sad statement to make."

Another difference from the pre-accident shoot was that there was now a major emphasis on safety. "When we came back and started the filming," said Clyde Baisey, "Bob Rosen stood up and the first thing he said, 'First topic we will talk about is safety. Clyde, you have the floor.' And we went through the whole safety process. What was gonna happen. The way things are gonna be done. New guidelines had been set up. How guns were gonna be handled. And that was the first thing discussed. Even before the first line of the script or the rewrites got done. And I was proud of him for that because safety didn't get put on the back burner. That got put on the front burner." Wardrobe supervisor Darryl Levine soon noticed that, for a little while, everybody was on their best behavior: "Everybody was making sure there was nothing wrong."

For Baisey, this was all a marked contrast to the pre-accident shoot when, "They went through the steps, but nobody ever danced to the tune. Now everybody's dancing to the tune that hadn't even been pronounced yet. So, the second time around was a lot different. The atmosphere was different. It wasn't the same crowd. It wasn't the same crew. Everybody was affected by this. And I think the way it affected everybody was to move to a positive from a negative. Lot more people became more safety-conscious than they were initially."

Now, there was a full-time armorer hired to handle the weapons. This was Jim Moyer, who had previously been hired to look after the semi-automatic weapons during the big shoot-out scene at Top Dollar's lair. JB Jones was glad. "After we had this problem, then we hired Moyer just to do everything. And when I brought the guns back, I signed them over to him, and he was responsible for them."

In addition, the second unit was expanded and separately resourced, so that they didn't need to keep borrowing items from the main unit. The money added to the budget due to the accident made this possible. Also, because in the meantime the movie had been cut together, it was much easier to be specific about exactly what the second unit was going to shoot. One of their major tasks would be to shoot a series of backing shots, which would enable Brandon Lee's image to be digitally removed and added to new scenes.

The hardship and strains of the past few months, not only because of Brandon's death but also because of the difficult conditions of the shooting before the accident, had left an indelible mark on the company. But it had also brought them closer together in their common effort to finish the movie. "There'd be times," Ken Arlidge recalled, "where certain crew members would break down crying, and we'd just comfort them and continue. You'd walk around a corner and see someone sitting down and just having a little sob for themselves. And you could see the pain in [Brandon's stunt double] Jeff Cadiente's face from day-to-day and I think that pulled us closer together." Laurence Mason also saw that his fellow workers had the same feelings he had. "Everybody'd gone through the same thing I did. Everybody had that look in their eyes like they'd seen something. And in a way that was comforting. Because like I said, I went back by myself to New York, and really had no one to relate to. In a way that was comforting, because these were the guys that were there when it happened. And we *know*. That was okay."

Many of the cast and crew thought, like Robert Zuckerman, that the atmosphere was "eerie, strange." Perhaps this was because attitudes were different. In contrast to the previous joking around, Laurence Mason found that now they all went by the book. "It was business. Let's get this done." Lance Anderson also noticed the difference. "The whole second shoot was at a different pace," he recalled. "More solemn." Ernie Hudson thinks it was "weird and odd and uncomfortable and all the above." Angel David said, "This was going back to finish a film where a really good person was killed. So, it changed."

Adding to the pressure on the crew, the media was still in full pursuit of the story. Photographers hung around the studio gates, and journalists called the crew members and actors. But they had to get on with their jobs, and they could never get out of their heads the reason they had stopped shooting and the reason they had returned. "Absolutely it was different," recalled Darryl Levine. "It's a marked film. Guy died on that movie." Nobody was more aware of that than Bob Rosen: "You're going back to places and scenes, and you're going back to the set where the accident took place, and you're going back to the back lot and everything else where you had been a short period before, with Brandon there. And now he's not there, and you know what's happened. It was never pleasant to deal with that. It was an amazing thing for the professionalism of everybody involved to get it done, because everybody's emotions were right on the ragged edge."

They had to deal with their feelings as much in their time off as when they were at the studio. "When we went out drinking, we spoke often about Brandon," said Ken Arlidge, "and just how much everyone liked him. In essence it was just a celebration of Brandon. A very dark, emotionally troubling time, as well as a drive to finish the film and pay a tribute to him, and certainly I was a small part of that. But if you look at people like Alex and Ed Pressman, and the power that really controlled the film, I really have to give them credit for pushing forward and doing their best to make it a good film."

On sound stage 4, the loft set was reassembled. It looked much as it did in the early hours of March 31, when Brandon entered through its front door. And now, each member of the cast and crew had to pluck up their courage and revisit the same four walls in order to finish *The Crow*. "Here we are on the set where Brandon was shot and effectively where his character first died and then was resuscitated," recalled Ken Arlidge. "Shooting scenes of empty doors opening, and mirrors and corners of the room that Brandon was later digitally cut out and placed into." For him, "Even the color of the walls . . . the interior of the loft . . . the paint . . . had a slightly reddish tint in it. I still get a chill thinking about it. It was such an awkward, unnerving position to be in, and I just wanted to shoot the shots and get out of that set as quick as possible."

Sandra Orsolyak, who had not come back to *The Crow* and had taken a job as makeup artist on another film shooting in Wilmington (the TV movie *The Birds II: Land's End*), found herself on the lot one day and was momentarily drawn back onto the fateful set. "I snuck in, listened and made sure there wasn't anybody there, got up there and said my only prayer, and snuck out again."

Knowing that he would have several scenes to shoot there, Angel David entered the empty set to allay his misgivings and calm his nerves: "I walked in there myself, just to get a sense of how I was gonna feel and just to sort of, in my own way, as bizarre as it sounds, in my own way, just to talk to Brandon and tell him, ask him, that I hope it's all right that this is going on."

Returning to finish the movie, Laurence Mason had convinced himself that time had passed and that he wouldn't be bothered by returning to Wilmington. And he wasn't, until he went to the studio. "I'll tell you, when we stepped on that set again, I got chills. When I stepped on that set, I had to take a minute and just think about it."

On the fifth day of shooting, June 1, 1993, the cast and crew assembled on the set. It was time to re-shoot the murders of Eric and Shelly. "I'll never forget that day," recalled Randy LaFollette. For that scene, he was given the responsibilities of the First AD, because his boss, Steve Andrews, "just couldn't handle it. It was, emotionally, very hard for him and he asked me to do it for him."

But the scene had been re-thought. It would eventually become a montage in the editing room, and it would be shot in such a way that the audience would never see Eric Draven's face. His part would be played by a stunt double, and only his body or shadow would be seen, or the camera would sometimes cover the action between Shelly and the thugs, from Eric's point of view.

Even though Eric Draven was still to lose his life in this scene, the sequence of deadly events was slightly changed from what had been planned on the night of the accident. Jeff Most recalled that now, as Draven enters the loft, "Brandon was not shot, and in fact it was a knife that was thrown at him by Tin Tin, just to erase any memory and any association with the actual event." But the disassociation with the gun was short-lived. The scene subsequently called for the wounded Eric Draven to be picked up by Skank and Tin Tin and held in a crucifixion-like pose. He is then shot several times by T-Bird and Funboy, who throw his body out the window. At that point, "There was a dead silence," LaFollette remembered. "And when we did that scene and we had to call for the real weapon . . . I'll never forget that in my life. You could hear a pin drop. You could feel the emotions bouncing off the walls." The "real weapon" used here was, of course, not the same gun that had killed Brandon. That gun was still held as evidence and was being put through ballistics tests.

Although almost all of Eric and Shelly's dialogue scenes would be cut or shortened significantly, more footage of the couple was still needed. In the absence of Brandon, Sofia Shinas filmed montages. "It was hard to do, because I had to just sort of act into a camera with no actor or anything like that." Shinas was asked to laugh and flirt into the lens, to depict Shelly and her "funnest, happiest moments." She recalled being directed here, not by Proyas, but by the director of photography: "Derek did a lot. I mean, Derek was quite helpful. Moving the camera, and he was really instrumental when we went back."

Rochelle Davis also found herself acting solo on the loft set. "If Brandon had been alive, it would've been me and him, like having a little picnic in front of the fireplace, talking, just talking about things. And he was gonna tell me that he couldn't really hang out with me or talk to me because that wasn't what he was there for, and he didn't wanna get attached or something like that." The original scene had been a two-hander, but it was now done as a single shot of Sarah in the loft, looking through old still photographs, and "a little monologue of me walking around in circles."

An entire section at the beginning of the movie still remained to be shot. Although the camera angles and script details were re-thought, the scenes explaining how Eric Draven rediscovers who he is and comes to understand his mission of retribution were impossible to leave out of the movie. Now, in order to finish the movie, Brandon needed to be doubled not only facially, but also physically. A great deal of this would be done by using new digital effects and special effects makeup. Although Brandon's stunt double, Jeff Cadiente, would continue to do many of the remaining shots, yet another double needed to be cast, someone whose body bore a closer resemblance to Brandon's. This was especially crucial for the many bare-chested shots of Eric Draven when, after being resurrected from the grave, he returns to the loft.

The production team initially decided to interview dancers. "Alex wanted the guy to be very light on his feet," Jeff Imada recalled, "and fluid and things like that. He didn't want a guy who was real clunky and stiff, because that's not how Brandon was." Unable to find anyone suitable, Imada approached them with another suggestion: "There's somebody that I know that's from the martial arts academy. He's a little bit taller, but proportion-wise, he's the same as Brandon, and we could work with him to move like Brandon. And another thing was that he knew Brandon, they were friends, and so he also knew how Brandon worked." This was Chad Stahelski. He had an interest in stunt work, but no real experience. Ultimately it was Chad's athletic and acrobatic abilities, and his physical resemblance to Brandon, that got him the part. Stahelski recalled, "Out of the first fifteen minutes of the movie, quite a bit is doubles. I'm not gonna tell you which parts, but quite a few of them are me."

Professionally, *The Crow* was Stahelski's break: "I had done a lot of low-budget, chopsocky stuff 'till then, and then *The Crow* was my first big one." After *The Crow*, Stahelski's career took off. He became a highly sought-after stuntman, appearing in big movies, such as *Escape from L.A.* (1996) and John Carpenter's *Vampires* (1998). Then in 1999, he became Keanu Reeves' stunt double and coordinator on the *Matrix* film series and moved on to direct Reeves in *John Wick* (2014) and all three of the hit film's sequels.

As soon as Stahelski arrived in Wilmington, he was given the tapes of all the dailies, "All the footage of Brandon and stuff. [They] stuck me in a room and said, 'Okay, watch it.' It was like a three-day weekend, and I just stayed in my hotel room and had a video camera and just walked up and down the hallway trying to get his walk." By comparing his own videotape with the movie footage and getting helpful critiques from Jeff Imada, who would tell Stahelski, "Brandon was a little bit more like this or like that," Stahelski began to successfully mimic Brandon. Regardless of skill or practice though, Stahelski admits his firsthand knowledge of Brandon was indispensable, "Because I saw him. I got to watch him work out a lot, and that's where you really see guys move, and how they sit and how they talk to you, his motions."

The biggest scene, which required both Stahelski and Cadiente, was Eric Draven's return to the loft. Here, Draven rediscovers who he was through flashbacks triggered by the images in the loft: still photos of him and Shelly, and their cat Gabriel, as well as other props. In between the flashbacks, all of which had been shot with Brandon, we see Eric Draven violently moving around the loft, experiencing the painful memories of his former life.

Since the cameras were primarily focused on Stahelski's chest and back, special makeup effects artist Lance Anderson had to painstakingly re-create the bullet wounds that Eric Draven received before he was killed on the body double. "Those took a long time just to glue on," recalled Stahelski, "because without the shirt, you always see these little bullet scars, front and back."

In addition to the bare-chested scenes, Stahelski recalled doing "all the stunt stuff, like in a tight shirt, some of the fights, anything that required real close stuff." These were primarily small shots needed to complete scenes that had already been filmed.

One of the trickiest shots was where Eric Draven recalls that he was thrown to his death from the round loft window. He grabs a section of window frame and swings himself through the opening as if he is going to throw himself out into the street, but then swings back in again. Once he swings back inside the loft, we see a close-up of his cut hands, sliced by the shards of glass left in the frame of the broken window, which heal themselves before our eyes. This is a turning point, the moment he realizes he is superhuman, invulnerable.

Because Alex Proyas wasn't sure whether specific sequences would be better if they used Cadiente or Stahelski, he would often shoot both men going through the same action. This was very helpful for Stahelski, who often got tips on mimicking Brandon from watching Cadiente.

When Stahelski got on the loft set, he realized that stunts were only a small part of what he was being asked to do. "And I was looking at it like, I'm just a stunt guy, and Alex is walking me through the scenes going, 'Yeah, and here you're going to do this because you're pinned up on the cross, you're being crucified. And here he feels shock. I need pain. And now you're thinking about your fiancée and you're crying.' And I'm nodding to him going, 'Yes sir, absolutely. Yes sir.' And in my head I'm going, 'Did he know I'm just a stunt guy?' So, we go for it," Stahelski continued, "and Alex is all happy: 'That's not bad, that's pretty good.' It took more out of me than any stunt I've ever done because of all the energy."

Stahelski couldn't avoid the personal emotional strain of playing his dead friend either. This was why shooting this scene was one of the hardest things he would do on *The Crow*: "Just doing that scene, because it was a big learning experience, emotionally. It was one of the first scenes that I did when I was there and I took Brandon's death kind of hard, you know. I felt pretty weird about it."

Stahelski noticed that this scene was also a tremendous strain on Imada. "He had to talk about Brandon every minute. He said, 'Okay, Brandon would do it more like this. I think you have to put your shoulder . . .' So you just can't put that in the back of your head and move on, because every second you're being reminded, okay, we're on the set that he just died in, and you've gotta continue the scene. What are you gonna do?"

It was "all a little freaky" for Stahelski. "I wasn't in the wardrobe that he was killed in, but I was in the other stuff. I mean, you try to be tough and you're cool and you're all calm, cool, and collected. But then you're in your little room and putting the clothes on and it's weird, you know. And it hits you. And you're busy, but there're those moments when it hit me a little bit. You know, buddy's dead and I'm doubling a dead guy. Okay. It's a little freaky."

The irony of the situation and even some guilt soon settled on Stahelski. Months before, when he had originally heard about the movie from Brandon, he had thought, "What a great thing to work on. And then, kind of like, the dream came true a little bit. But only through one of the biggest misfortunes you could ever have. It made me feel like shit." But the support of the crew made the experience a little easier for the first-time actor. "The key departments, the effects and obviously stunts, they were right there . . . 'You're gonna get it, and it's going to be good. We'd do it for any film but this film has a special meaning.' Even Alex, the director, he was just like, 'I'm going to do it and dammit, it's going to be good.' And that's pretty cool. You see movies about that kind of shit but you don't really see it in real life."

Nevertheless, Stahelski feels that the reality created a "sad feeling" that pervaded the set, and that it was impossible to be immune to the significance of the place: "You get the lump in your throat sometimes, and your stomach drops. And there's a couple times, you know, you wrap for the day and they turn off the lights on the stage and you forget your stunt bag and you go back and get it, you're like, 'Okay, where we going tonight for drinks? Time to get out of here. Let's go!'"

Now, perhaps because some of the time and budget pressures had been removed from the production of *The Crow*, or because it was crucial to get this scene right, Alex Proyas was able to take great care in directing Sta-helski. "He was like, 'Okay Chad, what's going on in this scene? You've read it. Brandon's character's doing this, this, and this, and the camera's right here,' and he's really good at telling where the camera was. 'So I need you to, as you come in, kind of turn away a little bit, so we hide your face, and turn back.' Real explicative. I thought he was great."

In the loft sequence, we almost never see the returned Eric Draven's face. Most of the shots are in profile, shadow, or tight close-ups on hands or body. Although both Jeff Cadiente and Chad Stahelski doubled as Brandon here, it is impossible to know who is who. Fortunately, Stahelski thought, he and Brandon both had high cheekbones. "I mean, facially we were close enough that they could shoot profile and over the shoulder, so it kind of worked. But I'm not Brandon. You're still limited."

In order to finish the movie, this limitation would have to be over-come. There were remaining shots that required seeing Eric Draven's face. Perhaps the simplest of the solutions was to put the doubles in the Crow makeup and shoot them far enough away so that their individual features could not be seen. Stahelski is convinced that, "When they took a picture of me, Jeff, and Brandon next to each other, like Polaroids, once we were all made up and unless you were working on the film, you couldn't've told us apart. I mean, straight on, facially. The makeup, with the hair the right way, can't tell us apart." In the remaining scenes that were shot of Eric Draven running across the rooftops, Jeff Imada said, "I had to remind the doubles to turn their face towards camera because they were moving. I mean, you could see him, but because of the makeup and stuff like that, you couldn't tell."

Stahelski soon discovered, "My makeup tripped people out a little bit. I was even told I was freaking people out too. And that's understandable."

But another, more lifelike solution to doubling Brandon would disturb some of the crew even more. Using the face cast that he had taken of Brandon to design the Crow makeup months before in pre-production, Lance Anderson now made a rubber mask to be worn by Jeff Cadiente. "I had to take a plaster cast of Jeff's face," Anderson says, "and his face was the negative, and then Brandon's face was the positive in it that fit right over him. Very thin. It only filled out places where Brandon has a very strong jaw." Anderson would then apply the Crow makeup over the mask.

"That portion of the shooting was as tough as it gets," said Bob Rosen. "You're seeing somebody in the wardrobe who looks remarkably like Brandon at times, who obviously wasn't." Angel David recalled that the mask was especially difficult for the other actors: "They had to deal with being in character, dealing with a character that was played by another actor who had died all of a sudden, and is being played by someone that has a mask of that . . . It's just too fucked up." Rochelle Davis said, "They didn't want me to see him, because they thought it [the mask] would spook me, and I think a lot of people, the crew members, told me it totally spooked them."

Great efforts were made to shoot around the facial close-ups in order to use the mask as little as possible. And when the mask was necessary, Anderson said that, between the takes, "they kept him in the shadows, because this was kind of nerve-wracking."

"They came to me and said there's a scene where Brandon was to jump in my car and he sort of hides under the dashboard while I drive him away from all this shooting," recalled Ernie Hudson. Though Brandon's dialogue in the scene had to be cut, they asked Hudson, "'Would it be okay if the actor would be made up like Brandon?' Would I be okay with that? And I said, 'Fine.' They didn't tell me that they had made up a face mask so he looked . . . It was Brandon—every little pimple, everything. And then he [Cadiente] felt a little odd, I think, because it was so awkward. . . . When we weren't shooting, he'd kind of pull into himself, and he'd sort of sit in those little doorways."

"It was a pretty emotional thing and it was also kind of strange," remembered Robert Zuckerman, who was explicitly told not to take photos of Cadiente wearing the mask: "They just felt it was inappropriate, plus they didn't want to reveal it." Ken Arlidge felt great admiration for Jeff Cadiente. "Jeff was going back to a dark space to fill someone's shoes and finish a picture," Arlidge said, "and I think that would be hard for anybody, especially someone who was as close to Brandon as Jeff was. A very difficult situation."

The world's media was still swarming around the production, all wanting details of exactly how the film could be completed without its lead actor. Concerned about the devastating effect any more bad press could have on *The Crow*, serious precautions were taken. "They had us sign that we wouldn't talk to anybody or interview with the reporters, which is understandable," Chad Stahelski remembered. Even on the set, discussion of the ongoing legal battles over Brandon's death were taboo. "I don't think the accident was talked about too much," Stahelski added. "It was weird at the time because there were lawsuits, investigations." Lance Anderson said, "It was just the eeriness of the whole thing. Everybody wanted to just be as subtle about this as they could, to get through the film."

Andrew Mason, now wearing his other hat as visual effects supervisor, had always intended to use digital compositing to create the backgrounds for some of the scenes in the movie. When the film was being planned, Mason had talked to digital expert Mark Galvin (who received an executive producer credit in the final film) about, "A relatively simple process of mirroring some miniature city he was gonna shoot, to some live-action plates, which is something that we take somewhat for granted in our business." This would mean that miniature sets would be built, filmed, copied digitally, and combined digitally with other images (a technique called compositing) before being printed back onto film.

Before the use of computer digital visual effects, compositing had been done by combining different film negatives, which was a relatively crude process, often done on a hit-or-miss basis, and not susceptible to supervision by a director as it happened. The combined negatives were then recorded onto a new negative. So, the first time that anyone could see the result would be when the new negative was processed. Now, the director can watch the process as it happens, altering the size and position of images as he or she wishes. These techniques are now commonplace, but in 1993 they were new, indeed, cutting edge.

Mark Galvin's company, Motion Pixel Corporation, was called in after Brandon's accident and asked if there was any way they could help them salvage the film based on a new script. This would involve taking Brandon out of some shots and inserting that image of him in others. Galvin told them, "Without seeing any of the footage or seeing what you're talking about, it's really hard for me to tell you. I can tell you, 'Yes, it can be done.' The question is, can it be done at a reasonable price?" The reason that the price was in some doubt was that new ground was being broken: "And that was putting one human's face or likeness onto another human or lift a character out of a scene and put him into another scene without properly choreographing that. It was all being done with elements that were found, much like going back to old movies."

This switching of images was done most strikingly to create a shot of Brandon inside the loft apartment, and for this Galvin used an exterior shot of Brandon walking in the rain that had not been used in the movie. "It was basically after he had been brought back to life," said Galvin, "and he was walking down an alleyway. Well, he was on his way to his apartment. That scene being gone and the Skull Cowboy being gone, they needed some way to get him to his apartment. They needed a hookup. So, we suggested shooting a plate [a background shot into which another shot can be inserted] of the doorway to his apartment." Ken Arlidge shot the clean plate of the apartment door opening: "We had someone walk through as a reference, and then the door opened."

So now they had a shot of a double walking into the loft and a separate image of Brandon's face from the discarded shot. Galvin then copied Brandon out of the alleyway scene. This was a complex process called "rotoing," in which the image to be extracted is outlined by hand, frame by frame. The final step was to combine the two shots, which was made more difficult because the alleyway shot was unsteady and "was rainy and wet, and he had water dripping on him and the whole bit," so that Galvin was, "Trying to steady that shot out, CGI [alter the image digitally] pull out as much of the rain as they could, to give the impression that he's actually walking inside the apartment."

Another vital part of the script that also remained to be shot was the scene in which the resurrected Eric Draven transforms himself visually, with makeup, into the Crow. Jeff Most explained the significance of this scene: "When Eric Draven returned and witnessed flashbacks of his own death, that the makeup is motivated by the stream of blood that's spilled from his eyes and particularly from his mouth. So that's what he references. And then that, combined with the masks of Tragedy and Comedy which are on the wall, gives him the impetus to create the Crow makeup." In this scene, the enraged Draven breaks a mirror. In the shattered image of the mirror, Draven sees himself. Then we see the process of the character putting on the makeup in shadow, shot from the back of the mirror, without seeing the reflection. There are also close-ups of hands picking up the white pancake base and the black liner. Finally, the audience sees him, for the first time, as the Crow.

The shots of the mirror being broken were filmed using Chad Stahelski's hand. Ken Arlidge shot, he said, "Images of fragmented mirrors, with Jeff's face used as a guide for the digital people, to later take Brandon's face out of another scene and cut and paste it into the fragmented mirror." To get Brandon's image onto the broken mirror, Galvin and his technical supervisor, Tim Landry, used a shot of him that was on the editing room floor. "We lifted him, rotoed [copied frame by frame] him out of that element [shot], and now needed to put him into a cracked mirror." This was a problem because of the many refracted edges of the mirror, but according to Galvin, Landry "turned everything to black and white and delineated by grayscale the value of the different refraction angles with the light on the set. Then he imported the image of Brandon that he had rotoed out, and then laid that image back over it, creating a refraction map that equals a mirror. And then laid him in, and it was quite amazing when he was done. I don't know if it had been done [before]. It had never been done that way. I can guarantee you that."

One of the key images of the film is when Eric Draven, realizing he is superhuman and ready to take on his killers, walks toward the large, round broken loft window, with the crow perched on his shoulder. The film then cuts to a shot of Draven from the front, standing in the window in shadow, looking out of the broken window where, a year before, he was thrown to his death. The camera widens to encompass the whole building and the dark, ominous skyline. This is a signature shot of the movie. Then, suddenly lightning flashes, and for the first time we see the full Crow makeup. But Brandon had been killed before this shot could be done, and it now had to be done digitally, very laboriously and expensively.

The shot from the back was a shot of Chad Stahelski. Indeed, the shot from the front was also Stahelski, but in the final movie, Brandon's face was superimposed on the shot. This was one of the few times that Stahelski's face was filmed straight on: "The one shot where he walks right into the window, that's myself, the bird flies on his shoulder, but with Brandon's face CGI-ed on." Positioning the bare-chested Stahelski at the window, Randy LaFollette recalled they had to move in perfectly. "We also had to find frames, because what happens if you're here and you move in here, all of a sudden, your face is bigger, so to get that, they had to steal frames from other existing shots of Brandon, to make that step by step."

After the scene with Stahelski was shot, Galvin's computer crew, he said, "Had to hook our miniature camera up to a plate [a background shot] of the body double at a window, track Brandon Lee's face onto the body double, add lightning bolts to make it spooky and rainy, and then do what I believe ended up being a several minute pull-back, to a flight over the city. Which ultimately became a combination into a matte painting, which became a thirty-second piece which became the opening to the film."

Seeing the final result, Stahelski thought it was seamless: "Myself and Jeff are probably the only ones that really know when it's me. I fooled my mom with a couple of shots. She didn't know who it was."

Editing and Digital Effects

25

A T LAST, THE SECOND SHOOT of *The Crow* was finished, and in June 1993, post-production began in earnest back in West Los Angeles. In the cutting room, things were not going well between editor Scott Smith and Alex Proyas. Everyone, including Greg Gale, knew that they did not see eye to eye. Gale was now in a new role as the post-production supervisor: "I think there was the creative difference. I think Alex wasn't getting what he really wanted out of Scott." But they soldiered on, switching shots around and doing everything they could to make the movie work as well as it could.

In this editing process, many of Sofia Shinas' scenes were lost. There was a rumor among the crew that Brandon's fiancée, Eliza, was disturbed that Shinas was the last person Brandon had been intimate with during the love scene that had been shot a few days before his death. Gale thought that Ed Pressman and Alex Proyas wanted to respect Eliza's wishes: "They had made certain editorial decisions, especially about scenes in regard to Sofia. I know there were additional love scenes between Brandon and Sofia as her character in the project that certainly might've bothered Eliza, had they been edited in. We could get around it and still get the thought of the story that these two characters, Eric and Shelly, were in love and they had special times. But I think with the length we had in the original shooting, the passionate scenes they had were cut down to flashes." Almost all the romantic flashback scenes included Brandon as the living, vibrant Eric Draven. Jeff Most wondered if perhaps Proyas found it too stressful emotionally to take the sight of the fit, living Brandon, and that was why he had a hard time including them.

Sofia Shinas was certainly disappointed with the loss of certain moments and the way that some of her scenes had been edited. They were broken into a montage, instead of being used complete. "They were short scenes, but they were still scenes," Shinas said. "There was a beautiful scene between his character and my character, where I'm telling him how much I love him and how much he means to me. And him telling me how much I mean to him, and how he would do anything for me, and how he'd be willing to die for my character and it's painful for him to even imagine anything happening to me. That's a great scene. They should have used that in the film." She also remembered, "Going up the ladder, the ring, the engagement process, a bunch of stuff, redecorating the apartment, cooking together. Everything you saw and more, but it wasn't actually *shown*."

Inevitably, as any movie is edited and scenes or shots are dropped from it, the people who have worked on it are bound to discover that certain of their own favorite moments have disappeared. Jeff Imada, dropping into the cutting room occasionally, missed several things that he thought were important. He missed some of the fight action in Top Dollar's lair, because Brandon had some interesting moves that were cut out. He also regretted the loss of the scene where Massee's character, Funboy, comes back and starts to slash at Brandon. "Michael Massee comes up from behind him and, with a straight razor, starts slicing him all up. That's how the tape gets on him, the black tape, the electrical tape. This part of the scene is missing. I can understand why they took it out, but it doesn't explain the tape. But nobody's ever questioned why he had tape on him. But it became a story point character thing [in the original script] where, because he helped Darla and pulled all the heroin out of her, and because he interfered with somebody's life other than what he was supposed to be there for, then he became a mortal person for a period of time. And that's when he was able to get slashed up."

While the editing process was proceeding, all the extra material involving the miniatures and other special digital effects had to be shot. This was such a daunting task that Greg Gale had no idea how they were going to finish. "Even when we got the film back, I was just wondering how in the heck is this all gonna fit together, until we really started to get the effects built into it and shooting the miniatures out in Dream Quest [a studio near Los Angeles], which was a major undertaking."

The miniature sets, which had been built in Wilmington, had been shipped to Dream Quest Images' facility in Simi Valley, where they took up two, and sometimes three, stages at a time. They usually worked with computer-controlled "motion control" cameras, which were extremely precise but very slow, since they usually shoot frame by frame. That way, it could take days or even weeks to create one single shot. The extreme precision of the motion control cameras was enhanced by the extremely steady mechanism they used to transport the film inside the camera. This steadiness was crucial when shots are combined because the audience may not notice a slight floating motion in a single shot, but they certainly notice when one shot floats against another that has, for example, been superimposed on it. Andrew Mason, in charge of the process, persuaded the crew that was shooting the miniatures to work at a speed unknown in their field. His concept was to use the cameras without their motion control, but on motion control tracking rails, which were 20,000-pound, laser-accurate railroad track.

Mark Galvin recalled, the result was "These miniatures on our stage were shot, I think superbly and quite honestly, by our own crews at that point . . . , but they shot in Andrew's style, which was much more loose, and much more quickly. Instead of shooting a shot a week, he had us shooting *shots* per day!" Andrew Mason accomplished the work at a fraction of the cost and in three weeks, instead of the twelve that would normally have been required.

Galvin explained the problem they faced in shooting the scenes of the crow flying: "When you've got a set that isn't a set, it's a miniature, when all your locations aren't locations, they're miniatures . . . The only thing to do is either fly a miniature crow around or to composite the [real] crow in." The decision had already been taken in Wilmington to shoot Larry Madrid's real birds flying up against the powerful air current of the wind machine. This in turn meant that Galvin could now fly over miniatures. "We could have the crow with us, or just in front of us, or go to a crow-vision look [seeing the action from the bird's point of view], which was one of the other things they had us incorporate and make it very believable. And you always thought the crow was flying over a city."

Eventually, the miniatures were all shot, all the digital composite work was completed, and the entire film was cut together by Scott Smith, working with Alex Proyas. Jeff Most went to see it and was stunned. "It was one of the darkest films I'd ever seen," he said. "I think partially it was a painful experience for Alex, having gone through all that he'd gone through, and it came out on the screen. And I remember seeing the first director's cut, and I did have tears running down my face, because it was so bleak and it sent shivers down my spine." Of course, he missed the romantic scenes between Brandon Lee and Sofia Shinas, which had represented the Crow's humanity to him: "I could conjecture about a lot of reasons as to why they weren't there, in the first editor's cut, the director's cut. It was just extremely bleak in my mind."

Cutting the movie, Proyas and Smith had not gotten along very well, and now there was a cut of the completed film that pleased nobody.

"Down the line, Alex decided that he needed to have someone else on this picture," said Greg Gale, "and I know Ed Pressman had a feeling about Dov Hoenig." Dov Hoenig was a highly skilled editor with a reputation for saving movies. Before *The Crow*, he had cut *The Last of the Mohicans* (1992), *Under Siege* (1992), *The Fugitive* (1993), and *Street Fighter* (1994). Gale found him a true perfectionist in whatever he did: "He became part of the story. Dov is an editor that just isn't going to edit from what's on the script. Dov becomes part of the story and makes the story. He has his thoughts on how to change the story, moving something from one spot to another to give a better feel to the story. He takes those spots and applies them and then presents them to the director, and there may be some discussion with him, but he's very aggressive in the way he edited and that was the beauty of Dov."

Since Gale was up against constraints of time and money, which meant nothing to the perfectionist Hoenig, he was also to find that Hoenig was a difficult man to work with. "When I first met him, I was really leery," Gale recalled. "I can't tell you the numerous arguments me and Dov Hoenig got in over the way he was abusing time and overtime, and other things, on the project."

When a film is being changed radically in the cutting, the editor and the director often want to keep checking each big alteration they make. In the case of *The Crow* (shot on film that needed to be developed), they ran the cut every three or four days. This may have meant making extra prints of shots that had been mutilated by being cut several different ways and then joined again, or it may have required making temporary mixes of the sound [temp dubs], just to see that it's all coming together properly. "Dov had certain ways of doing additional prints and cuts," Gale asserted, "and he was going through a lot of additional prints, which was running up our budget. And he wanted to do his own temp dubs before we even brought on the talent team to do temp dubs."

Hoenig got along fine with Alex Proyas though, and they produced a new version of the movie. This new version moved much faster, while using the romantic scenes as flash cuts, which Greg Gale described as, "flashes in your mind, like wham! wham! wham!" According to Gale, Proyas knew very specifically how he wanted these sequences to look. He wanted a contrast between the virtually monochromatic look of the bulk of the story and the intensity of the flashbacks. "When we printed these scenes, they were oversaturated with color. Only the flashback scenes. And it was kind of difficult with the color-timing of the project and we had problems in the lab. It took a long time to color-time that picture to where we got it."

To get around the problem of the explanatory scenes with Brandon that had never been shot, another innovation was to use narration from the character of the little girl, Sarah. This also added some light to the overwhelmingly dark mood.

For Jeff Most, Hoenig was definitely an improvement. "Dov Hoenig came in and, I believe, salvaged the picture by adding in a great deal of the heart which the picture now possesses, by including the flashbacks in a well-dispersed manner, and by going back to our original approach: that there was a lightness that followed heavy scenes."

The impact of this new version of the movie was entirely different. In contrast to his previous depression, when Most saw this cut, he felt, "'My God, this is a work of art! This is what we set out to make.' And I mean, I was, inside, so moved by Brandon that at the same time it was a sense of grief. It was a sense of exhilaration over it all coming together so that we could actually show the world once and for all what a magnificent job he had done on the film."

Bob Rosen was also pleased with the progress that had been made: "There were a lot of changes and a lot of improvements from the first cut to the final. Lots and lots and lots. On the other hand, the things that anybody objected to in the first cut, they probably would have objected to in the final cut. I don't think it changed that much. Things were better. Things got better. Things got clearer. Things got sharper. Things got more exciting!"

Things were to get more "exciting" still when the producers showed a cut of the movie to Paramount, who was contracted to pick it up.

James Janowitz was at the crucial Paramount screening, and the head of production was present. Janowitz recalled, "Sherry [Lansing, then chairwoman of Paramount Pictures] saw it, was very complimentary of the work and of the director and felt that the film was too violent! At least, that's what she told us . . . that, as a result, they would not distribute it."

Speculating about Paramount's real reasons for rejecting the film, Jeff Most is of the opinion that Brandon's death had frightened them away. "This was a very awkward situation. I guess they didn't want blood on their hands, so to speak." Bob Rosen's analysis is similar: "At that point in time, I think their biggest concern was, we had made a picture where this accident occurred. Is anybody going to come see the movie?"

Contractually, of course, under the pick-up deal's terms, Paramount was perfectly within their rights to turn the movie down. It was now a different film from the one they had agreed to buy: It did not contain the full performance of Brandon Lee, the script and story had been changed materially, and it was not ready on the agreed date.

Whatever Paramount's reasons for rejecting the film, *The Crow* now had serious financial problems.

To keep money from the bank flowing, fueling the continuing process of post-production, the production had to persuade their insurance company to, "Stand in the shoes of the distributor," as Janowitz said, "and pay the bank the money which that distributor would otherwise have paid, because otherwise the bank wouldn't give us any more money."

The only consolation they had was the very powerful responses that the movie seemed to generate. Bob Rosen was at a couple of runnings of the film after the Paramount people dropped out. "And you could talk to two people who saw this running, and one would say, 'That's going to be the biggest hit in the world!' and the next person's saying, 'You're crazy, you can't complete that picture!' And they just sat next to each other watching the same movie." The producers had to hope that they would find a distributor who would take the former view.

SOUND OF *THE CROW* 26

Jeff Most always had an interest in music, even before he worked on the TV show *Top 40 Videos*. One of the things that originally attracted Most to *The Crow* comic was that James O'Barr shared a lot of his musical taste and that was expressed in O'Barr's work. "*The Crow* character," Most saw immediately, "was drawn after Peter Murphy, the lead singer of Bauhaus. Funboy was drawn after Iggy Pop. There were strong musical tie-ins and lyrics that were printed, bands like The Cure in the comic books. And the series had been dedicated initially to Ian Curtis, the lead singer in Joy Division, who in fact had been an inspiration to James O'Barr." John Shirley had spotted the same musical connection with the comic book: "I mean, Marilyn Manson is huge. You think there's no connection between Marilyn Manson and *The Crow*? Of course there is. He'd totally be on *The Crow*'s first soundtrack."

Most knew that something special could be done with the soundtrack of his movie, and he knew exactly what it was: "The musical through-line of the piece was something I felt very strongly about. And in trying to fashion something that was very special, I came up with the idea of doing an album of all unreleased songs, which at the time was unheard of. You usually license songs that were hits in doing movies. I felt that to make the music organic to the film, and to be memorable on its merits as being music from *The Crow*, that every song should be a song that no one had ever owned or heard before."

John Shirley greatly admired Most's determination to make his soundtrack concept a reality. "I remember Most poring through hundreds of new bands and hot bands and looking for things that were kind of listenable industrial sounds."

Working with Jolene Cherry, the movie's music supervisor, Most went to his heroes when he was assembling the soundtrack: "The first artist I went to, to request a song for *The Crow*, was Trent Reznor of Nine Inch Nails, who agreed to record an Ian Curtis (from Joy Division) song, 'Dead Souls.'" Though Trent Reznor and his band were unable to appear in the movie performing their song as Most had originally wanted, they did record "Dead Souls" for the soundtrack.

However, the first song that was delivered for the movie's soundtrack was from Stone Temple Pilots. Jeff Most had heard their first album and "fallen in love" with it and asked them to write a song for *The Crow*. Sadly, because of its title, it didn't make it on to the movie's album or soundtrack. "They wrote a beautiful song called 'Oh, Me Dying,'" recalled Most, "that we ultimately, by mutual decision, did not move ahead with or put on the album, because of the loss of Brandon." Instead, they recorded another song, "Big Empty."

Most was proud of the many "firsts" that he had on the movie's soundtrack. "The Cure wrote their first-ever song for a movie, 'Burn.' Robert Smith had only, to my understanding at the time, *licensed* [existing] Cure songs, never *released* a [new] song to a feature film."

Most would go over his choices with Brandon Lee: "Brandon took a great interest in the music. He would come into my office and say, 'What have you gotten in?' And I would play various songs and he really dug the music, as did the director, and played the songs for people, so that everyone had an idea of what exactly we were going to be integrating. Music was certainly something he knew. I was placing a great prominence on it, and I know he loved the songs from [My Life with] the Thrill Kill Kult, the band that appeared on stage with their song 'After the Flesh.'"

Of course, the songs for the album also had to be integrated with the music the director wanted for the movie. A New Zealander, Graeme Revell, wrote the movie's score and was responsible for that integration. Revell had his own punk/industrial band on the Australian scene in the 1980s and knew Proyas from dates he played and from clubs in Sydney. Jolene Cherry was his music publisher, and she told him that he was Proyas' only choice for the job: "She said, 'You're the only name that's come up.' I said, 'Great, love to do it.'"

Revell was hired unusually early on. "While they were still shooting, definitely. And I started writing really early. I got the scenes quite early, I think, from dailies, of Brandon on the rooftop. And I had to do the hand sync [synchronization] to him playing the guitar, even though I had no idea what he was playing or even if he played anything really."

Revell's job was tricky: to incorporate Jeff Most's original songs, to accommodate Alex Proyas' wishes, and to use his own artistry. "I'm the only person that knows where all the pieces of the puzzle are at this point," said Revell, "because it's in my head. And because what often happens or mostly happened in Alex's mind is, 'I want a piece of music here to achieve such and such emotionally, and this song by Helmet doesn't do that for me.' You say, 'Okay, but if I'm doing those other things that you wanted to achieve emotionally and Helmet does what it does in the middle, which is energy, aggression, then it's okay, right?' 'Yes, it's okay.' So that's what happens."

As the music track developed, Revell felt that he was getting too much credit for original songs, but when he told Jolene Cherry that, "She said to me, 'Graeme, just take the credit.' And that's actually stuck with me, because I actually can't understand why people fight tooth and nail about credit, because there's so much credit to go around." Revell was also sympathetic to Cherry because he knew that she was having a "somewhat difficult" relationship with Alex: "I think probably, just because Alex was so busy with all the other issues on the show, by the end it was very hard for him to focus with what happened to Brandon."

The songs that Jeff Most was so proud of certainly helped to make the movie's music album a success. But it was Revell who came up with the strange sounds that embodied the decaying, urban battlefield of the back lot. "What I decided was, 'Well, what is the sound of Detroit going to be like?' And I came up with this mixture of somewhat Arabic, somewhat Mongolian influences in there. Just a wild kind of World theme, but it's not like the World Music as we usually hear it, it's really mixed with grunge, rock 'n' roll, Industrial, and all that kind of stuff. But I think it gave a really otherworldly mood to the whole thing."

Initially, Proyas resisted many of Revell's ideas, such as the World Music ethnic feel. But with music, description means little, so Revell played the ideas to Proyas, and "when he heard it, he really got what I was talking about, and that was kind of the idea."

Revell enjoyed his work on the movie because he was able to give it a different character from other movie music, which generally must hit specific points of action. "But with *The Crow*, it was less about hitting little movements and cuts and things like that, than actually getting the feeling across. And so, in some ways it was a lot freer. You can write musically a lot more freely, and so I would just start to slide things around and see how they worked in different places." In the end, Revell felt that he had made an important contribution to *The Crow*: "The film sort of grew with the music, I think. I've never seen a film grow like this one did."

But the music is only one element of the final soundtrack of a movie. There are always extra voices to be added later.

For some scenes, where the sound that was shot at the time was disturbed by interruptions, such as passing aircraft, the actors would go to a sound studio and re-record their dialogue. But with its star not available, *The Crow* faced an unusual problem. The only solution was to find another voice that sounded like Brandon. Alex Proyas and his editors listened to literally hundreds of voices before they finally found not one, but two that sounded like Brandon. In the end, they used both voices for different scenes.

The editors tried to rescue as much of Brandon's real dialogue as they could and used the other two voices only for the voice-overs, which had in any case been re-written. But getting the voices to sound exactly right was not easy. Greg Gale remembered working on the voice-overs the evening before Thanksgiving 1993. "It was on a dubbing [sound-mixing] evening that was going into the holiday weekend, and Alex just wasn't getting the performance that we wanted, and we went into triple, quadruple golden time."

They were getting more and more over budget on the sound. And as soon as they got started on post-production, the bond company had brought in their own post-production person. "Michael [Harker]," said Gale, "stayed laid-back of everything and, in fact, he was a great helping hand whenever I asked for it. He never wanted to step in." Still, after all the other problems that had beset *The Crow*, Gale was faced with the movie apparently sinking further and further into the red on post-production. "We were eating up the clock at Skywalker Sound, so that I couldn't tell you how many hours of overtime we put in. It was six days a week, doing just the dubbing [mixing all the different sounds together]."

The situation got tougher and tougher for Gale: "Oh, they [the bond company] wanted to take over the picture. They threatened every which way, any way, to take over the picture!" There were constant audits going on, battles between the bond company and Crowvision's own accountant working at the post-production offices. It was a continual struggle, and Gale needed his own accountant on hand. "We needed checks and we were spending money every day."

Costs were out of control for two principal reasons. The second segment of shooting in Wilmington had gone at a much more leisurely pace than the first, and it was also more difficult, because all the shots that were needed to handle the problem of Brandon Lee's absence had to be so precise. Also, the sound effects took a great deal longer than had been envisaged. "The result was that we were running twelve-, fourteen-hour days on the dubbing stage," said Gale, "and normally you don't run twelve-, fourteen-hour days on the dubbing stage. You're talking a lot of money, and it was six to eight weeks too."

By this time though, the producers had very favorable reactions to screening the unfinished versions of the film, and they were able to hang tough. Without sacrificing any single aspect of it for economy, they finished the sound, and they finished it on their own terms.

DEBUT 27

As *The Crow* Flies

ARAMOUNT WAS OUT and the financial clock was ticking in overtime. *The Crow* needed a new distributor, fast. Everybody connected with the movie was showing it to anyone they had a relationship with. "I had the picture shown at Sony, and I had the picture shown at MGM," said Bob Rosen, who had "two contacts of mine at those individual places."

As they went around trying to make a sale, it became clear to Rosen what the big problem worrying distributors was: "Whether it be Columbia, Sony, or MGM, they were looking at a movie that was headlines in the [*Hollywood*] *Reporter* that day. It was a question, and a good question. By the way, if I were them, I'd probably have the same question: 'Does anybody want to see this?' You know. 'And can anybody stomach the idea that it's life imitating art?' And so that's a viable concern."

But Ed Pressman's contact was with Miramax. Miramax, which had just been acquired by Disney, was at that point a maverick New York company started by two brothers, Bob and Harvey Weinstein. (They named the company after their parents, Mira and Max.) Pressman screened *The Crow* for them and Miramax wanted the movie. So, after a few financial hiccups, Janowitz and Pressman did a deal with Miramax and *The Crow* finally had a distributor for North America.

Of course, this being *The Crow*, there's another version of how Miramax became interested in the movie. In October 1993, Ian Jessel, a celebrated film executive, fluent in several European languages and known for his expertise in international distribution, hadn't yet seen the film but remembers being in the back of a cab, with the now infamous convicted sex offender Harvey Weinstein, at MIFED, the Milan film sales festival, telling him "he should really take another look at the film." Jessel's view, unlike Paramount and many other companies that turned down *The Crow*, was that the negative publicity could be useful in selling it. Jessel also knew that Harvey was more interested in Oscar material and Bob was more interested in genre films, so Harvey referred it to his brother's attention, and Bob Weinstein took another look at *The Crow*.

Whatever the Weinsteins' true motives, *The Crow*'s producers, who had been getting nervous, were glad the situation was resolved. "Everybody in town viewed the movie, and we kept being turned down by almost everyone," recalled Jeff Most. "And you know, Bob Weinstein and Harvey Weinstein . . . they felt that it was a marketing challenge that they were able to take on."

Always down to earth, costume supervisor Darryl Levine took a more cynical view: "Bad publicity is good publicity. Perfect! Is there any publicity that's bad? Nothing like this. This is unfortunate, but it's what people live for." Contrary to Levine's opinion at the time, eventually, Harvey Weinstein would fully come to appreciate the devastation, and burnt-ash desolation, resulting from the wrong publicity.

The final cut of *The Crow* was, in industry jargon, already locked by January 17, 1994, the day sound was finalized and the film's titles were completed. All that remained was for the laboratory to make the first print. Unfortunately, January 17, 1994, is a date better remembered in Los Angeles as the day of the Northridge earthquake, which registered 6.2 on the Richter scale at its epicenter, killing seven people and damaging 27,000 buildings.

In *The Crow*'s cutting room, at the same moment the building's water main burst, the severe shaking threw film cans from the storage shelves. Much of the film ending up on the floor was destroyed. If any pre-QAnon fanatics were looking for the curse of *The Crow* to strike again, this was their moment.

As quickly as he could, Greg Gale dashed to the labs. "I was dealing with everything going on, you know, gas outages, phones down, and everything else." At the laboratory, it was the day they were scheduled to screen a print for Gale, so that he could judge its color-timing. He had been present when Alex Proyas and Dariusz Wolski had been through the entire film, shot by shot, to select the exact lightness or darkness and tint of each shot in the film. Now Gale was to see how well those decisions had been carried out.

Fortunately, the film in the cutting room that had been destroyed was print film, so it could be re-printed. The negative was in the laboratory vault, and although a vault wall had collapsed, the precious material was undamaged. Gale could hardly believe it: "You go through the Storm of the Century on the East Coast, and you've got the big earthquake out here that wipes out half your editing room. Thank God we were at a final cut!"

In any event, the print was satisfactorily color-timed and the production was at last able to arrange the traditional Hollywood cast and crew screenings. The first one was in Santa Monica. Even after having waited almost a year to see their labor of love, for many of them the excitement was tempered with apprehension. "It was tough," Robert Zuckerman felt. "People were there, but it was really tough for me to watch it."

The initial reaction among the audience, thought Greg Gale, "Was that whole aura: 'Wow, Brandon's up on the screen.'" Second unit DP Ken Arlidge thought, "It's new. It's fresh. It's unique. It's dark. Therefore, it will have an audience." But for Arlidge, this could never be just another movie he had shot. "Unfortunately, I'm also walking out of there with all my memories and my emotional attachment to the film."

Summoning up her courage, Arianne Phillips also went to the screening. "I went mostly to see the other people, because it was like going through a war together. It's like you got this weird fucked-up bond." But she was dismayed: "A lot of people hadn't been invited. I remember Jeff Cadiente, he was one of Brandon's close friends, and he wasn't even invited to the cast and crew screening!" She did recall, however, seeing several movie stars, including Jean-Claude Van Damme. "I show up to the cast and crew screening, and there is a red carpet and tons of press. It was a première, but they called it cast and crew. I was disgusted. I almost wanted to leave, then I thought, 'No, I want to go and see Ed Pressman and tell him how disgusting it is!'"

Making an occasion of the traditional screening for those who had worked on the movie was especially infuriating to Phillips: "Eliza specifically asked for them not to have a première of the film and made it very clear that if it would be a celebration of the film, she couldn't support that. Ed Pressman promised that he wouldn't do that."

Creatively, however, Phillips was deeply fulfilled: "It is very rare that your sketch becomes realized, and my work really became realized from concept to screen."

Lance Anderson was also proud: "I was a contributing factor to the look of the movie from the very beginning to the end, the main character, and a lot of the effects and all of the makeup effects."

Sofia Shinas was certainly "affected and moved by Brandon's performance," but she had brought with her the gut feeling that, "They were going to try to limit, downplay, the relationship between Shelly and Eric to show respect in memory of the relationship that Brandon and Eliza had in actuality."

Her fellow actor, Angel David, saw the movie for the first time in a special screening at New York's Planet Hollywood. He was, "Awestruck, because every element that Alex was talking about was in the film." Unlike Shinas, Angel David was "really, really pleased that Alex put most of my stuff in there and just left it there."

Laurence Mason missed the New York screening but recalled being given a special video copy by screenwriter David Schow. "I had a director's cut, which was cool. And he gave me a tape and I went home and I watched it. A zillion times. And I was very happy with it."

Randy LaFollette was extremely excited to see the movie on which he worked so hard and which he felt so close to. Adding to his anticipation was his expectation of, for the first time, seeing his name in the main credits instead of in the roller at the end: "I'm in Seattle. I go and take all my family and we go and see the movie, and I get this huge shared card with Steve [Andrews, the first assistant director], which means there's two names on the whole screen and big huge letters and it's like, 'Wow!' And they misspelled my last name! [It is spelled 'LaFoulette' in the credits.] A typo!"

In Philadelphia, Rochelle Davis decided to see her movie on the night it was released in theaters. "I thought, 'I wanna go as a regular person and see how the crowd looks and reacts to this film.'" When she arrived, she was shocked at what she saw. In the first three rows were young fans dressed like the Crow. "I mean, they had put all this time into making their costumes before they even saw the movie. They were totally into it. And like, it was a première night of the movie and these people were already dressed in these Crow outfits. And I went up to the front, I said, 'Hey, guys!' It's the end of the movie, and they were like, 'That movie rocked!' And they're all screaming and I'm like, 'Hey guys!' They all looked at me and went, 'Oh my God!' and immediately knew who I was."

Around the country, audiences wearing Crow costumes flocked to the opening night of the movie. Claudio Miranda went to the famous Mann's Chinese Theatre on Hollywood Boulevard: "The cool thing is a lot of people were actually dressed for the thing. They're all in their white makeup and the little black lines. That was obviously great." But he was distressed to see that the controversy over Brandon's death was still raging outside the theater, where protesters paced up and down the sidewalk. "They were picketing the fact that the film was being released. I don't even know if they were union or not. But they were picketing the fact that if it was a union movie, Brandon would be living. That's not necessarily true!"

Much later, more than a year after the initial release, Darryl Levine rented the video at the insistence of his children. "It really touched me," he admitted, "but I wasn't ready to deal with it. I didn't want to see it." Levine found himself faced with difficult questions from his son. "He said, 'When did he get shot?' And everybody wanted to know how we did so much stuff without him, and actually we didn't [do that much]."

Beyond their personal difficulties, almost all the cast and crew were proud of their work on *The Crow* and felt that the movie had retained its integrity and was a fitting tribute to Brandon.

The senior creative team had approached the first public screenings with some doubts, some fears, and a lot of hope. "The first screening we had with civilians," Bob Rosen recalled of that occasion, "is when I knew we had something. And they were with the movie to the point that they lost themselves in the movie and weren't thinking about, 'Where was the sequence where he was shot?' And I didn't feel that at all. That between the action and the look, and it was something that they had never seen before, they got carried away with the movie. And I thought, from the very first preview . . . I recall saying that to Ed, I said, 'Wow, I think you've got something here. You've really got something here!'"

The next task was to market the film, which is usually the time when the star and director of a movie go out and promote it. In Brandon Lee's case, of course, this was impossible, and Alex Proyas seems to have made it a rule not to talk to the media. This was not simply because of the tragedy on *The Crow*; he has given few interviews on his subsequent films.

Not surprisingly, Jeff Most was hounded by the press, who had to make do with promotional efforts from James O'Barr, Ed Pressman, Ernie Hudson, and Most himself. They all found the interviews difficult because the media's focus was on Brandon's death, whereas the filmmakers wanted to talk about their movie. "It was certainly not something I wanted to take advantage of in an exploitative manner," admitted Most, "by discussing the tragic events surrounding Brandon's loss."

Ernie Hudson's movie with Wesley Snipes, *Sugar Hill* (1993), had just been released, and he felt that he was particularly useful in promotion because he was the best-known actor in *The Crow*. Perhaps more importantly, he had not been present when Brandon Lee was shot, and so could not be questioned about the incident.

Hudson had not seen the movie, and since the production wanted him to promote it, they set up a special screening for him. "When I saw it, I was sure that it was Alex's movie. And I'm sure the editing and the reason it turned out to be what it is today is totally, totally Alex." But he was also very disappointed by something he saw on the screen. He had been told earlier that they wanted to put all the cast and crew credits at the end of the film, so that the front credit could be used to dedicate the film to Brandon Lee. Hudson had originally contracted for a "starring" credit at the front of the film, but since everyone else had agreed to this change, he went along with it: "Except when I watched the movie and it's dedicated to Brandon, and then the film goes on, and they didn't even put the actors' credits to begin with. They put all their bullshit credits, all the production credits, in front of ours. And then they put my name in the wrong position, on top of all the rest of it!" Although this clearly irritated Hudson, he decided that he would do his best to promote the movie. He thought it was a good film, and that he should promote it for Brandon. "Brandon wanted to show people that he had what it took to be a star, and I thought the movie certainly showed that. And I thought people should see it."

A promotion tour was put together and on occasion Rochelle Davis joined it. How effective the publicity efforts were will never really be known, as there was already such a buzz about the movie, both because of the kind of film it was and because of the strange death of its star and of his father.

Jeff Most was now prepared for the worst: "All through the process we had so many naysayers on every front that it was beyond belief that we did as well. It's like a battered child, or a battered wife, whatever . . . We never let our spirits drop, and we gave it every ounce of energy we could, to make certain that it was presented in the finest fashion possible, and a non-exploitative manner."

Challenging all superstitions, *The Crow* opened in May 1994, on Friday the 13th, to mainly favorable reviews. *The New Yorker* thought the movie showed a "frightening mastery" from Alex Proyas and had "melancholy power." *Entertainment Weekly* liked its "kaleidoscopic rock-video fervor." The Hollywood trade magazine, *Variety*, said that the movie took place in a "most imaginatively rendered world" and that Brandon was "perhaps a star." *Playboy* thought the film was "a triumph" and that Brandon had "vivid presence." Similarly, the *Los Angeles Times* thought Brandon had a "phenomenal presence," in contrast to the bad guys, who the paper described as "world-class scum."

The Crow was an immediate hit. On its opening weekend, it was the number one movie in America.

After the long journey from first reading James O'Barr's comic, through the saga of pitching the project and eventually getting a deal, and the nightmare of production, being banned from his own set, and the ultimate tragedy of Brandon's death, Jeff Most was proud that, "We opened to $11.9 million, a record for its opening weekend."

Greg Gale was not surprised by the opening weekend. "But when it kept on holding number one for a few weeks, I was just like, 'My God!' It was elating to have a picture go number one for as long as it did." Like many other people on the crew, Gale had been so dazed by the process that he couldn't judge the result. "I was blinded into thinking it was not any good, as far as any kind of real content. But when it was released and it hit number one, I said, 'God, I guess this is the hype from the publicity.' 'Are we gonna see Brandon on the picture? This is his last picture. Is the scene going to be in there?' Even though it was said quite specifically, 'The scene's not going to be in there.' But the next weekend, number one again!"

The fear had been that the initial audiences had come out of ghoulish curiosity, and everybody knew that that feeling could not sustain the film at the box office. But the movie did sustain and remained high at the box office for several weeks.

It was satisfying for Jeff Most to see the passion for the film in the audience. "And you know, it started getting termed a 'cult movie' virtually after its opening. And I suppose at $50 million . . . over $50 million at the box office, you're no longer a cult. At $115 million worldwide, that's a big, successful Hollywood movie."

For Bob Rosen, it was not simply an artistic vindication, but a personal one. "It showed that there was an audience for a picture like this. It also, I think, showed that a picture that was as . . . I don't know . . . *ambitious* as this picture was, in terms of the production and the opticals and the physicality of the picture, could be done for a price with the right person directing it. As I say, I go back to those first meetings, I think about it a lot before I go to sleep at night, at Paramount where everybody told me I had lost my ability to function here, thinking we could make the picture for this price."

Actors have their own, different agenda and satisfactions. Angel David was, he said, "Walking down the street, and there were two or three women that were coming up the street and they were like, 'You were in *The Crow*, give me your autograph, here's my number'!"

The soundtrack of the movie was released at the same time as the film and was also a huge hit. Most, who created the album with Jolene Cherry, was again vindicated by the excellent sales, which, of course, helped to promote the movie. "I put so much effort into the music, so when that became a big success and a number one album, voted Best Soundtrack of the Year by fans and critics, I took a great deal of pride in that. The response by fans thrilled me." To date, the soundtrack has sold more than ten million units worldwide.

Laurence Mason thought that the marketing of the soundtrack was ahead of its time: "It was slick. Grunge was really big, and it was just making an entrance then. It was a very timely flick. And it has a little of everything: it's a little love story, a little action, little drama."

It quickly became clear to everyone who had worked on the film that Brandon's death alone could never account for such a big success, that the movie had touched some sort of chord in its audience. Actress Bai Ling, who felt very "happy and proud" with her performance, saw the film as "timeless. It's about love, it is about life, death, and being human. . . . It's about redemption. That love never dies. That's something very beautiful and powerful." Most had his own explanation: "It's a mythological thing, that I think people can imagine that they themselves were up on the screen. That [if], God forbid, this happened to one of their loved ones or themselves, that the light at the end of the tunnel is that an angel can return, and an angel can put things right. And that there is an afterlife, and that there is a strength of a bond of love that can overcome anything."

A Murder of Crows   28

Wᴵᴛʜᴵɴ sᴵx ʏᴇᴀʀs of *The Crow's* phenomenal film debut, the trilogy that Jeff Most dreamed of became a reality, albeit reimagined without Eric Draven. The two additional films that Brandon was originally signed to do had been made: *The Crow: City of Angels* in 1996 and *The Crow: Salvation* in 2000.

New comic stories published by Kitchen Sink Press had already opened the door to the idea that new characters beyond Eric Draven could embody *The Crow*, including an American Indian in *The Crow: Dead Time*, a federal conservation officer in *The Crow: Flesh and Blood*, and a man battling the Chinese mafia in *The Crow: Waking Nightmares*, though none of these were translated into film sequels.

Wanting to capitalize on the success of the first film and reinvent the franchise without the character of Eric Draven, out of deference to the legacy of Brandon Lee, *The Crow: City of Angels* was released in 1996. The hero, played by relatively new, European actor Vincent Perez, is resurrected by the Crow to exact revenge for his own murder and the slaying of his son. Now an adult tattoo artist in Los Angeles, the character of Sarah (played by rising-star Mia Kirshner), from the first film, reappears to help the hero realize his mission. Notably, a couple of the original film's key creative talent were rehired, including production designer Alec McDowell and composer Graeme Revell. One of James O'Barr's favorite music icons, Iggy Pop, appeared as one of its villains.

After shooting, the film was mired in creative conflict when pioneering music video director Tim Pope and screenwriter David Goyer clashed with Miramax execs who rejected their unique, darker vision and insisted the film more resemble the original.

The modest $13-million production opened number one at the box office, setting a record for the Labor Day Weekend and recouping 54.6 percent of its total costs. But the high expectations of a hit like the first film swiftly fizzled, as this new iteration was quickly fading at the box office as most reviews considered it a thinly veiled, inferior remake.

After being included in the *City of Angels'* soundtrack, legendary rocker Rob Zombie was hoping to make his directorial debut with his own Crow sequel in 1998. His screenplay, *The Crow 2037: A New Age of Gods and Monsters*, portrays a future boy and his mother murdered by a Satanic priest on Halloween. Subsequently, as the brand demands, the boy is soon resurrected as the Crow to seek revenge. Pressman Films ultimately abandoned the project.

Also in 1998, the made-for-syndication TV series *The Crow: Stairway to Heaven* brought back several franchise core characters, especially the lead character of Eric Draven, played by future *Iron Chef America* host Mark Dacascos, who began his career starring in numerous low-budget martial arts action films. Under the same premise as the original film, Eric Draven is resurrected by the spirit-guiding crow but now is condemned to exact vengeance on a disparate assortment of villains (spanning twenty-two episodes) in an ongoing quest to reestablish the balance of good and evil before he can be reunited with his fiancée in the afterlife.

The Canadian-produced series performed well, and the last episode ended with a cliff-hanger, assuming a second season. But, when the show's production house, PolyGram, was bought by Universal, the series was abruptly canceled. And by this time, the third film in the originally planned trilogy was gearing up. *The Crow: Salvation* (2000) starred newcomer Eric Mabius as a man wrongly convicted and executed for the murder of his girlfriend, played by the rising young actress Kirsten Dunst.

Although *City of Angels* performed moderately well at the box office, Miramax, the film's distributor, chose to release the third film directly to video. According to Jeff Most, "Bob Weinstein [the head of Miramax's genre division, Dimension Films] liked the film a lot but felt since the biggest name involved was Kirsten Dunst and it was difficult to market on the female lead in a Crow movie." Nevertheless, *The Crow: Salvation* did appear in some cinemas internationally and was reported by the *Wall Street Journal* to be one of Blockbuster's top five direct-to-video rental titles for 2001.

In 2000 and 2001 an attempt was made to produce what would have been the fourth *Crow* film. Set in the rap music world, *The Crow: Lazarus* planned to star major music artists DMX in the title role and Eminem as his manager who plots to kill him. "I wanted to combine the murders of Tupac Shakur and Biggie Smalls. I had this idea of, you know, what if a hit went wrong," recalled Jeff Most. The plot ensues as the assassin's bullet accidentally kills both characters, who are then resurrected into a good Crow and bad Crow character fighting it out to settle the score and put things right.

With hot music video director Joseph Khan attached and a budget of $11 million, production was set to start in Montreal in April of 2001, but by March, things started falling apart, as Eminem was put on trial for gun charges in Michigan. After seeking to push back the start date to accommodate the rapper's legal troubles, Most recalled, "The bond company said, look, there's a pending SAG [Screen Actors Guild] strike. You can't extend this and there's no way of knowing with a trial. You cannot move forward with Eminem in this role." Efforts to find a new bankable lead actor, in such a short window of opportunity, failed.

In the meantime, DMX's movie stardom was rising. He had signed a three-picture deal with legendary producer Joel Silver at Warner Bros. and now wanted to renegotiate his fee on *Lazarus*. "DMX wanted to get $6 million and we would have certainly given the same to Eminem. But, frankly, this was four times more than we had them attached for originally at $1.5 million each, so all of a sudden, their fees went up from $3 million in total to $12 million. Miramax's Bob Weinstein said 'No way. Not gonna happen. You know, I'm not paying for that.'"

After Miramax backed out, efforts to raise more money with other studios marched on. Eminem went on to star in his semi-autobiographical film *8 Mile* (2002) and DMX went on to star in *Cradle 2 The Grave* (2003), where he ironically collaborated with Eminem on the movie's soundtrack. Ultimately, *Lazarus* was never resurrected.

In 2005, after a delay in production, in part due to the general reluctance to make violent films in Hollywood following the devastating terrorist attacks on the World Trade Center in New York and the Pentagon in Washington, D.C., on September 11, 2001, *The Crow* spawned a third sequel: *The Crow: Wicked Prayer*. This fourth installment of the franchise was loosely based on writer Norman Partridge's Crow novel of the same name, set on the Arizona-Nevada border. Starring Edward Furlong, David Boreanaz, and Tara Reid, with appearances by Dennis Hopper and Macy Gray as featured villains, it boasted the biggest-name cast of any of the previous films. In one final curious twist in this exceptional Hollywood tale, it also starred the only cast or crew members to work on all four Crow films: the crows (or rather ravens) themselves, lead birds Magic and Baby, guided by their trainer, Larry Madrid.

The complicated plot of *The Crow: Wicked Prayer* portrays a new character: Jimmy Cuervo, a down-on-his-luck ex-con who returns from the dead after he and his girlfriend are murdered by a satanic ritual. Described as a "Spaghetti Western," the battle between good and evil is waged amidst witchcraft, Satanism, the Four Horseman of the Apocalypse, Native Americans, and shamans. With so many larger themes at work, compared to previous sequels and the core franchise, the film was critically panned and went direct-to-video.

The contentious odyssey of *Wicked Prayer*'s script started with Ed Pressman hiring Lance Mungia as screenwriter and director. Mungia was a novice filmmaker who had written and directed the low-budget indie post-apocalyptic musical satire *Six-String Samurai* (1998). The film made a splash at the Park City Utah film festival, Slamdance, a brand-new indie festival showcasing low-budget, cutting-edge, and art-house fare, right in the backyard of the well-established Sundance Film Fest, in hope of stealing some of the spotlight, and more importantly, some of the industry's deep-pocket acquisitions dollars annually flooding the picturesque locale.

According to Jeff Most, after ten weeks, and two weeks overdue, "He [Lance Mungia] calls me and goes, 'Jeff, I really need to see you.'" The deadline had passed for his contracted first draft and, with only four or five disconnected scenes written, Mungia agreed with Most to collaborate and finish the script. After moving into Most's Hollywood Hills home's guestroom, Mungia and Most worked nonstop and finished a draft in fifteen days. According to Most, "We sent it into the executive at Dimension and they literally loved it."

But upon receiving the script and seeing Most's name as co-screenwriter, Ed Pressman wanted to do his own rewrite. In turn, Pressman had Mungia come and live in his guesthouse in Connecticut and create another version. After the new draft was done and reviewed by Pressman's staff, Pressman called in a friend, the late actor/screenwriter/producer L. M. Kit Carson (most noted for his adaptation of Sam Shepard's *Paris, Texas* (1984) and writing *The Texas Chainsaw Massacre 2* (1986)) to do a rewrite. Ultimately, Carson was not listed as a writer but given a token co-producer credit.

The script continued to change hands. Not the concept they had signed onto, the studio (Dimension) rejected this new draft. A stalemate ensued. A script was needed to satisfy both Dimension and Pressman. Sean Hood, another novice screenwriter, whose major credit was *Halloween: Resurrection* (2002), was enlisted and ultimately received a screenwriting co-credit. But of greatest significance, the failure of *Wicked Prayer* damaged the essential relationships of the core creative team that had shepherded *The Crow* from the very beginning. "It was very, just disheartening. And, you know, very, very upsetting experience," recalled Most.

Though producer Jeff Most would ultimately be credited as a producer and co-writer on the awful mess that became *Wicked Prayer*, he felt, "When you find that your baby, that you gave birth to, you wrote the original options and treatments on and it's been spun into whatever . . . Frankly, I was very, very disappointed with the script that was going forward. I felt like so much of what made *The Crow* unique, and a touchstone emotionally had been lost."

Reflecting on the genesis of *The Crow*, Most said, "Maybe we made a mistake by not continuing on with the original character in the first place, but we just were so devastated with the loss of Brandon and just didn't want to tarnish his memory."

So, this became the moment. If the brand ever experienced a pause, this was it. Finally, *The Crow* fell back to earth.

But this is Hollywood. The very mutable laws of Life, Death, and Box Office can lead to an unexpected rebirth no matter how costly, painful, or colossal the original failure might have been. More often than not, for hardy and resilient IP, the respite can be surprisingly brief.

THE CROW REBORN 29

A LTHOUGH *CITY OF ANGELS*, *Salvation*, and *Wicked Prayer* were less successful than the original, Miramax/Dimension decided to release a glossy box set of the three sequels in 2005. Regardless of the films' lackluster performances, the Crow franchise was still thriving through a constant flow of published *Crow* books, comics, merchandise, and the popular twenty-two-episode TV series, *The Crow: Stairway to Heaven*, that still ran in syndication.

Time passes and Hollywood reflects society at large. It has a short memory, which makes the current state of the industry deeply inclined towards remakes and reboots. For good or ill, the process seems inevitable. But opinions may vary.

The Crow's story, an antihero avenging injustice to set the flawed world right and then pass into the awaiting Nirvana, transcended its sequel failures and created a resilient, consistently renewing fan base as well as a never-ending list of dedicated, A-List filmmakers ready to reimagine the story.

Ravens (the type of birds that played the crows through all the films) can live a half century in captivity, a longevity nearly mirrored by the efforts to reboot *The Crow*.

Fast-forward three decades after the release of the original film, and a remake of the original story of *The Crow* comic by James O'Barr is anticipated to be released in 2024.

For some who've been involved with *The Crow*'s long saga, this effort seemed impossible, a doomed project. For others, it was strangely inevitable.

Actress Bai Ling felt the reboot is a mistake: "It's an industry and whatever they think is sometime can make money and also can retell the original story. They can then adjust to the moral sense of it. In my sense, this [The Crow, 1994] is so original, so authentic. That is the power, so pure, so magical. They should not touch it. It can never be as good. This one can never be better."

Jeff Imada, Brandon's good friend and The Crow's stunt coordinator, felt, "The Crow was great and, just like other films, they want to feel like there's a guarantee of some sort for success. They don't want to take a lot of chances. But again, Brandon had a lot to do with it. It's like redoing Enter the Dragon (1973). Why would you want to do that when the project was good, but Bruce Lee was the one that carried the project."

However, The Crow's special makeup effects artist, Lance Anderson, had a different opinion. "You probably could do a sequel if you follow the comic book. They kind of got away from that in the movie [The Crow, 1994]. I think it would be more interesting to follow the comic book. That's where the fans are. If you look at the book, you get a sense of more real darkness and strong graphics."

The reboot saga started in in the mid-2000s. Pressman Films recognized the enduring interest in the evergreen story of the The Crow and that the stigma of the on-set tragedy had dulled with the passage of time. Plus, the original film had grossed more than $100 million worldwide and become a cult classic.

A decade-long-plus revolving door of creative hires for The Crow reboot ensued, disillusioning fans and promoting skepticism as the film industry would report the projects' ongoing failed attempts.

In 2008, momentum was building. Focused efforts by Pressman Films to reinvent the movie were underway. Sought-after Blade (1998) director Stephen Norrington was attached, and Pressman made a deal with Relativity Studios for three Crow films with an option to begin production within three years. To differentiate his reboot from the original film, Norrington told Variety, "Whereas Proyas' original was gloriously gothic and stylized, the new movie will be realistic, hard-edged and mysterious, almost documentary-style." A 2010 production schedule and 2011 release were announced.

In June of 2010, Ed Pressman told MTV that Norrington's script was "Terrific" and that "Stephen is a very talented fellow and I'm very excited to work with him. I think it's a very different conception."

A Hollywood minute later in 2010, Ed Pressman hired iconic musician and acclaimed screenwriter Nick Cave to rewrite Norrington's script.

Swiftly Norrington departed the project, telling *Mania* (a now defunct publication) in October 2010, "As I had gotten involved explicitly as a writer-director my exit was inevitable. I was bummed. I had developed a genuinely authentic take that respected the source material while moving beyond it."

In 2011, *28 Weeks Later* filmmaker Juan Carlos Fresnadillo was hired to direct with Bradley Cooper reported to play Eric Draven. But by the Fall, Bradley withdrew due to a scheduling conflict as did Fresnadillo shortly after. Industry rumors also circulated that Mark Wahlberg, Channing Tatum, Ryan Gosling, or James McAvoy were being considered as the lead. A rights dispute over worldwide distribution for *The Crow* franchise between Relativity Media and Miramax erupted, further bogging down the reboot's already rocky development.

By 2012, the distribution squabble was resolved and *Before the Fall* (2008) director Javier Gutierrez was hired. Actors Tom Hiddleston and Alexander Skarsgard were reportedly considered but Luke Evans emerged as formally attached to portray *The Crow*.

More stalls and no production/greenlight. In December 2014, *Deadline* reported that Gutierrez moved on to make the next film in the *Ring* (2017) franchise.

Ed Pressman then hired music video darling Corin Hardy, who had just made his feature horror film *The Hallow* (2015).

While publicizing the film, Hardy told horror film fan magazine *Fangoria*, "I was obsessed with *The Crow* when I was growing up. . . . And now that I have gotten the chance to do it, I'm very much going back to the graphic novel, particularly looking into the illustrations themselves as much as the story, and picking out all those beautiful ideas and details that haven't really been used yet."

Oddly still attached two years later, Luke Evans exited in January 2015 due to a scheduling conflict. Immediately, Jack Huston, of HBO's hit series *Boardwalk Empire* (2010–2014) was enlisted to play the new Eric Draven. Pre-production was set to begin in Wales, only to see Huston leave the project in June 2015, like his predecessors, citing schedule conflicts.

In July, Hardy in a statement told *Variety*, "Jack Huston is unfortunately unavailable to continue with us on *The Crow*. *The Crow* is an amazing project, and I am grateful that we have the time and patience to get it right. We look forward to unveiling our new lead and starting to film over the next several weeks."

A month later, Relativity Studios filed for bankruptcy. Additionally, their $2.5 million rights option for *The Crow* signed with Pressman Films was still set to expire in a year and a half unless principal photography commenced.

Responding to concerns for the project's viability after this announcement, James O'Barr told a comic con audience in New York State, "The day Relativity announced that they were having financial problems, there were like a dozen other studios that called about getting *The Crow* property. It definitely will happen."

With production stalled, the rights dispute heated up as Edward Pressman issued court papers that would prevent Relativity Media from making any sequel, prequels, or remakes of *The Crow*.

Ed Pressman's longtime personal attorney, James Janowitz, directed the efforts to take back control of *The Crow*; "I was approached by a number of investors who were interested in making the film, including the French company led by Samuel Hadida." Davis Films, established by seasoned producer Hadida, best known for producing the hit film *True Romance* (1993) and the *Resident Evil* film franchise, and who died in 2018, wanted the rights to *The Crow*.

Nevertheless, creative efforts continued. Actor Jason Momoa broke the news that he was tapped to play the role with an Instagram post on August 6, 2016, of him gleefully drinking Guinness with director Corin Hardy. "The only way to officially seal the deal as men is a pint of black-beauty. ALOHA ED!"

Indeed, in 2014, even before he had any relationship to *The Crow*'s meandering development, Momoa proactively shot test footage of himself as the character. According to producer Jeff Most, "He decided when he was in Europe on another film to have some stunt and makeup people help him and he filmed himself being Eric Draven." It wouldn't be until 2021 when the video surfaced online.

Most said that Momoa reached out to him to help persuade Pressman and Relativity after Momoa's agent failed to garner his consideration for the role. Most recalled, "I was just blown away by the extent to which he went to make clear that he could embody this character."

Though Most had years before ended any meaningful involvement with *The Crow* franchise, he enthusiastically pitched Momoa. "I was rallying behind somebody that I really believed could make a difference much in the way that we felt Brandon would in the role."

But the new producers passed, insisting that, according to Most, "'Momoa wasn't a big enough star'" with only the box office failure *Conan* (2011), which incurred a crippling $75 million in losses for its studio, Lionsgate, and his one hit, HBO's gamechanger of a series, *Game of Thrones*, as his biggest credits.

It would take two more years slogging through development hell and Momoa's casting as Aquaman, a DC Extended Universe franchise character, before the newest Crow team recognized his star power.

Re-enforcing the forward motion, at the end of 2016, Relativity Media never recovered financially and called it quits, selling all its holdings to Davis Films. The creative team was fueled by a positive new start. "I was able to make a deal to acquire the rights back to the film from Relativity, despite the fact that it was in bankruptcy," recalled Janowitz.

Perhaps, Janowitz knows the saga of *The Crow* franchise better than anyone: "I have dealt with it pretty much without break well, since it came out. There has never been a year in which I wasn't working on this property."

In November of 2017, Momoa posted on Instagram a fan's drawing of *The Crow* saying, "I've been waiting for sooooo long. @corinhardy let's do this brother."

At least one of the visionaries responsible for the original film thought the story of Eric Draven and Shelly Webster should be left alone. In December 2017, Alex Proyas posted a photo of a young Brandon Lee with his father, martial arts legend Bruce Lee, with a statement titled: "WHY I THINK *THE CROW* SHOULD NOT BE REMADE."

"I was privileged to know Brandon Lee—he was a young, immensely gifted actor with a great sense of humor and a bright future ahead of him," the post began. "I was also privileged to have been able to call him a friend. Our working relationship as actor/director went beyond mere collaboration. We crafted a movie together, which has touched many people.

"I did not take a 'film by' credit on *THE CROW*. I wanted it to be Brandon's movie, because it was, and because he would not be able to make any more movies. He brought all his passion to the movie and it has lasted as his legacy. It is a film I know he would have been proud of.

"I finished the film for Brandon—struggling through grief, along with the hugely supportive cast & crew who all loved Brandon, to complete it in his absence. We were imbued with the strength of Brandon's spirit and his inspiration. Not only Brandon's wonderful work as an actor and a filmmaker, but as a man, whose humanity had touched us.

"*THE CROW* would not be a movie worth 'remaking' if it wasn't for Brandon Lee. If it wasn't for Brandon you may never have even heard of this poignant little underground comic. It is Brandon's movie. I believe it is a special case where Hollywood should just let it remain a testament to a man's immense talent and ultimate sacrifice—and not have others rewrite that story or add to it. I know sequels were made, and TV shows, and what have you, but the notion of 'rebooting' this story, and the original character—a character Brandon gave life to at too high a cost—seems wrong to me. Please let this remain Brandon's film."

In early 2018, an October 11, 2019, release date was announced. "I loved the graphic novel," Momoa told *Entertainment Weekly*. After insisting the new reboot would follow the comic more faithfully than the original film, Momoa said, "I just got a first edition. I got it signed . . . It's an honor to play it."

Momentum was building. With a new working title of *The Crow Reborn*, Sony reported to be signed on as a distributor, the script finished, Momoa and Hardy in place, at last production was set to start in Summer 2018.

Then, a little more than a month before the filming, Hardy, and then Momoa announced their departure from the project, rumored to stem from a financial dispute between Davis Films and Sony.

On May 31, 2018, Momoa posted on Instagram, "I've waited 8 years to play this dream role. I love you @corinhardy and @sonypictures unfortunately I may have to wait 8 more. Not our team. But I swear I will. James O'Barr sorry to let you down I won't on the next. This film needs to be set free. And to the fans. Sorry. I can't play anything but what this film deserves and it needs love. I'm ready when it's right. Love u Corin aloha."

The next day, Hardy confirmed his disappointing departure by posting an earlier snapped, playful photo of him and Momoa in *The Crow* makeup: "I knew from the off, that the idea of making a new version of *The Crow* was never going to be for everyone, because it is a beloved film. And I say that as someone in love with it myself. But I poured everything I had into the last 3.5 years of work, to try & create something which honored what *The Crow* stood for; from James O'Barr's affecting graphic novel, to Alex Proyas's original movie, with great respect to Brandon Lee and with the desire to make something bold and new, that myself, as an obsessive fan, could be proud of. And with @prideofgypsies Jason Momoa, and my amazing team of artists & filmmakers, we came SO close. But sometimes, when you love something so much, you have to make hard decisions. And yesterday, deciding it was time to let go of this dark & emotional dream project, was the hardest decision of all." He ended the post with a signature quote from O'Barr's graphic novel/the original 1994 film, "Buildings burn, people die, but real love is forever."

In September 2022, Janowitz recalled how close the deal was to coming together: "Sony wanted to produce the film, we came close to a deal but, that deal failed. Then a smaller group of investors bought it and they are the people who put together the shooting in Prague and Pressman remains producer on the film."

By 2021, Hardy had moved on to work on the hit series *Gangs of London*, but he told ComicBook.com, "It's [*The Crow*] a story that I'm just in love with and wedded towards and I put three and a half, four years of life into and love and blood and sweat and tears, and I have a ton of materials, so I don't know whether one day . . . I suppose I'm not really wanting to show them because I still believe there will be a Crow sometime, but we'll see.

"I do think both James O'Barr's original *Crow* graphic novel and the subsequent other iterations of that character in the comic books, there's no reason not to do a lot more with that character, the concept of *The Crow*, the mythology of *The Crow*, and the tone and what that represents is still unique within the world we're in at the moment."

On April 1, 2022, the *Hollywood Reporter* reported that *The Crow* reboot was imminently resuming with an entirely new team, while still enduringly overseen by Pressman Films. Bill Skarsgard (best known for his performance as Pennywise from *It*, 2017) was announced as the new Eric Draven, with Rupert Sanders (*Snow White and the Huntsman* (2012), *Ghost in the Shell* (2017)) directing. The script was written by Academy Award–nominated *King Richard* scribe Zach Baylin.

Fan sites were abuzz with understandable suspicions that this announcement was an April Fool's hoax.

With a budget of $50 million, shooting of the reboot finally commenced in June 2022 in Prague and Munich. Notably, the production chose Munich's Penzing Studios, Europe's leading state-of-the-art virtual production facility and the world's first zero-emission film studio.

In June at the Cannes 2022 film pre-sales market, *The Crow* reboot package was reported by ScreenDaily.com to have "lived up to pre-market expectations." The definitive film market that happens the week following the star-studded, legendary Cannes film festival is a traditional indicator of a film's production viability and is a crucial industry test of a film's future possible success. Then, in November 2022, Ashland Hill Media Finance came aboard to co-finance the film.

The Crow reboot was reported to have wrapped and, upon the writing of this book, is in post-production. Once again, death has proved surmountable. *The Crow* is reborn and set to be released in 2024.

Sadly, *The Crow*'s longtime champion, legendary producer Ed Pressman, did not survive to see this latest chapter in the franchise. According to his family, he died of respiratory failure on January 17, 2023, at the age of seventy-nine.

ENDURING FLIGHT OF THE CROW

30

IT COULD BE ARGUED that the enduring interest in anything Crow is due to the compelling nature of the story and the mystique of the distinctive, Christ-like hero's return to the living world on a holy quest wreaking vengeance upon the forces of evil. Certainly, as an entertainment property now more than three decades old, *The Crow* is unique.

The Crow's box office success on its original release certainly vindicated those who had believed in the project. More than three decades after it was made, *The Crow* still retains its hold over the imaginations of fans around the world and sparks the curiosity of many new fans. But it was surprising to discover the wide range of opinions the cast and crew had about exactly why the film has been so successful.

Was it Brandon Lee's tragic death that had attracted people to the movie? For the film's publicity campaign, Miramax and the producers made a concerted effort to shy away from any mention of the accident. Instead, the marketing focused on the music and the story. Despite this, by the time *The Crow* opened, a year after it had been filmed, the media frenzy over Brandon Lee's death had seeped into the mass consciousness.

Associate producer Greg Gale thought, "The publicity of the accident is what drove that film and made it what it was. And that's my true opinion." Brandon's close friend Arianne Phillips has a similar view: "Sadly, it had a big break because, in my opinion, the film got its notoriety because of the tragedy linked to it."

"I think it still would've had a big, huge following," said Rochelle Davis, "but I don't know if it would've been *as* big if he hadn't died, because I think that if you can go out and buy a costume and dress up like a movie that you've never seen before, you have to have a reason before-hand as to why you did that."

Producer Jeff Most, the man who found and developed *The Crow* and put together the hugely successful soundtrack, not unnaturally, had a different spin. "I myself believe that the film's success was not based on macabre curiosity. I believe that the strength of the film alone, and the word of mouth generated by the critical reviews, the music on all the radio stations and on MTV, all played their part."

Executive producer Bob Rosen has an even more ambivalent theory. "I think that there were as many people who were drawn to the movie because Brandon had died, as *didn't* come to the movie because Brandon had died. I think the picture stands on its own."

In the longer term, the film does stand on its own artistic merits. But had Brandon lived, *The Crow* would have been a very different movie. On many films, the working script at the start of production, changing constantly throughout filming, is very different from what ends up on screen. But in the case of *The Crow*, the loss of Brandon meant that many story points had to be drastically changed or omitted.

Some crew members, like Greg Gale, thought the film suffered as a consequence: "It would have been maybe a better story had it been the original story." Body double and stunt performer Chad Stahelski was very aware of the amount of Brandon's un-shot material that was removed. "They kind of tweaked it a little to fit the situation. Not really what they had in mind," he said. "I think it would have been bigger if he was alive. . . . They lost a big chunk of the film." Jeff Imada also believed that the loss of Brandon meant losing important elements from the screenplay. "It would have shown even more of him as an actor if he could have completed the scenes without the [Crow] makeup on," Imada said. "I think it would have given a more well-rounded look at his acting abilities, as far as being able to shift from Eric, a human being, being in love, rock star kind of guy, to being the Crow, cold and coming back for revenge."

Perhaps a more important question is whether Brandon's rising stardom would have made the movie more successful. To judge from the success of *The Crow*, and the positive and intense reactions to Brandon Lee from all those who came into contact with him, it is certainly possible that, had he lived, he could have become a major movie star. Brandon, like his father before him, was on the way up. It was obvious to many, including Bob Rosen: "This picture was the tip of the iceberg. I think Brandon could have been a superstar in this business, in movies not about martial arts. And the fact that we're never gonna see that is a shame."

There is little doubt that *The Crow* was Brandon's big break as a leading man. Ernie Hudson graciously admitted, for himself, "As an actor who's done a lot of supporting stuff, I don't have any film that I can point to and say, that's *my* movie. I think it's great that Brandon got that."

Costume supervisor Darryl Levine thought, "Had Brandon lived it would have been a bigger hit, because Brandon would have been *huge*. He would have brought more to it, I think." Hudson is certain that, "Brandon would have become whatever 'a star' means in Hollywood."

The mystique that surrounds Brandon and his father is pure Hollywood, in the tradition of Marilyn Monroe and James Dean. The unfortunate cost of such white-hot legendary status, and part of the reason Brandon and Bruce will remain enduring icons, is a sudden premature death, in their prime, before we had the chance to see them truly fulfill their destiny—to flourish or falter. Brandon Lee has left an image that is eternally young, handsome, and energetic. As costumer Roberta Bile recalled, "For years after, everybody wanted the shirt he was shot in. The jacket too. People were obsessed with him because they loved his father too."

The young audience that James O'Barr, John Shirley, and Jeff Most originally believed would want to see a movie of *The Crow* comic embraced the film on a scale no one could have predicted. It is easy to see how the dark story of revenge and idealized love appeals to angst-ridden teenagers. "It's almost like *Star Wars* on a smaller level," felt Angel David. "I knew that there was gonna be a following. I didn't know it was gonna be to the extent that it is now." *The Crow* has become a cult film, with fan clubs and dedicated websites all over the world. While Lance Anderson likened *The Crow* to *The Rocky Horror Picture Show*, he thought, "It's a cult film for a different reason, for a different group of people that can relate to this darker side to humanity. I think there's just an element to it that's not mainstream."

"I got a lot of fans finding me on the web," said Arianne Phillips. For years, she said she would occasionally "go online and talk to these kids on the websites. And none of them believe that I'm me! I talk to these kids because they're young. . . . and give them a window into how cool Brandon was. I figure the most I can do is humanize him."

Ernie Hudson, who admitted *The Crow* was not his most recognized performance, said, "There's a lot of young adults will come up and go on about *The Crow*, so I know that they're tuned in to the film."

Sofia Shinas was certain that *The Crow* and the death of Brandon Lee influenced the lyrics of U2's hit song "Who's to Blame" on their album

Zooropa. "It's a father talking to his son, a dirty deed is done, and it's so poetic and written in allegories."

For the original screenwriter, John Shirley, the movie's impact, including attempts to copy its style, vindicated his original view of the project. "They tried a few vague little imitations. I think that the longevity of *The Crow* shows that. They're still making *Crow* movies, the sustained interest in it, you're writing a book about it! Merchandising for it still sells. What does that tell you?"

A solid argument can be made for *The Crow*'s cult status by simply looking at the strange parallels between the movie and real life. "I think that certainly the idea that a character is killed and reborn in the film, and that Brandon Lee died during the filming of the film, in the scene where he actually gets killed in the story—actually killed on that set in that scene—and the fact that he's Bruce Lee's son, adds to some of the interest in it," Ken Arlidge said. "The nature of the film is cultish already," agreed Arianne Phillips, who saw *The Crow*'s cult status as a combination of, "The whole life-and-death, and ever-after, and all these kind of gothic themes, coupled with what happened to Brandon and the fact that Brandon comes from a father who died under questionable circumstances." Roberta Bile also saw the story-within-the-story as the reason people are drawn to *The Crow*: "This young guy who had everything going for him, he was gonna get married, and then he dies! And that's really what happened in real life, when you think about the story. It is bizarre."

Brandon's own fascination with death could be thrown into this equation. With his earnings from *Legacy of Rage*, he bought a 1959 Cadillac hearse. Robert Zuckerman recalled, "His friends said that he definitely had an interest in death and the dark side of things. And he liked to sort of dare, from what I've heard. Just physically he'd do things like riding his motorcycle in the middle of the desert at night with the lights off and his eyes closed."

The Crow shoot was surrounded with apparently strange events, and some of the cast and crew found strange things happening in their lives both just before they worked on the movie—like Ken Arlidge's odd experience with the crow Tarot card—and after. These things certainly happened, but without Brandon Lee's death, would they have been remembered or noticed?

On the morning he was due to leave for Wilmington to start work on *The Crow*, Laurence Mason was asleep in bed at home when he heard the roof above him begin to collapse. "I heard the break and reflex-whipped off the bed, gave myself a whiplash and got a huge gash in my back from the concrete [that fell on me]. And that was the first time I saw my dad cry." That experience and the ghostly apparition he thought he saw around the time of Brandon's death were the first of many experiences that left Mason convinced there is more to the world than you can touch and see. "I saw a ghost. I almost got killed the morning I left," said Mason. "That's kinda when I gave up saying things aren't related and things are coincidence. I just couldn't do it anymore. I'm not saying I knew what was going on or what was at work, but after that flick I just had to say there's something bigger than us. Maybe it started from James O'Barr's anguish, I don't know. I'm just saying these things don't disappear. They go somewhere."

Sandra Orsolyak had a bizarre experience too: "A year or so later, I was in my office doing something, and all of a sudden I see this bird fly by. Wasn't really a bird, it was kind of like a shadow. And it's like, 'What the hell is that?' And I hear the squawking noise. Well, you walk around and the bird's on the tree. You know what? A raven! So I chase it around the house. And it literally kept flying around my house. So I'm following this thing around. He comes back the third time, gets into close proximity to where it was before, like in a branch, and it just squawks and squawks, squawks, and by this time I'm laughing hysterically—thinking it has some relevance to something only I knew. It made sense to me."

Before *The Crow*, Robert Zuckerman said, "I had been reading this book of poems called *Crow with No Mouth*, which was basically a book of this fifteenth-century Zen master. And I think the opening of the book says something like, 'Hearing a crow with no mouth cry in the deep darkness of night, I feel a longing for my father before he was born.'" This line only became memorable to Zuckerman because, he said, "Of the intensity of the experience. It was hard to describe, but there's nothing else like it that I've been through. Not so much anymore, but for a long time after that film I really sensed Brandon's presence around me—I could feel like, his bare-chested, wet body. Sometimes I'd feel him riding in the car next to me or walking or sitting in a room with me. It was a weird thing."

Despite the strange stories, looking back at Brandon's accident, Ken Arlidge didn't see it as superstitious: "I think it was a series of circumstances that could've affected and killed anybody on that set. Had it been another actor with another scene, had the gun been used in another scene and another shooting, pointed at our camera for a close-up of the gun firing . . . Maybe it would've put a bullet right through our lens. Who knows?" No doubt, the thought crossed everyone's mind that they could have been in the line of that fateful bullet.

For those closely involved with it, the impact of Brandon's accident continued long after the event. Ernie Hudson recalled seeing Daniel Kuttner at a party a couple of years later: "Kuttner had really gone through a hard time over it too. I don't even think he's even doing props anymore. He took it pretty hard."

Hudson found a chance meeting with Michael Massee even more uncomfortable. "I was in a restaurant having dinner with a friend, and I saw Michael Massee come in and I did not want to deal with him," he recalled. "I just sort of turned my back to the door and bent my head down, trying to hide and hope he didn't see me, because the last person I wanted to talk to was Michael. And he saw me, and he came over and he sat down and we talked. And then I realized that he'd really gone through a lot of changes over it, and it had really been hard for him and that he wasn't to blame. Nobody was, as far as I understand."

Jeff Most and Massee remained in touch and "used to come over with his kids, etcetera."

After the accident on *The Crow*, Massee took several years away from acting. After then appearing in a variety of smaller roles (often playing bad guys) in TV and film, Massee died of stomach cancer in 2016, at the age of sixty-four.

For Hudson, though *The Crow* is not his "favorite rental" and it didn't help him get future parts, he nevertheless felt "very glad and proud to have been a part of it."

Although *The Crow* wasn't necessarily a major boost for many of the cast's and crew's careers, Roberta Bile recalled, "In job interviews, people were always interested in it because of what went on. The first question out of the mouth was, 'So what happened with the gun?' It's sort of cheesy."

"I have done a lot of films since then, you know, on my résumé," said Arianne Phillips in 2000, who at that point had gone on to design the costumes for numerous high-profile Hollywood films, such as *One Hour Photo* and *The People vs. Larry Flynt*, as well as Madonna, Courtney Love, and Lenny Kravitz music videos. But still, she continued, "I go in for an interview, they always ask me about the movie, 'What happened?' You know, people in the business, all kinds of people from high up to low, it just doesn't matter, they want to know from the film side. This is really, really hard!"

"People have seen it on my résumé and go, 'Oh, you worked on *The Crow*!'" said Chad Stahelski. "It's a talking piece. People are curious about it just because of the whole incident. They want to know."

Jeff Imada thinks people feel awkward sometimes to bring up *The Crow* because they are sensitive to his personal connection.

Despite other people's curiosity, Randy LaFollette had not spoken about *The Crow* until I originally interviewed him in 2000. "I'm not sure if I would or would not have before now, but I think that the timing is at a point where it's a good healing time," he said. "It's been enough time away from it that it sounded like a really good idea to me, being able to talk about it, because it's something that I don't talk about maybe other than to my wife, and I don't even do that too much, because it's not an easy thing to talk about."

For Brandon's good friend Jeff Imada, recounting his experiences on *The Crow* was not easy: "There's hardly a time that goes by where I don't think of Brandon. I feel that it's a big loss, not just for me and the family, but for people, audiences, not to see this young man show more of his talent at a point in his career where he's just coming into his own, feeling quite comfortable with himself. Not feeling like he's in the shadow of his dad anymore, and that he's his own man."

When Michelle Johnson finished working on *The Crow*, she said, "I packed all that stuff up in a big box. I never opened that box. Until one day, I decided, 'I can handle this,' and I went to open this box and what made me cry was that stupid ball of yarn and those crochet needles."

The Crow indelibly changed people's perspectives on life. Arianne Phillips said, "I was having this incredible experience, and all of a sudden it was totally shattered by this tragedy, having your heart broken. And I would say that I have a very cynical, very cynical side of myself to the film business ever since then, which was my first [movie]." She concluded, "It was one of the best experiences in my life. And definitely the worst experience of my life."

Angel David, who also went on to work steadily on films and TV, felt, "If it weren't for the tragic circumstances of Brandon's accident, it would've been the best experience I've ever had as an actor."

Greg Gale insisted, "It holds a high sense of accomplishment in my heart. Absolutely."

Similarly, JB Jones felt that his experience of working on *The Crow* made it one of his favorites: "I guess it would probably be second or third place. All of the heavy, big hard work that we did. It was a picture that you work hard on and when you get done, you hope that it comes out to somebody's satisfaction, and it did turn out good."

For Chad Stahelski, it's the work he was most proud of. "I think it came out the best. Not mushy or anything, but it does have a small emotional thing. I'm proud to help out a friend and to make Brandon's last film good."

Bob Rosen has produced big-budget action movies spanning five decades, but before retiring, one of the posters that hung prominently in his office is that of *The Crow*: "It will always remain pretty high up there only because of what happened and how difficult it was. Certainly not too much time goes by that I don't think about Brandon."

Laurence Mason, who's gone on to appear in several notable films, including the Oscar-nominated *Ali* (2001), *Artificial Intelligence: A I* (2001), and *City of Lies* (2018), and numerous hit TV series said, "It was my coming-of-age kind of thing. That's how I remember it. And also just, unfortunately, kind of a dark place."

For Darryl Levine, the suddenness of the tragedy that happened right before his eyes changed his life: "My life is still impacted to living our days to the fullest. I go home every night at six o'clock. My watch is set to the day at six. If I'm not on my way home at six, there better be a real good reason, and just being in this business is not it, 'cause I'm home with my kids and I help with their homework. I show up. I'm there for my wife. Those are all things that took a dramatic turn as a result of this movie."

Sandra Orsolyak also admitted, "It changed my life. It taught me something. Brandon taught me humor, in his own little way. He could stand in that freezing cold, bloody puddle, and coming out of it and sort of laughing—even though he's shivering, laughing. It's like you laugh along with him because *you* feel the cold." However, immediately after finishing work on *The Crow*, on the set of Orsolyak's next movie, she recalled, "They had a gun scene, and as soon as they pulled those guns out, I lost it. I totally lost it." When I spoke to her in 2000, she was unable to watch *The Crow*: "I have the video. I bought it. It still sits there, cellophane wrapper on. I haven't opened it."

For Ken Arlidge, who first realized the origin of the bullet that killed Brandon, "His death was hard to accept. I accepted it. But to believe that it actually happened, to believe that it somehow was so close that we could just reach out and change it somehow . . . My regret stems from the fact that, had a realization of my thought process and understanding of things happened earlier, it would've prevented the circumstances from carrying further. So I was an observer to something that I didn't recognize and that I couldn't change."

Jeff Most said, "It's my baby . . . It really was the culmination of something that I set out to do years earlier and I was turned away at every doorstep. And, in a way, it was a black sheep that nobody wanted to see turned into anything. . . . I learned so much of what I now do on that movie, and I felt close to everyone and to the project, and to the events that surrounded it in every respect. It'll always occupy for me a touchstone of who I am, what my career is about, and it'll always hold a special place in my heart. The tragedy aside I mean, the film was an experience that was magical."

Ed Pressman's longtime personal attorney, James Janowitz, attributes the continued interest in *The Crow* franchise to, "the original movie. And I must tell you, when I first read the script, I was terribly unimpressed with the script. And there isn't anything really unique about the story. I mean it's a romance. . . . I think it's really the execution. And the first film was a wonderful film. You know, it was extremely well made. Everybody was very talented, very touching, maybe even more so by the real-life tragedy which had a bizarre coincidence with the film."

Regardless of *The Crow* franchises false starts, personal and creative splits, and contentious rights battles, Janowitz said he "doesn't mind. There are certain things there are landmarks in my career. Well, that [*The Crow*] goes in the obituary . . . it will make possibly interesting reading."

The legacy of *The Crow* and the story of the making of *The Crow* has tangibly touched a new generation. Justin Manes, who executive produced and starred in the independent ultra-low-budget fan film *Crow* released in 2022 on YouTube, first saw *The Crow* in 2000 on DVD when he was twelve years old. "I watched it and it completely transfixed me. It was something that like I had never seen before. Certainly not in the realm of a comic book film. It was just the emotional core of it, you're just brought into like the world and the life of the characters. Not many other films have done that for me. I think my favorite film at the time was *Jurassic Park* (1993).

"I don't know if you would call it like a horror or an action or a fantasy or sci fi or comic book movie. It's kind of like a whole bunch of different things all rolled into one, which I thought was also really cool. I call it romance."

Though originally budgeted for only $3,500, *Crow* ended up costing Manes and his friends eleven thousand dollars. It was a labor of love and has logged hundreds of thousands of views.

Manes felt that diehard *Crow* fans are so passionate because they see the deeper meaning. "I think it's something instinctual. I really think it has a calming effect. Knowing that when you pass on or something terrible happens in your life, love is so strongest that it would carry you through

. . . I think at its core, it's about how you process grief. I think that's why it resonates so much today."

For actress Bai Ling, *The Crow* will always remain her introduction to Hollywood and a spiritual touchstone in her career. "I do believe our spirit is timeless in the Universe. So, in that way, that's why I love cinema. Because no matter what happened to our form, as human, that moment is captured, no matter how many years. That's why we're talking about it now and why it's relevant, still very important, and it made a big impact in Hollywood . . . It's about redemption. That love never dies. That's something very beautiful and powerful.

"I think *The Crow* will be there forever. And since what happened to Alec Baldwin [who accidentally shot and killed cinematographer Halyna Hutchins on the set of his 2021 movie, *Rust*], I think just people rediscovered it [*The Crow*]. And how unsafe it can be or how we should consciously be careful. . . . Life's fragile. We have to celebrate and enjoy every moment of it because it can take away like Brandon Lee."

AFTERWORD

O N OCTOBER 21, 2021, the accidental fatal shooting of cinematographer Halyna Hutchins on the set of the independent film *Rust* sent shock waves through the news media and entertainment industry. Nearly thirty years had passed since eerily similar circumstances killed Brandon Lee on the set of *The Crow*, thrusting the 1994 film back into the spotlight.

Twenty years ago, in the original edition of this book, and nearly six years after the release of *The Crow*, I wrote the following in the last chapter: *The unavoidable question left by Brandon Lee's death is, could it happen again?* Tragically, it has and under even wilder circumstances.

On October 21, cinematographer Halyna Hutchins was in an old church on the Bonanza Creek Ranch facility, rehearsing a scene from the movie *Rust*, when she was shot and killed, and director Joel Souza was badly wounded.

The film's star and producer, Alec Baldwin, had pointed what was understood, allegedly, to be a safe, single-action, Civil War–era Colt .45 revolver loaded with blanks at the camera when a single shot unexpectedly fired.

Beyond the ongoing headline news coverage, loud public outrage from celebrities, and legal finger pointing among the cast and crew, there are notable similarities to what occurred on the set of *The Crow*.

Originally, plans called for a small, tight, low-budget little film, shot in the desert. A minimal twenty-one-day shoot, budgeted at $7 million. That is barely money by today's Hollywood standards, buying, at most, six minutes of screen time for an episode of Amazon Prime's *Rings of Power*.

And by October 21, 2021, *Rust* was already in crisis and moving to meet its moment in history when the promising young cinematographer was shot and killed. The tangled web of contradictory and changing narratives from the key cast and crew on *Rust* continues to evolve. As of the writing of this book, there is much still to come out about what led to Hutchins' death. But at this time, there are strong indications that she was another victim of poor management and unsafe circumstances—an amalgam of carelessness, fatigue, negligence, penury, and incompetence.

The extensive details were published online November 1, 2022, in a 551-page event report prepared by the Santa Fe Sheriff's Office. Many of the report's key points are hauntingly familiar. Then on January 31, 2023, the Santa Fe District Attorney formally charged actor/producer Alec Baldwin and weapons specialist Hannah Gutierrez-Reed with two counts of involuntary manslaughter.

The formal charges explain how Alec Baldwin and *Rust* armorer Hannah Gutierrez-Reed did not follow safety procedures and acted in "a negligent manner."

The court document read, "In this circumstance it is common practice (and expected) for any actor handling or firing a weapon to check for safety." The filing added, "The armorer's role is to provide that proper safe handling and management in order for them to do so. Reed not only failed in this regard but was not even present."

According to the report, multiple crew members had formally brought up firearms safety concerns to the producers, including previous misfires on set. In response, six camera crew apparently walked off the set the day of the tragedy. Investigators say they found several violations of required firearms safety protocols and that even Baldwin failed to participate in mandatory firearms safety training. Most disturbingly, prosecutors say they discovered five additional live rounds on the set. One was even found in the gun in Baldwin's holster.

Though in both *The Crow* and *Rust* prohibited live ammo had made its way onto the set and into the gun's barrels, the scenes that killed Lee and Hutchins are vastly different. The gun that killed Brandon was intended to be loaded with a full-load blank and fired within a safe distance not directly at him, whereas the gun that killed Hutchins was supposed to be purely a prop during a rehearsal and never intended to be fired. Alec Baldwin was allegedly instructed to hold the single-action, antique-style revolver while Massee was told to fire a double-action Magnum .44 loaded with a blank.

Painfully similar to the tragedy on *The Crow*, it appears industry firearms safety guidelines were not followed. Published at least a decade before filming of *The Crow*, with its last minor revision made in 2003, *Safety Bulletin #1, Recommendations for Safety with Firearms and Use of "Blank Ammunition,"* issued by the Industry Wide Safety-Management Safety Committee, is extremely clear. All unions, including the Screen Actors Guild and the International Alliance of Theatrical Stage Employees, mandate that, among other things, safety meetings be held whenever firearms are used and that this guideline is attached to the call sheet any day a firearm is to be used on set.

"There hasn't been an update in the firearms one in years. But that's because they are adequate. You just have to follow the guideline. Right?" said Larry Zanoff, lead armorer at ISS, Independent Studio Services, one of the top national prop houses and the largest rental armory for film and TV production in the United States. A combat veteran of the Israeli army with university degrees in US law enforcement as well as gunsmith and firearms technology, Zanoff felt professionals like himself are not being accurately represented and took issue with the media and the public's inability to separate events in the real world from the fantasy world portrayed on screen.

"People that I work with are upset that the public perception now of working on a film set is, 'Oh my God, you take your life into your hands if you're stepping onto a film set.' It's untrue. We are professionals. We do correct things. We follow guidelines. It is a highly skilled group of people that do this and just because something happens in a headline that, you know, focuses on one instance of somebody who's not following the guidelines or is not skilled enough. It's a little bit unfair in a way."

In addition to his day job at ISS, Zanoff provides weapons training to the military and various government and law enforcement agencies. He has also served as armorer on big-budget studio projects such as *Django Unchained* (2012), *Captain America Winter Soldier* (2014), *Captain America Civil War* (2016), and *Babylon* (2022), as well as the TV series *Westworld* (2018).

Most important and alarming, under industry guidelines, live ammunition should not have been present on either set. Yet there it was, both times.

Just as when Brandon Lee was killed, entertainment Industry Safety Guidelines were, and remain, very clear, according to Zanoff. "'Blanks can kill. Treat all firearms as if they are loaded.' It is the primary protection for actors and film crews when productions use prop guns of any kind."

Just as in *The Crow*, having a prop person manage a single gun is common. From Zanoff's experience, it's not unusual for "the prop master to keep doing their job of doing props, and they might even be running, let's say, a single handgun. But if you've got a big shoot-out with multiple people and fully automatic weapons, you've got specialists there that tend to those particular items."

Another dangerous point of similarity for both *The Crow* and *Rust* was violation of Guideline #1 of Bulletin #1 of the Industry Safety Guidelines: "Refrain from pointing a firearm at anyone, including yourself." And while Michael Massee was a safe distance away from Brandon Lee and blocked to swing around in a wide motion and fire towards but not at Brandon in a wide shot, Baldwin was shooting a close-up only a few feet from the camera.

Climactic shots of guns being pointed into the camera lens are not uncommon in films and TV. To not only protect the crew behind the camera but the equipment itself in case of any already mitigated explosion, a plexiglass shield is sometimes placed in front of the camera crew. But according to Cinema Armorer/Film Firearms Safety Coordinator Charles M. Coleman III, "What they'll do now is just a remote-operated camera versus plexiglass. I still see from time to time, but it's not everywhere like it was in the '90s after *The Crow*. One of the problems you run into with plexiglass is if the actor's too close, the sparks and gas can hit the plexiglass and come back on them."

Coleman is part of the small Wilmington, North Carolina, community. Though he was in the first grade when *The Crow* was made and ironically his best friend's dad, Dr. McMurry, was the surgeon who tried to save Brandon Lee's life, Coleman has worked locally and in many states on many shows since 2007. His credits include: *Scream* (2022) and *Crime Story* (2021), and he holds an IATSE 491 Card and a Federal Firearms License with a Special Occupational Tax Stamp and numerous other safety-related credentials related to the craft.

On-set armorer and seasoned munitions tactical and safety trainer Bryan Carpenter was hired to do his own independent investigation of the set of *Rust* by the Hutchins family attorney a few days after the tragic incident and to potentially serve as an expert witness.

It was clear to him the top safety protocols of handling a prop gun were not followed. "Never put your finger on the trigger till you're ready to fire, never point it directly at anything that can be hurt, and always treat a prop gun like its loaded. . . . In order for the bullet to strike Halyna, it was obviously pointed at Halyna.

"A good armorer doesn't just look at the guns. They do a sweep of the set when they are working on location. You look in the drawers, you're looking around to make sure there's no random ammunition has been left laying out."

Over the years, Carpenter has himself discovered live rounds on sets inadvertently purchased as set decoration by inexperienced, well-intending crew members not aware of the hazard or Industry Safety Guidelines. After a sigh, he said, "There [are] a lot of near misses."

Carpenter's take of the accident on *The Crow* was that, "It was every safety violation that a professional armorer that was in charge of safety would have caught along the process."

With firearms-heavy hit projects such as the TV series *Interview with a Vampire* (2022), *Cloak and Dagger* (2018), and *Queen of The South* (2016) and big-budget films such as *Jack Reacher: Never Go Back* (2016) under his belt and more than three decades of experience as a private military contractor, private security for top celebrities, and training law enforcement, private entertainment industry security firms, and stunt professionals, Carpenter always follows a strict on-set routine. He also knows, "Safety is never redundant. And complacency kills."

According to his discoveries on the set of *Rust*, "One of my favorite ones of all favorite ones was, well, 'Hannah, the armorer, couldn't be in the church because of COVID violations.' You have hair and makeup. You have sixteen people inside of this teeny tiny, little church. When you're telling me that one more person couldn't be in there? Are you freaking kidding me?"

Carpenter strongly believes in best-practices and process. "After initial comprehensive training to cast and crew, I check the weapon out of whatever locked area that I have, and I check out the ammo [never real ammo, blanks] of whatever locked area that I have, and I keep it always with me."

When the scene is ready to shoot with the gun, Carpenter explained, "I offer the weapon to be seen by anybody that's going to be in the vicinity of that muzzle. That could be the director, the DP, the stunt people, anybody. At a minimum I show it to the actor holding the gun and the First AD. It's a two-part process. Two people are going to verify that that gun is in the state that it needs to be in. We shine a flashlight down the barrel. And we see that there's nothing in the barrel. Then we shine a flashlight on the magazine and see that nothing is loaded right now. And then I explained to him that you're about to shoot a couple blanks or whatever."

When they are ready to shoot the scene, Carpenter walks out to the actor, "And I say 'control' and I make them repeat the word 'control' back to me. It's just a little mental thing that I used to do on real-world training so that that person knows that they are in control of the safety of that weapon and everyone's safety around them." Only then, will he load the blanks.

After they call cut, Carpenter gets the gun "back immediately. I clear the weapon and make sure it's okay and I hold it till they are ready to go again. Then we go through the whole process again.

"Hannah had the guns laying out on a cart in prep for the scene unsecured, right. I never, ever leave guns unattended!" he insisted, referring to the armorer on *Rust*. In the event neither he nor his trusted skilled staff can be there, he says, "I have these lockable cages that are rollout and no one can get in except me."

Although safety guidelines remained the same, awareness did change after *The Crow*. Los Angeles–based armorer Michael Gibbons, who managed weapons on hit films *Tango & Cash* (1989) and *RoboCop 3* (1993), noticed that after *The Crow*, "When firearms are involved on the set, I saw a marked change in people's attitudes. But as far as written-down rules, nothing really changed."

Wilmington native and armorer Charlie M. Coleman III is keenly aware of the legacy of *The Crow*. "Then people forgot about it. It became myths and legend. 'Well, that couldn't happen again. We're in a modern age of internet and smartphones.'"

Zanoff said, "So I would imagine that before *Rust*, not many people knew that there even was a position on a film crew called on-set armorer. Now, of course, because of the celebrity aspect of it, that's become much more well known. Productions are being much more careful about who they hire as the armorer. There's a little more vetting going on. So, it's definitely been a heightened awareness as a result." After *Rust*, Coleman definitely saw the pendulum swing the other way. Disney suddenly insisted he use only airsoft or rubber guns on a show even when the actor was only shooting at bottles. "Just because there's the whole stigma of it. Meanwhile, Marvel is still using blanks. Hulu is still using some blanks."

But Coleman adds, "Some things are happening. You're seeing a lot of people that were established as armorers doing really well. And then you're seeing people that were up and coming for better or for worse, backing up. Because now the bar, just like in the '90s, the bar now is very high to be an armorer."

But memories are short, as long as nothing goes wrong. For film industry veteran attorney James Janowitz, "I think, you know, again, it comes down to enforcement and execution. There are career professionals in this area. In this case of *The Crow*, it was not professionals handling it as much as other kinds of productions. So, if you have good professionals, we're really careful. The likelihood is that nothing bad is going to happen. I'm surprised more people haven't lost their hides and gotten hurt on set, like getting hit by particles. People get hurt a lot on sets. You know, I mean, a number of people fall, you know, trip or, or get hurt."

Now an OSHA trainer and certified IATSE armorer, Charles M. Coleman III thought the most effective way to present firearms accidents on set would be, "shorter days." On both *Rust* and *The Crow*, crews were working long hours and became exhausted.

Coleman often finds, "Producers are ignorant or uneducated on film firearm safety. They hire someone who they think is good. This person means well, doesn't have the experience. Doesn't have the knowledge, doesn't have the command presence to say, 'No, Mr. Director, we can't do that. But we can do this.'" He added, "Sets are either professional or pageantry." These situations are often related to budget.

Just as was the case after Brandon Lee was killed, celebrities and filmmakers called for stronger safety measures pledging a wide variety of solutions after Hutchins was killed.

Dwayne Johnson, also known as The Rock, vowed that only rubber guns would be used on projects from his production company. *Knives Out* (2019) director Rian Johnson tweeted in support of using visual effects to illustrate gunplay in his films. Alexi Hawley, the showrunner of the ABC police drama *The Rookie*, told his staff to stop using live guns but keep BB-like pellet-firing ones. Eric Kripke, the showrunner of Amazon's series *The Boys*, vowed to stop using guns altogether and use only visual effects.

Awareness increases but no enforceable, stricter rules to fully prevent such firearm accidents in the future on sets have yet been enacted. As of the writing of this book, more than a year after these vows were made, these filmmakers have said nothing further and no industry-wide consensus has emerged. Unions and studios are still not able to agree on rules that would impose new requirements on training and qualifications for armorers, as well as penalties for those breaching safety protocols.

After the accident on *Rust*, Academy Award–winning actor George Clooney spoke out on the *WTF with Marc Maron* podcast. Since his good friend Brandon Lee's death in 1993, Clooney said, "Every single time I'm handed a gun on the set . . . I open it, I show it to the person I'm pointing it to, I show it to the crew. Every single take, you hand it back to the armorer when you're done and you do it again."

Referring to the long-instituted safety protocols on prop guns, Clooney said, "After Brandon died, it really became a very clear thing: Open the gun, look down the barrel, look in the cylinder, make sure. It's a series of tragedies. But also, a lot of stupid mistakes. . . . Why, for the life of me, this low-budget film [*Rust*] with producers who haven't produced any-thing wouldn't have hired, for the armorer, someone with experience," Clooney wondered, "because this is just infuriating."

Carpenter believed armorers should have a certification system but, at the moment no such system exists. "It's who you know. No license required." Since it's not usually required, many props or armorers don't carry a license. Carpenter wishes the level of professionalism he keeps was more appreciated. "I've got multiple instructor-level certifications for training with firearms through actually recognized military or law enforce-ment groups and recognized certification. I've got thousands of hours training, military, law enforcement, tactical and federal agent, different officers, etcetera, etcetera.

"I run into armors that haven't ever been to even one safety class but got the job because they knew a prop master or someone who worked at the studio. So, the playing field is very unfairly balanced."

Guns are often rented from big prop houses with huge weapons inven-tories like ISS, Extreme Props, HBR, or *The Specialist*, who contract with their individually approved prop masters and armorers. But there is no uni-form vetting process for renting firearms to productions across the United States. Having any firearms license is not mandatory in most productions barring some select studios. According to Carpenter . . . "only Marvel has asked me."

An attempt in the early 2000s was made by independent companies to manufacture guns only for the film industry that were sized to never accommodate real bullets and only their uniquely manufactured blanks. Though a successful solution for on-set safety, the cost of manufacturing and replacing the vast, existing inventory of real prop firearms was deter-mined too expensive.

Visual effects technology is rapidly improving, enabling more explo-sions, including gun shots, to be simulated in post-production. But these high-end and believable visual effects are often expensive and out of reach for independent productions with substantially lower budgets than studio films. And, according to Zanoff, the physical, human response is just not the same. "You can't do it with CGI at the level that the realism requires. We have HD now we have 4k cameras, 16 cameras, we've got a lot more knowledgeable viewers right now. They understand guns. We have a lot of military veterans that are coming out of their military service. We've actually used those guns, so they watch these films, and they can tell the difference between a visual effect and the actual gunfire effect. The realism, the aspect of that reality is what we're selling to the public. I think that a competent well-trained armorer goes out onto set with multiple options at their fingertips; real guns with blanks, rubber guns, replica guns. CGI or visual effects is one of those other filmmaker tools. None of the tools are able to replace totally all the others. They are all another tool for specific scenarios."

For Carpenter, who is now producing his own films, "It's still not at the point where you get the effects of the light bouncing off the room, the sound, and then you get into the action of the weapon going back and forth." But he added, "I think that eventually visual effects will get to the point that it's going to be good enough."

For Coleman, "It's cyclical, it depends on the project. It depends on how the nation feels about guns at the moment. And it comes down to a couple of opinions of people at desks. The older generation, the boomers, they were a little more familiar with blanks, whereas the technology people are kind of newer generations that have been exposed to technology or kind of just like, oh, well, let's computer it."

The business of production is always constrained and pressured to deliver the final project as promised, within budget and on time but, when budgets are very tight (usually with independent productions) safety is one of the first thing to go. Carpenter strongly believed, "that Hannah [armorer on *Rust*] did not have the experience that she needed to be working on a set that had that many moving parts that needed strong personalities. They didn't want to hire an armorer for the entire show so she was made assistant props and armor. So, she's running back and forth handling props and handling gun safety."

There were seasoned professionals present on *Rust*, including Baldwin, who served as star and producer, and First Assistant Director Dave Halls, who, according to some of the conflicting firsthand accounts, handed Baldwin the prop gun. Halls has worked as an assistant director in the industry for more than twenty-five years and has taken safety training. In a now bizarre coincidence, he had served as assistant director on *The Crow* sequel *The Crow: Salvation* (2000). According to the industry publication *Deadline*, Halls had opted not to be a member of the Directors Guild union, allowing him to work both in union and non-union productions. But this is not an uncommon move for many in the filmmaking community who need to stay employed.

If *Rust* had been shooting in Los Angeles, would the fatal accident been less likely? Beyond the iconic Western setting, *Rust*'s decision to shoot in the desert thirty miles outside of Santa Fe, instead of in or near Hollywood where similar locations exist, was clearly about cost savings. Just like *The Crow*, *Rust* needed to cut costs by shooting far away from a recognized industry hub. And while armorer Coleman asserts that had the production been staged closer to Los Angeles, the incident "would have been less likely," he also flat-out refuses to say it couldn't have happened: "Never use the word never."

On both productions, emergency medical personnel were many life-saving minutes away. Sadly however, both Brandon Lee's and Hutchins' injuries were so immediately critical, proximity would have most likely not saved their lives. It would have taken about thirty minutes for the closest ambulance in Santa Fe to reach the ranch.

Carpenter observed, "They could have had a trauma surgeon right by their side and still probably the same thing would have happened. The bullet struck Halyna laterally and passed basically through her chest cavity and exited above the top behind her shoulderblade. And that bullet is a 250-grain lead round and she was a small lady so yeah, that was just tragic."

Ultimately, safety guidelines are just that without any oversight or enforcement. Although a filmmaker's reputation for a good safety record is a powerful incentive in this small, competitive business, actual penalties or legal action is scarce except in the most catastrophic circumstances. Even so, media-worthy accidents only include higher profile stars and more serious injuries.

Oversight is largely peer driven. In a business predicated on avoiding conflict with the entity paying your salary tends to be a good methodology for continued, gainful employment, rank-and-file cast and crew might think twice about making the kind of waves that could derail or jeopardize a production.

And the march of history is a slow process, as Janowitz noted, "I tried to write some legislation for the state of North Carolina, which nobody seemed interested in, which would create a solution to this by simply not allowing guns on set capable of accepting a live round. That seemed a reasonable way to go about it."

The brutal fact is that no regulations were broken on *The Crow*, no legal proceeding resulted, and there was no reason to suppose that a similar accident would not occur again. Today, the way films are made in North Carolina or New Mexico is not necessarily more reckless than elsewhere in the United States.

The jury is still out on whether *Rust*'s pending lawsuits and criminal charges will have a lasting impact on the Hollywood motion picture industry and how their product is financed, produced, and distributed. Perhaps future onset firearms accidents might be prevented at last. Time will tell.

Abruptly, on April 20, 2023, the New Mexico prosecutors decided to drop the involuntary manslaughter charges against Baldwin, citing a need for further investigation. Upon the writing of this book, the serious charges remain against Gutierrez-Reed.

Notably, Baldwin's dismissal was announced the same day production of *Rust* resumed at a new filming location in Montana, eighteen months after Hutchins was killed.

The enduring fascination with the artistry of *The Crow*, enlisting new fans and inspiring new generations of moviemakers, has now spanned three decades and counting. This classic film has stood, and will continue to stand, the test of time.

I sincerely hope that the powerful and influential entertainment industry will finally come together for the sole purpose of drafting standardized, collectively bargained, enforceable rules for the required education and training of all cast and crew and for the safe control, storage, use, and maintenance of any firearms used on productions.

There is absolutely nothing preventing this idea from becoming a formal, negotiated solution. Except for the possible beliefs that it is not necessary given the low rates of catastrophic injuries. Statistically, it's much safer making movies for the people involved than it is for other people driving cars, parking on public streets, and seeing movies in theaters.

But the simple truth just might be that functioning guns of any kind no longer belong in the dream factory.

This part comes down to money, which studios really do hate spending, particularly on non-glamourous, invisible on-screen aspects that do not enhance first-dollar gross. Getting rid of modified, functioning firearms would incur additional costs. But if the banks and insurers, the bond companies insisted on a "No Guns" policy as a condition for underwriting any film, a new system would be adopted, virtually overnight.

Moving on from the subject of on-set safety, I've reflected much over the years as I've written this book. In the first year I spent researching and writing this book in 2000, I began to feel as if I actually knew Brandon Lee. As if the stories I heard about him, from the people who worked on the movie, had somehow brought me close to a man I never met.

Remarkably, just as I felt then, I feel now in 2022. Reading once again their many vivid accounts as I assembled this book, I found myself playing out their memories in my head, as if I was there, witnessing events. The coldness of the set, the wrenching attempts to battle the fatigue, the triumph of new, untried ideas, and the fascination of watching a young star pour his heart into the role of a lifetime.

A fantasy, of course. But I still wonder what he would have thought of this book.

Mostly, I sincerely hope he would have found it a true account of the making of his movie. And, in the end, the book's accuracy and integrity is the only genuine thanks I can give to all those who worked on *The Crow* and who opened their memories and their hearts to me.

Thank you for a most unexpected journey.

Bridget Baiss
Los Angeles, 1999
Updated, London, 2003
Updated, Washington D.C., 2022

APPENDIX I

The Crow Synopsis

O N DEVIL'S NIGHT—the night before Halloween—in an anonymous and desolate urban landscape, anarchy reigns and fires are being set. Rock musician Eric Draven returns to his loft to discover that a gang of deranged and violent criminals are raping his girlfriend, Shelly. Eric and Shelly, who were to be married the next day, were organizing their building's tenants. The gang—Skank, Tin Tin, Funboy, and T-Bird— have been sent by their boss, slumlord and gangster Top Dollar, to harass Draven and Shelly. But Draven is shot and killed by the gang, while Shelly dies the next day in the hospital.

One year later, to the very second, Eric Draven returns from the dead, emerging from his grave, to be met by a familiar—the crow of the title, who becomes his guide. Draven sets out to take his revenge.

In a confrontation with Tin Tin, Draven shows his indestructibility and in the ensuing fight leaves his adversary mortally stabbed.

Led by the crow to the pawnshop that is selling Shelly's engagement ring, Draven tells the owner to inform the remaining members of the gang that he will hunt them down. He then torches the shop. . . .

Draven now seeks out the street cop who investigated his murder, Albrecht, to learn more about his own death.

He then rescues Sarah—a young girl, once a friend of the dead couple, and the story's narrator—from in front of a speeding automobile.

In Funboy's apartment, Draven finds the thug locked in a drug-hazed embrace with Sarah's mother, a waitress, Darla. Draven tells Darla she must give up drugs and be a better mother to Sarah. Then he hits Funboy with a king-size morphine injection, killing him.

After hearing further details of his own murder from Officer Albrecht, Draven sends T-Bird to his death in a burning car.

In search of Skank, Draven bursts into a meeting of Top Dollar's gang. In the ensuing massive shoot-out, Skank and many other gang members are disposed of. Myca, Top Dollar's half sister and incestuous lover, later tells him that the only way to stop Draven is to kill his familiar, the crow, thus robbing the dead rocker of his supernatural powers.

Top Dollar later ambushes Draven and the crow, wounding and capturing the bird, thus rendering Draven a mere mortal once more. Draven is saved from a second death only by the arrival of Officer Albrecht.

During the firefight that follows, the crow pecks out Myca's eyes, while Draven chases Top Dollar to the roof of the church, where the slumlord has taken Sarah as his hostage. In the course of a spectacular sword battle, Draven frees Sarah and dispatches Top Dollar, who falls to his death, impaled on a gargoyle.

The original murders now avenged, Eric Draven is able to return at last to the graveyard, where he is re-united in a true and lasting death with his beloved Shelly. Sarah lays Shelly's engagement ring on the couple's gravestone, whispering, "buildings burn, people die, but real love is forever."

APPENDIX II
Film Credits

Brandon Lee *Eric [Draven]*
Ernie Hudson *Albrecht*
Michael Wincott *Top Dollar*
David Patrick Kelly *T-Bird*
Angel David *Skank*
Rochelle Davis *Sarah*
Bai Ling *Myca*
Laurence Mason *Tin Tin*
Michael Massee *Funboy*
Bill Raymond *Mickey*
Marco Rodriguez *Torres*
Sofia Shinas *Shelly*
Anna Thomson *Darla*
Tony Todd *Grange*
Jon Polito *Gideon*
Kim Sykes *Annabella*
Rock Taulbee *Lead Cop*
Norman "Max" Maxwell *Roscoe*
Jeff Cadiente *Waldo*
Henry Kingi Jr. *MJ*
Eric Stabenau *Speeg*
Cassandra Lawton *Newscaster*
Lou Criscuolo *Uniform Cop #1*
Todd Brenner *Paramedic #1*
Joe West *Paramedic #2*
Tom Rosales *Sanchez*

Jeff Imada *Braeden*
Tierre Turner *Jugger*
Tim Parati *Bad Ass Criminal*
James Goodall, Brad Laner, James Putnam, Eddie Ruscha, Elizabeth
    Thompson *Medicine*
Marston Daley, Laura Gomel, Rachel Hollingsworth, Charles Levi,
    Mark McCabe, Frank Nardiello *My Life with the Thrill Kill Kult*
[Michael Berryman (uncredited) *Skull Cowboy* (cut from film)]
Matt Adler, Charles Bazaldua, Jennifer Blanc, Theodore Borders,
    Joseph Chapman, Holly Dorff, Judi Durand, Greg Finley, Spencer
    Garrett, Barbara Iley, Kathleen Kane, Carlyle King, Phillip Lucier,
    Peter Lurie, J. Lamont Pope, David J. Randolph, Vernon Scott
    Additional Voices

Stunts

Jeff Imada *Stunt Coordinator*
Brandon Lee and Jeff Imada *Fight Choreography by*
Jeff Cadiente
Rich Avery, Bobby Bass, Ken Bates, Sandy Beaumen, Simone
    Boiseree, Troy Brown, Bob Brown, Steve Chambers, John
    Copeman, Chris Durand, Dale Frye, Al Goto, Buddy Joe Hooker,
    Brian Imada, Matt Johnston, Dean Mumford, Alan Oliney, Eric
    Rondell, Ronnie Rondell, Gilber Rosales, Lori Lynn Ross, Chad
    Stahelski, John Stonham Sr., John Stonham Jr., Ric Waugh *Stunts*

Filmmakers

Alex Proyas *Directed by*
David J. Schow and John Shirley *Screenplay by*
James O'Barr *Based on the Comic Book Series and Comic Strip by*
Edward R. Pressman and Jeff Most *Produced by*
Robert L. Rosen, Sherman L. Baldwin Executive *Producers*
Caldecot Chubb, James A. Janowitz *Co-Producers*
Dariusz ["Derek"] Wolski *Director of Photography*
Alex McDowell *Production Designer*
Dov Hoenig, ACE, and Scott Smith *Editors*
Graeme Revell *Music Score Composer*
Arianne Phillips *Costume Designer*
Billy Hopkins and Suzanne Smith *Casting Directors*
Gregory A. Gale *Associate Producer*

Grant Hill *Unit Production Manager/Associate Producer*
Steve Andrews *First Assistant Director*
Randy LaFoulette [LaFollette] *Second Assistant Director*
Ric Rondell *Unit Production Manager (Added Scenes)*
Jolene Cherry *Music Supervisor*
Andrew Mason *Visual Effects Supervisor/Second Unit Director*
Simon Murton *Art Director*
Geoffrey S. Grimsman *Assistant Art Director*
Marthe Pineau *Set Decorator*
Peter Pound, Hannah Strauss *Storyboard Artists*
William Barcley *Set Designer*
John Kretschmer *Leadman*
David Riebel *Assistant Decorator*
Jeffrey Schlatter *Construction Coordinator*
Thomas "Mike" Ryan *Construction Foreman*
George Simcox *Plaster Foreman*
James Martishius *Carpenter*
Jeff Tanner *Assistant Art Department Coordinator*
David Crone, Ken Arlidge *Camera Operators*
John Verardi, John Cambria, Fredrick "Chip" Hackler *First Assistant
    Camera*
George Hesse, Michael Satrazemis *Second Assistant Camera*
Ken Hudson, Mary Lou Vetter *Camera Loaders*
Charles Laughon, Mark McManus *Video Assist*
Robert Zuckerman *Still Photographer*
Buddy Alper *Sound Mixer*
Byron Eugene Ashbrook *Boom Operator*
Lance Anderson *Special Makeup Effects Artist*
Scott Coulter *Assistant Special Makeup Effects*
Gary Gero *Crow Wrangler*
Roger Schumacher, Larry Madrid *Animal Trainers*
Darryl Levine *Wardrobe Supervisor*
Marina Marit, Roberta Bile *Costumers*
Pauline White, Amy Lilley *Set Costumers*
Janet Schriever *Assistant Costumer*
C. J. Harris *Seamstress*
Sharon Ilson, Herita Jones *Makeup Artists*
Sandra Orsolyak, Tiger Tate *Assistant Makeup Artists*
Michelle Johnson, Mary Lampert *Key Hairstylists*
Shelly Hutchins, Rita Troy *Assistant Hairstylists*

Daniel Kuttner, Tantar Leviser *Prop Masters*
Charlene Hamer Assistant *Prop Master*
Jim Moyer *Weapons Specialist*
JB Jones *Special Effects*
James Roberts *Special Effects Foreman*
Claudio Miranda *Gaffer*
Steve Perry *Best Boy Electric*
Al Demayo *Electric*
Charles "Chunky" Huse *Key Grip*
Robert Hoelen, Scott Hillman *Best Boy Grips*
Jeffrey Howery, Scott Lefridge *Dolly Grips*
Sonny Baskin, Craig Woods *Additional Editors*
Matthew Booth, Richard Alderete *First Assistant Editors*
John Finklea, Patrick Mullane *Second Assistant Editors*
Tony Max *Apprentice Editor*
True Sound *Sound Editing by*
Dave McMoyler, John J. Miceli *Supervising Sound Editor*
Joseph Phillips *Supervising Sound Designer*
Brian McPhearson *Sound Designer*
Patrick Sellers, Jeff Watts, Glen T. Morgan, Dan Hegeman *Dialogue Editors*
David Kneupper *Crow Voice Design*
Peter Lehman, Chris Assells, Scott Mosteller, Amy Hoffberg *Sound Effects Editors*
Robert Batha *Foley Editor*
John Rice, Dan Marshall, Ishmell Curry, Rodney Sharp *Assistant Sound Editors*
Anthony Miceli, Kim Waugh *Additional Sound Recording*
Richard Bernstein *Music Editor*
Beriau Picard, Philip Tallman *Assistant Music Editors*
Tim Simonec *Orchestration*
Brian Williams *Music Sound Design*
Michael Harker *Post Consultant*
Sam Bernstein, Bill Rose Jr. *Production Accountants*
Grace Griffith, Steven Simpson, Jean Henri Ahearn Sr., Christopher R. Dotterweich *Assistant Production Accountants*
Gregor Wilson *Payroll Assistant*
Curt Schroeder *Financial Consultant*
Cornelia "Nini" Rogan *Script Supervisor*
Vick Griffin *Location Manager*

Jennifer Roth, Carrie Durose *Production Coordinators*
Cindy Gray *Production Secretary*
Danielle Rigby, Chemen Ochoa, Stephanie Adams, Jay Tobias,
    Cynthia Williams *Additional Second Assistant Directors*
Chad Rosen, Patrick Lawlor, Patrick Marz *Production Assistants*
Tad Winship, Bruce Hofert, Emily Zalenski, Michael Toay, Nina
    Dib *LA Production Assistants*
Eliza Hutton *Assistant to Mr. Lee*
Michael Radiloff, Christopher Otto *Assistants to Mr. Pressman*
Janice Biggs *Assistant to Mr. Proyas*
Stacy Plavoukos *Assistant to Mr. Most*
Leslie Reed *Assistant to Ms. Cherry*
Daniel Posener *Business Affairs Executive*
Lee Siler *Transportation Coordinator*
Jesse Smith *Transportation Captain*
Kerry Barden, Diana Jaher, Jennifer Low Sauer *Casting Associates*
Craig and Lisa Fincannon *Extras Casting*
Pam Plummer *Extras Casting Associate*
Barbara Harris *Voice Casting*
Jason Scott *Unit Publicist*
Reva Grantham *Craft Service*
Darryl Chan *Brandon Lee's Trainer*
Ruth Streszoff *Teacher*
Clyde Baisey, Dione Kirby *Medics*
Art Hoover, Ken Young *Caterers*

Miniature Photography
Photographed at Dream Quest Images
Robert Stadd *Producer of Miniature Photography*
Michael Talarico *Director of Photography (Miniatures)*
Terry Moews, Mac *Motion Control Programmers*
Scott Campbell *Motion Control Gaffer*
Richard Johnson, George Prior *Motion Control Technicians*
Gus Ramsden *Model Coordinator*
Eric Skipper *Chief Model Maker*
Richard Wright, Eric Skipper Jr., James McGeachy, Jinnie Eddlemon
    Model Makers
Deborah Wolff *Dream Quest Editor*
Shawn Broes *Dream Quest Assistant Editor*

Warren Farina *Coordinator*
Digital Compositing by Motion Pixel Corporation, a Division of Dream
    Quest Images

Digital Compositing Crew

Mark M. Galvin *Executive Producer*
David K. McCullough *Producer*
Melissa Cira Taylor *Production Manager*
Howard Burdick, Tim Landry *Technical Supervisors*
Karen deJong, Bob Scifo *Digital Matte Artists*
Heather Davis, Blaine Kennison, Ron Longo, John T. Murrah, Mary
    Nelson, Alexander A. Pitt *Compositing Technicians*
Olivier Sarda *Digital Roto Artists*
Jason Piccioni *Scanning/Output Technician*
Derrick Mitchell *Visual Effects Editor*
Kim Jorgensen *Visual Effects Assistant Editor*
Skywalker Sound *Post Production Services Provided by*
Matthew Iadarola, Gary Gegan, Tim Philben, Ken Polk *Re-Recording
    Mixers*
Grover Helsley, Thomas P. Gerard, Christian Minkler *Additional Re-
    Recording Mixers*
Robin Johnston *Stage Recordist*
Bryan Fowler *Stage Loader*
J B & Associates Inc, Todd-AO Studios East ADR & Foley Stages
Marilyn Graf, Paul Zydel *ADR Mixers*
Eric Hoeschen *Foley Mixer*
Brian Smith *ADR & Foley Recordist*
Joe Sabella, Doug Reed *Foley Artists*
Dan Sperry *Dolby Stereo Consultant*
Gary Burritt *Negative Cutter*
Steve Sheridan *Color Timer*
N T Audio Visual, Thomas McCormick *Optical Negative*
RTV Video *Video Transfers*
Acme Soundworks *Sound Transfers*
International Creative Effects *Optical Effects*
Color by Deluxe
Studio Facilities Carolco Studios Inc
Camera & Lens Equipment Joe Dunton & Company
Crowvision Lense by Joe Dunton

Special Thanks to Lynn Pressman Raymond

Payor, Cashman, Sherman & Flynn, James A. Janowitz, Karen Robson, Phyllis Haufman, Roger Hass *Production/Financing Counsel*

Great Northern *Brokerage Insurance*

Film Finances Inc. *Completion Guarantor*

APPENDIX III
Soundtrack Credits

"Burn"
Performed by The Cure
Courtesy of Fiction Records Ltd., Elektra Entertainment, Warner
   Music, and Polydor Records
Written by Robert Smith, Simon Gallup, Boris Williams, Perry
   Bamonte
Produced by Robert Smith and Bryan "Chuch" New

"Golgotha Tenement Blues"
Performed and Produced by Machines of Loving Grace
Courtesy of Mammoth Records
Written by Scott Benzel, Mike Fisher, Stuart Kupers, and Tom
   Melchionda

"Big Empty"
Performed by Stone Temple Pilots
Courtesy of Atlantic Recording Corporation
Written by D. Deleo/Weiland
Produced by Brendan O'Brien

"Color Me Once"
Performed and Produced by Violent Femmes
Courtesy of Slash Records
Written by Gordon Gano and Brian Ritchie

"Dead Souls"
Performed by Nine Inch Nails
Courtesy of Nothing/TVT/Interscope Records
Written by Ian Curtis, Peter Hook, Bernard Sumner, Stephen Morris
Produced by Trent Reznor

"Darkness"
Performed and Produced by Rage Against the Machine
Courtesy of Epic Associated
Written and Arranged by Rage Against the Machine
Lyrics Written by Zack De La Rocha

"Snakedriver"
Performed by The Jesus and Mary Chain
Courtesy of Blanco Y Negro/Warner Music UK Ltd./American
    Recordings/WEA International, Inc.
Written and Produced by William Reid and Jim Reid

"Time Baby Ii"
Performed by Medicine
Courtesy of American Recordings
Written by James Goodall, Brad Laner, James Putnam, Ed Ruscha,
    Beth Thompson

"After The Flesh"
Performed by My Life with the Thrill Kill Kult
Courtesy of Interscope Records
Written by Buzz Mccoy and Groovie Mann
Produced by Buzz Mccoy

"Milktoast"
Performed by Helmet
Courtesy of Interscope Records
Written by Page Nye Hamilton
Produced by Butch Vig & Helmet

"Ghostrider"
Performed by Rollins Band
Courtesy of The Imago Recording Company
Written by Martin Rev, Alan Vega
Produced by Theo Van Rock

"Slip Slide Melting"
Performed by For Love Not Lisa
Courtesy of Eastwest Records America
Written by For Love Not Lisa
Produced by Matt Hyde and Doug Carrion

"The Badge"
Performed and Produced by Pantera
Courtesy of Eastwest Records America
Written by Tom Roberts and Jerry Lang

"It Can't Rain All the Time"
Performed by Jane Siberry
Courtesy of Reprise Records
Written by Graeme Revell and Jane Siberry
Produced by Graeme Revell

INDEX

Photo insert images are indicated by *"p1, p2, p3, etc."*

O'Barr, James, xvii; cameo by, 143–44; Catholic Church and, 4–5; on cities, 5–6; at debut, 262; early inspiration and influences of, 3–5; girlfriend's death and, 4; makeup effects and, 75; in Marines, 5; in medical school, 6–7; movie options for, 9–16; music and, 8, 253; on reboot, 274; screenplay and, 17–27
Officer Albrecht, *p3, p4*; Eric Draven and, 139
Officer Albrecht (fictional character), 22, 136; casting of, 52–53
"Oh, Me Dying," 254
O'Hara, 33
Oldman, Gary, 47
Olin, Lena, 47
Olivier, Laurence, 80
One Hour Photo, 284
Orsolyak, Sandra, 95, 133, 173; on day of Brandon's death, 178; emotional aftermath of Brandon's death by, 223, 224; on endurance of *The Crow*, 282, 286; in final filming period, 237; on Funboy, 134–35; in hiatus after Brandon's death, 232; on set atmosphere, 114; at Stimmerman's, 124; on T-Bird, 132; on weapons, 155–56
Owens, Rick, xiii

"Pain & Fear," 7
Pandora, 43
Paradise Lost, 163
Paramount Pictures, 42–45, 251–52
Paris, Texas, 269
Parker, Charlie, 54
Partridge, Norman, 268
Patterson, John, 151
PEA. *See* pulseless electrical activity
Pennywise (fictional character), 277
Penzing Studios, 277
The People vs. Larry Flynt, 284

Pet Cemetery, 75
Pettus, Brian: on day of Brandon's death, 193–95, 200; at hospital, 200; investigation into Brandon's death by, 213–21
Phelps, Nigel, 48
Phillips, Arianne, 50–51, 71–73, 79–80; at Brandon's memorial, 225; at cast and crew screening, 260; on day before Brandon's death, 166; on day of Brandon's death, 173, 180, 183, 185, 191, 201; emotional aftermath of Brandon's death by, 224; on endurance of *The Crow*, 279, 281, 284, 285; in hiatus after Brandon's death, 232; Hutton and, 201, 205, 225, 232, 260; Lee, Brandon, and, 121, 166; on Proyas, 101–2; reaction to Brandon's death of, 204–5; Sarah and, 137; on set atmosphere, 113, 114; Skank and, 133; Tin Tin and, 134
Phillips, Lou Diamond, 224
Phoenix, River, 28
Pit Bar, 132, 135–36, *p1*; in investigation into Brandon's death, 216
Platoon, 54
Playboy, 263
Playhouse 90, 105
Poe, Edgar Allan, 8
points of view (POV), 174
Polanski, Roman, 30
police: on day of Brandon's death, 193–94, 200; investigation into Brandon's death by, 212–22. *See also* Officer Albrecht
Polito, Jon, 128, *p6*; Mason, Laurence and, 140–41
PolyGram, 267
Pootie Tang, 15
Pope, Tim, 266
Porky's Revenge, 69